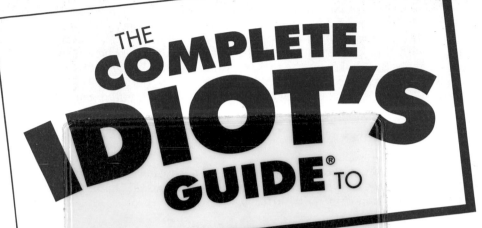

THE COMPLETE IDIOT'S GUIDE® TO

a Well-Behaved Child

by Ericka Lutz

alpha books

A Division of Macmillan General Reference
A Pearson Education Macmillan Company
1633 Broadway, New York, NY 10019-6785

Macmillan Publishing books may be purchased for business or sales promotional use. For information please write: Special Markets Department, Macmillan Publishing USA, 1633 Broadway, New York, NY 10019.

International Standard Book Number: 0-02-863107-2
Library of Congress Catalog Card Number: 99-62546

01   00   99   8   7   6   5   4   3   2   1

Interpretation of the printing code: the rightmost number of the first series of numbers is the year of the book's printing; the rightmost number of the second series of numbers is the number of the book's printing. For example, a printing code of 99-1 shows that the first printing occurred in 1999.

Printed in the United States of America

Note: This publication contains the opinions and ideas of its author. It is intended to provide helpful and informative material on the subject matter covered. It is sold with the understanding that the author and publisher are not engaged in rendering professional services in the book. If the reader requires personal assistance or advice, a competent professional should be consulted.

The author and publisher specifically disclaim any responsibility for any liability, loss or risk, personal or otherwise, which is incurred as a consequence, directly or indirectly, of the use and application of any of the contents of this book.

The Complete Idiot's Reference Card

The Twelve Disciplinary Elements

1. Pay attention to your child.

2. Respect your children and yourself.

3. Be reasonable, gentle, and firm.

4. Prevent and minimize problems through understanding, communication, and modeling.

5. Use positive reinforcement to encourage and reward proper behavior.

6. Teach ways to make choices.

7. Set reasonable personal expectations and goals for your child.

8. Set reasonable expectations for yourself and your family.

9. Communicate effective and reasonable limits.

10. Understand misbehavior.

11. Provide related, respectful, reasonable responses.

12. Be consistent.

Tips for Growing a Capable Child

➤ Instead of stepping in and taking over, check with her. Ask, "How are you doing?" or "Would you like help?"

➤ Let her figure it out, take risks, explore life.

➤ Encourage her growth, and discuss her ideas with her.

➤ Don't push her. Keep expectations appropriate for her, and celebrate her successes.

➤ Don't patronize or diminish her, her capabilities, or her accomplishments.

alpha
books

Tips for Talking With, Not At, Your Child

➤ Tell the truth.

➤ Keep complaints specific.

➤ Be careful with criticism.

➤ Stop yelling!

➤ Nix the nagging, lose the lectures, avoid the advice.

➤ Don't set him up.

➤ De-escalate the antagonism.

➤ Use "I" statements.

Effective Disciplinary Consequences

➤ Education

➤ Expressing disapproval

➤ Having a little discussion

➤ Ignoring

➤ Separation and replacement

➤ Time-outs (also known as "thinking time")

➤ Warnings

PARENTING MATERIAL

Funded by the

CHICOPEE COMMUNITY PARTNERSHIP FOR CHILDREN

Grant Round   FY 2000

Alpha Development Team

Publisher
Kathy Nebenhaus

Editorial Director
Gary M. Krebs

Managing Editor
Bob Shuman

Marketing Brand Manager
Felice Primeau

Acquisitions Editor
Jessica Faust

Development Editors
Phil Kitchel
Amy Zavatto

Assistant Editor
Georgette Blau

Production Team

Development Editor
Matthew X. Kiernan

Production Editor
Michael Thomas

Copy Editor
Faren Bachelis

Cover Designer
Mike Freeland

Photo Editor
Richard H. Fox

Illustrator
Jody P. Schaeffer

Book Designers
Scott Cook and Amy Adams of DesignLab

Indexer
Cheryl Jackson

Layout/Proofreading
Angela Calvert
Mary Hunt
Julie Trippetti

Contents at a Glance

Contents

4 Positive Reinforcement and Choices   43

10 Effective, Dubious, and Destructive Disciplinary Consequences 123

Foreword

The Complete Idiot's Guide® to a Well-Behaved Child is humbly titled, for it provides more than just the basics of good, solid parenting skills. This book offers insights and wisdom for parents on all levels—novice to expert (if there is such a person). In short, this book is full of solid information, sage advice, and necessary support to parents of all persuasions.

The book is an overview of the parenting years, at least to the years until your children move away from home, which is closer than most of us care to acknowledge. The author, Ericka Lutz, offers the reader some basic, tried-and-true principles to parent by, whether your child is two, twelve, or seventeen. At the same time, the author recognizes the developmental differences and needs of each age and is able, as a result, to offer practical advice and support for each age level. The principles of positive discipline that Ericka espouses are articulate and flexible enough to adapt to the needs of both the various ages and the various parenting styles, and she gives plenty of examples of this throughout the text.

At the same time, while the book is direct and informative, it is not moralizing. Implicit throughout is that parents must take the information the author presents and pass it through their value system to make it their own. Thus, in her examples, Ericka shows how different principles play out differently in a range of families. In this regard, I especially enjoyed her "Tales from the Parent Zone," as they illustrated real life frustrations, successes, and just plain-old muddling through, which is the reality of most parents. This book is no cookie-cutter approach to parenting, and it places ultimate responsibility where it belongs, squarely on the shoulders of parents.

Throughout your reading of this book you'll feel supported in what you are already doing well and compassionately challenged in the areas where you can do better. In other words, get ready for a wonderful read about real life parenting. Enjoy!

—Michael Riera, Ph.D.

Michael Riera has worked in schools since 1981 and, during that time, has worked with and spoken to over 25,000 adolescents and parents as a counselor and workshop leader. He has a Ph.D. in Counseling Psychology and is the author of *Uncommon Sense for Parents with Teenagers* (1995) and *Surviving High School* (1997). He is also an award-winning columnist on parent/teen issues and a consultant for CBS, as well as a regular contributor on the *Saturday Morning News Show* and *48 Hours: The Class of 2000*. He has appeared as a featured guest on *The Oprah Winfrey Show*; he is on the Advisory Board for *Teen People Magazine*; he is a nationally known speaker on issues regarding teenagers and parents; and he is the Director of Counseling at Marin Academy in San Rafael. Michael can be reached through the Internet at www.mikeriera.com. He is currently working on a third book, *Field Guide to The American Teenager.*

Introduction

Welcome! This is a book about raising the kind of well-behaved child who will some-day become the kind of adult you'd like to know—strong, reasonable, responsible, respectful, with a strong sense of values and ethics.

My approach to a well-behaved child focuses on preventing behavior problems through positive reinforcement and strong, safe limits.

But it's not so easy as that, is it? Problem behavior and children go together like coffee and cream, and prevention, no matter how essential, doesn't always work. You're frustrated, worried, and confused. You're no idiot—you don't want to resort to abuse—but how do you get your child to do his homework, stop slapping his sister, or get up at a reasonable hour?

This book is a hands-on guide with specific advice about dealing with problem behavior in a strong, reasonable, respectful way that works. I'm talking about Discipline—with a capital *D*. Not the kind that involves whips and leather (not the kind that involves slaps and screaming, either, but we'll get there), but the kind of discipline that uses clear communication, modeling appropriate behavior, and providing safe limits and appropriate, reasonable consequences to teach your children to become—yes!—the kind of adult you'd like to know.

Parenting is as individual as the individuals who practice it, and there's a lot of hope and guesswork involved. As you read the book, ask yourself, "Will this work for me?" "Will this work for my family?" I've provided a wide variety of suggestions and disci-plinary techniques to pick from, choose, reject, or inspire you to other ideas. Not all suggestions will work for every family—they aren't meant to. But understanding the concepts behind each technique will help you make stronger, clearer choices about your disciplinary approach.

What's in the Book?

The Complete Idiot's Guide® to a Well-Behaved Child is divided into sections. Each section in the book covers a broad area of discipline and positive parenting. Each of the sections is divided into individual, more focused, chapters. You can read the whole thing cover to cover, or you can just dip in and out to focus on the areas you are most concerned about right now. Here's what you'll find in each section:

Part 1: Setting Up for Success. Raising a well-behaved child entails paying attention, preventing as many problems as you can through a positive approach, and strengthen-ing your own parenting skills. In Chapters 1, 2, 3, and 4, you'll get an introduction to the tools and principles of positive parenting. We'll discuss the importance of paying attention to your child (and gain some communication skills to help you out). You'll learn about the Twelve Disciplinary Elements, and start understanding a bit about parenting styles and how to be an ally for your child. In short, the first section gives you the building blocks of positive parenting.

Part 2: Clearer Than Mud: Expectations and Goals. What *is* a well-behaved child, anyway? Understanding your child's temperament and development will help you adjust your goals and expectations to reasonable levels. In Chapters 5 and 6 we'll focus on expectations and goals—yours, your family's, your child's. You'll learn how to write your family's value statement (it's sort of like a mission statement) and define when a cleaned room is clean. Then, in Chapter 7, we'll look at limits—one of discipline's primary tools.

Part 3: Prevention's Great, but Sometimes.... Okay, okay, so you've been positive, used encouragement, established your expectations, and set the limits. But, something went wrong, and your child is misbehaving like crazy! Did something go wrong? In Chapter 8, we'll look at why your kid is "naughty" and in Chapters 9 and 10, we'll start building the tools to "fix" it. These are the chapters about consequences—good, bad, logical, and natural. We're in the heart of it now—learning which consequences work, which consequences sometimes work, and which consequences are really bad, ineffective choices.

Part 4: Putting It to Work. Parenting skills are like language: They gain fluency through practice. The four chapters in Part 4 focus on the daily doings of discipline. In Chapters 11 and 12, you'll learn what to do about specific problems. From bedtime to biting, from cheating to disastrous play dates—it's all here. Chapter 13 focuses on life (and your child's behavior) in the household, and Chapter 14 focuses on life (and your child's behavior) outside the house.

Part 5: Positive Discipline for Complex Families. Life's not all 2.5 kids, a mom and a dad, a dog, and a white picket fence, now is it? Part 5 focuses on complex and specific situations—little kids, adolescents, stepfamilies, team parenting. In Chapters 15, 16, 17, and 18 we focus on details, specific to you.

Part 6: The Hardest Parts. What about those really tricky situations? How can you raise a well-behaved child when your family is fighting all the time? Chapter 19 teaches you a number of conflict-resolution skills to make your family life a little smoother. What if you struggle with a particularly challenging child? Chapter 20 focuses on kids with a difference—spirited, divergent thinking, or diagnosed with attention deficit disorder. And what (oh, no!) about sex, drugs, addictions, crime, and depression? Chapters 21 and 22 focus on those. Yes, Part 6 is about tough stuff. You'll find information and support here.

Part 7: Finding Balance and Serenity. Chapter 23 focuses on getting your emotional act together—first, realizing ways to nurture yourself, rid yourself of parental guilt, and respect your own parenting struggles. Chapter 24 is about finding outside help for your family's troubles. Here are specific questions to ask a therapist before you hire her, and a discussion of support groups and parenting classes. Chapter 25, the final chapter in the book, focuses on building a strong, reasonable family (there's balance and serenity in that!). Pull away from the details, and focus larger. Your family exists in a community. This chapter has specific suggestions for teaching your child to use artistic endeavor, spirituality, and community service to bring her values out into the world.

In the back of the book, you'll find the appendices—more information for you! These recommended books and resources, glossary words, and exercises will keep you very busy.

Extra! Extra! Read All About It!

Besides the main body of text in this book (and the cute little pictures), you'll find additional information and statistics, special tips, vocabulary words, and warnings located in little boxes. Here's what they'll tell you:

Behave Yourself!

Children learn what they live, so if you behave yourself, they should, too! In this box, you'll find cautions and warnings. Look alert! Behave yourself!

It's a Good Idea!

This little box dispenses advice, reminders, and interesting details to accompany the main text. Follow these tips for good parenting, and a well-behaved child.

Words to Parent By

In this box, you'll find definitions of special disciplinary vocabulary. And, in Appendix A, all these terms are collected into one big, tidy list.

Tales from the Parent Zone

In this longer feature you'll read anecdotes, statistics and parenting stories—some even about my family.

A Special Note About Language Usage

The Complete Idiot's Guide® to a Well-Behaved Child is designed for both male and female caregivers, and kids of both sexes. Most examples and stories in the book can apply equally to both. In an attempt to use inclusive, nonsexist language, I've alternated gender pronouns and examples. (At times there are certain specific circumstances that apply to only one sex—and you'll know what I'm talking about when you get there.)

A Legal Disclaimer

Any information in *The Complete Idiot's Guide® to a Well-Behaved Child* is as accurate and current as we can make it. But hey, we're not lawyers or doctors (and even if we were, lawyers and doctors make mistakes). We really, really try to be right, but we're not always gonna be. This is a long way of saying we're not liable.

Acknowledgments

This book could not have been written without the wisdom, stories, and experiences of many, many parents and children, many of whose stories appear (sometimes disguised) in this book. When I submerged myself in this project, a lot of people went out of their way to pick up my slack. These slack-picker-uppers have my undying gratitude. They include, first and foremost, my husband Bill Sonnenschein, and my mother and father, Arthur and Karla Lutz. Life as a parent would have been *way* more difficult without the Archway After School program, Mariko Hibbets, Steven Kusch, and Saill White. As always, I depended upon the love, support, and advice (both discipline-wise and otherwise) of Anaya Lutz Sonnenschein, Tilly Roche, Ami Zins, Ailsa Steckel, Milo Johnson, Carolyn Brown, Jessica Lutz, Tillie Olsen, Julia McCray-Goldsmith, Peggy Roche, Annie McManus, Jim Higgins, Mark Hetts, Steven Rosenthal, Lew Levinson, and Andree Abecassis. Thanks, everybody. I couldn't have done it without you.

Special Thanks to the Technical Reviewer

The Complete Idiot's Guide® to a Well-Behaved Child was reviewed by an expert who double-checked the accuracy of what you'll learn here, to help us ensure that this book gives you everything you need to know about raising a well-behaved child. Special thanks are extended to Annie McManus.

Annie McManus has more than 16 years of professional experience working with children. She earned her Master's degree in developmental psychology at San Francisico State University and worked in the San Francisco Bay Area as a parent educator, family crisis counselor, child advocate, and early childhood educator. Ms. McManus is currently a full-time developmental psychology instructor at Parkland College in Champaign, Illinois, teaching early childhood education, child psychology, adolescent psychology, and human growth and developmental psychology. She frequently presents at professional conferences and for parent groups, speaking on a variety of topics including "Preschool Undercover: The Emergence of Sexuality, how to redirect the game of doctor and other challenges." Thank you, Annie McManus.

Part 1
Setting Up for Success

Ready to rumble? Let's go! In the first part of the book, we'll get down and dirty and talk about the root of the well-behaved child. Guess what? That's you, the parent! We'll look at parenting styles, and talk about becoming the kind of parent who has a well-behaved child. We'll talk about ethics and values, and the real skills of positive parenting.

The well-behaved child is raised on a solid, basic foundation of love, respect, and encouragement—so let's work on the basics of "positive parenting." We'll look at the importance of paying attention, how to prevent as many problems as you can through a positive approach, and get some tips for strengthening your own parenting skills. I've broken the components of discipline into 12 simple elements, called the Twelve Disciplinary Elements. You'll also learn about being an ally for your child, and some really easy, good, and effective communication skills to stop problems way before they start.

Chapter 1

How to Raise a Well-Behaved Child

> ## In This Chapter
>
> ➤ The complexities of raising a well-behaved child
>
> ➤ Understanding the Twelve Disciplinary Elements
>
> ➤ The importance of paying attention and respecting your child
>
> ➤ Raising an ethical child
>
> ➤ Relinquishing control and gaining trust
>
> ➤ Discipline, it's a discipline

Earlier this year my husband, Bill, our five-year-old daughter, Annie, and I found ourselves in a New York hotel room. It was late at night and we were all beat and ready to sleep. All except Annie who—wired and tired—was jumping up and down on her bed chanting, "I can do whatever I wa-ant, I can do whatever I wa-ant!" Welcome to the parent's nightmare.

What did we do? We tried to reason with her. We hugged her and sang to her. We lost our cool and yelled at her. We didn't hit her—but it took all of our resources to keep from doing it. Eventually, a while later, the behavior stopped and she slept. Bill and I were left frustrated, upset, confused, and wondering what we'd done right, what we'd done wrong, and what we could have done instead to salvage the evening, our blood pressure, and our moods. When a child is this out-of-control, it's hard to know what to do. Should we have smacked her? Let her continue to jump and taunt us? Hung her over Times Square by her toes? Taken away ice cream for a year? Popped her in a bathtub to cool down? Gotten all of us dressed and marched out into the night? The possibilities were endless, and endlessly frustrating.

Parenting Well: It's Confusing, for YOU!

The path to a well-behaved child isn't always intuitive—it doesn't come easy to most parents. How do you get a child to behave without resorting to screams and slaps? Are screams and slaps effective? How do you raise a responsible, resourceful child without becoming a tyrant? What works?

It's a Good Idea!

Remember: No one approach works with every child or every family.

Nothing is easy with kids, and nothing is ever going to be. Yet, with the right information and approach, it can be easier. I'm not a complete idiot and neither are you. All of us struggle in our quest to be better parents, to raise responsible, respectful kids, and just have a little *peace* around the house! In short, we'd like our kids to be well behaved.

I wrote this book for parents who want simple, effective, sensible, and gentle parenting tips on getting their kids to behave. Be aware, though, this is not a paint-by-numbers parenting book. It's not a formula, it's an approach. The technique I encourage is known as *positive discipline,* and is based on mutual respect, communication, and *effective* tactics that will make life easier for you, and for your kids. This book will help you now to prevent trouble later. And when you're feeling out of control or utterly confused, this book will suggest easy ways to calm down and get back on track. None of us will ever be a perfect parent, but we all can improve.

Words to Parent By

A *well-behaved child* is a child who is respectful, reasonable, responsible, resourceful, loving, eager to learn, and engaged by life. It's *not* a child who is beaten down, cowed by you, her peers, or the "system," or who is too frightened to express her feelings and ideas.

In this first chapter, we'll look at the job of raising a well-behaved child. I'll define positive discipline for you, and we'll start discussing some of the most important aspects of the approach.

What Is Discipline, Anyway?

Before we get any further, we should figure out what we mean by *discipline.* It's one of those words that has quite a few meanings. Take the Discipline Quick Check and see how you do (nobody said learning about discipline had to be *all* gloom and doom!).

Discipline Quick Check

For each question below, answer *true* or *false.*

1. Discipline has something to do with sharing information.
2. Most teachers are disciplinarians.
3. Discipline is not the same thing as punishment.

Answers:

1. *True.* If you look up the word *discipline* in Latin, you'll find that it's rooted in the word "disciple," somebody who takes away and spreads ideas he has learned.

2. *True.* A disciplinarian is somebody who teaches. Therefore, true, most teachers are disciplinarians.

3. *True.* Don't confuse discipline with punishment. Too often, people mix up those two words. Go ahead, look up *discipline* in the dictionary. You'll find that it has as much to do with teaching and learning as it does with cruelty, retribution, or whips and chains. The definition of discipline includes words like *instruction, teaching, learning,* and *to train or develop.* Discipline is the process of instilling values in your child. Now look up *punishment.* You'll find words like *suffering, pain, loss,* and *retribution.* Here's my suggestion: Forget about punishment. Even if you punish your child with the best of intentions, even when it's for your kid's "own good," you still risk lowering your child's self-respect. There's no doubt that self-respect is key to being a responsible, loving person, in short, a well-behaved child.

It's a Good Idea!

Challenging and discovering the world is part of being a human being, and it's a big part of your child's job to challenge you and discover your limits, rules, and opinions on issues. It's your job to respond to your child's challenges by being the most informed and educated parent you can, while providing love, respect, affection, safe limits, gentle correction, and consistency.

Good Behavior, Here We Come!

How do kids learn the kinds of behavior that will make them wonderful, kind, thoughtful adults who can make a contribution to the world? They learn through experience; they learn when they feel good about learning, and not before. Enter *positive discipline.*

Positive discipline involves positive feedback, and it involves consistency. It incorporates example, encouragement, praise, trust, and respect for children with setting firm, wise limits. It teaches them how to make their own choices, and to understand the consequences of their choices. When necessary, it provides related, respectful, and reasonable responses to misbehavior.

If you teach positive discipline to your children you shouldn't have to resort to punishment.

Words to Parent By

Positive discipline is an approach to raising a well-behaved child that incorporates encouragement, praise, trust, consistency, and respect for children with setting firm, wise limits. It teaches them how to make their own choices, and to understand the consequences of their choices. When necessary, it provides related, respectful, and reasonable responses to misbehavior.

The Road to Well-Behaved Children

Learning is lifelong, especially when it comes to behavior patterns. Nobody—not you, not your brother, not the woman cleaning the bank teller's booth 12 miles away—is completely and always disciplined. Discipline, and what it means, also needs to be frequently redefined. You're still working on yourself, your own discipline, aren't you? It's helpful to remember that *nobody* is perfect, and that discipline is a process, not a result. Keeping this in mind will help your peace of mind, and help your kids, too.

The Twelve Disciplinary Elements

Like most things in life, positive discipline happens all at the same time. If you're changing your approach to your children's behavior, it can seem overwhelming. My personal way of dealing with a seemingly impossible task that makes my anxiety levels soar is to break it into a whole bunch of little tiny parts, each one of which can be easily accomplished. My friend Ailsa calls these the "approachable increments of infinity."

Here then, are my Twelve Disciplinary Elements. Each one is doable. They're not steps, because you climb a flight of steps one after the other (unless you're like my 86-year-old grandmother and take them two or three at a time). They're pieces of a whole; once you get them working they happen all at once, and each element isn't fully effective without the others. In this book, we'll look at each element, and concentrate on making them work for *you*.

1. Pay attention to your child.
2. Respect your children and yourself.
3. Be reasonable, gentle, and firm.
4. Prevent and minimize problems through understanding, communication, and modeling.
5. Use positive reinforcement to encourage and reward proper behavior.
6. Teach ways to make choices.
7. Set reasonable personal expectations and goals for your child.
8. Set reasonable expectations for yourself and your family.
9. Communicate effective and reasonable limits.
10. Understand misbehavior.
11. Provide related, respectful, reasonable responses.
12. Be consistent.

Let's take a moment in this chapter to look at the first two elements of the discipline process, element number one: Pay attention to your child, and element number two: Respect your children and yourself. We'll look at the rest of the parts later on in the book.

Disciplinary Element Number One: Pay Attention to Your Child

Parenting *is* the art of paying attention, and element number one of the Twelve Disciplinary Elements is paying attention to your child. You can learn almost everything you need to know about parenting your children by paying close attention to them. It's not easy, especially in today's rush-rush world. Not many of us can take life at a leisurely pace, and I know I'm not the only parent who's made multitasking—doing a bunch of things at the same time—a lifestyle. I read in the bathtub. I talk on the phone while cooking or gardening. I'm writing *this* in a restaurant while eating Thai noodles with basil and chicken, and when my daughter Annie was a baby, I learned how to fax, phone, and change a diaper at the same time.

Multitasking is not always appropriate, though. Children require focused attention. No, not every moment, but much of the time. If you don't really know your child, how will you understand what's wrong when things go wrong? How will you pick up the clues when your kid is flirting with trouble? How will you understand how to make things right for your child?

It's a Good Idea!

Use your multitasking to free up time to spend with your kids.

Big and Little "Troubles"

The odd thing is that, contrary to popular belief and the dim, vain hopes of sleep-deprived new parents, parenting doesn't become easier as your children grow. When your child is a baby, yeah, you're changing diapers, nursing, and burping the baby every five minutes. Okay, as your kid gets older, the less minute-by-minute attention is required. Then again, though, with a baby, your worries are relatively small (and usually are centered around bodily functions). The older your child gets, the more can go wrong. School, friends, behavior, independence issues—as the old Yiddish saying goes: "Little children, little troubles. Big children, big troubles."

Now, more than ever, your kids need you to pay attention.

Behave Yourself!

No slacking! Parenting requires time. And effective, positive discipline requires paying attention to what is going on in your child's life.

Pay Attention! Easier Said Than Done

I can tell you the importance of both quantity and quality time when you're trying to raise well-behaved kids, but it won't do you or your kids any good if you simply clear your schedule or quit your job. It's not enough to be there, hands idle, ears perked.

Paying attention means more than being physically present. It means learning *how* to listen to your kids, *how* to talk with them, and *how* to respond to their actions. (Rest assured, you can still have a busy life and do all this.) Throughout this book, you'll find exercises and suggestions to help you improve your ability to pay attention to your child. Good, quality attention will improve the quality of your family's life—and there is always time for quality.

Disciplinary Element Number Two: Respect Your Children and Yourself

Element number two of the Twelve Disciplinary Elements is to respect your children and yourself. Positive discipline is based on mutual respect. Assume that children are basically reasonable human beings who want to do well, and treat them with the respect they deserve. Kids learn by imitation, and just demonstrating respectful behavior will take you a long way. The basic rule is: You get what you give. Sound familiar? Some call it the Golden Rule, and some call it karma, but the idea is the same: Treat your child as you would like to be treated and your child (eventually and usually) will treat you that way back.

How do you show respect for your child? By discussing her feelings and beliefs and acknowledging that they are valid—for her. By helping her improve her critical thinking skills and empathy by discussing other people's perspectives on the same issues. By respecting who she is, and the integrity of her body. By starting with the child, and moving forward from there. You don't show respect when you agree with everything she says or by letting her make all her own choices or decisions. Look, kids *don't* always know what's right for them. They're kids, after all.

You show respect for your child when you:

➤ respect her feelings;

➤ respect her opinions;

➤ respect her privacy;

➤ respect her temperament; and

➤ respect her body and personal space.

It's a Good Idea!

The fact that children are little, seemingly-irrational, and inexperienced shouldn't be held against them. Children should be held against you—gently.

It's a Good Idea!

Respect your child's challenges! Children test you to see how far they can go. It's not that they want total freedom, rather they want to know what the limits are. Setting reasonable (and respectful) limits for them will enable them to set their own limits as they grow older.

Values, Communication, Internal Discipline, Trust, and Problem Prevention

Before we continue going through the elements of discipline, let's look at some of the other qualities of positive discipline. Positive discipline also:

➤ teaches values;

➤ requires strong communication skills;

➤ develops internal discipline;

➤ builds trust; and

➤ prevents problems.

"Hey John, Here's What's Important"

Teaching discipline instills values in your kids, and you can't beat values into your kids with a stick. (Actually, if you try, you'll probably be reported to child protective services, serve time in the pokey or be forced to go to anger management classes, reinforce your child's violent tendencies, and lose all the trust your child ever had in you.) We'll look at spanking and striking kids in Chapter 10. Positive values are automatically imparted gently, every day, through example, information, and positive associations. (Negative values are imparted everyday too, so watch your own actions!) In Chapter 6, we'll look closer at ways to clearly define your own family's values.

Who's Talking? Who's Listening?

Communication is key in teaching your children discipline. To pay attention effectively, you've got to know how to listen. And to get a disciplinary message through to your child, you've got to know how to talk with him in a way he can hear (otherwise he'll never learn). Throughout the book you'll find exercises and approaches to improving your family's communication.

Internalizing Discipline and Building Self-Control

Discipline begins from the outside, taught by you, and moves to the inside, as your kid develops his conscience and sense of responsibility. A child learns discipline *from* you, but the main goal is to teach a child how to discipline himself, to *internalize the discipline*. A child whose disciplinary process has been internalized relies on himself to make appropriate choices. He probably also has developed his sense of ethics. (There's a bit more on ethics in a moment.)

Words to Parent By

Internalizing the discipline is the process whereby a child learns how to discipline herself.

Trust

As the child internalizes the discipline you've taught him, your job changes. Now you've got to let go and trust that what you've taught him is going to stick. Take a deep breath and let go. The more you show your trust, the more your child will strive to meet it. Kids want to be trusted.

It's a Good Idea!

Do it daily! Since positive discipline is a general parenting approach to preventing problems, it's gotta be used as part of daily life rather than as an occasional thing.

Steer Clear of That Problem!

Positive discipline is a preventative approach. Don't just sit back and wait for trouble to find you (because it will!). Yes, there's correction involved in positive discipline, but the main focus is on preventing trouble. Paying attention, effective communication, responding to your child's positive choices, and good parental modeling are your primary ways of preventing problems (there are other techniques, too, and we'll go into those in later chapters).

Raising an Ethical Child

Throughout this book we'll be talking about how discipline is the process of instilling values in your child. Ethics are how your child expresses the values she's learned. An ethical person *has* discipline—the courage to believe in something (whether political, social, or spiritual) and the strength to act on those beliefs.

Children need to be taught to be well behaved. Just because a child lies, for instance, doesn't mean she's unethical. Her ethics—her personal sense of right and wrong—are still being developed.

She learns how to be ethical as she learns to be disciplined, and she learns ethics from how *you* demonstrate your ethics in the world.

The Fantasy of Parental Control

Who's in charge in your family? Who controls your child? Do you? Come on now, do you really? Let me tell you a story, adapted from an old folktale.

The Mighty Ruler and the Baby

Once upon a time, there was a very strong and powerful ruler. "I'm so strong and powerful I can do anything!" he boasted and roared. "I can bend *anybody* to my mighty will I'm so strong that *nobody* can defeat me!"

"Nobody?" asked his grandmother, a wise woman, well tempered by time.

"*Nobody!*" he roared.

"We'll see about that," said his grandmother. "I know somebody more mighty than you." And she took him by the hand and led him to a neighbor's house. Inside, a baby was sitting in the corner, laughing. Her laughter enraged the ruler, who believed that everybody should be solemn and respectful around him.

"Stop laughing!" demanded the ruler. "Nobody laughs at me! I am the ruler of all rulers!"

But the baby kept on laughing.

"I will *injure* you if you don't stop!" yelled the ruler, who, as you already can see, had some rage-control issues.

At this, the baby stopped laughing, looked up at the ruler, and then began to coo and smile.

"I'm *scary!*" roared the ruler, and, determined to get a reaction from the impertinent little subject, began stamping his feet, waving his arms, making ugly faces, and growling.

The baby, bored with the display, lay down and went to sleep.

Here's the moral: Your grandma knows more than you do. Oops, wrong moral. Here's the real moral: You cannot control a child through sheer willpower, show of force, or bullying. In that New York hotel room with Annie, we could have smacked her until she cried, and stopped her from jumping up and down on the bed. But what message would we have given her, to have lost control over ourselves and have to resort to violence? And nothing, not even spanking, would control whether she'd do it again.

Source of Security: You!

You can provide your child with a sense of security without controlling her. Your child will feel most secure when she trusts that you are "in control" when it comes to making safety issues, setting appropriate behavior boundaries, and teaching her what your expectations are while still respecting her thoughts, feelings, and individuality. Kids rebel when their parents exert too much control. Parenting is negotiation.

It's a Good Idea!

Self-control—over yourself, over your life—is something to aim for. You cannot gain self-control by being "controlling."

What Does Control Mean to You?

As you think about your own parenting, it can be helpful to take a quick peek back at the past, to your own childhood. Take a moment to think about your own upbringing. Then write short responses to the following questions.

1. What's your history with family control?

2. Who was in charge?

3. Who wanted to be?

4. How was control exerted in your family?

5. What would you like to change about this picture with your own kids?

Focus on Positive Influence

You may never be able to "control" your kids (and, after all, the real goal is for them to have self-control), but you do have influence, and your influence is *very* important to your child. The older the child gets, the less overall influence you have. School, friends, siblings, the media, all influence who your child is becoming. But though it seems that the older they get, the less they want to listen to poor old *you,* it's really not true. You *do* matter. What you say and do strongly affects your child.

(Here's the other moral of the story of the ruler and the baby: It's totally maddening when a kid laughs in your face. In Chapter 15, we'll look closer at ways of dealing with anger.)

Letting Them Go

As a parent, you're doomed to spend the rest of your life trying to find the balance between being actively involved with your children and still letting them go toward their own, independent lives. There's no easy answer. We'll talk more about this process when we explore limits in Chapter 7.

Tales from the Parent Zone

Alicia and her daughter Toni were reading the Laura Ingalls Wilder books about pioneer life, *The Little House in the Big Woods, The Little House on the Prairie,* and so on. Parenting was very different then, Alicia had to explain, when they came to the part where Pa talked about taking a child behind the wood shed to "tan his hide" with a fresh willow switch. Alicia found it delicious, and a testimony to her own parenting style, that her five-year-old daughter didn't know what the words "spanking," whipping," or "beating" meant. After Alicia explained corporal punishment, Toni looked at her in amazement that any parent would hurt a child so.

The Discipline of Positive Discipline

We use the word *discipline* frequently when we're talking about raising well-behaved kids. The word *discipline* is also used a lot by people who are involved in Eastern studies—meditations like Zen Buddhism, and martial arts like karate, judo, aikido, and tae kwon do. All of these Eastern studies focus, too, on paying attention, and on the process of learning, not just the results. I like to think about the process of teaching positive discipline to kids as a kind of combo meditation *and* martial art. You have to be focused and strong, and you have to practice a lot (and consistently). No Zen master became enlightened in a day. Those high kicks done by karate masters, the slow elegant moves of the aikido master, all took years to learn. Be patient.

Raising a well-behaved child by using positive discipline techniques can be slow going. You *will* see some immediate change, but for many behavior problems, there are no quick fixes. Sometimes behavior takes months or even years to change. Keep at it! Positive discipline is like learning to ride a bike—you'll fall down a lot, but once you know how to do it, you have that skill forever. (Come to think of it, riding a bike is all about learning how to balance. So is positive discipline!) By using encouragement, setting limits, and providing reasonable consequences, you'll be helping your child develop long-term self-control *and* self-respect.

Never give up on your child or on yourself. Setbacks don't mean you are failing. Get "Zen" about it. Change will come. Learn to practice positive discipline daily (Hey, you can take a moment to pay attention at any time!). Here you go! You are entering the discipline of positive discipline. With time, both you and your kid can earn your black belts.

The Least You Need to Know

➤ Kids learn to be well behaved through a positive approach of focused attention, consistency, modeling, and gentle correction.

➤ The main goal of positive discipline is to teach a child to discipline himself.

➤ For best results, pay attention to and respect your children.

➤ You have strong influence but ultimately no control.

➤ Teach your child as best you can, then let go and trust your child.

Chapter 2

Parenting Styles: Wimpy, Bossy, or Strong and Reasonable

In This Chapter

➤ The difference between being in control and being in charge

➤ Determining your parenting style

➤ Tips for being gentle, fun, and strong

➤ All about behavior modeling

➤ Choosing your battles

Who's in control here? I know, in Chapter 1 I convinced you that *you* aren't. I didn't lie—ultimately, you can be influential without being controlling.

But just because you're not the big control master doesn't mean being *out* of control. It doesn't mean giving *up* control. It doesn't mean being a parent who lets your kids stomp all over you while you lay back and tell them what a good job they're doing. "Excellent stomping, James!" That's not what raising a well-behaved child through positive discipline is about.

Positive discipline means establishing a parenting style that walks the wide road between being authoritarian (we'll call it *bossy*) and being ineffective and lenient (we'll call it *wimpy*). You can be strict without being bossy. You can be loving and patient without being wimpy. You can be a strong and reasonable parent—not controlling, but in charge. Every child needs a caretaker who will provide encouragement, guidance, limits, and unconditional love in a reasonable fashion. You can be that caretaker.

In this chapter, we'll look at you, the parent, at your style of parenting, and at tools that will help you teach discipline to your child while staying sane. You'll learn more about how to shift your parenting style toward strong and reasonable, and how to be gentle at the same time.

The Parenting Style Continuum

What's your style? Experts who study family dynamics and parenting have come up with a range of parenting styles. If you put them on a continuum they look something like this:

The Parenting Style Continuum

| Abusive | Conditional | Assertive | Supportive | Indulgent | Neglectful |

| BOSSY | | STRONG AND REASONABLE | | | WIMPY |

A Quick "Hit" on the Parenting Continuum

Imagine six parents, each with a different parenting style, sitting in the dentist's waiting room with their six children. The kids are running wild, acting out, and getting into trouble. Here's what the parents might say and do:

➤ The abusive parent says, "Get your ugly butt over here you little stupid creep!" (smacks, screams, tears).

➤ The conditional parent says, "I can't believe you would behave like this, you're embarrassing me, we're leaving. I told you we were going to go get ice cream later but I changed my mind. You won't be having ice cream for three weeks, young lady!"

➤ The assertive parent says, "Sarah, that is inappropriate behavior. Sit down right next to me. *Now* please. And now might be a good time to start that homework you brought."

➤ The supportive parent says, "Tommy, what's up? You can't behave like that, honey. Please sit down now. Are you bored? I brought your book and some stuff to color with."

➤ The indulgent parent says, "Ah, let them run, they're just kids having a good time."

➤ The neglectful parent says, well, *nothing*. The neglectful parent doesn't notice his kid; he's too busy reading *People*.

Keeping all these categories straight is pretty tough, so I've lumped them together into three styles: on one end, the bossy parent (conditional to abusive), on the other end, the wimpy parent (indulgent to neglectful), and in the middle, the strong and reasonable parent (assertive to supportive). No matter where on the continuum your parenting style falls now, it's a no-brainer to figure out which style I think you should aim for: strong and reasonable. Either of the other two styles in their extreme raise children who lack self-control and self-respect.

The Bossy Parent

The bossy parent's word is law. After all, she's the parent, and her word goes. She is good at barking orders, but rarely gives reasons for them. She rules by fear. Don't get me wrong, she's not necessarily cruel; she fears for her child's future. "If he's not scared I'll hurt him, he'll go bad," she might feel. The bossy parent's ideas of getting her kids to behave often backfire. Her kids may learn how to follow orders and be "good," but their discipline is all driven from exterior threat, rather than being internalized. Kids with bossy parents often have difficulty making decisions. How can they? They've had little practice. They tend to be immature, lack in confidence and resourcefulness, and act irresponsibly and impulsively.

The Wimpy Parent

The wimpy parent is the opposite: He steps away from asserting his opinions, values, and rules, and allows his child full responsibility for her own actions. He's usually very inconsistent, and may threaten consequences but fall down on the follow-through. Very often wimpy parents are rebelling against their own bossy parents. While the impulse to trust the child is positive, the lack of boundaries and direction leaves many wimpy-parented kids lost and confused. These kids often lack self-control—with no rules, they've never had to practice. Children whose parents have a wimpy style are often not very resourceful either. They have trouble determining whether or not their behavior is appropriate, and, if it is not, how to change.

The Strong and Reasonable Parent

Ah! Our hero! The strong and reasonable parent is in charge without being authoritarian, a companion to her kids without being a peer. She relies on knowing her children, is comfortable talking with them, and likes and trusts them. She isn't removed, cool, or dictatorial. She's involved, she's real. Her

It's a Good Idea!

The well-behaved child needs a strong and reasonable parent.

Behave Yourself!

Parents of *every* parenting style are occasionally furious parents. Anger is scary. There are very few parents who have never been so angry, hurt, frustrated, worn-out, or simply at the end of their patience that they haven't lost it—or come *this close* to losing it. Fury often brings the urge to *hurt* your child, out of revenge, or simply to make the behavior stop. ("Stop crying or I'll give you something to *really* cry about!!!") It's common to feel it, it's not okay to do it.

kids know she's human, they know her weaknesses and strengths. She's forgiving, occasionally indulgent, good at setting limits, excellent at applying appropriate consequences, and she doesn't let anybody push her around. Her children *know* that no matter what they do, she loves them and is on their side. Finally, the strong and reasonable parent knows that her ultimate goal is raising a resourceful child who can think for herself and make good, appropriate life choices.

Sound like something to aim for? I think so. (Sound too good to be true? Probably. I said something to *aim* for, not to expect to always be!)

Where Did You Get That Style?

Take a few moments to think about your relationship with your child, and your life way back in the dark ages when *you* were a child. Then answer the following questions. Be honest, now. You don't have to show this to anybody, nobody will ever know (unless you decide to blab). This is between you and you:

> What parenting styles did you experience as a child?
>
> How did your parents teach you to be well behaved?
>
> How did your parents discipline you?
>
> Did they always teach and correct you with anger?
>
> How did they encourage your independence?

List three things your parents did that you wouldn't mind repeating:

1.

2.

3.

List three things your parents did that you will never, ever, not-even-when-the-cows-come-home do to your children:

1.

2.

3.

Now think about your own parenting.

> How often do you criticize your child?
>
> How often do you provide specific, positive feedback?
>
> In what ways do you show your pride and enthusiasm?
>
> In what ways are you instilling your values, and your ethics?

Do you "rescue" your kids from difficult situations, let them work things our on their own, or help them with their problem-solving?

Do you find yourself charging up your anger before you talk to your kids when they've done something wrong? Note a time when a talk with your child felt more like a confrontation.

Unless they consciously make other choices, people tend to slide into the same parenting styles as their parents. (They've internalized their parents' discipline.) By looking at your answers to these sets of questions, you can begin to think about the parenting style that helped shape you, and how you parent now. You can begin to make decisions about adjusting your style. Self-knowledge is the secret, isn't it?

"That Approach Is Not My Style"

There's a difference between parenting *approach* and parenting *style*. Parents have all sorts of approaches to parenting, and there's room for positive discipline within all of them. Every family is different, and every family has its own values and customs. In all these examples, the parents are basically strong and reasonable, they just have different ways of applying their style:

➤ In Joanie's family, everybody yells all the time, and everybody is always in a hurry.

➤ Linda rarely raises her voice, and her kids get up five minutes later than they should every day.

➤ Doug's kids have to clean their rooms once a day, before they go to bed.

➤ Belinda and Tom's daughter is expected to straighten her room once every six weeks or so, before the cleaning lady comes in to do the heavy cleaning.

➤ Sarah and Lou weep with their son when he comes to them about his disappointments.

➤ Tony, who is Dave and Lee's kid, has been informed where the Band-Aids are kept. If it's a serious problem, he knows he can call one of his dads. Otherwise, he bandages up, and goes back to play.

When Parents Have Different Approaches

No two parents have exactly the same parenting approach, and even your styles don't need to be an exact match. Some people tend to be laid back and casual, some more strict. Some believe in organizing the household with operating procedures, guidelines, rules, and regulations. Ideally, of course, two parents living together should have a meeting of minds, or at least a balance of parenting styles and approaches. Have a little conference or two to discuss your household's approach. (There are details on family meetings in Chapter 6.) Whatever approach you decide on, make sure you are respecting your children, honoring their autonomy, and nurturing their needs.

About Boundaries

Positive parenting is *not* about being so goofy sweet that you allow the kids to walk all over you. There's a lot of talk these days about the horrors of "permissive" (otherwise known as "wimpy") parenting, and the damage it's done to kids who were never "punished."

On the other hand, returning to a model of punitive punishment and "parents are king" isn't a viable option. It's cruel, and it simply doesn't work. You cannot "control" the situation by asserting control. Guide, yes, control, no.

And somewhere in the middle is the fact that *you* need to be comfortable with your own parenting style and approach. As you determine what that's gonna be, keep in mind that you have rights here. Patricia Jakubowski, author of *The Assertive Option*, writes that a parent has the very basic right:

1. To act in ways that promote dignity and self-respect as long as others' rights are not violated.
2. To be treated with respect.
3. To say no and not feel guilty.
4. To experience and express feelings.
5. To take time to slow down and think.
6. To have a change of mind.
7. To ask for what he wants.
8. To do *less* than she is humanly capable of doing.
9. To ask for information.
10. To make mistakes.
11. To feel good about himself.

Disciplinary Element Number Three: Be Reasonable, Gentle, and Firm

You can be a strong and reasonable authority figure and still be fun, as well as gentle and affectionate. The first task is to give up on perfection. Go on! Take perfection by the hand, lead it to a tall bridge over deep water, hoist it up the railing, and *push it off!* You are not a perfect parent. Guess what? You aren't going to be.

Now that we have that out of the way, let's talk about being reasonable. You cannot be perfect, but you *can* be reasonable. A reasonable parent:

➤ Tries hard and cares.

➤ Works hard to model the behavior she'd like to see in her kids.

➤ Sets her expectations and disciplinary goals for herself, and for her family, at reasonable, realistic levels.

➤ Defines reasonable limits for her children's behavior.

➤ Identifies and discusses natural consequences that occur and provides reasonable, logical consequences when things go wrong.

➤ Is reasonably consistent about it.

➤ Understands that change takes time, and gives herself and her kids a break.

Words to Parent By

A *reasonable parent* is an informed and compassionate parent who relies on reason as well as emotion to understand his developing child.

You, the Gentle Giant

The word *discipline* often calls up for me the image of a woman with a bullwhip, a man with a belt, a fierce, mean face, and a couple of terrified children, afraid to squeak for fear of "getting it." Okay, we know that discipline means "teaching," and we know that teaching works *best* when kids want to learn. Since kids learn best when they are engaged, active, and having fun, *dump the attitude* and join the learning! You can be fun, and you can be a disciplinarian. Correction *is* correction without the screams. You're not being lenient when you're gentle and kind, you're imparting knowledge in the most effective way. And it's a lot easier on your blood pressure.

It's a Good Idea!

Did you ever think you were going to grow up and become so *reasonable?* Kids aren't always reasonable, it's not in their job description. Adults aren't always reasonable, either, but it's something to aim toward. In many ways, a reasonable parent is automatically a good parent.

No matter what style you begin with, you can change and become more gentle, stronger. The first step is becoming aware of how you treat your children when you are angry at them. Try the following:

➤ Take a deep breath and cool down before you leap into telling your kids why you're mad at their behavior.

➤ Remind yourself you don't have to *look* or *act* angry to get results.

Remember, It's Funny!

Humor is a big part of reasonable parenting, and of positive discipline, for a few reasons:

➤ Laughter breaks the tension.

➤ Humor is a good way to deal with stress (it's better to laugh than to scream).

➤ Teasing and sarcasm don't count as reasonable. Be gentle.

➤ You don't have to *impose* your limits and consequences with a heavy hand and a heavy heart. Actually, being too heavy can often work against you (who wants to listen or learn from a mean, grumpy horrible person?).

Behave Yourself!

No sarcasm! Sarcasm is a mean form of humor, designed to slice, rather than soothe. Kids often don't understand sarcasm. Laugh with the child, not at him, and keep that humor gentle!

Just because you're laughing or smiling doesn't mean you're not taking something seriously. Humor is a great way to keep a sense of perspective about things—really now, on a scale of one to 10 of terrible behavior (with 10 resulting in doing time in San Quentin for assault and murder), blowing milk out your nose barely counts at all! Laughing may sometimes be unavoidable—don't worry, you can laugh and still correct your child.

Quantity Time, Quality Energy

Discipline is your parenting style in action. Remember that old debate about quality time versus quantity time? This just in: Both matter. You really need at least *some* quantity to achieve quality. If, on the other hand, you are together with your child all the time but never pay attention, there's no quality to your quantity. Arghhh! It's an issue of balance. I'm beginning to think it's *all* an issue of balance!

How can you get both quality and quantity into your busy life? It's not always easy. This is an insane time for most parents, and your schedule is probably stretched thin as it is. Don't waste valuable time feeling guilty: Prioritize! The more quality time you have in your life, the easier it will be to predict trouble.

It's a Good Idea!

How do you know if you're spending enough quantity and quality time with your child? Why not ask her?

➤ Take an hour of your usual TV watching time to spend with your child (turn that set off!)

➤ Include your child in your day-to-day errand running (keeping in mind your individual child's errand tolerance level—some like errands, some tolerate one, some three, and some *hate* them all). Use the transportation time to chat.

➤ Instead of listening to the news, the traffic update, and music in the car, turn the radio off and listen to each other. (There's more on *this* in Chapter 3.)

Let Your Child Do It

The strong, reasonable, gentle parent teaches self-reliance by expecting self-reliance and competence, and by letting children make mistakes. Trust that your child can do it. Show your trust, encourage progress, and don't "rescue" your child! If you constantly step in to save the day when a child is in a minor jam, he won't learn how to work his way out of his own problems. Sometimes this means letting small mistakes and minor disappointments happen. They're learning experiences. (Hey, I'm not saying abandon your baby to the wolves—just teach him how to avoid wolves, and then watch him do it, standing by in case of disaster.)

Tales from the Parent Zone

"The hardest thing about parenting is watching my son Ramsey stumble and fall and learn from his mistakes," Lisa says. "But I know I'm not always going to be around to hold his hand through life." Lisa is wise. As Dorothy Fisher once said, "A mother is not to lean on but to make leaning unnecessary."

The Loving Parent

The *most* important aspect of being a strong and reasonable parent is showing unconditional love for your child. There's a tight correlation for children between experiencing unconditional parental love, and having a sense of self-respect. Unconditional love is loving a child for who she is no matter what she does or how well she succeeds in life. This kind of love promotes self-acceptance and self-confidence. The child who knows she's loved, who is encouraged, and who has experiences of mastery and success, will grow to respect and cherish herself. She'll have the tools to make positive choices all through life.

Words to Parent By

Unconditional love is love that has no conditions attached to it. The person loved unconditionally doesn't have to be anybody, or prove anything, or act in any particular way to be loved, and love is neither withdrawn for "bad" behavior nor bestowed for "good" behavior.

Disciplinary Element Number Four: Prevent and Minimize Problems Through Understanding, Communication, and Modeling

In order to prevent behavior problems, you've got to understand your child's point of view, you have to be able to communicate with your child, and you need to model the behavior you want to see. We'll talk more about problem prevention and

Words to Parent By

Behavior modeling means demonstrating, through your daily actions, the kind of behavior you expect your children to demonstrate. (This takes a certain amount of discipline of your own.)

It's a Good Idea!

If you're struggling with a certain issue or behavior, don't lie about it, and don't hide it from your child. The struggle is an important part of the process and you're teaching him that, though you're not perfect, you're working hard to improve yourself.

It's a Good Idea!

Model effective and appropriate talking and listening skills. "Don't you *&%$-ing talk to me like that, young lady!" doesn't cut the mustard. Work on it. A family that communicates well has fewer problems than a family that doesn't.

understanding your child's point of view in later chapters, and we'll talk about communication later in this chapter. Now, let's talk about behavior modeling.

Here's the thing about modeling: You don't have to decide to begin modeling behavior, you already are. You simply need to realize *what* you are modeling now, and decide what you want to model in the future. My parents, simply by being who they are, modeled a very strong work ethic and interest and joy in what they were engaged in. I learned that it's important to do work that feels valuable and I learned to work at my work very hard. I don't remember them telling me this—in words. They told me it everyday, just by how they were living their lives.

One of the most effective ways to get your child to be well behaved is to model the correct behavior. What you *do*, and who you *are* will sink in, eventually. (Please note that modeling is a daily process, and there are some results you may not fully see for *years*. Fifty years from now your doddering old daughter will be saying, "My parents taught me everything I know.")

Negative Modeling

Modeling works the other way too. If you model the incorrect behavior, it doesn't much matter *what* you say. Forget "Do as I say, not as I do"—actions speak louder than words. That means that if you want your child to lose the foul language, you'll need to model good language yourself. I know, what about the occasional swear word that slips from your lips? My best friend Tilly's mom always recommends this approach: Teach your children the difference between "family words" and "public words." "Family words" can sometimes be angry words (they make people angry when they hear them) and can cause trouble for us if we use them outside the house.

This, of course, is a matter of family approach. Other families *never* want to hear cursing. They might make that desire explicit in their family value statement (and there's more on this in Chapter 6).

It's the Golden Rule

Modeling behavior really comes down to one rule: Be who you want your kids to emulate. Be considerate and your kids will learn consideration. It's simple, really.

Who's the Grown-Up Here, Anyway?

Just because you're the grown-up, that doesn't make you the boss or the heavy in the family. Be the voice of reason.

You are the adult in the family, no doubt about it. You have more hair, more wrinkles, more money, and more experience than your child. Your child isn't your peer, that's clear, but she isn't your inferior, either. She's younger than you, less experienced, and she needs your help to learn about the world, and how to act in it. It's not useful to be competitive with your kids about who is more important, you or your kids. They matter just as much as you do but that doesn't mean their needs come first. It doesn't mean *your* needs do either.

The FamilyMind Tool

Jeanne and Don Elium, authors of *Raising a Family,* have developed a great concept called *FamilyMind.* When things feel stressful, ask yourself the FamilyMind question: "What does this family need right now, including me?" Don't forget the "including me" part, it's really important. Working toward family needs (as long as they include your own) reduces stress, and simply bypasses the pecking order struggles that are too common in families.

Behave Yourself!

The quickest way to rebellion is to assert too much control. That doesn't mean rolling over and taking abuse, and it doesn't mean letting your kids run wild without limits. The lion tamer *harnesses* that energy, he doesn't kill it. Neither should you.

Choosing Your Battles

Choose your battles. Choose what you will and will not let fly in your household. In our society, we all have an idea of "normal," but the range of normal is pretty large. In my friend Sophie's house, they agree that kids shouldn't bring food into their rooms, but they've decided not to enforce the idea. In my house, it's firm—eating in the kitchen *only!* On the other hand, Sophie and her husband are strict about not talking about anything gross at the dinner table. In our house, we know it's not polite, but it sometimes happens anyway. Once again, which battles you choose to fight should be based on your personal and family boundaries. Making decisions about what battles to battle—choosing what is and is not okay—will make you feel more "in control." We'll talk more about setting family limits in Chapters 6 and 7.

Even once you've chosen, be prepared to lose occasionally. If you hate the idea of this, here's a technique to make sure you won't lose any battles—stop considering them battles! In a battle, two sides pit themselves one against the other, and one side wins, the other loses. In a discipline situation, your goal is not to defeat your child (or have your child defeat you). Back off on the competition, baby. Your goal is to have you *both* win by strengthening your child and helping him form his character. Sometimes it's better to let it go—just not mention it when the kid is breaking "the rules." Save your battles for when it *really* matters.

Enjoy Your Child

Here's another reason to slack off and let the little stuff go: It'll free you to *enjoy* your child instead of constantly looking for something to criticize and correct. Having fun with your child is a vital part of teaching him discipline.

The Least You Need to Know

➤ Just because you're not in control doesn't mean you're *out* of control.

➤ Aim toward the center of the parenting continuum—strong and reasonable.

➤ Your parenting style is not the same as your parenting approach—everybody's approach is different.

➤ Your child will model his behavior on yours.

➤ You can't win every battle. Choose the ones that feel significant, and let the rest go.

Chapter 3

Setting Your Child Up for Success

In This Chapter

➤ Why and how to be always on your child's "side"

➤ The importance of hugs and other affection

➤ Tips on how to effectively listen to your kid

➤ Talking strategies

➤ Helping your child succeed through patience, justice, and love

Want your child to grow well in life? Show her you are on her side. Respect her. Assume she will do well. Listen to her, show patience. Work for justice. Love her unconditionally, and teach her to love and respect herself and others.

In this chapter, we'll talk about what a well-behaved child really needs from you, and how you can help him become confident, respectful, well behaved, interested in learning, able to achieve personal goals, and ready to leap zestfully at life.

This means discipline. Doesn't everything?

Tales from the Parent Zone

How do you measure success? Mr. B.G. Mouth has money, a big house, three luxury cars, and a staff of 40 catering to his every whim. His wife, Lauda Mouth, has political power and fame. Yet the three Mouth kids are miserable, socially inept, and in trouble. Let's get a little more internal, and consider success on an interpersonal and personal level. The best thing a parent can do is to teach a child the tools for creating her own successes.

Be Your Child's Ally

Your child will become a well-behaved child when she knows deep down in her bones that you are there for her as her ally. An ally is somebody who is on your side, who assumes that you mean well, and who trusts and believes in you. You need to be your child's ally. The world out there is mean and cruel! "Of course I'm on my child's side!" you might exclaim. But think about it for a minute. Are you?

Some parents automatically side with other grown-ups, roll their eyes at their own child's behavior, and believe it instantly when another adult criticizes or accuses their child. "Your Billy hit my Angela." "Billy! Get over here right this moment!" (smack!). That's not right. Your child needs to know that there is at least one person in the world who believes in him, no matter what happens. That's you. If you're in a situation where you must leap to assumptions, assume your child is right. Two things will happen:

1. You'll realize that it's true, at least 50% of the time.
2. As your child realizes how much you trust her, she'll take care to do things to get your approval—and she'll take time to actually *be* right.

Words to Parent By

An *ally* is somebody who is on your side, who looks out for you, and who you can trust to be there when the chips are down.

An Ally Is Unconditional

Be your child's ally in good times and bad. Your child really needs to rely on you not to laugh at her, insult her, or love her less when she has done something wrong, or when she is angry, frightened, or confused. If she fears you're only "on her side" when she acts like a good kid, she'll hide, she'll pull away, and lie to you. Stay open to all aspects of your child. You are her champion for better or for worse! If you're truly her ally, she'll remain open to you.

An Ally Doesn't Always Approve

Yes, indeed, you can be somebody's ally and disapprove, be furious, or be hurt by their actions. As a matter of fact, it's part of your responsibility as an ally to help the person take responsibility for his actions (especially when you are both an ally and a parent).

The Ally's Goal: Mutual Respect

Ah, respect. Look at that, we're back to the second element of the Twelve Disciplinary Elements! I know, we looked at "respect" in Chapter 1, but I've got a few more things to say about it, in the context of setting your child up to be successful. (And then I'll shut up. I promise.)

Respect, respecting, and self-respect—it's all intertwined. In order for a child to be successful, she needs to be respected and to have a sense of self-respect. In order for a child to respect *you,* she needs to first feel *your* respect. Self-respect is key to success. It's your job to help build your child's self-respect by standing up for her.

You communicate respect for your child's body and personal space, temperament, privacy, needs, and opinions by observing her carefully, listening well, and taking her seriously.

Kids respond when they feel respected. It's like the story of the first grader who kept talking about her new friend on the school bus—the bus driver. For days her imaginary play was filled with busses and drivers, and she looked forward to going to school and coming home on the bus every day. What was the big draw, her parents wondered. Finally they asked her what was so special about this new friend. "I like him," the little girl said, "because he treats me like a people."

Kids today when asked why they got into a fight often respond, "He dis'ed me," meaning "He disrespected me." Though kids may not themselves have a fully formed notion of just what respect means (for example, it's a two-way street, among other things), they demand respect and resent its absence. This should be a signal to parents.

Treat your kid like a "people," and he'll return the favor.

Behave Yourself!

Respect is a two-way street. If you travel the road toward your child, he'll travel the road toward you. Here are three common but disrespectful parental phrases that interfere with traffic on Respect Boulevard: "Because I say so, that's why," "Do as I say, not as I do," and, "Shut up." Don't cause a traffic jam!

Assume a "Good" Child

Assuming your child is a "good" kid is part of setting your child up for disciplinary success, and is a big element of positive discipline. Nobody wants to be "bad," and every human being wants approval.

Kids are as likely to rise to meet your expectations as a helium balloon will float from a toddler's hand. (They'll also sink to meet your expectations like a dropped Rolex will fall to the ocean floor.) What you expect, you get. Assume that you have a well-behaved child, and your child will generally meet your expectations. If you assume negative behavior, I guarantee that that's what you'll get.

Tales from the Parent Zone

All kids are driven by the need for approval—if not from their parents or school, then from their friends. Bobby got nothing but criticism from his dad, and his teachers all considered him a disruptive influence. Yet to his friends, Bobby was brave, noble, and true, and they let him know it. (Guess who he listened to when things got rough? Obviously, his friends rather than his parents or teachers.)

Tales from the Parent Zone

I assume my daughter will behave in grocery stores, and most of the time she does. There are always glitches, though—we're talking about kids, and kids test their parents. Just the other day I had to drag Annie down from the high shelf she'd scaled with a package of Skittles clenched in her teeth. This was totally unacceptable behavior! (And she was tired and angry at me for rushing her.)

Here are a few ways to assure that you're assuming yours is a well-behaved child:

➤ Before you go on an adventure, don't present a list of negative behaviors you *don't* want the child to do. Assume she will be well behaved.

➤ Reinforce the assumption of "good" by noticing out loud what she is doing well.

➤ Don't confuse *good* with *perfection*. A child is childish, expect nothing less! She's acting appropriately when she pushes you to the limit, experiments with rebellion, repents and surprises you with kindness, sweetness, and responsibility, and then suddenly gets wild again.

➤ Assume, if she behaves badly, that there is a reason for her behavior. Is she hungry, tired, overwhelmed, unready to deal with this experience? Is she trying to communicate this to you but having a hard time expressing that in words?

Assume a Resourceful Child

Expect and trust that your child is capable and resourceful, and avoid doing for the child what she can do for herself. Rely on her to excel—and let her show you she can. Children feel great about themselves when they *can*. "I can do it, Mommy!" a toddler will announce. "Am I old enough to do it?" an older child might ask. When you do too much for the child, when you correct her actions, you send her the message that she is inadequate. The parent who "rescues" too much, who doesn't allow his child to try and fail, is being unfair to the child's abilities (more on rescuing in Chapter 9). No, this doesn't mean having a baby, and then throwing it to the wolves as soon as it can walk. Of course not. But even very young children can begin to build skills toward taking care of themselves.

Here are some tips for growing a capable child:

➤ Instead of stepping in and taking over, check with him. Ask, "How are you doing?" or "Would you like help?"

➤ Let him figure it out, take risks, explore life.

➤ Encourage his growth, and discuss his ideas with him.

➤ Don't push him. Keep expectations appropriate for him, and celebrate his successes. (We'll get to expectations in Chapters 5 and 6.)

➤ Don't patronize or diminish him, his capabilities, or his accomplishments.

All You Need Is Love

Well, maybe not *all*. But love, attention, and affection are essential elements of raising a reasonable, well-behaved child. Discipline happens best in an environment where a child feels loved, needed, and approved of for herself, with her individual personality quirks and temperament. True discipline always includes love and affection. Your child needs to feel utterly secure that no matter what mistakes she makes, or how angry you are at her, that you love her. There are two ways you can convince your child that she is loved and cherished for who she is: Show her, and tell her.

Behave Yourself!

It's not optional; your child *needs* your approval. Children who believe their parents are disappointed in them lose confidence in themselves. Lack of confidence may actually slow development.

Showing Your Affection

Teaching discipline is best done with one hand gently rubbing tension from a kid's shoulders, with a kiss on the nose, a squeeze of the torso, and a love pat on the back. Physical affection matters. A lesson imparted with a hug will be remembered far longer than a cold, distant lecture, because it will be associated with good feelings of parental love.

Here are a few tips for showing your child affection:

➤ Eye contact across a crowded room, smiles, winks, and thumbs-up.

➤ Hugs in the morning, hugs at noon, hugs at night (yes, even those smelly 10-year-olds, yes, especially those gawky adolescents).

➤ Hold hands walking down the street.

➤ Kiss your kid good-bye and hello.

➤ Model an affectionate relationship with your partner.

Appropriate and Inappropriate Affection

Kids don't always want physical affection, nor is it always appropriate. Part of respecting your child is to accept and appreciate when he doesn't want to be touched. You can help him build a sense of boundaries when you teach him to:

➤ Establish his boundaries. At the age of two, my daughter Annie already knew how to tell people, "Please don't touch my body." Once you teach your child to establish his own body boundaries, respect them.

➤ Respect the body boundaries of other people, whether family or friends.

➤ Know with whom and when it is appropriate to have physical affection. Family and friends are fine to hug (if he feels comfortable with it), strangers are not. Some places and times are *not* appropriate for hugging and kissing.

➤ Listen to his own discomfort level no matter *who* is doing the touching. Unless it's a medical or safety matter, a child should always be clear that physical affection is his choice.

➤ Understand that stepfamilies are sometimes a different story, and that physical affection is not always appropriate (there's an entire chapter about stepfamilies—check out Chapter 17).

Telling Her Your Affection

Kids need to hear that they are loved. In order, though, to talk effectively with a child, it's important to understand a bit about communication, and, especially, about listening. It's all about communication.

When we're talking telling a child about your affection, we're talking about communication! Before you start talking to your kids about affection, or discipline (or about anything else for that matter), it's best to listen. It's not enough to be born with ears, they don't guarantee a good listener. Listening is a skill, it takes time. It's the rare person who really knows how to listen effectively without first learning some basics and practicing.

Easy Listening

Listening—it's not as easy as it sounds. It's often uncomfortable to really *hear* somebody else's point of view (especially if it's your child and she's right and you happen to be wrong. It could happen, you know!). You might hear something you don't want to hear. It's uncomfortable to be challenged. You might hear something that challenges your belief system, or makes you question your assumptions about life. You might hear something that will make you want to *change.*

Listen up now, here are some reasons to work on your listening skills:

➤ Listening carefully is how you gather information about what's going on in your child's life and head.

➤ Listening effectively builds strong relationships.

➤ Listening thoughtfully shows respect.

➤ Listening is always the first step in solving problems.

➤ Listening to your child's perspective will teach you a lot. Kids are smarter than most grown-ups think, and they generally know what they need. Listen to your kids, and they will teach you how to raise them.

➤ If you want your child to listen to you, you'll need to first listen to her. A child who is listened to learns how to listen. And until she learns how to listen to you, it's the same as telling your problems to the bathroom mirror— no matter how eloquently you express yourself, nobody will be hearing you but you.

It's a Good Idea!

There's only one rule for being a good talker: Learn to listen.

It's a Good Idea!

A greedy communicator "takes" from instead of "talks," or adds to a conversation. The main difference between taking and talking is one little *l.* That *l* stands for "listening." To talk with somebody, you've gotta listen.

Here are the keys to improve your listening skills:

➤ Listen first.

➤ Always listen.

➤ Create a special time and place for listening.

➤ Use active listening.

Listen First

Listen first, and listen well, before reacting. The true story may take a while to emerge, the real feelings may take time. Okay, hotheads, this one will be a challenge for you! Can you count to 10? Practice! (And then turn to Chapter 8 for "The Strong and Reasonable Parent Responds" section of specific tips.)

Always Listen

I know, you've got a million things, people, and animals to focus on. And I'm telling you to always be aware of listening opportunities? Alas, yes. Kids aren't always organized, and kids with emotions (and last time I checked that was all of them) are even less so. It's hard for a child to wait until an opportune time to raise an important issue or disclose some vital information about how she got sent to the principal's office or that Toby beat him up because he accidentally shoved him into the garbage can. Sometimes a child will fret over telling you something important—and let it slip out just at the moment you are least expecting it. Perhaps you're on your way out the door to a board meeting, or making a left-hand turn into the most dangerous intersection in town, or checking that the soufflé hasn't fallen. Trust me, when you're least prepared is when the most vital information will slip from your child's little lips like a sigh.

Carpe diem—seize the day! Keep a constant low-level awareness, a sense of priorities. If Bobby is in hysterics or Sally is desperate to tell you about her date, perhaps you *can* rearrange your morning (and your life) and listen. (Can you call in sick? Cancel the carpet cleaner? Get somebody else to pick up for the carpool? It's important!)

It's a Good Idea!

If you already have established special time with your child (see Chapter 6) you *might* use that time to listen to your child. But remember that not all truths or confidences require a big listen. Some announcements, important truths, and confidences need a response of silence, or need time to sit and breathe.

Create a Special Place or Time for Listening

And sometimes you can't rearrange things. You're not superhuman, you know, and sometimes listening—which does take time and requires full attention—will just have to wait. If you need to delay the listening:

➤ Acknowledge the child's need to be heard. Stop for 5 seconds, 10 seconds, a minute and look your child in the eyes. "This is not a good time, Paula. Let's talk about it later." (It helps to name the "it" you're planning on talking about specifically so the child really feels heard, acknowledged, and seen.)

➤ Make an appointment. Any child over three will be able to understand the concept (even though the younger ones' senses of time aren't very good yet). "Paula, may I make an appointment with you to talk about this after lunch? We'll sit on the porch. Okay?"

➤ Follow through. It's up to *you* to remember, and it's vital that you appear at the established time and place, ready to listen. Don't be a flake—kids hate that. Why should they trust and respect a flake?

Active Listening: Your First Line of Defense

Here's a tool that works especially well when you feel stalemated or frustrated with a conversation. You can actively listen anywhere, as long as you pay full attention and do it deliberately. You can do it by first announcing you'll do it, or you can do it without drawing attention to the technique. Either way is effective.

Here's your three-step active listening formula:

1. *Focus your attention.* Have the child talk to you. Listen to the child's thoughts and feelings until he is finished.

2. *Paraphrase the thoughts and feelings you heard back to him without interpretation.* That means simply repeating back what he said and what you heard. "You say you hit Angela because she's an ugly girl. You were angry with her. Did I get that right?"

3. *Allow the child to correct what you've said.* "No, I meant that I hit her after she said I was ugly, and I said she was ugly, and she made me cry. Why did she say that, Dad?" (See, the conversation has opened up already!)

What are the direct results of active listening?

➤ *Active listening helps the child explore his own feelings and thoughts on a deeper level.* Sometimes feelings are so complex or overwhelming that a child may not know *how* he feels, especially if he's very upset at the time. Active listening can help you help him figure it out.

➤ *Active listening raises a child's senses of self-worth and self-respect.* You are listening to him, you are respecting his feelings and ideas, you are taking the time to find out what really matters

Words to Parent By

Active listening means trying to understand the child's thoughts *and* feelings by listening silently and then paraphrasing—saying back again as closely as possible *without interpretation*—what has been said.

to him. Getting respect increases his self-respect, and not just a little bit, either! Paying attention and listening well are the things that matter *most* to a child!

➤ *Active listening helps build your sense of empathy.* When you've truly heard the child's ideas, thoughts, and concerns, you'll be able to feel what he is feeling.

➤ *Active listening gives your kid the opportunity to correct you.* After you paraphrase, he can tell where you've misheard, and correct your misunderstandings. By hearing his words reflected back at him, he can clarify *to himself* what he means.

Beware: Evils lurk in the house of active listening. Don't open these doors:

➤ *Watch that you hear what is being said,* not what you *expect* to hear, and not what you *want* to hear. Expectations and desires can be seductive and dangerous.

➤ *Watch that you aren't focusing on the method of delivery.* It's not *how* it's being said, but *what's* being said. Ignore the swear words, the finger in the nose, the mumbling, and the slouched posture, unless they are part of what is being communicated.

➤ *Listen with more than your ears.* Nonverbal signals are important, too, and meaning is transmitted through *all* of our senses.

➤ *Don't be too literal.* Some kids exaggerate, some use slang. Listen for the message.

➤ *Be careful not to let your feelings about what is being said interfere with your listening.* Kids know just how to bug their parents, and they'll try to, at any given opportunity.

➤ *Be careful not to let your beliefs and attitudes interfere with your listening.* Even if you are hearing things that totally offend your moral values, complete the exercise. You can process, judge, and respond later—your job here is to gather information and understand what the child is saying. Let your own ideas go, just for a moment! Stop, take a deep breath, concentrate, and just listen. Listen to the child's perceptions. You need to *hear* to understand.

➤ *Don't ignore the emotion.* If you're listening only for the facts, you'll likely miss some important information. When you paraphrase, include how you think the child is feeling (and let him correct you if you are wrong). How the child feels about what he's telling you may be just as important as what he's saying.

It's a Good Idea!

Talking *with* your child means creating a dialogue—true communication between two people. When you're talking *at* your child it's merely a monologue. It's a rare monologue that can hold a child's interest (or an adult's, for that matter).

Let's Talk About Talking!

Listening, active or not, is only half of verbal communication. Talking is the other half. While we've all been talking from the time we were toddlers, there some specific verbal skills that we can all improve on. In this part of this chapter we'll look at ways to talk *with* instead of *at* your child.

Tips for Talking With, Not At, Your Child

Here are eight quick tips on ways to improve communication with your kid. (Hint: Nobody likes lectures, nobody likes to be yelled at, and nobody *learns* when the communication is antagonistic.)

➤ Tell the truth.

➤ Keep complaints specific.

➤ Be careful with criticism.

➤ Stop yelling!

➤ Nix the nagging, lose the lectures, avoid the advice.

➤ Don't set them up.

➤ De-escalate the antagonism.

➤ Use "I" statements.

Tell the Truth

If you ask most parents what qualities and behaviors they want to see in a well-behaved child, honesty is right up there. Here's a modeling issue—if you want your child to be honest, you must tell the truth yourself.

Now, we all know that there are all sorts of "truths": the whole truth; the half-truth; the gist of it, "the words are true but it's misleading." What do I mean, tell the truth?

➤ *Truth-telling with kids doesn't mean confessing all, but it does mean not lying.* Being honest about your feelings and your experiences doesn't mean always telling all or publishing it on the Internet. You can be reserved and dignified. Nobody needs to know all your gory details.

➤ *Honesty in front of the kids counts.* Be a good role model—if you let them see you lying, cheating, and stealing, you can expect to see them doing the same. (This makes it sound like I'm saying to lie, cheat, and steal when they're not looking. I'm not!)

➤ *Sometimes cruelty is a wolf disguised in a sheep's wool of honesty.* "I have to be honest with you." Honesty doesn't mean being tactless, or telling hurtful truths for the sake of being truthful ("I gotta tell ya, Joe, you're looking pretty lousy.").

➤ *Truth includes emotional honesty.* You have a responsibility to be truthful about what you feel.

➤ *Your child is not your psychologist or your confession-taking priest.* It's talking *at* instead of *with* your child when you tell them a truth just to get something off your chest and onto his.

Keep Complaints Specific

Keep complaints specific, to the moment. Lumping the whole world into one conversation or fight is known as "gunny sacking"—pulling all your old complaints out of the sack where you store them—and it's a sure way to close a child's ears. You'll know you are gunny sacking when you hear *always* and *never*. Be specific about what changes you want to see. Not, "Be more respectful!" but, "Please work on remembering to use a tissue, not your sleeve."

Tales from the Parent Zone

I know a woman who can't get started protesting one action without dragging every complaint, injustice, and old hurt into the conversation. You can imagine how her son feels— Mom can't ever just complain about Jerry leaving the refrigerator door open (again). He ends up hearing about the time (last year) that he was two hours late ("You have no *respect* for me!") and the time he got a "C" in chemistry ("You never pay attention!"). And he ends up not willing to respond to the initial problem (the refrigerator door).

Be Careful with Criticism

You may *think* you are helping improve your child's behavior when you sit down for a good critique session. You are probably wrong. Criticism tends to put people on the defensive, and defensive people aren't open to learning, or change. Criticizing too harshly or too often can damage a child's sense of self. Try encouraging your child first (that's in the next chapter). If you do use criticism:

Behave Yourself!

To avoid gunny sacking and to improve communication with your child, never use the word *never*, and always avoid the word *always*.

➤ Make it *very* specific.

➤ Be gentle.

➤ Don't go on and on.

➤ Be very clear and explicit that it is the *behavior* you are criticizing, not the child. You should say this, not just assume the child understands.

➤ Stop *yelling!*

Q: What do parent/child talks have in common with large warehouse stores?

A: Volume discounts.

Your child cannot hear you if you yell at her. (There's that *at* again! Very rarely will a parent yell *with* a child.) Keep the volume down. It's a well-known fact that a whisper is often louder than a scream.

Nix the Nagging, Lose the Lectures, Avoid the Advice

Nagging never made a child change his evil ways, and it's most likely to result in major, unbearable attitude. And no self-respecting kid is going to listen to yet *another* lecture on what she should or shouldn't do or be. While you're at it, cool it with the advice. Nobody asked you (unless they did). Kids are deaf to stories with a moral. I know, it's a challenge. Rise to meet it, it's important.

Don't Set Them Up

You're on your child's side, right? Then why are you trying to trap her like a little mouse in the cheese? It's not right to trick your child into a confession, and it's also wrong to force her into a situation where she must lie to save face or protect herself. When you trick or manipulate your child into a trap, you are showing a basic lack of trust and respect. You're trading immediate results for later resistance, recrimination, and loss of trust and respect.

> **It's a Good Idea!**
>
> Family communication happens best when it happens every day, each time family members interact with each other. Every communication with your child should communicate respect, affection, and your expectations and goals.

> **Behave Yourself!**
>
> Two other verbal messages to banish from your vocabulary when talking with your child: "You should" and "You have to."

De-Escalation

You're the parent, you (presumably) have more insights, long-term perspective, wisdom, and patience than your child. Therefore, it's *your* job to keep squabbles from escalating into wars. The hotter the fight, the fewer the positive results. How can you prevent "discussions" from becoming "arguments"? Try these preventive measures:

➤ *Take a deep breath.* The tenser you get, the shallower your breathing gets, and the more distressed you become.

➤ *Help your child breathe.* When Annie gets worked up, I hold her gently by the shoulders and tell her to blow out. A couple of deep breaths, and she's usually able to verbalize what is wrong without screaming and losing it.

➤ *Count to 10 or 100.* In other words, focus for a moment on something else to stop yourself from reacting.

➤ *Take a little personal time-out.* Excuse yourself to the bathroom (try not to slam the bathroom door). Splash some cold water on your face, breathe, count, and don't forget to flush.

➤ *Announce a general time-out.* "Okay, everybody run around the block! We'll talk about this again in seven minutes in the kitchen!"

➤ *Crack a joke* to diffuse the tension with laughter. Warning: This only works before people get *too* tense. People have died because jokes have misfired. Make sure your joke is funny, and never, ever, ever, ever, ever laugh *at* your kid. (There's that *at* again!) In other words, be Bill Cosby, not Don Rickles.

All About "I" Statements

Kids hate listening to a parent who is accusatory and self-righteous. As a parent trying to talk *with* your child, danger lurks when you use *"you" statements,* that is, statements that begin with the word *you* ("*You* make me feel unhappy," "*You* always,"). If, on the other hand, you begin statements about your perceptions, feelings, or preferences with the word *I,* you don't seem accusatory, and you're obviously speaking only from your own point of view.

Words to Parent By

An *"I" statement* is a declaration of your feelings, views, needs, likes, or dislikes that begins with the word *I.* "I" statements tell the listener that you're speaking from your own point of view. A *"you" statement* begins with the word *you* and can appear to be accusatory or self-righteous.

Behave Yourself!

"You" statements are risky, especially when your child comes back at you with another "you" statement. Escalation! Blame! Misery!

"I" statements:

➤ Imply that you're willing to at least *hear* another opinion or perception.

➤ Help you to clarify your own perceptions, feelings, and preferences.

➤ Don't call special attention to themselves. You can do them anywhere, anytime, without announcing it.

➤ Imply that you're open to hearing your child's perspective.

➤ Avoid the risk of escalation, blame, and misery associated with tit-for-tat "you" statements.

➤ Used in response to "you" statements can de-escalate tensions.

➤ Open, instead of close, conversation.

The "I" Statement Formula

"I" statements are easy to build. They're always a variation on the following: a description of an occurrence, your emotional reaction, and your desire for the future.

"When (the event) happened, I felt (emotion). Next time, please (action/response)." Try it out!

Patience Is an Eight-Letter Word

Don't you *hate* it when people tell you to be patient? I do. Patience is twice the length of a four-letter word, and sometimes twice as nasty, but it happens to be one of the important ingredients to raising a well-behaved child. Your child needs to know that you will wait for her, and with her. It takes time for people to change, and by "people" I mean both you and your child. It's unrealistic to expect yourself to suddenly become reasonable. It takes time to learn new patterns. It will also take time for your kid to change her patterns. Be patient! Allowing a reasonable amount of time for change to occur is reasonable. You'll also need to have a reasonable response when it doesn't happen immediately, or without resistance.

I've found it's easier to be patient when I believe that change *will* come. So let me tell you right now—change *will* come.

Justice and Fairness

You can help your child be a disciplinary success by working for justice and teaching him to work for justice, too.

A quick semantic note about justice and fairness: Kids often confuse fairness (dividing things exactly equally) with justice (making things *right* for the entire family). "Daddy! But that's not fair!" is a whine that echoes from coast to coast and beyond, especially in families with more than one child. But things can be just, that is, *equitable and right* for the family as a whole, without being exactly fair.

Keep in mind that:

➤ Life ain't always fair! The good news is that some frustration and disappointment is necessary for development.

Behave Yourself!

It's not an "I" statement if it describes your opinion, rather than your feelings. Try changing the word *feel* to *think* in that "I" statement and see if it makes sense. ("When you eat in your room, I think you're a sloppy pig.") Oops! Try again: "When you eat in your room, I know that there will be a big mess and I feel angry that you expect me to do extra work." That's better.

It's a Good Idea!

Change is a process, it happens gradually, and it takes time. Try to see in small increments. Let me say it again: Change takes time!

Words to Parent By

Justice is a combination of integrity, virtue, and equity. Fighting for justice means fighting for righteousness.

> ➤ Kids remember injustices. For longer than elephants. And elephants live a long time.
>
> ➤ You'll all do better when you forget about the concept of fairness and work for justice! Teach your child to fight for it as well.

Unconditional Love

Unconditional love means loving a person *no matter what*. No matter what happens, or what she does, you will love her. You may hate what she does, but you love her. With unconditional love, a child's entire house may fall, but she'll always have a foundation to rebuild on. A kid who is loved unconditionally, who is shown respect, who is trusted, and who is guided with gentle correction will grow to be a respectful, self-confident, trustworthy individual who likes, respects, and believes in herself, and in others. In short, a success.

It's a Good Idea!

Justice and fairness are not always the same thing, as parents who have more than one child know full well. Life is not always "fair" (otherwise known as exactly equal) and kids need to learn that. Justice, on the other hand, is something to fight for.

The Least You Need to Know

➤ Your child needs you to be her unconditional ally.

➤ Treat your kid like a "people," with love, respect, and open communication, and he'll return the favor.

➤ Active listening and "I" statements can improve your family's talking and listening experiences.

➤ Strive for patience, work for justice.

Chapter 4

Positive Reinforcement and Choices

In this chapter, we'll concentrate on the specific things you as a parent can do on a day-to-day basis—using positive reinforcement, instituting natural and logical rewards, and teaching your children to make effective choices—to prevent behavior problems.

Disciplinary Element Number Five: Use Positive Reinforcement

Using positive reinforcement to encourage and reward proper behavior is the fifth element of the Twelve Disciplinary Elements. Here are a couple of universal statements: Everybody wants approval for who he is and for what he does. And, everybody wants to please, especially children, and especially *your* child who wants to please *you*. Can that really be? Then why do children misbehave? We'll tackle that big question later (in Chapter 8) but until then, take it from me and the experts, kids just wanna be good.

How can you "let" your kids be good, increase positive behavior, and decrease and prevent misbehavior quickly and painlessly? Here's a start: by accentuating the positive. (Remember that old song by Harold Arlan and Johnny Mercer? "You've got to accentuate the positive, eliminate the negative, latch on to the affirmative, and don't mess with Mr. In-Between.") One terrific way to accentuate behavior you like to see (and take the emphasis off negative behavior) is by using positive reinforcement.

It Works Like This

Positive reinforcement is a simple, reality-based technique that can help turn your child's behavior around—often *very* quickly. Here's the recipe:

1. Your child wants your approval very badly.

2. You notice and comment on specific positive behavior and provide natural and logical rewards.

3. Your child feels noticed, validated, and approved of, the good behavior increases, and misbehavior is prevented or decreases.

4. Your child also begins to recognize the value of his own positive qualities and actions.

Words to Parent By

Positive reinforcement reinforces what the child is doing right rather than concentrating on what the child is doing wrong. It increases the likelihood that the behavior will be repeated. It supports your child's positive deeds and qualities through enthusiasm, descriptive encouragement, and natural, logical rewards.

Positive reinforcement is at play every time your child brings home his report card, or every time you get a bonus at work. But positive reinforcement works best when it isn't a once-in-a-while thing; the more it happens, the more effective it is. That means daily.

For instance, comment when your child for once does something without being told. Focus on positive behavior ("John, I noticed you remembered to take your clothes off the floor. Now the puppy won't be able to chew them."). Don't focus on the negative ("You hung up your jacket, for once!"), and don't link it to a judgment on the child's personality ("What a good child you are for hanging up your jacket!").

Tally Ho!

Just how much positive reinforcement do you offer your child? You probably offer some already, most parents naturally do. Yet no matter how good at it you think you are, you may be surprised to find that, in reality, most parents focus on the negative. How much negativity is creeping into *your* parenting?

Learning to parent well is a process, and there is always room for improvement. It *is* helpful to look at the problem areas. Here's an easy little exercise inspired by the work of James Windell (author of *8 Weeks to a Well-Behaved Child*) that lets you clearly see how many negative and critical remarks you make. (Hey, try the exercise! You may be pleasantly surprised!)

Get a little notebook at the supermarket. A *little* one. Smaller. One that can fit in a pocket or a purse. Get a pen, too, and put it in the pocket or purse next to the notebook. Ready to begin?

Every time you make a critical or negative comment about your child, open the notebook and make a little mark. If you have time, write down what you said and the circumstances. Do it for five days, and don't try to change what you are doing, just make notes. That's it! (Well, that's almost it.)

➤ Don't share this exercise (or the fact that you are doing it) with your child. That may mean excusing yourself to the bathroom frequently, or dashing off to another room to make your tally marks, but if you share the fact that you are doing this little experiment, your kids might get upset, you'll start adjusting your behavior, and the exercise's results won't be accurate.

➤ If you have more than one child, label a page for each one, and keep a separate tally.

➤ Make sure you count feedback that starts out positive but includes a "but" as in: "I really appreciate you doing the dishes, Samantha, *but* please try and rinse the soap off better next time."

➤ Pay special attention when you are angry, disappointed, tired, or hungry (people tend to get *very* crabby and critical when their blood sugar levels are low).

At the end of five days, take a deep breath and add up your tally. There's no magic number—whether your reaction is "Arrghhh!" or "Wow!" it doesn't matter. Knowledge is necessary (even when it is painful). What did you find? Have a lot of tally marks in your notebook?) If you're like most parents, you parent more through criticism than through positive reinforcement. We simply expect kids to behave themselves (without giving them a lot of tools to know how) and then when they don't, we hit the roof. Sound familiar? Look again at your tally sheet. Don't feel bad, this is just a place to begin. Nobody but you is counting your tally (aren't you glad you kept it private now?) and you can tear up the pages in that teeny notebook, if you like.

Most of us are in fire-fighting mode most of the time, trying to get things done, get through life

Behave Yourself!

No wimps allowed! Not everything your child does is great, and if you pretend it is, you're doing your child a disservice.

It's a Good Idea!

Pay attention to what's going on with your child's heart, mind, life, and you'll be able to prevent a lot of discipline problems.

relatively intact, and put out the behavior fires as they flare. It seems easier to notice what's annoying or troubling than it is to notice how wonderful your child really is. Some parents are so afraid of raising a stuck-up little monster that they bend over backwards to never give a compliment, or describe positive behavior. Not a good idea.

Doing an exercise like Tally Ho! will help you become aware of your expectations for your child, and your patterns of treatment. If you have more than one child, the exercises will show you the differences in treatment and expectations. Once you become aware of it, bingo! You can change!

The "Let's Get Positive" Exercise

If you're used to focusing on negative behavior, it can be hard to start using positive reinforcement techniques. Let's practice being positive. In order to give positive reinforcement, you need to recognize specifically what to reinforce. Once you recognize the positive behavior, you can use descriptive encouragement. Here's a quick exercise for you. Just for the next day or so:

➤ Make a list of things your child does right or well.

➤ Blow off the negative (let it go free!).

➤ Frame each positive thing in positive terminology ("He got dressed easily and got along with his sister at breakfast") instead of in the negative ("he didn't fight getting dressed, for once, and he didn't whack Nikki at breakfast").

➤ Notice how the behavior of even a "misbehaving" child is mostly positive.

Tales from the Parent Zone

Every morning, when I get into my car to drive my daughter to school, the most obnoxious beeping noise occurs until I buckle my seat belt. This is "negative reinforcement," and it can be an effective way of encouraging proper behavior. In order to get rid of that bleeping beep, I buckle up. A balance between negative and positive reinforcement is important for a child's development.

Prevent Problems with Descriptive Encouragement

If you tell a child he's a pathetic, sniveling worm, he'll either go to the garden and start eating dirt, or he'll rebel, move to the other coast, and never speak to you again (and good for him!). If, on the other hand, you support and encourage him, he'll do his best for you. When you're using encouragement:

➤ *Keep it very specific.* "I noticed you worked for an hour on your homework." "You certainly emptied the dishwasher fast and well!" The more specific you get, the more your child will learn to figure out for herself when she is doing a good job.

➤ *Say it deliberately.* Remind yourself to comment on positive behavior. It takes awhile to make this kind of commentary second nature, so it will have to be deliberate for a while. It may even feel forced. That's okay!

➤ *Effort counts.* You can give descriptive encouragement for effort even if the results don't turn out so well. "You worked very hard on your homework, Adam. I'm sure next time you will get the right answer."

➤ *Focus on improvement.* "Your arms have gotten much stronger from all the swimming practice you've been doing."

➤ *Say it often.*

It's Not Praise, and It's Not General

When you're using encouragement, steer away from the following pitfalls:

➤ General encouragement, "You're a great kid!" and "You're so smart!" is nice to hear, but it isn't very effective at promoting change. General encouragement too often shows that you aren't really paying enough attention to the child, or her process, to make thoughtful, helpful, respectful comments about her behavior. Some experts think too much praise or general encouragement can even be damaging, making a child dependent on others for positive feedback. In other words, "How am I doing, Mom," replaces, "Wow, I'm doing great" or, "I kinda flubbed that test, I'd better work harder."

➤ There's a school of parenting (I think it's affiliated with Wimpy University) that praises kids all the time. "Excellent job walking down the street, Emily." Too much of this constant, empty praise, and your child will stop trusting you, or even listening. "Great job!" becomes empty, unless you mean it.

➤ Never lie to your child about how he's doing. If you tell a kid what a scholar he is when he's earning the lowest grades in the school district, you're lying, and both of you will know it. Your child is not stupid. Encourage the positive ("You're working hard to do well next time," or "It took courage to risk and fail")—but don't *lie*.

➤ There's nothing wrong with hearing that you're a great kid (it promotes a general sense of being loved and approved of), but it works best when it's very specific. Telling a child, "Wow, you're so mature" puts a lot of stress on a child to be mature, to never be immature, and to never disappoint you. Children under this kind of stress tend to rebel, hard.

Reward Positive Behavior

Rewarding your child when he has done a good job, made progress on a tough problem, or achieved something he's worked for is a great way to accentuate positive behavior (and prevent problem behavior, too). A rewarded child learns, "When I do well, I'm appreciated and rewarded." (Rewards are related to consequences. You'll learn more about those in Chapter 9.)

It's a Good Idea!

Rewards for positive behavior are best when they are *not* tangible, material objects. If you want your child to internalize his achievements, use encouraging words, or, better yet, throw him a party! Parties and celebrations are great consequences of a job well done (and they can become part of your family culture).

Behave Yourself!

Be very careful before linking food with *any* kind of reward, bribe, or negative consequence. It's vital to teach your child how to be a disciplined eater, that is, to know what she likes, feel when she is full, and understand what makes a healthy diet. Using food as a motivating force or reward will compromise your teachings.

Natural and Logical Rewards

Rewards are best when they are a natural or logical extension of the behavior. The best rewards are natural—and you don't have to provide them (though noticing them is wonderful, positive reinforcement). A child who works hard in his swimming class is rewarded by increased skills, bigger muscles, the great feeling of improvement and ability, and, eventually, permission to swim on his own. For a child, the sense of "I can do it!" is the best reward in the world.

A logical reward is provided by the outside world in response to a child's actions. Getting an "A" on a studied-for test is a logical reward. A logical reward might be used like this: "Sarah, I really appreciate how hard and well you worked with me fixing up the laundry room today. I thought we could go to the hardware store tomorrow and get you a tool box so you can start your own tool collection." Sarah's reward is directly related to her actions. You *bet* she'll be eager to help you again, not because she expects more tools, but because she knows you really see and appreciate her efforts. (Note: Tangible or monetary rewards should be used warily. Often the best reward you can give a child is the honesty of your pride in her achievements.)

Rewards Versus Bribery

Many child development experts recommend rewards but have a conniption fit when you mention bribes. So what's a bribe? How does it differ from a reward? A reward happens after the fact, in return for a kid doing the best she can. The child isn't working *for* the reward, she's working hard for the pleasure of achievement. The reward is a little bonus, a special treat. A bribe, on the other hand, is used to motivate a child in advance.

A bribe is an outside motivator to get the child to do what you want. "If you're a good child, I'll get you an ice cream." It might work, and forgive me, it works with dogs, too. "Down, boy. Sit, and I'll give you this doggy treat."

Bribes are also often negative motivators, and they're often related to or combined with threats. "If you don't flunk algebra this year, I'll buy you a car. Otherwise, it's reform school for you, Buddy." Or, "Be a good little boy and don't use naughty words with Aunty Susan and once she's gone I'll get you ice cream. If you call her a poo-poo head, you can't watch *Sesame Street* tomorrow."

What do you want your child to achieve? Do you want Buddy to pass algebra so that he can have a car, or a future? Do you want your little son to learn that the only reason he should have a "clean" mouth is so he can watch TV, or so that he learns what kinds of language are acceptable?

Here's the big disclaimer: Almost every parent I know has resorted to bribery. I know I have. It's usually done in public, and it's usually done out of sheer desperation. Bribery is a short-term solution, and sometimes the short term wins out. Sometimes you just need results. Just keep in mind that bribery works *best* when it is used very occasionally. Used as a regular technique, it loses its teeth, and throws you firmly into the camp of wimpy parent.

Disciplinary Element Number Six: Teach Ways to Make Choices

Teaching your child to make choices is element number six of the Twelve Disciplinary Elements, and it's one of the most *important* elements of raising a well-behaved, resourceful child.

Let's talk about choice for a moment.

I love science-fiction stories that deal with alternate choices ("The Fork in the Road Not Taken" stories), where the hero or heroine suddenly is plunged into an alternate reality—a reality that could have happened had he or she made a different choice of action somewhere, sometime, before. That theme always points out to me how *much* choice we have in life. From big choices ("Should I take the big PR job and move to New York or go back to the land and become an herb farmer?") to little choices ("Ice cream or salad?"), every move we make has ramifications.

How Do Choices Prevent Problems?

Part of being self-disciplined is understanding and taking responsibility for making life's choices. Helping your children learn the difficult skill of making positive, appropriate choices is a big part of parenting well. A child who is skilled at consciously making choices will understand her own needs, and gain a sense of control over her own life. Choice-making also helps teach internal discipline, organization, and prioritizing. (You're not going to have a lot of problems from a kid this empowered.)

Children learn how to make big choices by watching you do it, and by gaining experience through making little choices. Here are some tips about teaching choice to your child:

➤ *Never give a choice you aren't willing to follow through on.* That means if you say, "Either you clean your room or we are not going out to dinner tonight," you should be prepared to start cooking. It also means if you say, "Clean your room and I'll take you to the fanciest restaurant in town," you need to be prepared to pick up that phone and start making reservations.

➤ *It's your responsibility to keep your child safe and healthy.* Keep food choices healthy, and allow your child to choose what to eat. If your kid chooses to eat only cookies and ice cream, stop having them as a choice.

➤ *Unless your child is very skilled at choice-making and your budget is unlimited, never offer choices without parameters.* Give them an "either/or" if they are young, or up to several options if they are older. You're looking for trouble (and you're not teaching choice) if you say, "You can choose where we're going on vacation," or "Whatever you want for dessert, it's your choice." (Whee! We're going to Bora Bora to eat a carload of chocolate mousse topped with champagne cream and gilded with gold leaf!)

➤ *When a child is making choices about her behavior, you can point out the choice and the consequences of it.* "Jonah, I notice you have chosen to play Nintendo before dinner instead of doing your homework. I hope you are aware that you have chosen to stay home and finish your homework tonight instead of going to the movies with your friend Jeremy."

➤ *Older children can use choices to learn how to prioritize.* You can say, "Your laundry needs to be in the hamper, Rex needs a walk, and your book report is due tomorrow. You can choose how you arrange to get it all done." (You might add, "If you would like some help organizing your time, I'll be happy to take a couple of minutes with you at any point this evening.")

➤ *Once a child makes a choice, lay off on the options, don't continue to offer choices.* ("Well, maybe not Bora Bora, perhaps Kathmandu.") That's what a choice is, it's a decision. It's part of choosing to live with all the ramifications.

➤ *Once a choice has been made, be clear as to when it becomes final.* ("The special price on those discount tickets expires at midnight, so we need to be prepared to buy before bedtime.")

Which brings us to the question, What if your child doesn't like her choice? That can be hard for a wimpy parent to watch. It can even be hard for a strong, reasonable parent to watch. Nobody enjoys watching a child be disappointed. But making a choice entails learning to live with the choice that's been made. Don't "rescue" your child from her experiences; it may make her feel better in the long run, but it ultimately won't teach her anything at all. Disappointment is a good teaching tool, and discipline is teaching.

Choice Expands with Age

As an adult, you have free choice about many aspects of life. You've earned that. Children start out unable to handle anything but the simplest choices. Think of the challenge faced by the kid in the ice-cream shop: "Chocolate or vanilla?" As kids get older, the choices become more complex, and they should.

Free Choice?

No matter what you say, do, or try to control, your child does have choices. Yes, they can be restricted choices, but your child can *always* choose noncompliance. I say it's better to provide a variety of choices instead of letting the extreme choice of noncompliance be a child's only option. You'll do best and be happier when you embrace choice and learn how to work *with it* (since it exists, you might as well make it work for you). When choices and the choice-making process are made explicit, there is less room for misunderstandings to occur.

Behave Yourself!

Why so negative? It's better to plan for success, rather than failure (It's been said that people who expect success are more likely to achieve it than people who expect to fail). Provide choices that will work for your child.

It's a Good Idea!

Take a deep breath, step back, and trust your child's choices. He is learning what he wants, needs, and values—these things can't be forced. Model your values, then let your little bird fly.

Choice Builds Strength

The world has its dangers, and try as you might, you cannot protect your child from all of them. A child's best defense is the ability to make safe, wise choices, and this is a skill that takes practice. Help your child by guiding her through the choice making process. That's really all you can do, and that's often more than enough.

Other Trouble-Preventing Techniques

There are numerous other trouble-preventing techniques that take a positive, proactive approach. Here are three: If you want your child to do something, try asking nicely. If your child is having trouble controlling himself around a desired toy or food, you can prevent problems by simply removing the temptation. Finally, if your child is behaving in a way you don't like, try ignoring him. (As my dad used to say, "Hold your horses!" I'll explain what I mean by these three approaches in a moment.)

Just Ask Nicely

You have no idea how often parents leap to commands and fury without making their desires clear in a nice, polite way. Here's a basic, positive, problem-prevention parenting technique: When you want something done, ask! People—and that includes kids—will often respond better to a request than they will to a command. Many is the parent who has tried this technique with a recalcitrant child who they daily do battle with, and bingo! It's truly amazing what a little bit of polite respect will get you.

Of course, this won't *always* work, but it's the right place to start. If you ask nicely—"Allison, please set the table"—and a few minutes go by and nothing happens, Allison is still playing Power Rangers, the next move is to say calmly, "Allison, I asked you nicely to set the table. I'm not asking now. Please come into the kitchen immediately and I'll help you begin."

The "just ask nicely" technique is valuable for more than saving your vocal cords, it teaches kids how to clearly request what they want or need. You are the model, they will follow your lead in the world.

Words to Parent By

Self-control is the ability to deny oneself immediate pleasure for one's longer-term good or for the good of somebody or something else. Self-control becomes an issue for kids in many areas: homework (do it now or watch TV), money (spend it or save it), food (eat it all or leave room for dessert), and so on.

Remove Temptation

Self-control takes time to learn, and it's not fair to test kids on their self-control before they've really learned it. The spirit may be willing, but the flesh is too often all too weak (just ask otherwise intelligent and well-disciplined politicians). If your kid is not allowed to watch TV except on weekends, don't leave the TV in his bedroom. It's not helpful (and it sets up terrible conflicts) to say, "No sweets or soft drinks," and then stock the cupboards full. Why set your child up for failure? The child that fails the lure of temptation because it was too accessible will feel terrible, and learn to *hate* self-control.

It's a Good Idea!

Don't lie! If you're angry, hurt, or disappointed in your child, express it in a calm and honest way, and *don't* let it slide. Ignoring behavior doesn't mean lying about your reactions. Show your child respect by letting her know how you feel.

Ignore It, It Will Go Away

"Minor" problems and irritants sometimes go away fastest when you simply ignore them. Nose-picking, tuneless whistling, belching, rudeness, bratty "testing" behavior—sometimes the best thing you can do is to avoid feeding into it. These are things that, if you begin making issues out of them, often get worse.

No, don't ever ignore behavior that is cruel or dangerous. But sometimes kids are just trying to get a reaction from you, and the best response is no response. This can be harder than listening to fingernails scratching on a blackboard—kids seem to have an innate knowledge about what most irritates their parents, and then they go for it.

Ignoring negative behavior is more than just a technique for stopping misbehavior. It's more profound than that—it's part of the shift from noticing the negative to accentuating the positive, from being your child's opponent to being her ally. As much as possible, notice the good and refrain from criticizing. (There's more on ignoring as an effective disciplinary technique in Chapter 10.)

Society's Child

I sorta hate to tell you this, but you may matter less to your child than you think you do. You're not the only influence on your child's life, and the older your child gets, the less your opinion matters. (As a matter of fact, there's a new critique of child development literature that re-evaluates the standard belief that a child's main influence are his parents, not his friends.)

Okay, enough of that. Whether you are primary or secondary, you do matter, what you do matters, and how you respond to your child *definitely* matters. But the point is, so does the rest of society. Your child's teachers, your child's friends, the media, the times we live in, all have strong influences on who your child is, and who he will become. You have little say over what influences creep into your child's life. Do the best you can—and let the rest go.

The Least You Need to Know

➤ Problem behavior is far easier to prevent than correct.

➤ Positive reinforcement is very effective at preventing and correcting misbehavior.

➤ Use choice-making to teach responsibility and prevent trouble.

➤ Rewards work best when they are natural and logical (and not material objects). Be wary of bribes!

➤ Sometimes, just asking nicely works best!

Part 2
Clearer Than Mud: Expectations and Goals

In Part 2, we'll take a closer look at your child—her stage of development and her temperament. Once you understand these things, then (and only then) can you create appropriate goals and expectations. What's important for your family? Different families need different things from their kids. To help you clarify your family's expectations, you'll work on a family value statement (it's kind of like a mission statement).

Now that your expectations are clear and your goals are set, you can start imposing the limits—the behavior boundaries and support system for your child. Remember, even light has a speed limit! Oh yeah, remind me to talk about reminders, too.

Chapter 5

Expectations for Your Child

In This Chapter

➤ Setting expectations through understanding your child

➤ Tips to your child's temperament

➤ The Quality Time Quiz

➤ What to do when your child is a perfectionist or an underachiever

➤ Disciplinary goals—setting ones your child can meet

➤ What the world expects from your child, and what she expects from you

---

Want a healthy, happy, reasonable and resourceful child whose behavior matches your expectations *most of the time?* Here's what you've gotta do: Show your child how much you love her, understand your child, and expect and trust that your child means well, is capable, and will do fine in life. Easy as pie, close the book, that's that.

Stop! It's not really so easy, is it? Depending on your temperament and your experience with your child (who may be a challenge), it may be very tough. Your expectations of your child will deeply affect who your child becomes, though, so it's important to set your expectations in the proper place—somewhere between sinner and saint. And it's hard to place trust in a child who has been giving you a lot of trouble.

This chapter focuses on ways to set your expectations at reasonable levels, and teach your child how to build realistic expectations for herself. That matters, too. You'll get tips on understanding your child and teaching her to believe in her own capabilities. We'll also talk about setting disciplinary goals for your child that are specific, achievable, and limited.

There are three basic types of expectations: personal expectations, family expectations, and the world's expectations. In this chapter we'll talk primarily about personal expectations (these are your achievement-based expectations for your child and your child's expectations for herself in areas such as academic, athletic, and developmental growth). We'll also look a little at what society expects from your child. In Chapter 6, we'll concentrate on family expectations (moral and value-based expectations about how people in the family should behave and treat each other).

Behave Yourself!

Don't judge a person by whether they see the glass half-full or half-empty—neither way of living is wrong: Pollyannas aren't always realistic, their blithe high expectations may put a lot of pressure on their kids to achieve, and their endless cheeriness can get on your nerves. Eeyores are deeply entrenched in reality, but they can live a life of self-fulfilling prophecy. People who walk around expecting to get whacked by life often do.

What You Expect Depends on Who You Are

Some parents are glass-half-full people, optimists, "Pollyannas" who see only rainbows on a rainy day, and look at the bright side of all dim situations. They'll naturally tend to expect the best from their child. In some cases, they may even expect too much! Other parents are glass-half-empty people, pessimists, "Eeyores," who expect life to strike them down, and expect little from their kids but grief. (They haven't singled their children out for this honor—Eeyores expect grief from everybody and everything.) It was an Eeyore who invented the bumper sticker, "S%$# Happens, and Then You Die."

Disciplinary Element Number Seven: Set Reasonable Personal Expectations and Goals for Your Child

No matter your general mood, having positive, realistic expectations for your child's achievements and behavior *is* something to strive for. When parents' expectations for their kids are set at the right level—not too high and not too low—kids do very well in life indeed. Here then, are some specific tools for setting reasonable expectations that even the gloomiest donkey can follow.

➤ Assess your kid as an individual.

➤ Understand your child's developmental stage.

Who Is Your Child?

You can't set a personal expectation or goal for your child without taking that individual child into consideration. It's very attractive to try, especially if you've been reading the charts in too many child development books or have older kids. ("Eliza was washing her own hair by the time she was four, Tina should be doing it, too.") Forget all the other kids, forget the books, ask yourself some simple questions: What is reasonable to expect from this child? What are her abilities, needs, accomplishments? What's her basic temperament? What's her stage of development? In order to set appropriate expectations for *your* child, you have to really know her (and that leads us right back again to part one of the Twelve Parts of Positive Discipline: Pay attention!).

Adjust to Your Child's Level

When you're assessing your child for "reasonable" behavior, take temperament and development into consideration, and adjust your expectations to meet his capabilities. If your child can't tolerate an elevator ride to the top of the Empire State Building, then chances are he won't tolerate the wonderful plane ride to Disneyland, either.

Behave Yourself!

Be very careful about comparing your child to others. Every child develops at a different rate.

Charts, Graphs, Uneven Development

It's also helpful to know what to expect *in general* from children at certain ages. A friend of mine who has a daughter with a nonverbal learning disability was delighted when I overheard little Posie swearing a blue streak at her sister and taunting, "You're just a ba-by!" "That's so typical," I said. "Doesn't the constant taunting of five-year-olds drive you nuts?" "You mean your daughter taunts?" Her eyes filled with tears. "Of course," I said, "it's developmental." My friend, who had been spending nights stressing out about her daughter's rudeness and lack of social skills suddenly relaxed, as she realized that her child's mocking—while not very nice—was completely and utterly developmentally appropriate for her age group.

Charts, graphs, and development books are not fail safe, always true, or always helpful to a parent trying to set reasonable expectations for *his* child. Charts, graphs, and the like deal with averages, means, and norms. They don't track individuals.

If you don't believe me, visit any sixth-grade classroom for 10 minutes. Check out the desks—some are filled with children so filled out you'd think twice about carding them if you were a bartender. Other desks hold scrawny kids who look as though they sleep each night with teddies clutched in their arms. Development and maturity in children is often uneven, too. Your son might be

Behave Yourself!

Stop trying to fit your child into a mold. Social scientists and child development specialists have been studying enough children for long enough that they've quantified their data into big charts and graphs to tell you what's "average"—physical, social, and intellectual—for a child of a particular age. In reality, there's no such thing as an exactly "average" child.

excelling in math, great in swimming, and still sucking his thumb at night. Your daughter might be terrific at art, brilliant at computer programming, but so absent-minded that when people ask her what her name is, she often replies, "Ummmmm?" You get the picture.

Tales from the Parent Zone

Jane's son Patrick has a wide spread of abilities (he's got a firm grasp of planetary environments and has mastered the subjunctive tense, but he struggles to write his name). Patrick has what's known as a "jagged" profile. I say *viva la jag!*

We all want our kids to achieve and excel, and it's hard to step back and let them develop at their own rates. But from toilet training to reading to swimming to dating to getting a job, every child is on a different, individual timeline, physically, mentally, and emotionally. Your child *will* test older than average in some areas of the development charts, and *will* be younger than average in others. Try to accept her for who she is.

Personality-Appropriate Expectations

When you're trying to set reasonable personal expectations for your child, it's also helpful to think about their temperamental style. *Temperament* is the way a person approaches the world. Temperament is inborn. It's considered the "how" of behavior rather than the "why" or the "what." The "temperament trackers" use 10 characteristics to analyze a person's emotional style, and to assess how well they adapt to situations. The 10 characteristics are:

➤ *Adaptability:* "We're going where? Cool!" or, "This wasn't on the itinerary!"

➤ *Energy level:* "Wowie zowie, let's go!" or, draggin' a loaded wagon.

➤ *Environmental sensitivity:* Eagle-eyed nature-lover, or, "Ooh! I broke a nail!"

➤ *First reaction:* Deep-end pool diver, or, inch by tiny inch.

➤ *Intensity:* Roller-coaster emotions! or, "Whatever."

➤ *Mood:* Here's Eeyore and Pollyanna again.

➤ *Perceptiveness:* "You moved the curtains an inch," or, "You painted the house? Whoa. Didn't notice."

➤ *Persistence:* "I think I can, I think I can," or, "No? Okay. Onward."

➤ *Physical sensitivity:* "It's a bed of nails? That must be why I was a tad restless last night," or, "Stop breathing so loud. I can't hear myself think!"

➤ *Regularity:* "Noon? Time for lunch. *Now.*" or, "Did I eat today?"

(You'll notice that intelligence, charm, or compassion aren't on this list—they're personality traits, but not temperament traits.)

It's All Temperament

Kids are born with temperament—you can't order it up like a Blue Plate Special ("I'll have one kid, over easy, light on the hysterics and make sure her regularity is well done."). Some kids are generally easy-going, positive, and calm. Others are high-spirited, sensitive, or moody. Everybody has some temperament traits that can be labeled "easy" or "difficult." Assessing your child's temperament (and your own) can help you take it less personally. "That's who Sally *is*," you can say. (More on this in a moment.)

That said, your kid isn't stuck for life; she has certain temperamental tendencies, but those tendencies can be channeled: high energy into enthusiasm, sensitivity into poetry, regularity into organization.

It's a Deadly Combo

How does your child's temperament differ from your own? Two kids from the same family can have completely different temperamental traits, and both of them may be utterly different from you.

When you compare your temperamental traits with those of your child, you'll probably find some areas where you're two peas in a pod, and others where you could be aliens from different planets, you think *that* differently. (You can compare your temperamental traits in Appendix H, "What's Your Temperament?") If you have a child whose temperament is very different from yours, take solace. Nothing is wrong with your child. You are not inadequate as a parent. You simply are very different people, and there are lots of ways of being in this world.

Words to Parent By

Temperament is a way of analyzing a person's adaptability and emotional style. Temperament is inborn. The 10 characteristics—adaptability, energy level, environmental sensitivity, first reaction, intensity, mood, perceptiveness, persistence, physical sensitivity and regularity—all refer to the way a person approaches the world.

Behave Yourself!

It's your way or the highway—or is it? When you look at the world through your child's eyes, with his temperament and development, you'll gain understanding, empathy, and patience. There are many ways of living. Know your child's temperament—and your own.

Say you're quiet and deliberate and your son is high-energy and impulsive. Or you're highly emotional and your daughter makes ice cream seem scalding. Some combinations of kids and adults mesh better than other combinations—and it's not always tied to genetics. Understanding the differences between you and your child's temperamental approach can be a big help in figuring out your relationship, your expectations for your child, and what you can do to help him achieve success.

Temperament: Take a Positive Approach

If your house is filled with tension because of the constant fights with Augustino to get him to clean his room ("He lives like a pig!"), take a moment to reassess. He may not be as environmentally sensitive as you are. Maybe he's having trouble prioritizing tasks, and he's just not getting around to the room. Maybe try a new tactic.

Tales from the Parent Zone

Annie's good pal Alonza is a great, zesty kid—social, high-energy, bossy, and always covered in mud. Her mom is retiring, generally calm, and very respectful of Alonza. "She is who she is," Saill says. "If I was to try and make her completely obedient, quiet, and timid, Alonza would spend a lot of unhappy years. It's my job to help her be the best 'Alonza' she can be. Even if I wanted to, I can't make her into somebody like me." Saill is a wise mother, working *with* instead of *against* her daughter's temperament.

The better you understand your child's temperamental traits, the easier it is to reframe them in a positive way—for both yourself and your child. (There's more about positive reframing in Chapter 8.)

Negative Temperamental Frame	Positive Temperamental Frame
"Tommy must be very troubled. He doesn't want to go to the first day of his fantastic new school!"	"Tommy has a hard time dealing with change, and he's feeling trepidation about starting a new school. I'm sure once he gets used to it he'll be as excited about it as we are."
"I can't take Rebecca to the movies; she refuses to stop kicking the chair in front of her!"	"Rebecca is very high-energy, and sitting still that long is physically painful for her. Let's go ice skating."
"Alice is lazy. She takes forever with her homework.	"Alice is deliberate and thoughtful with her homework. She takes her time, but she comes up with great, original thoughts."
"He's totally hyper."	"He's very athletic."

Understanding Your Child

A big part of establishing appropriate expectations involves really knowing your child. How do you learn her? You put in quality, undiluted, alone time with her.

Special Time with Your Child

Special Time is one-on-one time—one parent and one child. Family togetherness is very important (and there's more on this in Chapter 6), but don't ever sacrifice your time alone with each child. To effectively teach discipline, you need to establish that special rapport. Besides, most parents find that tensions dissipate, boundaries fall, and troubles fly away—at least until special time is over. Special time is:

➤ Best if it's regular.

➤ Fun when it's spontaneous.

➤ Dangerous when it *always* involves food treats.

➤ *Not* special time when it involves errands, "have-tos," or make-work.

Special time is an opportunity to hang out, or do special activities with your child. Special time pays off—in closeness, in rapport, in stress reduction. It's a minivacation. It needs to be special. Don't confuse special time with the casual conversations you have while you're folding laundry. Special time is supposed to be *fun*. No chores allowed.

It's a Good Idea!

Understanding a problem *is* the hardest part of solving it.

It's a Good Idea!

Don't neglect Special Time with your older children when there's a new baby in the house. I know, you're up to your eyeballs in diapers, milk, and sleep-deprivation. All the more reason to focus a little attention on the older kids.

Special Time Ideas

Stumped? Let these ideas generate ones of your own:

➤ A monthly downtown lunch date complete with fountain Cokes at the old drugstore.

➤ A trip to somewhere *you've* never been (an aviation museum at the airport, the race track, a tour of the city sewer system, a working milk farm).

➤ A midnight pizza run!

➤ The movies, with a slow stroll afterwards to chat about it. Rushing there and back (with the focus on the movie in the middle) doesn't fill the bill, Bill.

➤ Sign up for a dance class together. A science class? An Italian class? Make sure the class meets a discussion-length drive away.

➤ Turn on the sprinkler, and take turns getting soaked.

➤ Take the A train. Take a ferry ride. Ride the metro to the end of the line and back.

➤ Go horseback riding. Take a hike (take your child).

➤ Surf (no, not the Net, the ocean!).

➤ Be spontaneous. One day you'll look at little Paulette and *know* she needs special time, and she needs it now. Call in sick, cancel the appointments, turn off the phone ringer, get in your pajamas (yes, I know you just got dressed, but what the hay!), and climb into your bed with hot chocolate. Paulette will soon be spilling her guts (better her guts than her hot chocolate) and soon you'll both feel much better. When the sobs stop, *then* you can watch a video.

So, It's All About Confronting Issues and Gut Spilling?

No! No! No! And, of course! It is, and it isn't. Take the word *confront* out of it. Special time works like this: Remember that special time is fun time—fun without guilt. Sharing pleasant experiences will bring you emotionally closer to each other. Closeness leads to talking, *if* you don't push it. Let discussions bubble up like the fizz in freshly poured strawberry seltzer. Don't push for intimacy (it will push right back).

How Quantity Is Your Quality?

Don't get defensive now, I'm not reading over your shoulder. I've just noticed in my day-to-day dealing with parents that when the time crunch is on, special time is usually the first thing to go. It's easily compromised, especially when things get nuts. (Among my own family and the families of most of my friends, "nuts" is the normal state of things.) The next thing to disappear is all that other "quality" time with your kids that isn't quite so special—the discussions over shelling peas, the discussions in the car about Grandpa's cancer. Look, I know you're crazy-busy (and you have *no* idea how much I can relate), but how much time *do* you spend with your child these days? How "quality" is that time?

The Quality Time Quiz

Minutes a day, seconds a day, far too many hours? During those minutes, seconds, and hours, how much of that time is your attention shared with other kids, laundry, the report to the board, trimming your toenails? There's no recipe about the number of hours or quality time spent with your kids. It's not a simple formula of more equals better. (I'm one of those parents who goes bonkers if I don't have time *away* from my child, and it's truly no reflection of how much I love her, or enjoy being with her.) The interesting thing is that few parents truly know how much time they are actively parenting, and how much of that time they are focused on their kids.

Since, as they say, knowledge is power, let's get a little knowledge.

Get out your eeny teeny notebook (remember the Tally Ho! exercise in Chapter 4?) or copy the chart in Appendix F and get ready to write. Every day for a week, write down how much actual time you spend with your child, who else is there, what you do or talk about, and what else is going on while you're together. I suggest doing it for a full week so you can include a weekend. When you're done, look it over. Surprised? Most parents are.

Minimum Quality Time in Two Minutes Flat

Guess what? In an emergency, quality time can be short—very short. Of course, it isn't as good as a major, laid-back hang-out or adventure, but just by focusing and paying attention, you can still really connect with your child. Anthony E. Wolf in his book *Why Did You Have to Get a Divorce? And When Can I Get a Hamster?* writes, "Obviously, two minutes a day is not enough. But even a little of special just-you-and-them time touches a place deep within kids. More often than not, parents already provide it—usually at bedtime. But it can be anytime."

The World's Expectations

Parents get blamed for a lot, but we can't take responsibility for every part of a child's experience in life. Your child is a citizen of a country, a resident of the town or country she lives in. She goes to school, to play dates, to the park. Unless you're doing the hermit-family thing and are holed up with your kids somewhere without other input, your child will have expectations placed on her by many people and institutions; school expectations, societal expectations, gender-related expectations, her own expectations of herself, and so on.

Gender-Related Expectations

We're a sexist society, and a gender-divided society. We have different expectations for boys than we do for girls, not only for their futures, but also for who they are as kids. We expect different interests, energy patterns, ambitions. Many people subscribe to what I call the "testosterone theory," that boys and girls have such different hormones and brain structure that we should have different expectations for them. Others disbelieve that theory. No matter what you believe, one thing is true: All kids are different, and you should gear your expectations to your child, not her sex.

My daughter loves imaginary games, stuffed animals, swimming, and trucks. If I expected her to play with dolls (which leave her utterly cold) and be interested in only wearing dresses to school (like many of the other little girls in her class), I wouldn't be doing justice to who she is, and what she is interested in. Barbara Mackoff, in her terrific book *Growing a Girl,* stresses that parents, instead of focusing on society's gender expectations, should look at each child in terms of their individuality, while at the same time, wearing "gender glasses" and teaching their daughters to be aware of society's gender biases. Mackoff suggests we aspire to be "equalist" parents, who create more equal opportunities for their daughters through loving exposure. You can be an equalist parent for your boys, too, by seeing and supporting your son for who he is, not for who society expects boys to be.

Your Child's Expectations for Himself

It's not just about you. Your child will set expectations for himself, and though you have influence over these expectations, once again, you have no control. The older kids get, the more objectivity they have about themselves, and the clearer they can see their own paths.

You can help your child define who he wants to be and how he wants to behave. The biggest influence will be your own expectations for him. It's not an easy task to get your self-expectations balanced. (Look deep inside yourself and tell me, is it?)

The Perfectionist

Some kids are perfectionists, always *needing* to get everything right. Perfectionism is painful—the perfectionist child never satisfies herself. You can help her get her self-expectations in line:

➤ *Assess your own expectations*—no, not just for her, but for yourself, too! Are your own expectations too high? Does she see you flip out over the fear of failure? Do you *drive* yourself to succeed? (Might be time to *drive* yourself to the woods for a walk, or else you'll *drive* yourself crazy!)

➤ *Show her that you aren't perfect,* and that you've made mistakes but have survived and are striving to do well in life. Let her see you make mistakes (little kids *love* to see grown-ups mess up!), and talk with her about times you've utterly failed, flunked, messed up, offended everybody and his brother, slipped on a banana peel in front of the queen. (What? You've never failed? Then you've never risked.) Admitting your mistakes is *especially* important for parents who are in recovery from drug or alcohol abuse.

➤ *Help her prioritize her tasks*. Sit with her and talk it through. The perfectionist is so worried about getting a task right (and convinced that she'll fail) that she often has a hard time even beginning. ("If you *know* you'll fail, why begin?" the perfectionist reasons.)

➤ *Encourage her as she finishes*. No false praise, but real encouragement (to bone up on encouragement techniques, see Chapter 4).

It's a Good Idea!

A perfectionist can be recognized by the following signs: easily frustrated by tasks, gives up quickly, procrastinates beginning tasks, and has trouble completing projects.

The Underachiever

Some kids have such low self-expectations that they don't think they can do anything. A child with no confidence in his abilities or talents will stop trying.

That's not to say that all kids should be ambitious or goal-driven. Not at all. He's a kid—let him enjoy exploring the world at his own pace. Many an easygoing, emotionally secure child seems unconcerned about the future. That's a *good* thing. He's got years and years of time-starved work-driven life ahead of him.

If your child seems as though he's given up or he doesn't believe he *can* do anything, it's time for you to step into action. Try active encouragement. Involve your child in activities that will give him a sense of his ability *to do:* sports (if he likes them), dance classes (for girls *and* boys), rock climbing, gymnastics, music, art, 4-H, chess club. It doesn't matter *what* your child gets passionate about, it's the passion that's important. If your kid feels good about one ability, no matter what it is, he'll do better in *all* areas of his life. Remember that what works for one kid won't work for another, and you may need to plow through a number of extracurricular activities before you find a match. Do it. It's vital.

It's a Good Idea!

Extracurricular doesn't mean expensive. There are terrific free or low-cost classes for kids almost everywhere. Check out the museums, recreation departments, community centers, community colleges. Look on bulletin boards. Ask other parents in the park or at your child's school. Good luck!

Setting Reasonable and Achievable Disciplinary Goals for Your Child

Goals are expectations in action. They are specific, they are real life. When you and your child are thinking about behavior changes, remember that success breeds more success. The goals your child should aim for should be ones he can reach successfully.

When defining disciplinary goals:

➤ Make sure you are specific and explicit about the goals *with* your child. Say the goal is for your son to clean his room every Sunday before bedtime. If you think cleaning his room includes vacuuming and windows, and he thinks it means shoving all the little Leggos into a box, you've got trouble. Talk about it. (Also see "Clear Expectations in Action: A Clean Room?" in Chapter 6.)

➤ Make sure they're achievable.

➤ Keep them limited in number and scope.

➤ Make sure they're defined—or at least approved—by the child.

➤ Understand that the goals are the child's, not yours.

You Goal, Girl!

Say that you and your daughter Laura are frustrated by her behavior. You sit her down for a little chat. You've been reading this book, so you know about and have been practicing your "I" statements (you learned about "I" statements in Chapter 3).

"Laura," you say, "I hated our fight this morning. When you are that belligerent and unhelpful, I feel very angry. I value our relationship very much, dear. In the future, I want you to do what I tell you, and stop being so rude. Please do your chores and study hard."

Laura agrees. "I will, Mom. I hated our fight, too. From now on, I'll do what you tell me and I won't be rude and I'll do my chores and I'll study hard."

Tales from the Parent Zone

"I want Sherri and Tommy to be more resourceful," their dad told their mom. "I agree, but how?" After much conversation, the parents decided on specific goals: "Sherri is old enough to begin packing her own lunch" and "Let's let Tommy decide in what order he'd like to do his homework." These well-defined goals were the first step on the way to more resourceful children.

Behave Yourself!

Too much pressure on a child to achieve can backfire—you may end up with an A student, but she may be a nervous, miserable A student terrified of failing and terrified of disappointing you. Celebrate effort and progress, not the end results.

You and Laura have now defined some behavioral goals. Perfect, right? Smooth sailing ahead?

Well, not exactly. Yes, you've defined some goals for Laura, and she's agreed (she wants your approval, and she wants to feel good about her behavior), but are these goals specific enough? Is she likely to be able to achieve these goals? Are they limited enough in number and scope? Have your given her enough direction? (Just how *is* Laura going to do all these things?) In this case, the goals you've chosen are vague, and it will be hard to measure Laura's progress. Some might require skills Laura may not have yet, and willpower alone won't work for her. It's a long list of goals too: obeying, being polite, completing chores *and* doing homework. Such a change in behavior will feel overwhelming. You and Laura risk being disappointed when she fails. I think you should start smaller.

Start by targeting a specific goal. *One*. One you know Laura will be able to achieve. For instance, "Laura needs to complete her homework before dinner." Or, "Laura may not use curse words, and if somebody talks to her, she'll, at the least, acknowledge his presence with words."

Now Laura will have a chance at success.

Whose Goal Is It Anyway?

Your child may, from the time he is very young, have different personal goals than you would choose. He's him, you're you. You have certain things you would like your child to achieve, but it just won't occur if your child doesn't want it, too. When setting up goals with your child, make sure that it's *with*. It's ludicrous to set up goals *for* him. He should be part of the decision-making process. Ideally, disciplinary goals should come from the child, in response, or as part of a conversation with you. Some parents have kids sign contracts about behavior issues. For most kids, in most situations, a verbal agreement is enough.

It's a Good Idea!

When setting up disciplinary goals, keep in mind your child's development and your child's age.

What Your Child Expects: From You!

It's simple—well, it's simple to list, anyway. Your child expects a parent who:

➤ Shows her unconditional love, respect, enjoyment of her presence, and who appreciates her for who she is.

➤ Demonstrates your pride in her.

➤ Isn't too lenient, isn't too harsh, and gives her the support and limits she needs.

➤ Is her ally.

➤ Keeps expectations reasonable.

Don't Overexpect

Expectations must constantly be dealt with. Keeping your expectations for your children in line ("Down, Doggy!") is very tricky. We want the best for our kids, and we expect they deliver. Keeping expectations in line with a child's capabilities and development is difficult, especially with eldest or older children. Final tip: Want answers? Look to your child.

The Least You Need to Know

➤ Strive for positive, realistic expectations for your child.

➤ Everybody is born with temperament—understand the temperament, and you'll have clues to understand the child.

➤ To effectively teach discipline, you and your child need to spend quality time together.

➤ Don't base expectations on age or gender; look to the child.

➤ When setting disciplinary goals, understand that the goals are the child's, not yours.

➤ Keep your expectations reasonable.

Normal or Naughty?

In this chapter, we're going to talk about your family—the basis and location of all this disciplinary action. We'll talk about what the members of your family expect from each other: family values, family rules, and family goals.

Expectations, again? Yes! It's not enough to set reasonable expectations for a well-behaved child, you need to set them for yourself and for your family, too. And that means some soul-searching, some decision-making, and some family input. Relax! I'm not asking for anything outrageous here—this chapter will help you define what's normal and expected from members of your family, give you a few specific tips and tasks to make life more serene, and help you with your discipline. Really. I mean it.

Disciplinary Element Number Eight: Set Reasonable Expectations for Your Family

Element number eight of the Twelve Disciplinary Elements widens the scope of discipline outside of you and your child. Your child doesn't exist in a vacuum, he lives in your family, probably with you.

Since you want to be the reasonable, respectful, well-behaved parent of a reasonable, respectful, well-behaved child, it makes sense that you want to have a reasonable, respectful, well-behaved family. A reasonable, respectful, well-behaved family is a group of people who care about each other, who are allies for each other, who listen to each other, who tend to live with each other, and who are doing the best they can. (Keep in mind that we're not talking perfect here. Keeping your expectations reasonable is vital!)

Words to Parent By

A *family* is a grouping of people—usually but not always biologically or legally related—who may live together, and who love and rely on each other.

It's a Good Idea!

Every family has its own expectations about things like manners, cleanliness, and acceptable language. As a reasonable, respectful parent, teach your child the "when in Rome" principle—follow the customs of the natives and respect other families' values and rules. It's just a question of respect.

To have a family that respects each other, it needs to start with you. You're the adult here, remember? I know too many people who think that a family is a good place to kick back, away from the world. "I don't have to be on my best behavior with *them*, they're just my family." Yes, you can relax, but remember that this is the place where you should be the *most* considerate, thoughtful, and kind. These are the people you love, remember? Show them a little respect.

What's Normal for You?

Every family has a different expectation of "normal" behavior. When I as a kid, I used to love to go over to other people's houses for dinner because every house was so different. At Rowena's house, we said grace before we ate. At Alison's house, we had to clean up—really well—after we ate. At Tilly's house, we ate chicken with gravy, homemade pie, and occasionally had a food fight. At Milo's house, her parents had wine with dinner (and she thought it was odd that at my house we drank water and ate mung-bean-and-brown-rice casseroles and huge bowls of green salad).

All the rules were different, too. My parents liked a quiet house, and the radio was usually on low playing classical music. At Tilly's house we could watch TV, at my house we didn't have one. And so it went. The rules and customs you establish for your household and family may be completely different from what's happening at the Joneses down the block. There's no one "normal," but it's helpful to have your family's "normal" explicitly defined so your child understands the behavior expectations.

Who Is Your Family?

Families come in all sizes and configurations. Your family might include biologically related members, nonbiologically related members, people who live together, and people who don't, of all ages and genders. The definition of your family depends on you—if you say you're a family, you are. I believe it's the love that matters, not the shape of that love.

Families are more than a configuration of people who love each other. Families have a family identity, shared values, shared rules of behavior— shared expectations.

Some families are very clear about what these expectations are, but in most families, the expectations are just sorta understood. But are they? Problems arise when some family members assume that others know and believe in the values and rules. Those others, who've never really had the expectations clearly explained, may be utterly clueless. When expectations aren't clearly talked about, there's also no way to work out differences in opinion and values. And then they fester. Ugly, dark family dynamics begin rising like a north-caster, and it's time to take cover.

Far better to spend a little time explicitly building your family identity and defining your family's behavior expectations. To do that, it helps to make your family's values and your family's rules explicit. We'll do that later in the chapter.

If You Can't Beat 'Em, Join 'Em

There's another shared element of family identity: family loyalty. While family identity often comes with loyalty built in, I think it's important to make a special mention of it here. Most people have strong expectations around family loyalty. But sometimes it can take all of us by surprise.

Behave Yourself!

If there's food that your child can't or shouldn't eat due to allergies, values, or religion, teach her to remember two little words: side dishes. If served food she can't eat she may explain simply without making a big deal out of it. She should expect her values and restrictions to be respected by her host but she shouldn't expect other food. So, she's a little hungry for a few hours. She'll survive.

It's a Good Idea!

To truly set family expectations at a reasonable, attainable level, it helps to be deeply involved—and communicative—with your family.

Have you experienced this?: You're *very* annoyed at a family member. Let's say it's your mother. You complain to your friends. You whine to your partner. You're tired of her garbage. You hate her. Then, somebody else says something unkind about your mother, and whoa! "Hang on buddy, don't you talk about my mama that way! Those are *fighting* words!" Your blood boils, your loyalty emerges, your very family identity is challenged. You are ready to go to war and give your life over the very person you were so furious and disappointed with just moments before. The "I can say it, you can't" phenomenon happens in more than family situations (it happens with friends, at school and on sports teams, even between countries), but it's a good sign that there is healthy loyalty and family identity at work.

It's a Good Idea!

When you model being an ally, your children will learn to emulate you.

Being an Ally

Just as you are your child's ally, you also should be your family's ally. There are forces, evil forces, trying to tear your family apart. Maybe they are people (that cute young thing coming on to your partner), maybe they are work schedules (70-hour work weeks tend not to be good for family health). Be on the side of your family, and your family will be on the side of you.

Keeping It Private

The children of celebrities learn this one early: You don't air your dirty laundry in public. This is not a plea for secrecy or for skeletons hidden in closets; this is a suggestion for keeping family matters private. By all means, share them with your family therapist (if you have or need one). Confide in your trusted friends. Sometimes it's important to let your child's teacher in on family issues. But there is no call for sharing your family's struggles indiscriminately with every stranger or acquaintance. It's not very respectful to your family. (And it doesn't make you, the blabbermouth, look very good, either.)

What Does Your Family Expect?

Kids, and people in general, do best when they clearly know what kinds of behaviors are acceptable and expected of them. To get your disciplinary expectations clearly defined and reasonable, start by asking yourself the following questions about what you *already* expect and need from your family regarding discipline.

Take a few minutes to think about each of the questions below. It helps to write down the answers—there's something profound about seeing these things written down. Be honest with yourself, now. Nobody, and no family, is perfectly behaved (including you, and including your partner). What are the important areas? What do you let slide?

It's a Good Idea!

Your family's expectations of your child are based on your family's values.

1. When do you need family members to be on their best behavior (daily, business calls, family events, around certain family members, and so on)?

2. What kinds of "misbehavior" does your family tolerate (occasional cursing, food fights, messiness, lateness, sloppy eating, all, none, and so on)?

3. What kinds of behavior are *never* acceptable?

By looking at what kinds of behavior expectations your family has, you're also beginning to look at your family's values.

Writing Your Family's Value Statement

There's family values—that's a political agenda—and then there's *your* family's values, which are your family's personal beliefs and behavior guidelines. (In some cases, these two kinds of family values may be the same thing. In *most*, they will not be.)

Here's a fact: Just by living we impart our values to our children. Most parents have a vague sense of their values and how they want their kids to be, believe, and behave, but far fewer have crystallized them into words. That's what we're going to do now; write your family value statement that gets it all down into a series of behavior guidelines. Later in this chapter, you'll be turning these values into a set of family rules and goals.

Start by getting a piece of paper and a pencil. You can do this exercise at a family meeting if the kids are old enough to focus on it (we'll talk about these meetings in a moment), with your partner, or by yourself. It's best, but not vital, to have everybody involved.

What's a family value statement? It's a set of guidelines based on your beliefs about how family members should behave. It has little to do with specific instructions (it's not, "The guys need to put the toilet seat down"—that's a family rule, and we'll get to those later). The statement you are creating is more like a company's mission statement. The family value statement applies to everybody—not just the parents, not just the kids, and not just Cinderella in the corner.

Here's a sample statement developed by Karen Renshaw Joslin, author of *Positive Parenting from A to Z:*

1. We use words to tell others how we feel. We do not name call or use bad language.

2. We do not hurt others physically or emotionally.

3. We do not hurt each other's property or our own.

4. We work to get out of a problem, not stay in it.

You can use her statement (it's a good one), you can add or subtract, or you can build your own. As you are discussing your statement, think about the following set of questions:

Words to Parent By

The *family values statement* lists a general set of beliefs and behavior guidelines that apply to everybody in the family—for example, "Our family does not use violence to settle problems." It is based on your family's deep-seated beliefs.

It's a Good Idea!

Organization, structure, and specific understanding of family rules, expectations, and goals makes children feel more secure.

➤ As a family, how do we like people to express that they are upset?

➤ How important is it for us to spend family time together?

➤ What do we feel are important manners in this household?

➤ If somebody is really angry, is it okay to hit? Do we feel it's okay to curse?

➤ How do I like my things to be treated?

Keep your list fairly short and basic and, when you're done, post it somewhere visible, where people will see (and read) it on a regular basis.

Family Rules, the Family Jewels

How are your family's values put into action? Through personal limits (we'll do those in Chapter 7) and through family rules. Family rules define what is and isn't allowed in your family. They apply to everybody. (Waiting for something that says only Joey can't cross the street by himself? That's a personal limit, and that's in Chapter 7.)

Defining your family rules can be helpful, especially if you're having disciplinary problems. It's not required. Some families don't believe in having specific family rules. Done right, the family value statement (no matter how short) should cover the territory. If a behavior doesn't fit into your family's value statement, it is against the rules, and that's that. Other families rely on clearly defined family rules. It's a matter of your family's approach to life.

Use Family Rules Sparingly

Louanne Johnson, author of *School Is Not a Four-Letter Word,* tells the story of her first few years of teaching: yards of rules that she, and her students, were constantly fighting over and forgetting. Finally she tore up the rule sheet and wrote a new one, with only two rules:

1. Respect yourself and the other people in the room.

2. No insults against anybody's race, religion, skin color, ethnic background, gender, or sexual preference.

Behave Yourself!

Too many family rules and your family will start focusing more on what it *can't* do rather than what it *can,* and that's not very positive now, is it?

Johnson makes a point of noting that rule number two is included in rule number one, but she wanted to stress it. Behavior in her classroom was measured against these two rules. Spitting is disrespectful, therefore it was against the rules. With this simplified approach to behavior, Johnson's whole classroom dynamic changed.

If you look closely, Johnson's rule number one is a value statement and rule number two, which is more explicit and precise, is a rule.

Family Rules Are Your Family Values in Action

Family rules are more specific than the values expressed in your family value statement. They are how the general values are expressed in the real world. To define family rules for your family, sit down with your partner (yes, just the two of you for this discussion; it's not a kid thing) and go over the list of suggested topics below. You'll see that the potential for rules is endless. Some of the topics you may want to write a rule for, some not, and there may be a variety of topics I haven't included here. Remember:

➤ Keep your rule list sparse; the fewer there are, the more power each rule will have.

➤ Developing your list will probably take you more than one sitting.

➤ Write down your rules and review them the next day.

➤ The very process of discussing these issues with your parenting partner may lead to some very interesting conversations—and potential conflicts to be resolved. It's worthwhile to air these differences before they become household issues, even if you decide not to have any "official" family rules.

➤ Remember that family rules apply to *everybody*. If the rules are only for the kids, or if they're supposed to be for everybody but you break them, you're saying, "I'm the one in power (ha-ha, you're not)," "I'm an adult so I matter, you're a kid so you don't," and "Just wait until you grow up. Then you can break all the rules you want." Say you make a family rule that everybody's room has to be kept presentable. If your bedroom remains swallowed by piles of clothes, old papers, and dirty dishes, you're just about assured that your child's will look the same.

Even if you *love* rules, don't even begin to think you can make family rules to cover every contingency. As a matter of fact, the fewer rules the better!

Family Rules Definition Exercise

Use this work sheet to begin your exploration of your potential family rules. Try to phrase your rules in the positive, rather than in the negative. "Eat only in the kitchen" means the same thing as "No eating in any room with a rug," but it tends to be more effective.

It's a Good Idea!

All this talk about expectations, values, rules, and limits is really just a way to determine your family's approach to discipline. Defining them helps you answer the vital question, "How do we want this family to function, and what should we do about it when things break down?"

Household responsibility and participation.
Rules?:

_____

Mealtimes.
Rules?:

_____

Snacking.
Rules?:

_____

Other food concerns.
Rules?:

_____

Privacy.
Rules?:

_____

Language.
Rules?:

_____

TV and video games.
Rules?:

_____

Homework.
Rules?:

_____

Other school issues.
Rules?:

_____

Indoor physical activity.
Rules?:

_____

Extracurricular activities.
Rules?:

_____

Sibling behavior.
Rules?:

_____

Forbidden activities.
Rules?:

_____

Telephone.
Rules?:

_____

Computer and Internet use.
Rules?:

_____

Reading.
Rules?:

_____

Pets and pet care.
Rules?:

_____

Allowance.
Rules?:

_____

Earnings.
Rules?:

_____

Savings.
Rules?:

_____

Family functions.
Rules?:

_____

Guests.
Rules?:

_____

Permissions.
Rules?:

_____

Modesty.
Rules?:

_____

Car.
Rules?:

_____

Smoking.
Rules?:

_____

Drinking and other drugs.
Rules?:

_____

Curfew.
Rules?:

_____

Dating.
Rules?:

_____

Sexual activity.
Rules?:

_____

Religion and religious practices.
Rules?:

_____

Family Goals

Now that you've defined your family values and rules, you can move on to establishing your family's goals. Where is your family going from here? What would you like to see happen? Here are a few suggestions:

➤ *Keep goals very specific,* not vague and general. "I want us to be happy, healthy, and rich" is way too vague. What do you mean by happy? Vague goals are so overwhelming as to usually mean nothing.

➤ *Goals should point the family in a positive direction.* They should imply an action to take, and a way to begin. "I want this family to go to counseling, and start an investment program" is far more specific. Progress will be easy to measure.

➤ *Keep family goals realistic.* Start small, with a specific goal you *know* you'll be able to reach, like, "Let's get a couple of loads of laundry done today" instead of "Let's clean up this entire pigsty this afternoon!"

➤ *Keep goals limited in number.* Too many goals can feel overwhelming, and your energies will be diffused.

➤ *Discuss goals with the entire family.* Everybody except the dog can participate in making them into reality.

➤ *Keep goals visible.* You may want to post them (right under the family calendar, right over the family value statement). Discuss with the entire family.

➤ *Make sure that everybody shares an understanding of the family goals.* Try some active listening to make sure that you're all on the same page.

Family Meetings

How does all this happen? You're leading busy lives—what family isn't? Few of us are used to sitting down together and working on lists of values, rules, and goals. First, *don't try to do it all at once!* Schedule a few sessions to do it.

A good place to write your family value statement and define your family's goals is during a family meeting.

Family meetings aren't just for making lists. In general, they're a great way to pay attention to the inner workings of *your* family unit, and to help build inner discipline, or structure, into your family life.

Family meetings aren't required for healthy families, but, especially if you have a big, busy family, they are worth considering. They work best when they are regularly scheduled events, not just called when there's a family crisis. Here are a few uses for family meetings:

➤ To coordinate the running of the household; schedule car pools and rides, chores, special events, vacations, and holiday planning.

➤ To get input from everybody about larger family decisions that will be made by the parents.

➤ To announce family decisions.

➤ To discuss serious family issues, come up with new ideas, and problem-solve.

➤ To recognize and celebrate each family member's biggest accomplishments since the last family meeting.

➤ To kick back with each other, eat, drink, and be very merry.

Tales from the Parent Zone

The Green household is thick with tension. Nobody seems to have anything good to say to anybody else, and few conversations occur without sarcasm or yelling. The Brown household, on the other hand, is a mellow, enjoyable place to be, because family members seem to generally respect and appreciate each other. Besides being reasonable and respectful, it's nice to have a family where the feelings are generally positive, and the tensions relatively low, most of the time (are my expectations getting unreasonable or unrealistic yet? I don't think so).

When scheduling family meetings, remember:

➤ Plan the agenda ahead of time.

➤ Schedule meeting times far enough ahead of time that that particular time slot is empty on *every* family member's calendar. Family meetings are for everybody.

➤ Set up the agenda in advance so everybody can have input, and to avoid squabbles (stick up an agenda idea list in the kitchen).

➤ Keep family meetings to 30 minutes maximum. Otherwise, you'll achieve maximum burnout truly fast, and you'll be *very* sorry.

➤ Take turns planning and facilitating the meetings.

➤ Focus on the positive. Family meetings aren't only gripe sessions focusing on *issues*. Take some time each meeting to eat popcorn, sing, show off silly costumes, enjoy your family.

Clear Expectations in Action: A Clean Room?

Where do expectations and reality most often clash in families? The issue is called: a clean room. Families often run into trouble right here, somewhere between the sheets and blankets and the toys and clothes covering the floor. What's your expectation? Who is expected to clean? What does that mean? And whose room is it, anyway?

Privacy Issues

Patty's junk is all over the floor. If you tossed a pencil onto the floor, it would immediately be swallowed into the mass of clutter writhing and seething on the rug. The shades have been drawn for months, and you're sure that there are mushroom colonies sprouting and sporing in the corners, if you look hard enough. You're tired of asking, you're tired of nagging. So one spring day, when Patty is over at a friend's house, out come the trash bags, the broom and dust pan, the gloves, the Ajax, the furniture polish, the rags, and the sponges. And you go to work. Hours later, the room is glowing and spotless. "Patty will be so happy," you think. "It's so much more pleasant, now."

Patty comes home. Is she thrilled? Well, there are screams, but they are not screams of pleasure. Patty feels betrayed, embarrassed, humiliated, her privacy invaded. Was she right? Were you?

She was. Unless she was told that you were going to clean her room for her, you had no right to invade her privacy. Her room is her room, and she should be able to be the queen of her castle, no matter how small. But you were right, too, in one way, because her room was becoming a health hazard. Mushrooms and mold are not healthy, and her cleanliness (or lack of cleanliness) was affecting the whole household.

It's a Good Idea!

Children have the right to a private space of their own, no matter how small, where nobody can intrude. This could be a cubbyhole, a special trunk, or a bedroom. Respect her right to privacy. This might include allowing a certain degree of chaos. A child's room doesn't always have to be ready for photographers from *Architectural Digest.*

Here are the essential points:

➤ Every child is entitled to her privacy.

➤ Health and safety issues override privacy issues.

Ideally, you should have pressed Patty to do the work, helped her do the work (this is really the only approach that works with small kids), or at the least, informed her that if she has chosen not to do the work, you were, but you weren't very happy about it, and there would be some other consequences as well.

Tales from the Parent Zone

Back when I was a teenager who procrastinated a great deal, my dad's final threat was always, "Clean up your room, Ericka, or I'll do it." Terrified of losing my privacy, this threat prompted me into immediate action. Especially after the time I didn't listen, and he made good on it. My papers, organized wrong. My scraps of important papers, tossed out. My innermost secrets, exposed!

What Are You Modeling?

If you treat the whole house as your closet, your child will, too. If you are a neatnik, your child will probably be tidy, too.

Making Cleaning Possible

Cleaning is not an intuitive skill. Nobody is born knowing how to attack a messy room and turn it to serenity. Few of us can effectively wield a broom, dust pan, or dust rag without a lesson or two—and a lot of practice. Making beds takes time. Here are some suggestions for making clean bedrooms possible, and defusing the dust bombs.

➤ Teach your child *how* to clean by incorporating him into your own cleaning.

➤ Cleaning can be a lonely task, and for the social child, it may feel like a punishment instead of a way to contribute to the family. Become the clean team—make the jobs go faster by working together. Your child helps you clean your areas of responsibility, you help him with his room (you're excused for a cup of afternoon tea while he hides all the pictures of the *Baywatch* beauties—and worse).

➤ Plan a special activity or adventure for the family to celebrate a successful day of cleaning. It's not really a bribe—it's a treat!

➤ Be clear about what you mean by "a clean room." Check out the clean room checklist, below.

Clean? What Do You Mean?

We all know what a truly clean room looks like, but how do you get from here to there? How much of it is your child's responsibility? "Go clean your room" could mean tossing things in the closet until company has gone. It could mean clearing the toys from the floor and sorting game pieces into their boxes, throwing the dirty clothes in the hamper and pulling up the bedspread. It could mean changing the bed, dusting, and vacuuming. It could mean polishing the windows and mirror until they sparkle. Here's your choice (you're balancing on a high crag in the wind, choose now, parent, choose now!): Define, or face the conflict!

Below, I've broken down the process of cleaning a filthy bedroom into small, manageable chunks. You can use these suggestions (and others!) to create an individualized bedroom chore list for each member of the family. If this is successful for you, consider making a chore list for other areas of your home.

When you make chore lists for your child, always take your child's age and development into consideration. A five-year-old can get the books back on the shelf and the clothes in the hamper, but she won't be able to do much with the bed. A 12-year-old can do his own laundry with some supervision. Remember, your expectations will change as your child matures.

Using the list will help you define your expectations. It will help your child organize his time and remember his tasks. You'll have an easy, stress-reduced way to check if things have been done. Keep the list small. Better to have too few things on the list than too many (aim for success!)

Here are two quick hints: Separate the job into straightening and cleaning, and don't clean before you've straightened, you'll just make yourself frustrated; and, a filthy room is like an archaeological dig. You've gotta approach it in layers.

Behave Yourself!

When it comes to clean bedrooms, keep your expectations *very* low. Few kids have clean rooms. They like them dirty, it's the only place where they have control over their environment, and for some kids, a dirty room is a point of honor! This may be an area where something needs to give, and that something may be you.

One, Two, Clean!

Here's the ideal order to get from disaster to gleaming in as short a time as possible:

1. *Tackle the clothes first.* Fold the clean ones or put them on hangers, and put them away in an organized fashion. Put the dirty clothes in the hamper. Put all shoes (neatly) in the closet. Once the clothes are out of the way, you may be able to see a patch or two of carpet. There's hope!

2. *Clear the garbage and clutter.* Return all dirty dishes to the kitchen, and wash them. Bring in a large plastic trash can bag for the trash. Don't forget to empty the wastepaper basket.

3. *Strip the bed* and put the sheets and pillowcases in the hamper. Remake the bed with clean sheets.

4. *Start laundry load number one,* if you have in-house machines.

5. *Put away the toys* and the fragments of toys (oh, those puzzle pieces!).

6. *Put away all books, tapes, CDs, videos, computer programs.* Library books go in a pile near the door ready to be returned. Tapes, CDs, and so on, all need to be in their *proper* boxes, and *then* put away. You *won't* get to it later.

7. *Clear the desk.* Organize the desk so that homework and books are accessible. Throw away old clutter and scrap paper. (You may need to empty that wastepaper basket again.) Stuff the (now full) trash can bag in the kitchen garbage can or, if you're really ambitious, take it out to the trash cans or dumpster.

8. *Now we make the shift between straightening and cleaning!* Get your dusting supplies handy! (If you keep pets and plants in the room, you might want to "excuse" them, now.) Straighten and dust surfaces (dresser, bedside table, vanity, shelves, and so on). You do this surface by surface—clear the surface of objects, dust, and return objects neatly. Starting to look pretty good, huh?

9. *Clean the floor.* Sweep, or move furniture aside and vacuum. Don't forget to vacuum the dust from under the bed!

10. *It's wall time!* De-web the ceiling and corners with a broom covered with your dust rag or the vacuum cleaner. Scrub the bad spots off walls with spray and a rag. Make sure all posters are still securely attached.

Hot dog! It's a clean room!

The Least You Need to Know

➤ Different families have different "norms": values, rules, and behavior expectations.

➤ Understanding the family values and rules makes children feel more secure.

➤ The fewer explicit family rules, the stronger each rule becomes. Allow the family values statement to determine behavior expectations.

➤ Family meetings are a great way to build a strong family.

➤ The "clean your room" issue becomes less of a battle when you make your expectations very specific.

Chapter 7

Even Light Has a Speed Limit

In This Chapter

➤ Providing personal limits for your child

➤ Making limits that pass the Limit Test

➤ Communicating and sticking to the limits

➤ Changing the limits to reflect your child's growth

When contractors build a house, they pour a solid foundation. Then, as the walls are slowly going up, they use props—solid boards to keep the walls in place. Once everything is hammered, glued, and sturdy, they slowly remove one prop at a time. Voilà! A house! As your child grows, she, too needs a foundation and props. Love, trust, and respect provide the foundation. Personal limits, consequences, and consistency are your child's props. As they grow older, you'll be able to slowly remove them, and your child will remain standing, a strong, architecturally gorgeous structure.

In this chapter, we'll look at the personal limits, the props, that you can provide your child. (We'll look at consequences and consistency in depth when we get to Chapter 9.)

Give That Child Some Limits!

Kids not only need personal limits, they actually crave them (though sometimes they'll tell you just the opposite). Personal limits provide boundaries and supports they can lean against. For many parents, setting limits, sticking to them, and following up (that's the consequence and consistency part) is the hardest part of parenting. There's no doubt that it's hard to say no, especially to those droopy little puppy dog eyes. Try to remember (before you give in yet again), providing clear behavior limits will make your child feel secure and more confident.

Tales from the Parent Zone

The cartoonist Gary Larson once drew a "Far Side" cartoon called "The Boneless Chicken Ranch." Groups of boneless chickens lay flopped on the ground. Without bones, the chickens' muscles had no structure, nothing to flex against, and they had no way to stand. Now imagine a boneless child. Flop. This is your kid without limits—structureless, unable to stand. Give your kids a skeleton, okay? Provide them with personal limits. (Just as bones grow alongside the growing muscles, blood, and brain, so, too the limits you set should not be static—they should be adjusted to accomodate your child's growth.)

Sounds Like a Family Value! Or Maybe a Rule!

A child's personal limits reflect your family's values, and exist within the family rules. But whereas the family values statement (Chapter 6) and family rules (also Chapter 6) apply to everybody in the family, personal limits are customized for each child, at each stage of her development. A personal limit is a specific behavior boundary: Annie can play with the parakeet when there is a grown-up around, or Tony must be home by dinnertime.

Words to Parent By

Limits are behavior boundaries. Some are set by nature (humans can't fly, I can't keep track of my sunglasses), some by the state (you can't drive the wrong way down a one-way street), and some are set by you. It's up to you to define and make explicit each child's limits.

Disciplinary Element Number Nine: Communicate Effective and Reasonable Limits

The limits you set for your child should be effective, reasonable, and well communicated. Kids do best when they have structure in their lives, both daily routine and behavioral structure. Children do best when they understand what is acceptable, what isn't, and what will happen if they push the boundaries too far.

Defining Limits for Your Child

Any limit you set for your child has gotta pass the Limit Test—it's gotta fit inside your family's values, and it can't contradict your family rules. Here are all the qualifying considerations of an effective limit:

➤ *Does the limit fit within your value system?* Look at your family values statement. Say you have a statement that reads, "We solve our problems with words, not violence." If so, this limit *wouldn't* pass: "When John is fighting with Eliza, he's only allowed to punch her on the arms, legs, and torso. He's not allowed to punch her in the nose."

➤ *Does the limit contradict a rule?* Review the family rules. Here's a sample contradiction: Say you have a rule that you turn off the lights when you're the last person leaving the room, and Joey has a limit that says, "Joey can only have 12 lights on in the house at a time." (Silly example? Who am I to say what kinds of limits certain families create? Every family and every child's rules and limits will be different.)

➤ *Is a particular limit really needed?* Is it a limit just for the sake of having some limits? Sometimes overeager parents start going wild with arbitrary limit-setting, just for the sake of having something on the books. Chill, baby. Let it breathe. Don't panic, your child *will* be well behaved. You don't need to discipline for the sake of discipline.

➤ *Are you dogmatic about limits?* Limits are not laws. There are times when you need to be flexible about limits.

➤ *Are you setting new limits after the fact?* Ideally, set limits ahead of time. You'll save everybody agony.

➤ *Does your child understand the limit?* Once you've decided on a limit, make it explicit—the child should be informed exactly what the limit is.

It's a Good Idea!

Limits are extensions of your family values, and writing your family value statement (Chapter 6) will *massively* help you understand and define limits for your child.

Planning Ahead

How do you set limits ahead of time? Okay, I'll confess, planning isn't one of my strong suits. I'm a one-day-at-a-time woman, rather spontaneous, who wouldn't know a five-year plan if it hit me in the face. Look, in our family we rarely plan *dinner* until half an hour before our starving stomach rumbles disturb the neighbors. Yet, even *I* recognize the value of choosing limits for children ahead of time. It's a matter of paying attention, thinking ahead, and *talking about it*.

Of course, you can't plan ahead for all situations, and children make unforeseen leaps in development

It's a Good Idea!

Limits are set by parents and other concerned adults, and all involved adults should *know* the limits. There's more about working with a parenting partner in Chapter 18: "Double Discipline: The Tag Team."

that require sudden, new limits. When something new comes up, by all means create a new limit for the future (if it's needed). But a child shouldn't suffer the consequences of exceeding a limit she didn't know was there.

Limits and Modeling

When you start defining personal limits for your child, one of the things to keep in mind is *you*—your modeling, your example. "Do as I say, not as I do" is not a very respectful approach to parenting. (Of course there are times when it's appropriate, like when you're enjoying a glass of wine with dinner. Enjoying wine with dinner is an *adult* thing, and when your child is grown up, he'll be able to have a glass as well.)

If you limit your 12-year-old to two cookies, it's cruel to sit in front of him finishing the box and licking your fingers with joy. Doing that sets up a pecking order, with you on top. Be aware, and be sensitive. You want those limits to feel like strong, loving arms, not barbed wire fences topped by guard towers armed with machine guns and searchlights.

Tales from the Parent Zone

Tamara grew up in a family where she was expected to set most of her own limits. Her parents believed that this was the best way to teach her responsibility. As an adult, Tamara doesn't wholly disagree with her parents' method, but she tells tales of flailing and pain that could have been avoided had her parents stepped in and said, "Enough, here's a limit for you." Because her "wimpy-style" parents weren't assertive about their limits, at times, Tamara even questioned their love.

Making Limits Totally Clear

Here's the deal, it's not a limit if your child doesn't know it's there. If you don't communicate limits to your child, she won't understand where the wall is until she smashes head on into it. Invisible force fields are *not* a great idea in a family home. Spending a little time to first think about and decide on appropriate limits, and then talk with your child about them, will save her from crashing and burning. Making your child's limits clear will help you too: You'll avoid that horrible trip from calm to hitting the roof in five seconds flat.

Once you've got a limit defined, it's time—as much as humanly possible—to let your child know what it is. You've made up *your* mind; sound like it! State the limit with a clear voice, as though you are presenting an algebraic theorem: "One more chapter, and lights out." It takes practice to sound strong and reasonable. (Here's a tip: Drop the pitch of your voice at the end of the sentence.)

Processing the "Can I?"

What happens when your child asks for permission to do something when no limit has been overtly established, or your child wants existing limits stretched or bent? Here are some tips:

➤ *Don't leap to No!* When your child begins a question with "Can I," or "May I," he's asking you to define, reiterate, or change a limit. Especially if he's asking about an area that hasn't been defined before, try not to leap to No! It's easy to say no, and most parents do it almost absentmindedly. Kid asks question, and halfway through, parent mumbles, "No." Is this you? Stop. Listen. Do you really mean it? Sometimes no slips out, even when there's no reason for it, and once you've said no, it's kinda hard to say yes. Try not to say no unless you really mean it—you'll save yourself the agony of either being unjust or backing down. We'll talk more—a lot more—about the importance and pitfalls of consistency in Chapter 9.

➤ *Don't leap to Yes!* without thinking about it, either. Many parents feel as though unless it's explicitly not okay, well, why not. I guess I'm just saying, think about it!

➤ *Don't react, respond!* Take a breath, step back, and think about the request. No matter how absurd, ridiculous, or morally offensive, there's probably *something* positive about the request. Say it's, "Mom, can I skip my homework tonight and go to the movies with the kids up the block?" Instead of jumping to "Absolutely not!" start with a "yes" statement. "I'm delighted you're making friends, honey, and maybe you should ask them if they can do it Saturday. But tonight is out."

➤ *Stall, stall, stall!* Don't be afraid to take your time making a decision. Rarely do you need to make a decision *so* fast that you can't take time to think it through. Getting pressure? Try saying, "I'm not sure how I feel about that. I need some time to think about it. I'll let you know after dinner." Or, you can ask your child to tell you why she wants to do something.

➤ *Confer with your parenting partner.* (I'll have a whole section about this in Chapter 18.)

It's a Good Idea!

Patience. It may take a while for limits to sink in, especially if you're new at imposing them. Give all people involved a break—that means the limiter and the limitees here. You might be too harsh or inconsistent. Your limitee might forget or rebel. Whatever you do, don't hate yourself, don't hate your kid. Change takes time.

Tales from the Parent Zone

Back in my early 20s, I was an au pair for a family in France. The three kids *weren't* well behaved, and their specialty was the internationally popular childhood sport of whining. The culprits here?: *Madame et Monsieur.* In that household, *non* didn't mean no, it meant, "Keep bugging *moi* about it until I say 'Okay, just zis one time, Cherie.'" Don't get me wrong, changing your mind can be a good thing—it teaches your child how to own up to mistakes, and the benefits of flexibility. But too much waffling leads to whining, now and forever.

Behave Yourself!

Reminders are not the same thing as nagging. Nagging is characterized by an unpleasant tone of voice, and constant repetition. Kids' ears all come equipped with an "N" chip that filters out nagging. They simply *cannot* hear it!

It's a Good Idea!

It takes energy to set limits, but the payoff is worth it. Your child will feel reassured, and life at home will run smoother. Added bonus: a dive in the number of "Oh Pleeeaazes" and "Whine-nots?"

Using Reminders

There's a lot of life in life, and in the middle of all the daily hullabaloo, it's easy for kids of all ages to forget their limits.

Using reminders is a gentle approach to keeping kids in line. Repetition is a vital part of learning. Reminders, when repeated, simply and clearly bring the limit to your child's awareness. Before entering the mall with Paul, you might remind him that he can select one pair of gym shoes, and they need to cost less than $60. Or, say Tony has a 9 P.M. bedtime, and at 8:45 you watch him pulling out an elaborate game. Saying, "It's 8:45, dear," and leaving it at that is probably more effective than, "Tony, how many times do I need to tell you to be ready for bed at 9? How can you possibly think that you can play that game now? How many times do I need to tell you not to start something new so late!" and so on.

The Wiffle-Waffle and the Waffle-Wiffle

There's a type of parent who has a hard time setting and sticking to limits. There's another type of parent who leaps to No! And then there's the wiffle-waffle and the waffle-wiffle whose favorite answer is, "We'll see."

➤ Wiffle-waffles say, "We'll see," and the answer is always no. They're uncomfortable asserting themselves, or they don't want to hurt their kids' feelings. Is this you?

➤ Or perhaps you're a waffle-wiffle, whose, "We'll see," can be translated as an inevitable yes. Waffle-wiffles are afraid of seeming too lenient.

Remember, you don't have to be tough or overly solicitous—just firm.

Stay Flexible

Trees that bend do a lot better in storms than their more brittle, rigid cousins. Life, and parenting, are never predictable, and flexibility is one of the greatest strengths you can build in yourself. Firmness is not the same as rigidity. Don't enforce limits just because once upon a time you decided it was a limit—you may need to reevaluate, or provide exceptions in cases of need.

There's a Limit to Limits!

You can't raise a resourceful child if your limits are too tight. Limits are vital and needed. Too many limits, though, can make a child feel crunched and, well, *limited*. How will you know if you are being reasonable, or if the limits you are setting are too extreme? Easy. Watch your child's reactions:

➤ Resistance and grumbling are normal. No self-respecting child is going to let you know how much she craves limits.

➤ Continued outrage or full-scale rebellion over a limit are your clues that something else is going on—perhaps your limit *is* too stringent and unjust. It may not be age or developmentally appropriate anymore. Are the limits expanding as she grows? Or perhaps your reason for the limit, or the values behind it, haven't been communicated clearly enough. Are they explicit? Are the purposes of the limit clear?

Not Sure About a Limit?

Is it time to expand the limit? How can you be sure?

Behave Yourself!

Don't create arbitrary or unhelpful limits. Limits should be as logical as consequences.

It's a Good Idea!

Snake skin doesn't stretch, which is why snakes shed their skins as they grow. One day the old skin simply splits (rrrippp!!!), and the snake wriggles on out of it, wearing a clean, shiny new skin underneath. Sometimes parents and kids don't always realize a limit is too tight until it suddenly, and with force, splits open. Growing up isn't always smooth and ripple-free.

➤ *Keep evaluating your child,* keep looking at who your child is *this* month, keep on talking.

➤ *Ask your child what limits would feel appropriate.* After you get past the initial part of the conversation ("No limits, Dad!"), you'll probably get a few ideas. If your child takes part in the limit-setting, he's more likely to live comfortably within their boundaries. (Kinda like the difference between your building a fence around your property for privacy, and somebody else fencing you in.)

➤ *Check out Junior's friends' limits.* Let's get clear, here, "Everybody *else* gets to," is *not* a reason to let Junior do something. Find out though—it's purely informational. You'll discover what other parents consider developmentally appropriate, and why Junior may be pushing for a change.

➤ *Do your research.* Hit the library and go get overwhelmed by the sheer number of parenting books (and check out the suggestions in Appendix B). You'll discover some vital information from child development experts. You'll also learn that everybody has an opinion, that most opinions are a matter of opinion, and that you can trust your own opinion.

➤ *Talk with your child's teacher.* She's one of your parenting partners. She's involved in your child's life, and she'll see your child from a completely different perspective than you do. Involved parents are the number-one factor for how well a child will do in school. Don't wait until conference time or until the principal's office calls—get involved! Call for a conference today!

Tales from the Parent Zone

Marissa doesn't understand why you won't let her walk home from school by herself. "I'm *old* enough. You don't trust me! You never let me be independent! You're punishing me for growing up!" she cries, and ditches her escorts. Marissa doesn't understand that you do value her independence and respect her growth—you've imposed the limit because you are worried about the safety of your neighborhood. Perhaps you can demonstrate your trust and respect by loosening the limits in other areas—and having a heart-to-heart with Marissa about your concerns.

The Limit Changing Test

Before you *do* change your mind on a limit, put it through the "Limit Changing" test, a very simple, two-part exam that will tell you whether you can change a limit—or not.

There are two areas where limits are nonnegotiable:

➤ Is it a question of safety?

➤ Is it a question of values?

"One, Two, One, Two, Flex and Stretch"

Here's a sentence that should rarely come out of your mouth: "Well, maybe just this time." Limits should change for reasons, not because your child has worn you down. Sometimes a limit needs to be breached, once, because of an emergency situation (Grandpa had a heart attack, we're racing to the hospital, and no, you don't need to finish your homework or clean your room.).

It's a Good Idea!

Some limits are short term. Andy's having trouble staying dry at night, and, at age seven, his bed-wetting is becoming an issue for him. An effective short-term limit might be to limit how much water he can drink at night.

Expand-a-Limit!

As your child grows, you can help her build her internal resources, learn self-control, and "internalize" the discipline she is learning by allowing more lenient limits, letting her try new things, and giving her more responsibility. The little child who can step onto the porch without supervision, but no further, now is going to slumber parties and meeting her friends at the movies.

Here's the thing: The fewer limits you present, the *closer* you need to watch your child. Keep checking in. This is *not* a time for you to slack off on your paying attention. As a child learns responsibility and safety, she still needs your help defining her own limits, her values, and her ethics. And, of course, when it comes to safety or your family's values, *keep those limits firm and explicit!*

Reinstating a Limit

Two steps forward and one step back. Progress, learning, and growth do not proceed at a steady pace, and backsliding is common. Sometimes you'll change a limit to include more privileges and responsibilities, just to learn that your child really *isn't* ready for that big a step. Okay, back up. But be careful not to make your child feel punished, or that she has failed. This would be a good time to have a problem-solving/brainstorming session (more about these in Chapter 19 and Appendix E). A creative solution will give your child the limits and structure she needs without making her feel like a big, bad failure. Perhaps you need to establish a series of gently expanding limits, rather than trying for too much at once.

Rosie's Dance: Working with the Limits

James, a single dad, had never set a limit for what time his 14-year-old daughter, Rosie, needed to be home at night. Frankly, it had never come up. Rosie came to James one Friday night and said, "Dad, I'll be out until midnight at the dance. See ya, I've arranged for a ride."

Now, James knew Rosie was going to the dance, he had even given her money for the tickets. If he had thought about it, he would have realized that the dance was going to go fairly late, and that it was possible Rosie would want to go out to eat with her friends afterwards at a 24-hour coffee house. (That was the tradition when James was Rosie's age.)

Oh, if he had already discussed with Rosie her limits ("Rosie, you're 14, and I think you're old enough to stay out until 10 o'clock"), then she would have known her parameters, and known that she needed to try to renegotiate with you ahead of time. Because he hadn't thought about limiting the time Rosie was due back in, her announcement caught him by surprise. He wasn't comfortable with it, at all. The more he thought about it, the more uncomfortable he felt. He didn't want to arbitrarily assign her a time to be home and ruin her well-organized plans. He knew if he let her go, he'd spend a miserable night, stewing and brewing and worrying.

James sat Rosie down and expressed all of his feeling. "I know, Dad," Rosie said, "I'll call when the dance is over and we're going to Denny's, I promise I won't drive with somebody who's been drinking, and if they aren't ready to go by 11:45, I'll take a cab home and pay for it out of my allowance.

James breathed a sigh of relief—his daughter *was* growing up, and, in this case, she was happy to work out a limit that worked for both of them. Ah, the wonders of communication!

The Least You Need to Know

➤ A child without limits is structureless, unable to stand.

➤ Any limit you set for your child must pass the Limit Test: It must fit within your family's values and rules.

➤ As much as possible, set your limits ahead of time.

➤ A limit is not a limit unless it's been communicated.

➤ Use reminders to reinforce limits.

➤ Flexibility is a vital trait for the strong and gentle parent.

➤ The fewer the limits, the closer the supervision.

Part 3

Prevention's Great, but Sometimes...

You are terrific! You've done a great job as a parent, and you child is one lucky cookie to be so supported, loved, and strongly parented. So why is he still misbehaving?

Look, kids misbehave. To respond appropriately, we first need to know why he's misbehaving, and then we need to know what to do about it.

Part 3 focuses on consequences—what happens when the apple drops from the tree (it hits Newton on the head!). You're about to learn about natural and logical consequences, and things like making your consequences satisfy the three R's: related, respectful, and reasonable. You'll also learn the details of which consequences really work, which ones might (given the right circumstances) be appropriate, and which are big, bad no-no's. And here it is, the great spanking debate.

Why Is Johnny Naughty? What Am I Gonna Do?

In This Chapter

➤ When bad isn't that bad—and when it is

➤ Dealing with your child's misbehavior

➤ Proactive listening—getting the goods on what happened

➤ Understanding what your child *really* needs from you

Raising a well-behaved child is all well and good, until the next time your child misbehaves. Then you've got a naughty kid, a headache, and, often, a bad case of confusion and despair.

Misbehavior is normal. Your basic well-behaved child isn't a human being unless he spends a great deal of time being irresponsible, overly dependent, and irrational. (Show me the perfect child, and I'll show you a pod person.) Yet, when your kid is misbehaving, how *are* you going to respond? To teach your child to be well behaved, you have to understand misbehavior. In order to find the most appropriate action, or consequence, to fit a misbehavior, you first must understand the misbehavior and the problem driving it.

In this chapter, we'll look at "naughty" behavior—*mis*behavior—and try to understand what is *really* going on. I'll give you a number of ways to put a more positive spin on some fairly negative behavior. (Hang on, I'm not apologizing for bad behavior or trying to explain it away! Understanding *why* misbehavior is happening is the first step to making sure it doesn't happen again.) We'll look at your process—the appropriate steps a parent can take when responding to misbehavior, including a special "proactive" listening technique to find out what is *really* going on.

Relax! Naughty Is Normal

Look, kids test you to your limits. They exasperate, they annoy, and most of all, they misbehave. It's all part of their job description.

Help Wanted

Immediate openings for children. Room, board, and occasional spending money. Excellent benefits package (talk to our recruiter about our college saving program and inheritance plan). Many of our wonderful opportunities also include a weekly allowance! Required: entry-level skills in testing, bugging, mischief, driving parents nuts, and all-around misbehavior. Must be willing to be trained. Applications available from Dr. Stork, 100 Cabbage Leaf Blvd. Join NormalKid Enterprises today!

It's a Good Idea!

The child who is disobedient may be seeking clearer limits or consequences.

Behave Yourself!

Don't leap to judgment! "Bad" behavior is often a matter of the circumstances. What is appropriate at home might not work at a fancy restaurant, what kids do at school doesn't always wash at home. Kids don't always understand what is appropriate when and where (which is why they are notorious for embarrassing their parents). It's an education thing.

Occasional Disobedience

It's hard to remember that bad behavior is often a season. Your child is acting up. Your child is stealing, or biting, or blowing curfew, or fighting with his sister. Your previously charming child now can't be taken to restaurants without causing glares and raised blood pressure in you, the servers, the table busser, the chef, the maître d', and every diner. Every time your kid misbehaves, your imagination goes crazy, and suddenly it's not your little Joey taking pennies from your nightstand to buy gum, it's big bad Joe doing hard time for grand larceny. You imagine little Amanda (last seen teasing and smacking her little sister) carved with black, homemade tattoos, running with a gang, and calling herself Vampira. It's no longer just her sister she's hurting, she's up for grand theft auto for stealing a neighbor's old four-runner and turning it into a convertible. Your mind goes wild. You see yourself in front of the judge, pleading for mercy. You wonder about visiting hours in San Quentin—do they let parents hug their kids?

Parents, parents, get a grip, relax. These are the facts:

➤ Kids misbehave.

➤ The fact that kids misbehave does *not* doom them to a life of evil crime and hard time.

It's hard to remember, but kids *do* go through phases, and phases pass. When I was eight, my friend Lori McAdams taught me how to take stuff. We stole scented candles from a candle shop. Decades later, instead of calling my parole officer every week, I'm a reasonably upstanding citizen writing books about how to raise well-behaved children. My husband, Bill (reasonably upstanding, himself), confesses to once roving with a band of boys, breaking off the antennas of parked cars. He may not have been ethical then, but now, I consider him the most ethical person I know.

Yes, we were wrong, and I'm not condoning our behavior (it may even have been better if we had been caught; it might have done us some good to have been actively corrected), but no, it didn't mar either one of us for life. In each case, whether through time, correction, or the realization of basic conscience, we stopped the misbehavior. Whether it's not feeding the dog, "losing" a poor report card, or trashing the visiting team's locker room after a lost game, most kids will get over the behavior.

Chronic Disobedience

It's true, too, that most criminals *do* begin with the petty. It's not all right to ignore most misbehavior, but try to keep some perspective—*most* misbehavior passes.

Yet, say something new or chronic is occurring with your child's behavior, something very troubling. It's time to figure out what's going on. First assess the parts of her life you are directly involved with. Is there a lot of fighting, hitting, yelling in your household? Changes? Stresses, strains, unusual money worries? When chronic or very troubling behavior occurs, it's time for a little increased attention to, and talking with, your child.

➤ Be honest—tell her you're disturbed by her behavior, that you sense she's having a hard time, that you want to know what's causing the behavior, and to help her figure out how to stop it.

➤ If life at home is rough, especially if it's rougher than usual, talk about it with her. Commiserate and/or problem-solve (there's problem-solving guidelines in Chapter 19).

➤ Ask about school, use active listening (Chapter 3) and proactive listening (later in this chapter) and let her rant and rave.

➤ Listen hard and well. Let her know you're an ally, not an enemy.

➤ If necessary, seek out counseling. There are suggestions for finding help in Chapter 24.

Everybody goes through hard periods in life. Don't leap to scenarios of gloom and doom. Unless there's a strong pattern forming, unless your child becomes stuck in the behavior, he's probably not

It's a Good Idea!

Kids are curious. Life is a science experiment, and sometimes you're the field of study. How far can I push Mom until she goes off the deep end? And what happens then?

on his way to forming his own evil empire. Do what you can, worry about the immediate, and let the future take care of itself. Most people make it through.

"Good" Behavior, Plus or Minus 10 Percent

Now that you're reading this book about raising a well-behaved child, you're probably seeing the need for discipline every time you look at your child. That's natural—when you start looking closely at your kid, you'll no doubt see dozens of areas that can use improvement.

Warning: Don't go overboard here. It's not as bad as you think—you're just noticing all the flaws because you're looking really closely. (It's like looking at your face in a magnifying mirror under a bright light. Scary!) Don't get so picky, don't crack down on every misdemeanor. Choose your battles, allow some leeway. Do you really want a totally obedient, perfect, every-hair-in-place little child? Let your kids take some risks, express zest, dissent, criticize, tease, bore you with bad jokes, whine, and rebel. Any child with a questioning spirit, with a zest for life, with a strong sense of self is going to test, experiment, and exasperate. You *want* that! It's a tough world out there, and they'll need every ounce of that spirit, zest, and sense of self to carry them strongly through life. The most "challenging" kids are often the big achievers in life.

The Strong and Reasonable Parent Responds

Okay, realistically now, you're not always going to be cool, calm, collected, and totally wise when your kid misbehaves. Ideally—and I mean *ideally*, this is something to strive for!—your responses will go something like this:

1. React ('cause you can't help it).
2. Cool down and gain a little distance.
3. Separate the *deed* from the *doer*.
4. Listen to your child, look for the message behind the action, and determine the child's needs, figure out how to "honor the impulse," determine your own needs.
5. *Then* respond.

Whoa! There are a few steps between *react* and *respond!* That's right (that's why I stress *ideal*). And to make it even more complicated, you'll need to work on not expressing your reactions so heavily, and using your anger *for* not *against* your child.

I feel you gulping. I sense your discouragement. Hang in there, it's *not* impossible. Let's take it one step at a time.

First, You React

Your child has stolen a candy bar, skipped his chores, or spoken to you harshly. She comes home with a disappointing grade, or sports a black eye from fighting. You get a call about his behavior from a neighboring parent, the school, or the police station. Whatever the misbehavior, your first response is likely to be, what? Anger, right? Anger is one of the scariest emotions, and learning to effectively deal with it is truly important. I've got a lot of ideas and suggestions in Chapter 19, but, until you get there, just keep this in mind—the ideal first reaction to misbehavior is to make sure your reaction doesn't get in the way of your eventual response.

What's the difference between reactions and responses? One of the ways scientists determine whether something is living is whether or not it is responsive to stimulus. Any *thing* will react (reactions are chemical), but only living things will respond. A rock will react to sunlight by getting warm, but a plant will respond, it will turn toward the sun. Reactions are chemical and passive—you don't choose your reactions. Responses are deliberate and active. You can choose your responses.

Of *course* you react—you hear the news, and panic or rage surges through you. You yell. Or your first impulse is to somehow simply stop the behavior, prevent your child from ever doing it again, and, maybe, to "teach her a lesson." Most of us need practice to keep our reactions from being so extreme, from getting in the way of good parenting. Try this: Feel the panic? Feel the rage? Breathe! Count to 10, now count to 20.

It's common to feel horrible about overreacting. All is not lost. If you apologize, your child will have a lesson in being gracious. Either way, your child will learn that you aren't perfect, and that perfection is not required to be a good person.

Try to Cool Down and Gain a Little Perspective

Perspective makes all the difference. Remove yourself from the situation for five minutes. Go into the backyard and stare at the sky. Do *something* to ground yourself back in your body, and relinquish the sense that you have to *do* something immediately. Remember: No matter *what* you do, you *won't* be able to prevent it from ever happening

Behave Yourself!

Don't react, respond.

It's a Good Idea!

What if you did flip out? Did you ruin the entire experience? Have you destroyed your relationship? No, and no. Parenting is a daily thing, which means that you get another chance tomorrow, or the next time your little angel misbehaves.

Behave Yourself!

Don't label your child. ("You're a thief." "Andy's a biter." "Sarah's lazy.") Labeling a child makes the child, and those around her, assume the behavior is an immutable personality trait, part of her identity. A child who is labeled often gets "frozen" into the misbehavior.

again. You just don't have that much control over your child! Face it: You are not in control. You have influence, but ultimately no control. If you can understand that—and it's a hard one to get—you are halfway there.

Blood pressure lower? On to the next step.

Separate the Deed from the Doer

Separate the behavior from the personality. Remind yourself that you don't have a bad kid, you have a kid who did a bad thing.

It's *very* easy to condemn a kid who behaves badly as a "bad kid." "That Jones boy," you'll hear people say. "He broke three windows with a baseball bat. Is *he* a bad seed, or what?"

Probably "what." Yes, in this society child-on-child violence may be growing. But in a vast majority of all cases, the problem is not *who* the child is, it's what he's doing. Kids have good intentions. Even children who are acting "bad" are trying, sometimes desperately, to be seen and approved of for who they are. Kids who behave poorly feel bad about it. Sometimes they are looking for attention. Sometimes they are expressing frustration. Sometimes bad behavior is a diversionary tactic. Your job is to *not* withhold approval and affection and to look behind the negative behavior to see what is driving it. Separate the deed from the doer, and look for clues.

Tales from the Parent Zone

Twelve-year-old Tanya can't read, so she picks fights right before reading every day in order to get sent to the principal's office. That way nobody will witness her shame when she's called on to read in class. Six-year-old Elizabeth isn't very good at the fine motor skills. She kicks other kids and runs around like crazy when she's asked to put together puzzles. Why is *your* child misbehaving? Look for the patterns.

Disciplinary Element Number Ten: Listen, Look for the Message, and Determine the Child's Needs

Element number 10 of the 12 Disciplinary Elements is to understand misbehavior. Take it from the experts, there's a reason for every misbehavior, and when you figure out the reason, you're more than halfway home to stopping it. Fine. So why is your child misbehaving?

Gathering Information Through Proactive Listening

Take your good-but-misbehaving kid aside, take a deep breath, and listen to his side of the story. You want to hear about what was happening when the incident occurred, what happened before and after, and how he feels about it.

Listening effectively—especially when you've been upset by disturbing news—is very difficult. Kids are often the *opposite* of clear (they often don't understand their actions, themselves). Listening takes practice, and most of us don't have much experience. Don't expect perfection the first time you try it. Practice, and determination, are the key.

Here's a "guided" listening technique called *proactive listening,* developed by communications expert William Sonnenschein. It takes *active listening* (introduced in Chapter 3) one step further, and it's most useful when there's specific information (like *why* Tommy cut off all of his sister's hair) that you need to elicit.

In active listening, you, the listener, are in a passive role. In proactive listening, you, the listener, guide the course of the conversation through asking pertinent, probing questions. Remember, though, it's still a *listening* (rather than a talking) technique, which means it's your job to hear what your child says, not to control the content. Here are some reasons to try proactive listening:

➤ *To get and keep the conversation on track.* You're on the hunt for information, and your child may not know what's important to say. As an effective proactive listener (silent and stealthy) you can gently steer the conversation over to the important subjects.

➤ *To delve deeper into the depths of detail.* Your child may be glossing over important facts because he doesn't know what you need to hear. Or he might be trying to hide information (the little scamp!). By asking the right questions, you can cut through to the deep details.

➤ *To help your kid express himself.* By directing him with your questions, you hear what he is trying to communicate and he (bonus points!) may begin to better understand his own thoughts and feelings about the incident.

> **It's a Good Idea!**
>
> Discipline is learning, and the path to learning never runs smooth.

Ready? Here's how:

1. *Ask an open-ended question.* The best proactive listening questions can't be easily answered with a simple yes or no. Say, for instance that you're trying to understand why Tommy chopped Belinda's hair off at the roots. You might ask, "What were you feeling before you cut Belinda's hair?"

2. *Don't react to the answer!* Say Tommy says, "I was really happy because I wanted to get back at her and I knew this would make her cry." *Don't* stop the "exercise" to make judgments or criticize—you'll have lots of time for that later. It won't help for you to scream, "You were *happy* to make her cry? You insensitive little—" Listen quietly. Allow time for the child to fully finish.

3. *Get more information.* As you listen, find a cue to an area you feel needs to be explored, and ask another question about what has been said. "What did you want to get back at her for?" Now you're getting some information. (Hey, this isn't the end of it, you can't let Tommy just go back to chopping hair—but that's the only part we're dealing with here—the information-gathering aspect. We'll talk about consequences in Chapter 9.)

Look at Family Dynamics

Proactive listening is one way of figuring out what is going on with your child. Another way is to look at your family dynamics. What has been happening between you and your child? Between your child and the rest of the family? Between you and your partner and other family members? Family tensions frequently manifest in misbehavior. (It's become almost a cliché for teachers to ask parents, "Is there anything happening at home?" whenever a child misbehaves. It's a cliché based on reality, though.)

Look for the Message Behind the Action

As you seek to understand your child, it's important to look a little deeper, at your child's underlying motivations. As you go through the process of responding to misbehavior, think about the incident and what it might mean to and about your child. Psychiatrist Rudolf Dreikurs developed an important theory of child development based on his belief that a child who is misbehaving is discouraged, and believes both that he lacks significance and that he doesn't truly belong. Of course, this may be the *child's* perception, but hey, it's the perception that matters.

The Four Mistaken Goals of Misbehavior

Jane Nelson, author of many wonderful books on positive discipline, has taken Dreikurs's discovery that a child's misbehavior is based on one of four mistaken goals: undue attention, power, revenge, and giving up, and created a powerful tool for responding effectively. Nelson writes that all misbehavior is a child's method of saying, "I am a child, and I want to belong."

Here's an adapted version of Jane Nelson's tool for understanding and responding to misbehavior. As you look carefully at your child's misbehavior, apply it to the categories below to figure out which "goal" your child is trying to achieve.

Child's Mistaken Goal: Undue Attention

If your child is acting out or bugging you for undue attention, she's saying, "Notice me! Involve me in your life!" The methods she's choosing, however, are more likely to make you feel annoyed, worried, and guilty. You may find yourself coaxing your child, or simply doing things for her that she can do herself.

The child seeking undue attention only believes she belongs and is important when she's being noticed, or getting special attention.

She needs to be noticed and involved. Help her by giving her assurance and immediate redirection. Give her useful tasks, tell her you love her but you're busy and set up a special time with her (and keep it!). Touch her without words to show her you love her but can't be distracted. Be firm.

Behave Yourself!

Ever catch yourself growling, "Do you need a spanking, young man?" If so, consider what your kid might really need: attention? affection? independence? nurturing? limits? privacy? responsibility?

Child's Mistaken Goal: Power

The child seeking power is trying to say, "Let me help! Give me some choices!" If, however, anybody (including your child) is challenging you to a power struggle, you're gonna feel challenged, provoked, threatened, and possibly defeated. You may fight, find yourself thinking, "You won't get away with this one!", want to *make* the child behave, or give in and feel cowed and powerless yourself. You'll probably react to the threat by wanting to be proven right.

The child seeking power believes he belongs only when he's in control. He's a kid on a mission: to *prove* that nobody can boss him around.

This child needs you to withdraw from head-to-head conflict, calm down, be the "adult," let him help you with tasks, offer limited choices, and acknowledge that *you can't control him* (nor can he control you). This child needs limits set, and firmness around the limits—but do it kindly! Don't rise to the bait!

Child's Mistaken Goal: Revenge

A child seeking revenge is really trying to tell you, "I'm in pain! Help me, I'm hurting!" The child who has been hurt may try to retaliate or "get back" at you or others. You may feel disappointed, hurt, disbelieving, or even disgusted at the behavior. You may try to get back at the child—to retaliate yourself—or feel a loss of control and despair: "How could you do this to me?"

The child seeking revenge is hurting and doesn't believe she belongs, so she wants to make others feel like she does. She doesn't believe she is good, she doesn't believe anybody could like or love her. (She probably doesn't like or love herself.)

Your task: to avoid punishment and retaliation, to demonstrate understanding and empathy, to talk with your child about her hurt feelings, to apologize. Encourage her strengths. Allow her to voice her pain. Try not to take it personally.

Tales from the Parent Zone

In fourth grade, I shoved Anthony because he was bugging me, and he fell off the desk where he was perched and landed, rear end down, in a wastepaper basket. All the kids laughed. "I'm gonna get you," he said. After school, I hid in the girls' bathroom until I thought he was gone, but, no, I came out and he was waiting. "Do you know what 'revenge' means?" he asked. I shook my head. "This is what revenge means," he said, and socked me as hard as he could in the stomach. What a way to learn a new vocabulary word!

Child's Mistaken Goal: Giving Up

The child who gives up is saying, "Believe in me. Don't give up on me." When a child gives up, quits, doesn't try, and moves passively through life, you may feel hopeless yourself, despairing, disappointed, and inadequate as a parent. You may react by doing everything for the child, expecting nothing, or expressing your disappointment.

It's a Good Idea!

At different times, the same kid might express different "mistaken goals of misbehavior."

The child whose mistaken goal is to give up doesn't believe he belongs, thinks he's hopeless and incapable, and does his best to convince everybody else of these "facts."

You must show him your faith in him. Start small and take small steps. Show him how to do things. Encourage any effort. Encourage the progress. Be his ally, his champion, his cheerleader. Enjoy him and believe in him.

Many Misbehaviors, Many Reasons

Your child's misbehavior may be spurred by her need to achieve one of the "four mistaken goals of misbehavior." She might have other reasons as well:

➤ testing

➤ saving face

➤ seeking respect

➤ needing more independence

➤ avoiding unpleasant or scary tasks

➤ experiencing a moment of thoughtlessness or being unclear on how her actions affect others

➤ expressing a serious emotional problem

Whatever the reason, your job is to analyze the situation and try to deal with it in a positive, nonpunitive way. Remember, punishment is short term, and ultimately an ineffective way of dealing with misbehavior.

Honor the Positive Intent

Parenting is truly tough; it calls on *all* your resources, and demands you to be the best, noblest, smartest person you can possibly be.

Your challenge is to try to understand your child and treat her *as you would like to be treated* at the same time as she's treating you worse than a hideous bug crawling on the floor. As she stomps and screams, your job is to model appropriate behavior. Part of *your* appropriate behavior may be to express how angry it makes you to be treated like an ugly bug, and to insist on better treatment.

How do you do this? If it were truly easy, you wouldn't be reading a book about it. One way to meet this steep challenge is to look for, and honor, the positive intent in your child.

Jane Nelson and Rudolf Dreikurs assume there is always a message of need behind a child's misbehavior. Jeanne Elium and Don Elium, authors of *Raising a Son, Raising a Daughter,* and *Raising a Family,* go even further. They teach parents that kids always have a positive intent—an underlying positive meaning—even when they are misbehaving. Finding the positive intent within negative behavior can help you with your own frustration level, and help feel friendlier toward your child.

Here's an example of positive intent:

Maya was way too old to be throwing food on the floor. She was almost five. Yet, when she didn't like something, or when she was finished with her dinner, she grabbed handfuls of spaghetti, rice, or beef Wellington and flung it on the linoleum. That's not okay. What was the positive intent here?

It's a Good Idea!

There's an old saying that the road to hell is paved with good intentions. I've always said that so is the road to heaven.

Words to Parent By

Positive intent is the underlying positive meaning behind any action. It's a theory (developed by Don and Jeanne Elium) that assumes that people mean well and strive for the best.

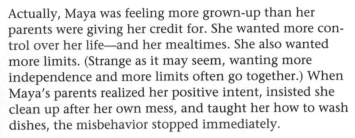

Actually, Maya was feeling more grown-up than her parents were giving her credit for. She wanted more control over her life—and her mealtimes. She also wanted more limits. (Strange as it may seem, wanting more independence and more limits often go together.) When Maya's parents realized her positive intent, insisted she clean up after her own mess, and taught her how to wash dishes, the misbehavior stopped immediately.

Here's another example of positive intent:

Jenny was caught scrawling graffiti on the school wall. Her parents were scandalized—defacing property! Hanging with the wrong crowd! Yet, when they stopped to honor her positive intent (she wanted to express herself creatively, and she wanted to be accepted), they were able to channel her energy into something far more productive: community service, art classes, and a school mural project. Jenny thrived.

Determine Your Own Needs

Okay, with me so far? Your kid has misbehaved but you haven't flipped out yet. You've cooled down and decided she's not evil, she's just misbehaving. You've listened to and elicited your child's story, you've determined her needs and intent. Now what?

Well, where's the *you* in here? You're not perfect, you're not a saint, you're not selfless—you have needs, too. Yes, you do! The more you understand your own intents, needs, and values, the better you'll feel about your parenting—in times of good behavior and bad.

Respond

You've gone through all the steps, and you're ready to respond. Aha! I fooled ya. You *have* responded—the only thing left to do, if appropriate, is assign consequences for the behavior (or let them occur.) And that's the topic of the next chapter. See you on the next page!

The Least You Need to Know

➤ Misbehavior is normal and necessary for the well-adjusted child.

➤ Hang in there! The vast majority of misbehavior will pass.

➤ Practice responding, not reacting.

➤ Separate the deed from the doer. Your child's behavior is bad—*she's* not a bad kid!

➤ There's a reason for every misbehavior. When you figure out the reason, you're more than halfway home to stopping it.

➤ Every misbehavior has positive intent behind it.

➤ Part of figuring out an appropriate response to misbehavior includes acknowledging your own needs and feelings.

Chapter 9

Consequences: Natural, Logical, and Consistent

In This Chapter

➤ Understanding natural and logical consequences

➤ The 4-Rs—related, respectful, reasonable and rewarding

➤ Choosing consequences—in advance and on the spot

➤ What makes a consequence inappropriate?

➤ The importance of consistency

You've done *your* job. You've balanced your parenting style and, you're pleased to say, you can now consider yourself a strong and reasonable parent. You've worked with your parenting partner to establish strong, safe limits, and you've clearly expressed them to your children. You have family meetings weekly, special time daily, and your ability to remain cool and collected in the face of kid chaos is the envy of all the *other* parents in your community. You understand *why* your children don't always behave, and hey, you're down with that. You're hip, cool, positive, and ready to rumble. Congratulations!

Then it happens—the dreaded call from the principal's office. The crime? Cheating, fighting, and cutting class. You catch your littlest princess with a pen in her hand, a smirk on her face, and scribble on the walls. There's homework left undone, your daughter wipes her rear with a hand towel, the phone bill arrives with several hundred dollars in calls to a sex hot line "900" number, Junior tells you *and* his grandfather to "Shut the %#!@ up," and Juniorette won't stop slapping you every time she gets annoyed.

Words to Parent By

Consequences are what happens as a result of a behavior, good or bad. Consequences can be pleasant or unpleasant—they are simply the outcome of an event or a course of events.

Words to Parent By

Natural consequences are the natural outcomes of behavior. The natural consequence of taking an hour-long shower is having to rinse your hair with icy cold water because you drained the water heater. A natural consequence of throwing your favorite toy against the wall is that it breaks. It's a cause and effect thing.

Yes, you read Chapter 8, but so what? You lose it! You have fantasies of throttling your child, hauling out the belt! Tying the kid to the whipping post! Forbidding dessert for a year and a day!

Nope. Uh uh. Cool out. Slow down—take a deep breath. Remember our slogan: Don't re*act*, re*spond*. Okay, so your child has misbehaved. That's what children do. It's your job to *teach* them. Here's what you gotta do: Be the voice of reason, and either apply, or let occur, related, respectful, reasonable responses.

In this chapter, we'll focus on those responses, otherwise known as consequences. We'll talk about what they are, how to apply them, and how to be consistent.

What's a Consequence?

Consequences are simple to understand. They are what happens as a result of an action. When we're talking about misbehavior and discipline, consequences are what occurs when a limit is exceeded.

Consequences Are Not Punishments

It's far too easy to let the word *consequence* become a synonym for the word *punishment*. "John, stop that or you'll get a consequence!" Consequences can be good, they can be bad, and they work best to change behavior when they just happen, as reliably as gravity. The apple falling from the tree is neither a good thing nor a bad thing—it just *is*. If you can reach the point in your parenting where consequences just *are*, you get an "A" in positive discipline!

Natural and Logical Consequences

The best teaching tools are *natural* consequences (if you stay up late, you'll be tired the next day) and *logical* consequences (abuse your television privileges and you won't be able to watch for a week).

It's Only Natural!

Natural consequences are highly effective teaching tools. When natural consequences are available, by all means, use them! Using natural consequences generally requires some restraint on the part of a parent, you have to allow the consequence to occur, and stop yourself from "rescuing" your child (remember the concept of "rescuing" in Chapter 2?). Of course, some natural consequences are inappropriate. The natural consequence of diving into a pool without water is a cracked head—yes, your kid will learn never to do that again. If she lives! Safety is *always* a consideration.

Tales from the Parent Zone

Recently, my daughter, getting ready to go to her swim lesson, flat-out refused to put her street clothes back on over her suit. Instead of putting the clothes on her by force, getting furious, or refusing to take her to class, I decided to teach her why clothes were a good idea through using a natural consequence. I smiled and told her she didn't have to wear her clothes, but that—if she chose not to—she would be wet and cold on the way home. She easily got into the car wearing only her suit and sandals. On the short trip home from class she began shivering and turning blue. "Why do you think you are so cold?" I asked her. "It's a natural consequence!" she announced (quite happily) through chattering teeth.

Logical Consequences

Natural consequences are not always available, safe, or convenient for dealing with misbehavior. If they aren't, make your consequences logical. Diving into a shallow swimming pool and cracking his head would certainly teach your son not to dive into the backyard pool, but that's hardly an acceptable way to teach a lesson. Logical consequences, though not as "natural" as natural consequences, should still have the same sense of inevitability as gravity. They are direct extensions of your child's actions tied to the misbehavior through logic. Using logical consequences will help you avoid power struggles with your child. Kids have a strong sense of justice, and they respond well to logical consequences because they are related to the misbehavior, and they have a real, logical basis. They aren't just arbitrarily applied by you, the big, mean parent flexing your muscles.

Words to Parent By

Logical consequences have some human intervention—and are logically related to the behavior. If Polly throws a ball in the house, it's a logical consequence for Dad to remove the ball. If Dave gets up late and misses the carpool, the logical consequence is that he walks to school. And if Anselm sneaks in an extra TV show or two after he's been warned, he loses his TV privileges for a week.

Disciplinary Element Number Eleven: Provide Related, Respectful, Reasonable Consequences to Misbehavior

The 11th element of the Twelve Disciplinary Elements is to provide consequences to the misbehavior that are related, respectful, reasonable, and rewarding—what I call the 4-Rs.

Related Consequences

Whether the consequences are logical or natural, when your child misbehaves, the consequences should be related to her actions. An unrelated consequence risks confusing the child. Related consequences can be either natural consequences that you allow to happen to teach your child a lesson, or logical consequences that you decide on, and that relate to the misbehavior. If your child refuses to hang up her clothes, keep the consequence related to clothes, tidying up, or chores in general. An unrelated consequence would be: "Since you're such a slob, you're gonna miss your piano lesson." That teaches nothing, *nada*, zip.

On the other hand, if she's been told to pick up her room or she won't have time to go to her dearly-loved piano class, then you've already tied the consequence to the action—and it *would be* related to tell her, "I'm sorry, but I told you we're on a tight time schedule today. You chose not to pick up your room on time, and since it *must* be done now, you won't have time for piano."

Some other, better-related consequences for not hanging up her clothes might be:

➤ To work with you in doing the ironing that weekend (she'll learn the effort that goes into making clothes neat).

➤ Not allowing her to have kids play in her room until it's picked up (she'll learn that your family values tidiness).

➤ Letting her go to school in wrinkled, dirty clothes (she'll learn that a natural consequence of not taking care of her clothes is that they become wrinkled and dirty). Watch this one, though, it's risky: She might not care, others might judge her, she may be humiliated.

Keeping the consequence related to the action is vital for your child's education. When he's an adult, it will be more useful for him to think, "If I don't get this job in on time, my clients will take their business elsewhere" rather than, "If I don't get this job in on time, I won't get to pet my puppy tonight."

Respectful Consequences

Any consequences imposed on your child must be respectful of who he is—of his personality, of his individuality, of his body. Consequences that injure your child or have long-term ramifications are *not* respectful. Take care of your kid. Letting him discover the natural consequences of not brushing his teeth ("See? Cavities and a root canal!") is not respectful of your child's body. Making him go to school without a shirt because he ripped his up is not respectful either—it is humiliating.

Reasonable Responses

It's a fact: Unless a consequence is reasonable, your child will not learn from it. Go overboard too much, and hoooo boy, all your kid will understand is that you are angry, that you are unreasonable, and that there's no reason in the world to refrain from doing the behavior again.

You can react with anger to the little things (you don't need my permission, most people do it all the time). Feeling angry when you are irritated is a reasonable reaction. I mean, you're *irritated!* What you do with your irritation, how you respond and what consequence you assign, is another issue.

How do you know if a particular consequence is reasonable? Here's a few clues: If it's not respectful, it's not reasonable. If it's not related, it's probably not reasonable either. But "reasonable" also refers to the degree of severity. In order to figure out how severe the consequence should be, you'll have to determine the severity of the misbehavior.

➤ *Weigh it on the severity scale.* With all the hurry-scurry and stress of life, it's sometimes hard to keep your child's behavior in perspective. Some experts suggest establishing a severity scale. On this scale, a minor irritant would register a 1, and a felony would be 100. When your kid misbehaves, hold the behavior up to the scale. Where does it fall? The vast majority of your child's misbehaviors will fall below 10. Looking at things this way may help you keep your consequences reasonable.

➤ *Keep it short!* Reasonable consequences are usually short term. Forbidding your child to watch his favorite TV show for a week because he flatly refused to lower the volume would be reasonable. Forbidding him to watch his show for the rest of the season would not be reasonable, it would be too severe.

Behave Yourself!

Warning: The severity of misbehavior *cannot* be judged by the intensity of your reaction. We all have our areas of zero tolerance and pet peeves, but just because I *hate* it when people leave the toilet seat up doesn't mean it's a major crime.

Rewarding Consequences

On top of making your consequences related, respectful and reasonable, it's also important to make them rewarding.

What? How can you make consequences rewarding?

Stop: I'm not talking about chocolate, flowers, or gold medals. Remember that discipline is not meant to be punishing, and that unless your child reaps some benefits from the consequence (a reward) they won't learn from the experience, and they won't have *any* reason to begin to discipline themselves.

It's a Good Idea!

Encourage your children to notice and value the positive and negative results of their actions. It's a skill that will help them make positive choices throughout life.

I'm talking about knowledge and understanding. Knowledge about natural and logical consequences, how the world works, is a strong, fine, satisfying reward. (That's why my daughter was so happy to be cold after her swim lesson. Kids *love* order, balance, and when the world makes sense.)

Remember, also, that all behaviors have consequences. Consequences are not innately good or bad, they just *are*, which means that many times a child will behave a certain way and the consequence will be positive.

Explicit Consequences

The best consequences are also explicit, that is, the child understands the *why* and *what* of them (and so do you). Whether it's a logical consequence or a natural consequence, your child will learn best when it's very explicit. Use this time as an opportunity. Talk to your child about the consequence:

It's a Good Idea!

You can often "choose" to use natural consequences as a disciplinary technique simply by allowing them to happen.

➤ State what it is.

➤ State *why* it's occurring.

Choosing Consequences

This part is not for the frail at heart. In fact, choosing appropriate consequences is very difficult for many parents (I know it often baffles me). I'll give you a few approaches here—things to think about, plans to make.

It's a Good Idea!

All this talk of choosing appropriate consequences sound heavy? I guess it is when you think about it. *Heavy* doesn't mean difficult, though. The best consequences are very simple, and, since they come directly from the misbehavior, are fairly straight forward. Stick close to the misbehavior, and you'll find your consequence.

1. Consider what you want the consequence to achieve. The point of all discipline is to teach your child internal control over her behavior. You're training her conscience, and her ethics. You're teaching her how the world works. Long after you're dead and buried, this conscience, ethical sense and knowledge of the world should *still* be instructing her on how to behave.

2. Consider whether you'll be able to follow through on the consequence. Saying, "That's it, we're not going on vacation!" is not only unreasonable, it's unrealistic. Yes, you *are* going on vacation. You need it, the tickets have been purchased, the hotel reserved.

3. Check it against the requirements—is it based in nature, is it based in logic? Does it fulfill the 4-Rs (related, respectful, reasonable, rewarding)? Will your child *learn* from it?

4. Can you support the consequence with your actions? Does it make sense in terms of your family's values? Say you value time spent together. If the TV is located in a central location, and the consequence is that the child is not allowed to watch TV (and therefore is banned from the living room while the TV is on), then don't sit and watch TV all evening. If you do, you're applying *more* than the stated consequence of separating the child from the television—you're separating the child from *you*.

Behave Yourself!

Your kid has misbehaved horribly! I can picture you now, thumbing frantically through this book, looking for the list of ways to choose a consequence. No, no, no. That won't do! I'm breaking it down into steps so you can *think* about it. This is *not* paint-by-numbers parenting!

Defining Consequences Ahead of Time

Whenever possible, it's best to define consequences ahead of time. It takes a little time, but the advantages are enormous:

➤ This forces you to think about it, right?

➤ It will get you away from that "I'll show you," punitive frame of mind, and back into the "Zen of inevitability." You'll be calm, cool, and collected.

➤ You won't have to think through a veil of red anger, or stall until you've talked with your parenting partner. Consequences work *best* when they are immediate.

Predefined consequences are the other half of family rules and personal limits. An easy way to predefine consequences is to sit down with any lists you've already made of family rules (Chapter 6) and your child's limits (Chapter 7). Take each rule and limit and rewrite it in the following form:

Rule or limit. If rule or limit is broken, then consequence.

Here are two examples:

We do not eat at the computer. If anybody eats at the computer, the consequence will be:

Robert's bedtime is 8:30 on school nights. If Robert doesn't go to bed, the consequence will be:

Setting up the consequences ahead of time doesn't always work, nor is it always appropriate. Here are two disadvantages of predefining consequences:

➤ *It puts you into a negative frame of mind while you're making your list*—everything is looked at in terms of what can go wrong, instead of expecting, assuming, and supporting that everything will go right.

➤ *It doesn't figure in the flexibility required.* There may be extenuating circumstances, or the consequences defined may not actually fit when the moment comes.

When You're on the Spot

When you're called upon to think up consequences immediately and on the spot, you can use a shortened version of the process I described in Chapter 8. This short, succinct, and highly effective technique is called STAR. It was developed by communication expert William Sonnenschein.

STAR stands for <u>S</u>top, <u>T</u>hink, <u>A</u>sk, <u>R</u>espond.

Stop: Breathe, calm yourself, take 10.

Think: Think about what is really going on, about what your child needs, and about her positive intent.

Ask: Here's where you can use active and proactive listening, to get your child's perspective (yes, this step is necessary!).

Respond: Apply a consequence that satisfies the 4-Rs.

It's a Good Idea!

Whenever you're applying consequences, take as much time as you need, remember to keep consequences close to the action, do your best, and forgive yourself for making mistakes.

Letting the Child Decide

Older kids who are experienced in making fun choices (ice cream or cake? Swimming or ice skating?) can start working *with* you to determine appropriate consequences. Before you start asking your kids to help you determine their own consequences, make sure they've had positive experiences with choice making, and are old enough to understand how consequences work (logical, natural, the 4-Rs, and so on).

Avoiding Inappropriate Consequences

There are so many varieties and examples of illogical and inappropriate consequences that I'm a little leery about bringing them up at all. If a consequence isn't natural or logical, if it doesn't fit the 4-Rs and it doesn't teach anything, then it's inappropriate. There's another kind of inappropriate consequence to watch for: the double-dip.

Here are some examples of double-dip consequences:

➤ *Disciplining your child because he was disciplined at school.* You can and should talk about what happened, chat about the child's feelings (and your own), and brainstorm ways of avoiding similar situations in the future.

➤ *Natural consequences often lend themselves to double-dipping.* Be wary! People have a tendency to scold or discipline a child for letting a natural consequence occur. If Maurice's favorite toy breaks because he threw it against the wall, it's double-dipping (and inappropriate) for you to scold and berate him for breaking it. He will learn more from the natural consequence if you simply talk with him in a kind, firm way about what happened, how he (and you) feels, and how to avoid the situation in the future.

Words to Parent By

A *double-dip consequence* is a consequence one step removed—a consequence applied because the parent is upset that a child has done something away from home that required somebody else to apply discipline. Double-dip consequences are very common, but highly inappropriate. An extreme example: A child is spanked for "earning" (and getting) a spanking from somebody else: unjust, unfair, and punitive.

Disciplinary Element Number Twelve: Be Consistent

Consequences must be consistent. You're aiming for consequences that feel as natural and strong as physical laws, right? Gravity and inertia are nothing if not consistent—that's why they're laws of nature.

Consequences should be applied not based on your moods, biorhythms, or whether the Sox won the game. Time is consistent—if sometimes a minute lasted a minute, sometimes 30 seconds, and sometimes a random hour, it would make it hard to schedule anything. Clock companies would go out of business. People would wait in endless lines. Frustrations would mount, empires fall. I exaggerate, but the point is this: Calendars are reliable because we can consistently count on a minute lasting a minute. Consequences and discipline work best when they are consistent.

But consistency is more than consequences, and it's larger than limits and rules. Consistency is a general parenting technique, and one of the main definitions of discipline. (Think about the religious disciplines—a big part of all of them is doing the same practices over time, consistently.) It's not just for misbehavior. Consistency is part of the structure of your child's life. It's the reliability of a

Words to Parent By

Consistency means sameness—the same rules and consequences over time.

It's a Good Idea!

Consistency applies to more than consequences. All of discipline must be consistent. Consistency is part of the structure of your family—your values, your rules, your limits, your consequences, your unconditional love.

weekly schedule, a set bedtime, a ritual birthday breakfast, and traditional holidays. It almost doesn't matter what the routine is—consistency gives your entire family something to rely on and lean against. If you promise a special treat, a consequence, a vacation, or special time together, then *do it*. Don't promise it unless you're going to deliver. Maintain that trust.

Inevitability, Not Severity

In some families, the most severe consequence ever handed down is, "That's it, I'm not telling you a story before bed tonight." That's fine—it's not the severity of the consequence that matters, it's the fact that certain kinds of behavior are not acceptable, and if that behavior happens, that consequence *will* occur. Kids get the message, and learn from it, when consequences are inevitable for certain behaviors.

No Waffles at This Breakfast Table

Don't set a rule, limit, or consequence *unless* you're going to be consistent in enforcing it. Easier said than done, especially if:

➤ Your kids are as cute and manipulative as mine.

➤ Your own upbringing was either inconsistent or overly structured.

Kids Make Your Wees Go Kneak

Kids are physically designed to be cute so that we respond to them. The big heads and eyes of babies affect all human beings with the desire to care for them. (It's the big head/eye thing that makes us love puppies, bunnies, and little lambs, too. We can't help it!) Babies need adults to do things for them—they can't walk, feed themselves, or pull down a living salary. Babies grow into kids, but it takes most kids a long time to grow out of their ability to charm. (Some people never do, and I'm sure you know one or two adults who bat big eyes, or give you that puppy dog stare and make you melt into submission.)

Because of the powers of children to make you get weak in the knees and grin uncontrollably, you have to be on your guard to maintain your consistency. Ignore the wheedling, the dewy sobs, the look like, "You're killing me, Ma" when all you're doing is enforcing a very sensible, explicit limit or consequence. Choose your position, and stick to it. Whining should make you firmer than ever.

Consistency: When It's a New Skill

For some parents, consistency is hard because they were raised by bossy parents, and they're *not* going to be so rigid, inflexible, and mean with their own kids. Parents rebelling against bossy upbringings want to please their kids, want their kids to love them, and don't want to come off as tyrants. You can be nice, loving, and consistent at the same time. Consistency doesn't equal rigidity or cruelty. It's a support system.

For parents whose own parents were wimpy, the struggle may be to discover what consistency and firmness really means in day-to-day life. I suggest more disciplinary advance planning. Sit on down, alone or with a partner, and work on your lists. "How *do* we want to deal with this issue?"

Follow Through

Stick to your decisions, stand confident in your responses, and your kids will respect and trust you for your fortitude and your consistency. They are relying on you to be firm—they don't yet know how to be. No matter which direction on the parenting scale you are coming from, remember that children *need* solid, firm consistency.

Remember my analogy of floppy, boneless bodies in Chapter 7? I was talking about the use of limits as a structure. Your consistency with your children is a form of structure, too. If your kids can't rely on their bones to be there to support them when they walk, after a few uncomfortable splats, they aren't going to move *anywhere*. Your kids are relying on you to provide solidity and structure, to be consistent in an inconsistent world. You're being firm for their sake.

> ### It's a Good Idea!
>
> Being consistent is in your own best interests, too. If they know you can be pushed around, you will be.

Faulty Consequences and Flexibility

Now that I've begged, pleaded, and lectured about the need for consistency, I've gotta tell you that sometimes you've got to change your mind.

There are those who believe that once you've made a stand and established a rule, limit, or consequence, you've gotta stick to it or you lose all credibility.

On the other hand, Ralph Waldo Emerson said, "A foolish consistency is the hobgoblin of little minds."

I say that there's a difference between throwing out idle threats and never following through on promises or consequences, and occasionally changing your mind, or realizing you've made a mistake and rectifying it. Sometimes a rule, limit, or consequence isn't right, or simply doesn't work. These are the times to be flexible. Part of being flexible is realizing you've erred and being willing to change. (Sometimes the act of confessing you've made a mistake opens a great dialogue with your child, and accomplishes exactly what the faulty limit or consequence did not!)

Be consistent, but make sure your consistency is not "a foolish consistency." Keep thinking. Be willing to change when you are wrong.

The Least You Need to Know

➤ Consequences are what happens as a result of a behavior—good or bad.

➤ Kids respond best to natural consequences or consequences with a logical relationship to the misbehavior.

➤ Keep consequences related, respectful, reasonable, and rewarding!

➤ Don't double-dip your consequences.

➤ Your child is relying on your consistency.

Chapter 10

Effective, Dubious, and Destructive Disciplinary Consequences

You've been very patient. Here, at last, is what you've been waiting for, the chapter with the down 'n' dirty details of discipline! Tools to use when your kid misbehaves! Consequences to apply when encouragement, rules, limits, and consistency don't work! Plunge in—you're getting a whole basket of techniques, as full and varied as the contents of your grocery cart after your weekly shopping trip.

Many of these techniques you'll be familiar with. Maybe I can give you more insight into them. Others may be new to you. No technique works all the time, or with all children, and no technique works if used incorrectly or at the wrong time. There's no clear answer about which will work for you and your child. You'll probably use a combination of techniques, and you may come up with others.

We'll also talk about spanking. Despite plenty of evidence to the contrary, some parents still consider physical discipline—spanking or occasionally swatting a child—

Behave Yourself!

Don't beat yourself up (or anybody else, for that matter)! No matter how hard you try, you're going to make disciplinary mistakes—no parent is perfect, no parent should try to be. The most important aspect of parenting is love.

a valid disciplinary technique. We'll get into spanking below—it's important enough an issue to warrant its own section!

Let's take a second, though, before we launch into whips and chains (oops, I mean gentle correction and consequences). I want to remind you of the disciplinary technique that works best, that works always: love. Love, and paying attention. Now, on to the techniques. Some will hit the spot, and some will make you want to cross the street when you see them coming from a block away. I've broken them down into three divisions: great, effective techniques; techniques you should only use with trepidation; and techniques that won't work, are cruel, and should never darken your doorstep.

The Effective Big Seven

Let's start with the effective big seven—the most effective, kindest, most positive disciplinary techniques out there. These are the ones you *should* be using. Here they are, in alphabetical order (so you won't think I'm ranking them by merit):

➤ education

➤ expressing disapproval

➤ having a little discussion

➤ ignoring

➤ separation and replacement

➤ time-outs (also known as "thinking time")

➤ warnings

Education

Education is a disciplinary technique, and I'm not talking about the normal use of discipline as a teaching tool. I mean using education as a direct consequence of misbehavior. Education is an opportunity to move your child to thought*ful* from his normal stance as thought*less*.

In many cases, a child's misbehavior is based in ignorance. Racial slurs, or physically risky behavior (like smoking and driving too fast), can often be corrected easier and more effectively by a specifically educational response than by other forms of discipline (like scolding or making rules).

A child caught drinking to excess a couple of times could be taken to an AA meeting to see firsthand the ravages of alcohol. A child participating in racist behavior could be shown the movie *Schindler's List,* brought to a lecture on Martin Luther King, or, better yet, the whole family could get involved in community activities where the child can meet and become friendly with people from diverse racial groups.

Education is *not* about lecturing, and, since your child may not be open to hearing the truth from you, an educational consequence may be best imposed by another adult he respects.

It's a Good Idea!

Natural consequences are educational opportunities, too. Don't compromise on safety, but within those limits, allow your child to learn through experience the consequences of her actions.

Expressing Disapproval

Perhaps the simplest and most effective way of changing a child's behavior is to let her know that you disapprove of it. State your objections clearly, and give reasons. "Judy, I don't like it when you hit your sister. It's cruel and thoughtless, and I want my children to be kind and compassionate." When your child hears your disappointment or disapproval, she may shape up. Your child *needs* your approval. Miss Judy will hear your anger, and resolve to change.

Disapproval works when it is stated clearly—once. Don't nag, rub it in, carry on, or hold disapproval as a grudge. What if you can't let it go? That's between you and you. Don't raise it again (and that means you!) Kids can hear a complaint or disapproval once—more than once erases the message from their little brains and closes their ears tighter than Scrooge's wallet.

Your disapproval needs to be expressed with conviction and passion, but without fury. Don't be wimpy or bossy:

➤ Wimpy parents tend to *feel* the disapproval, but express it so mildly and gently that no impact registers. Here's an example: "Honey, please don't pull Muffy's tail, dear. I really hate it when you do that, it's not a very nice thing to do, Sweetheart, and you want to be a nice little boy, don't you? Honey? Please stop for Mommy, dear. Mommy's getting a little bit upset and concerned," and so on.

➤ Bossy parents tend to come down so hard on the disapproval that they frighten, or make their child feel like a personal failure or a dirty rotten piece of scum. Make sure that your disapproval transmits the message that it's the *behavior* you don't like, not the child.

Having a Little Discussion

When something goes wrong, the first and best response of all is usually to sit down and talk about it. Often, open communication is all that is needed to change behavior, or to make sure that a certain misbehavior doesn't happen again. All through this book are communication techniques you can use in your talks. Check out active listening and "I" statements in Chapter 3, proactive listening in Chapter 9, and problem-solving suggestions in Chapter 19. You can talk with your child alone during special time (Chapter 3) and during family meetings (Chapter 6).

Use your discussions to point out natural consequences that might occur from the misbehavior. Kids sometimes need help seeing the chain of events, and understanding why they happen.

At times, simply "talking about it" is not effective. You may be "talked" out. You've had these little chats in the past and nothing has changed—Amy keeps borrowing your clothes without asking. Or the rules and limits around the unacceptable behavior are so explicit and well understood that talking about it is counterproductive. Norman knows perfectly well that placing crank calls to 911 is hurtful and dangerous (it's also illegal). Talking about it won't help—other consequences, applied swiftly and fairly (like removing all phone privileges for a while) will be far more effective. *Then* you can talk about it.

Ignoring

When you're faced with mild, irritating misbehavior, sometimes the best response is to ignore it. Ignoring is a very active behavior; it doesn't mean just letting it slide and neglecting your child. Ignoring a behavior requires:

➤ Making an active decision to ignore it.

➤ Paying attention silently while you are actively ignoring it.

➤ Developing a poker face—a relaxed body, and straight, unimpressed face—and refuse to get riled by the annoying behavior.

What kind of behavior can you ignore? Certainly, never anything dangerous or hurtful to the child, anybody else, or any object. Good types of behavior to ignore would include: nail biting, nose picking, tuneless humming, minor swearing, foot jiggling, gross jokes, annoying laughs.

Kids often try out annoying behavior patterns, and, the more attention that is paid, the worse the patterns get. Ignoring is gentle, and it works. It's based on the premise that, for your child, negative attention (getting a rise out of you) will give him more satisfaction than will getting no attention.

It's not a new concept. You probably have your own version of the following story. In eighth grade, Randy Humphreys kept teasing me. "Just ignore him. He's just doing that because he likes you. If you ignore the behavior, he'll stop." (Postscript trivia: Randy did stop. And at my 20th high school reunion, he apologized. "I was just doing it because I liked you," he said.)

While you're ignoring, make a special point to encourage positive behavior—the behavior that you hope will replace the irritating misbehavior. If even one teacher had said, "Randy, I like the way you let Ericka get ahead of you in line today," instead of, "Randy, stop bugging Ericka and get to the principal's office *this minute!*" things might have been very different.

If you choose to "ignore," grit your teeth and be prepared for the behavior to get worse before it gets better. Your child, who is really trying his best to bug you, will now pull out *all* the stops. If you slip and react, even once, you'll have to start all over again. Give ignoring a chance, perhaps a commitment of a week or two. It's gentle, it's nonintrusive, and, as I know from personal experience with both my kids and stepkids, it can be *very* effective.

It's a Good Idea!

The key to good discipline is flexibility—the ability to flex and stretch and use a variety of disciplinary techniques and approaches.

Separation and Replacement

Kids squabbling over an object? Take it away. (I used to hate it when my uncle did this to me and my cousins, but it sure was effective.) If you separate a child from an object, make sure you replace the activity with something productive. Putting the Nintendo on a high shelf without giving the kids something else to do will only leave them:

➤ Bored and ready to cause more trouble.

➤ Empty-handed—they'll have to fight each other.

Two rules:

1. Separation and replacement should never be done with glee ("Ha ha! I've taken away your favorite toy!").

2. Only separate a child from an object when the object is related to the misbehavior. (In other words, if Joe is whacking Todd with the truck, the truck goes up. But Joe's Teddy bear—which sat watching the whole encounter with glassy eyes—stays down.)

Time-Outs (Also Known As "Thinking Time")

Separation and replacement involves separating a child from an object. Time-outs are also a form of separation—separation from a situation. Time-outs (or thinking time) differs a bit depending upon the age and development of the child. The time-outs I'm describing here apply to school-age kids. If you're dealing with little ones, you'll find discussion and details in Chapter 15.

Time-outs separate a child from a situation in order to "break" the action and reset it on a new track. Time-outs take the child out of an environment that is reinforcing the negative behavior. For school age kids, time-outs shouldn't always be timed, they should allow the child enough time to change his mood on his own.

➤ Don't threaten time-outs, and don't think of them as punishments ("Hit me again and I'll put you in a time-out!"). They're meant to be used as an immediate, brief cooling-off period.

➤ Time-outs are most effective when a child needs help changing a mood.

➤ A time-out is over once the mood has been changed or the child has calmed down and regained self-control. Let the child determine when a time-out is over—she needs to learn to determine her own moods and rhythms.

It's a Good Idea!

Change the physical place, change the emotional space. I've heard it said that there are not geographical cures. Maybe not, but there *are* geographical remissions.

It's a Good Idea!

Try a little laughter! Jokes, humor, giggles, and gentle teasing can heal, relieve tension, de-escalate a gnarly situation and stop kids from acting out. Joking nicely about misbehavior can correct it without making it a "heavy" scene. If you're gonna use humor, trash the sarcasm and put-downs. And if your child is preadolescent, sensitive, or touchy, save the humor for another year.

➤ Time-outs are designed to remove a child from an environment where she is getting gratification for her negative actions. When she returns, *don't* let her resume her activity. Let her know that her actions were unacceptable. Move her into a more positive situation, and give her positive reinforcement. "The colors you're using on your self-portrait sure make me think of autumn!"

➤ Parents can take time-outs, too. (I do!)

Warnings

Your kid starts acting out, and the first thing you do is warn her: "Jasmine, cut it out or I'll take that paint brush away," or "Cody, I'm counting to 10. One, two, three...". In many cases, bingo! End of misbehavior! I'm warning you, warnings are *not* the same as threats (you'll learn more about those in the destructive techniques section later in this chapter). Threats are threatening; warnings simply put the child on alert that the behavior needs to stop, *now,* or there will be consequences. The best warnings clearly state the limit and the related consequence. Warnings only work if your child believes that you'll follow through. Be careful not to cry wolf. Be prepared for your child to call your bluff.

The parents who are the most successful with warnings (you know them, they merely need to murmur, "Andrew," and their child scampers to behave) are the ones who aren't afraid to follow through on each and every warning. Be consistent—it provides security for your child, and ensures that you'll be listened to.

The Dubious Six

Here are six disciplinary techniques that fall into the category "dubious." Dubious techniques *may* have their place, with certain kids, certain families, in certain situations. I present them to you with a lot of caveats. Read closely! (You'll find a few here that are often considered essential and effective.)

The dubious six disciplinary techniques are:

➤ assigned reading

➤ caring for a younger sibling

➤ chores

➤ constructive criticism

➤ grounding

➤ removing privileges

Assigned Reading

I know parents who use reading as a consequence for misbehavior, and I'm dubious. Yes, it's gentle, nonviolent, and educational, but I believe that reading, especially reading outside of school, should be *fun,* not linked in any way, shape or form to unpleasantness. Besides, it encourages children to change their behavior in order to avoid reading.

Behave Yourself!

Knock off the guilt trips! If you've used dubious or destructive disciplinary techniques in the past, don't beat yourself up about it. Work on changing. It's *never* too late to start using positive methods.

Behave Yourself!

Don't make the mistake of thinking that the "dubious" techniques are stronger, or harder hitting than the effective big seven. They are *less* effective, and more punitive.

It's not the child who loves to read who is likely to get into trouble for *not* reading, it's more likely to be a child who isn't enjoying reading, or is having trouble with it. Forcing this child to read additional material as a consequence for *not* reading makes *no* sense. Yes, it's related to the misbehavior, but it won't serve your eventual goals, which should include helping him improve his reading, and enjoying books. Good readers are readers who love reading, and kids who love books become good readers. Why jeopardize that relationship?

Here's a situation where assigned reading *might* be effective as a disciplinary consequence:

➤ Your child is a book-a-holic and there is no risk of assigned reading (no matter how dry) turning him off, *and*

➤ You are using the assigned reading as part of an educational consequence (see the effective big seven, above) where the book is educating him, enlightening him, or making him more sensitive to an issue.

Caring for a Younger Sibling

Parents often assign a child to care for a younger sibling as a way to teach responsibility. That's fine, but don't impose it as a consequence for negative behavior!

Making a child care for a younger sibling as a consequence for misbehavior will teach the child to associate the younger sibling with the misbehavior, and with behaving poorly. Your child will learn responsibility best when it makes him feel wanted and needed (and when the responsibility is satisfying and enjoyable. Don't associate family responsibility with coercion. (It's also unfair to the younger child. Would *you* like to be considered a punishment?)

Chores

Chores are on the "dubious" list because they tend to be used too often, and inappropriately. A chore should *only* be used as a disciplinary consequence if it's directly related to the misbehavior. If a child spreads papier-mâché goo all over the bathtub and leaves it, yes, she should have to clean the bathtub. Now. If a child doesn't feed the dog when it's her turn, she shouldn't have to clean the bathtub, she should have to feed the dog.

Tales from the Parent Zone

A couple of years ago I edited a technical specifications document for a company that builds construction materials. I learned that, before putting construction materials on the market, engineers give them stress tests to determine the "allowable load" (the maximum stress that can safely be imposed on the materials) and the "ultimate load" (the point when something breaks or the product reaches its maximum resistance). Kids are like those engineers; a child who is "bad" is testing your (and the world's) allowable and ultimate loads for reliability.

Constructive Criticism

Criticism is easy to do, hard to do well, and even harder to get your child to take without feeling angry, picked on, or inadequate. Even when you're *trying* to be constructive, it's difficult to criticize a child in such a positive, helpful way that he can correct his behavior while still feeling good about himself. If you're going to use constructive criticism as a disciplinary technique:

➤ Don't scold your child, put him down, or come down too heavy.

➤ Keep the criticism specific to the behavior (don't start attacking everything about him) and support, suggest and educate.

➤ Keep it brief.

➤ Reassure your child that it's the *behavior* you're critiquing, not him.

Grounding

Whoa—surprise! Why is grounding on the "dubious" list? Grounding—making a child stay home as a consequence for misbehavior—is one of the most commonly used consequences for older kids and adolescents. But just 'cause it's popular doesn't mean it's the best choice (said the parent to the teenager deciding whether or not to get a tattoo).

Most parents impose grounding as a *reaction* rather than as a *response* to a situation. "That's it! Maya, you're *grounded!*" But effective grounding entails far more than just making your child stay home.

Think about the other uses of the word *ground*. When you ground a loose wire, you give it a way to discharge its loose energy. Getting grounded also implies getting in touch with the earth, centering, getting balanced, and all those groovy things. Simply making a kid stay home doesn't do any of those things.

Below are some of the pros and cons of grounding. Don't leap to it! Consider well. It must *not* be overused.

Positive Aspects of Grounding	Negative Aspects of Grounding
Grounding demonstrates clearly that actions lead to consequences.	The way most parents use grounding, it's rarely related directly to the misbehavior.
When you use grounding correctly, as a consequence for a related lapse in judgment or a child's inability to regulate himself (he was late and he didn't call or he missed his curfew), the grounding provides guidance from you on how to regulate himself.	Simply forcing a child to stay home and miss social activities doesn't teach *why* his behavior wasn't appropriate.
Grounding can present a rare and valuable opportunity for a busy family to stop, slow down, and take some time at home to reconnect with each other. To get grounded, as it were, with all the positive implications of the phrase. This can turn into family time.	Grounding a child means grounding yourself, too.
	Grounding is rarely fully enforced. Most groundings are imposed in the heat of the battle, and rapidly forgotten about as soon as the weekend comes. Make your consequences consistent!

Removing Privileges

As your child grows, she's generally allowed more activities and responsibilities. Some of these are optional, and are known as privileges. The key word here is *optional,* and that's where the consequence of removing privileges usually runs into trouble.

Grounding is a form of removing privileges—the child loses her freedom for a short period of time. Or, if Theo has lost five library books in three weeks, it *might* be appropriate for you to take away his library card. But aren't there better ways of teaching responsibility short of removing it? (Establishing a corner of a bookshelf for library books, marking due dates on the family calendar, *you* taking control of taking them back—because the point is to have access to books.) Removing privileges is effective *only* when you make certain that you are not undermining something you are trying to encourage (like going to the library). Remove privileges only after deep consideration, not in haste.

Words to Parent By

Privileges are optional responsibilities or activities allowed your child.

Before you begin removing privileges as a disciplinary technique or consequence for a misbehavior:

➤ Think about more productive, educational, options.

➤ Don't make a removal of a privilege a punitive action.

➤ The privilege removed should be clearly in scale with the misbehavior.

➤ Remove privileges on a temporary basis, or this dubious consequence will lose its effectiveness.

Spanking and Why Not To

Spanking is a mild form of corporal punishment. The American Academy of Pediatrics (as well as many, many child development experts) strongly opposes *ever* striking a child. Whether or not parents believe in spanking their kids seems to be somewhat based on the time and place (in the Midwest in the '50s, spanking and much stronger physical abuse was simply an acceptable part of "child rearing"). It's also related to the education level of the parent (the more educated, the less likely they are to spank). Many parents occasionally hit their kids when they are frightened (the child has done something dangerous), or from sheer stress, frustration, or fear of having no other options.

Words to Parent By

Corporal punishment means "punishing the body." *Spanking*—swatting your kid once or many times on the rear with your hand—is corporal punishment. So is hitting your child anywhere on his body, softly or hard, with your hand, belt, or any other object, one time or 10 times, frequently or once in a while.

If, occasionally, you *lose* it and spank your child, you aren't going to damage him or your relationship forever. It's not an effective or positive approach to discipline, though. It's a more serious problem if you commonly spank your child, or if it's one of your dominant disciplinary methods.

I find it hard to justify spanking at any time. Here's why:

➤ It teaches your child that violence *is* an acceptable way to express anger and deal with conflict. This contradicts the rest of how you are trying to raise your child.

➤ It is painful. Deliberately instilling pain on your child is cruel (even if you believe it's "for their own good"). The slogan, "No pain, no gain" does *not* apply to child rearing.

➤ It's harmful emotionally for you. Have you ever felt wonderful after hitting a child? Spanking often leads to remorse, guilt, and doubts about the quality of your own parenting skills. Avoid the agony—resist the urge to smack. It's a very unpleasant sensation to feel like a bully.

➤ It's harmful emotionally for the child. Spanking is traumatic, makes a child feel as though there's something wrong with her (instead of something wrong with her behavior), creates resentment, and can lead to body image and self image problems.

➤ Spanking tells a child she is powerless. A powerless person will act out (see Chapter 8), leading to more problems.

➤ Spanking is disrespectful to the child, and it doesn't help teach respectful values or standards.

➤ It breaks trust and invades a child's sense of security.

➤ It halts effective communication.

➤ Where do you go from there? Once you resort to physical discipline, the only steps "up" are more, or stronger physical discipline. Don't start down that path.

➤ It doesn't work! In the very, very short term, you may stop the misbehavior. The backlash is *not* worth the very, very short term.

It's a Good Idea!

If you've spanked your child, you may feel guilty and contrite. Don't be afraid to express your contrition to your child. Use the experience to teach your child that everybody makes mistakes, and how to handle contrition, remorse, and restitution. This present-day mistake, rather than a tale from your past, can be a powerful teaching tool.

Tales from the Parent Zone

I've read dozens and dozens of books about discipline, and sometimes I feel like throwing one against the wall. There are authors who believe that corporal punishment *is* appropriate, and some try to make the case that, while a child needs to be spanked, a parent should never spank with her hand, that the hand should be reserved for loving touch. I find this entire argument appalling, disrespectful, and the opposite of positive discipline.

The Destructive Eight

Here are the destructive eight, all disciplinary approaches to steer well away from, no matter *how* terrible your child's behavior is. They vary from simply ineffective to very terrible, but what they all have in common is these techniques are all more destructive than constructive. I'm not including these to give you new ideas; they're here to convince you to eliminate them from your disciplinary tool kit.

The following eight "techniques" (tortures?) are *not* on the path to a well-behaved child:

➤ guilt
➤ humiliation
➤ hurtful talk
➤ physical abuse
➤ punitive and retaliatory action
➤ threats
➤ traps
➤ withholding affection

Guilty of Imposing Guilt?

"What are you trying to do, kill me?" While there *is* a positive aspect to guilt (learning to feel guilty when you are doing something wrong is an important aspect of learning self-control), imposing guilt on your child makes her feel resentful, and *too* self-judgmental. You want your child to have enough negative feedback to stop the misbehavior, you don't want her to wallow, grovel, and feel forever lousy. (Okay, maybe at this precise, angry second you do, but think about it, that's really *not* what you ultimately want.)

Why do otherwise wonderful parents lay guilt trips on their kids? Sometimes parents do it because it's what *their* parents did. It's sometimes an attempt to arouse empathy. It doesn't work.

Guilt is especially destructive when imposed on kids at the beginning of adolescence, when they're already deeply self-conscious and self-disparaging.

Humiliation Hurts

Humiliation (and by this I mean those forms of old-fashioned punishment like making a child stand in a corner with a dunce cap on, pulling down his pants and spanking him in public, washing his mouth out with soap, or sending him to bed without dinner) wears down a child's self-image and self-respect.

Humiliation teaches a child that you don't value him. Respect your child—his body, his mind, and his ego. Never underestimate the damage that can be done by humiliating a child. One of the most common triggers of suicide in kids and teenagers is a humiliating experience. His sense of self is a very delicate flower, easily stomped.

Hurtful Talk

Most parental "crimes" against their child come under the category of hurtful talk or no talk. Talking is very powerful. What you say to your child, and how you say it, matters tremendously. Talking can build a child up, or tear her ego down to rubble. Here's a list of verbal disciplinary don'ts. Don't use this list to beat yourself up. We're aiming to make you the best parent you can be; and I don't know a parent in the world who has achieved all the points on this list.

➤ *Cool the commanding and demanding.* Commands and demands are sometimes necessary for safety reasons ("Get your finger out of that socket *right now!*"), but they should only be used in emergencies. Commands and demands are a power show—parent over child. Instead of, "Get over here this instant," and, "Why? Because I say so!" try using requests. They'll go a lot further in fostering mutual respect. For kids who tend to be willful and push buttons, commands and demands will often get you exactly what you *don't* want—resistance when you need something done immediately. Enlist the child's help. In most cases, a gentle request will actually save you time.

➤ *Sarcasm sucks.* Here's the problem with sarcasm: Little kids don't understand it, and big ones do. Sarcasm is a way of putting distance between you and your child. It puts kids down, builds resentment, and it hurts. Consider what audience you are being sarcastic for. Often parents are at their most sarcastic when other adults are around—they're not really talking *with* their kid, their talking about her. This isn't right.

Behave Yourself!

If a tree nags in the forest, will it make a sound?

135

➤ *Nagging is another no-no.* Nagging is continuous harping about a task, a habit, or a personality trait. ("John, can't you ever pick up after yourself? Remember to get your shoes off the floor. I've told you a million times, John, your shoes are in my way! I can't believe that you *never* remember to pick up anything!") Bug, bug, bug. Nagging is a completely ineffective technique of getting a message to your child and, while it's not particularly damaging, it does tend to damage the communication pathways between parents and kids. I often use the example of the sense of smell. You can get used to rotten odors—just think of all the people who used to work in packing houses. They'd walk in, and the smells would almost knock them down. By the end of the day, no problem (with smells, anyway), their noses would have simply shut down. It's the same thing with nagging—your child will turn her ears off, and you'll be nagging at a wooden post. It's unpleasant, for *you,* to feel unheard. Avoid that sensation, say it once, say it again strongly, and then be done with it and move on to action. (Remember that nagging is not the same as reminding. There are more details about reminding in Chapter 7.)

Tales from the Parent Zone

A Great Dane and a poodle sauntered up to a spaniel that had broken free of his leash and was spending his afternoon hanging out at the local fire hydrant. "How's it shakin'? My name's Rex," said the Great Dane. "I'm Fifi," said the poodle, "what's your name?" "I'm not sure," the spaniel replied, "but I think it's Down Boy."

➤ *Shaming, belittling, labeling, and name-calling don't cut the mustard.* These are verbal forms of humiliation (often used by parents who would *never* use the old techniques) and they often include emotional humiliation, like mocking, or making fun of a child in public. "You lazy boy!" "Go ahead, eat that candy. You'll be sorry when your thighs get even fatter and nobody asks you to the dance!" and "Here's Marie, who takes after her aunt the slut." Remember, "Sticks and stones can break my bones, but names can *ever* hurt me!" Kids will live up to your expectations—good *or* bad, and they'll internalize your opinions of them. Keep your reinforcements positive.

➤ *No talk.* Shutting down and not talking to your child about what is bothering you or him, or about his behavior, is not effective in curing misbehavior or avoiding it in the future. Confrontation is *hard*. It's a truism, though, that if you talk about it, you'll all feel better afterwards.

➤ *Yelling isn't effective.* I've saved yelling for last on this list because almost every parent does it. Okay, it's not a crime. It's not, however, effective in solving problems or communicating *anything* except how frustrated you are. When you're yelling you're certainly not talking *with* your child, and too much yelling, or yelling that is too fierce, may cause your child to feel angry, intimidated, resentful, or shamed. Expect yelling, tears, withdrawal, or a child who learns to ignore you until you calm down.

Physical Abuse

However you feel about physical discipline, there is *no* doubt that punching, shaking, slapping on the face or hands, beating, whipping, hair-pulling, burning, binding, or any other physical attacks on children are *never* acceptable, no matter what the child's misdeed or attitude, no matter how frustrated or angry you are.

It doesn't matter what you intend—to teach your child a lesson, to correct him, or to get back at him. No matter *what* your intent, physical abuse causes terrible harm. Kids who have suffered physical abuse spend years fighting against lowered self-respect, mental health issues, and behavioral problems. They often become part of a cycle of violence as they, too, begin to suffer from delinquency, crime, and violent patterns as both abusers and victims. If you or anybody else in your child's life is resorting to physical abuse to handle your child, you need to change these patterns, and to do this, you need help and support. Immediately.

Take this book with you to the phone, *now*! and call the National Domestic Violence Hotline at 800/799-SAFE. The TDD/TTY number is 800/787-3224. I don't *care* what time it is, and neither do they. They're open 24 hours a day to talk with you, and help you through this.

Behave Yourself!

Don't correct or scold your child in front of her friends (unless you are catching *all* of them in a misbehavior). Making your child look bad in front of other people is embarrassing, and can be humiliating. You won't achieve your goal of correcting the misbehavior in a positive, respectful way. Save it. If something needs to be said *now,* pull your child aside.

Behave Yourself!

Shaking a child—even lightly—can cause permanent damage. Never, ever shake a child.

Punitive and Retaliatory Action

Getting back at your kid, or correcting with a punishing attitude, is *not* positive discipline. Your intentions and your attitudes *do* count, almost as much as your actions.

Threats

Warnings are an effective disciplinary approach (see the effective big seven, above), but threats are not. Threats have an element of coercion, and they make a child obey through fear or by threatening harm. Here's an example of the difference: "Lucia, you are getting late. Get dressed now or we won't get to the party in time for dinner," is a warning. "Get dressed or I'll rip up all your clothes and you'll have to go out in rags!" is clearly a threat. The child whose parents use threats will feel uneasy in the one place he should feel secure—his family. Kids who are threatened often get into lying or deceptive behavior. Since most threats are "empty," they also learn not to trust what their parents say.

Traps

Laying traps for kids, to see if they'll lie, lose control, or misbehave in a seductive situation, is unfair and disrespectful. Support your child. Plan for him to succeed, not fail.

It's a Good Idea!

You're a parent? Your job description includes: breathing deeply, keeping cool, and keeping your sense of humor.

Withholding Affection

Withholding affection ties your love to your child's behavior, and is completely opposite from the concept of unconditional love. A parent who withholds affection becomes cold and distant until the behavior improves, forcing the child to 1) suffer the lack of support, and 2) become an amateur psychologist as he tries to psyche out what is making you so upset. (This "method" tends to be paired with no talk.) Parents who withhold affection believe it will make their kids shape up—quick. In reality, the child will retreat, and, in anger and hurt, rebel against you.

Creativity Counts

Sometimes your first approach to dealing with a disciplinary problem doesn't work. Try another. Be creative and think it through! Try something, and then try something else. When all else fails, when there's big trouble in your family, you'll need some additional outside help to get your family back on track. I'll give you more information about last resorts in Chapter 22, and about finding help in Chapter 24.

The Least You Need to Know

➤ Base all your discipline on love.

➤ The "gentlest" techniques are also the most effective.

➤ Just 'cause it's popular as a disciplinary technique doesn't mean it works.

➤ Many parents *lose* it and occasionally spank their child. If spanking is very, very occasional and mild, you *may* not do damage, but any spanking *is* ineffective, *will* backfire into negative natural consequences (for both of you), and *will* make you both feel lousy. Don't do it.

➤ A child should never be subjected to *any* physical abuse or punitive behavior.

Part 4

Putting It to Work

In Part 4, it's time to talk detail. What specifically should you do when Joanie's stealing lunch money, Tommy is biting his sister, or Eliza's bathroom is a pigsty no matter how many times you remind her, scream at her, or just plain nag? And what about when you're on a vacation?

This part is designed to give you suggestions for a wide variety of behavior problems you might run up against. The first two chapters (Chapters 11 and 12) focus on daily doings and specific problems. Then it's on to general life in the household (chores and homework and so on) and life out in the big world. And yes, taking the kids to a restaurant or on vacation can be a blast! (I'll give you a few hints how.)

Chapter 11

Day-by-Day Discipline

In This Chapter

➤ Dealing with the daily details

➤ Mornings and evenings—how to wake and sleep in peace

➤ Secrets to avoiding house-leaving hassles

➤ What to do about green hair and dirty fingernails

➤ Playmates, lessons, and activities

It's the day in, day out daily grind of it that earns you your parental stripes. This chapter is devoted to solving the daily disciplinary hassles—applying some of the disciplinary techniques you learned in Chapter 10 to real, ordinary misbehaviors.

Raising a well-behaved child is not just about dealing with misbehavior and dealing with things when they go wrong. It's about avoiding problems (I *know* I've said this before, but it's important!). In this chapter, I've provided you with ideas and suggestions for keeping away from hassles, dealing with hassles, and making daily life run smoother.

Tales from the Parent Zone

The more you learn about your child, the better able you'll be to solve your disciplinary problems. My daughter gets belligerent when hungry—and she doesn't always know that she *is* hungry. Many of our problems are solved with a little food. My young friend Tanya gets sullen and resistant when there's too much noise in the environment. Her parents know that sometimes, getting Tanya to behave entails bringing her into a quiet room for 15 minutes. Voilá! A new child! It helps to understand your child's patterns, proclivities, and temperament (and there's more on this way back in Chapter 5).

The Well-Mannered Child

First, a word or two about manners. More than any other area of raising a well-behaved child, manners are a simple matter of training your kids how to act in the world.

As a parent, I would like my child to feel equally comfortable dining with princes and scarfing hot dogs at tailgate parties. What will make this possible (besides the opportunity to move in royal circles) is manners—knowing the appropriate way to comport herself in different social settings. All this takes time. The best way to teach your child manners is through:

➤ *Repetition*—"Say 'thank you' when somebody gives you something, Honey," and, "It's not 'give me a napkin,' Eliza. Please ask me nicely."

➤ *Modeling*—kids will imitate how you are in the world.

A note about manners: Sometimes the most important thing is that other adults see that you, the parent, are aware of good manners and are trying to train your child. People know that kids don't "train" easily, and a child's rudeness is understood and excused if the parent is seen to be making an effort. Say Timmy crashes into a woman in the store and doesn't say, "Excuse me." If you say, "Timmy, what do you say when you bump into somebody?" it will reflect less poorly on your parenting abilities.

Mornings and Evenings: Getting Them Up, Getting Them Down

Too often, the beginning and ending of the day are the worst parts of family life. Many a parent wakes up before the kids, and spends those lovely, early morning moments dreading the time when the little cranky monster will rouse (or be roused) from bed.

Bedtime in many households becomes fight time, as tired kids rile tired parents, and the day disintegrates into tears. Often, if you have a moody morning child, you also have a bedtime beast. How can you change the dynamics so mornings are serene, and bedtimes are cozy and heartwarming?

Moody Mornings

In some families, the kids are up at the crack of dawn, everybody has a leisurely breakfast together, and, right on time, they cheerily march out the door to work and to school. In far more families, days begin with the jangle of alarm clocks, clattering dishes, shouts ("Isabel, out of bed *now!*" and "If you aren't at the table by the count of three, young man!"), fights over the bathroom ("Mo-om! Jamie's been in there for 15 minutes and I've really gotta go!"), hair brushing, lunch making, writing excuse notes, searching for lost homework and clean clothes. There's always something forgotten, something late, somebody getting uptight. There are the screamers, grumpy but operating at full speed, and the mopers, sullenly staring at a coagulating egg while the clock ticks and ticks. Tears. Stress. Why are mornings so bad, and what can you do to make them better?

Whether your problem is with the stressed out, hyper child bouncing off the walls or the slug-a-bed moving in slow motion, if there's this much chaos, the whole family has a problem.

It's a Good Idea!

Kids are most likely to misbehave when they are stressed—isn't that true of all of us? Reduce a child's daily stress and you'll reduce her misbehavior (hey, and don't forget, boredom is a stressor, too!). Understanding your child's temperament will help you understand her stressors.

It's a Good Idea!

Reminder: Always judge the *behavior*, not the *child*.

When Mornings Are Miserable

Some kids just can't get up in the morning. Some don't like to be rushed. Some don't function well when they first wake up. Some are tired from not getting enough sleep. Moody mornings are closely related to bedtime battles (we'll get there in a moment). Assess your child's natural rhythms (they're part of her temperament), and your own. Some people are morning doves, some are night owls. In our family, I wake fairly easily, and my idea of a good time is getting into a cozy bed at 10 P.M. Bill and Annie, on the other hand, can party the night away. I like the early morning hours. Bill only wants to see dawn from the wrong side.

Tales from the Parent Zone

Cool it with the judgments, forget all the old sayings. "Early to bed and early to rise, makes a man healthy, wealthy, and wise," made sense when we all were farmers and needed to get up and milk cows. Ditto "The early bird gets the worm." ("Who wants a worm?" groans my husband the night owl as he buries his head deeper into the soft, warm bedcovers.) In these days (and nights) of overcrowding, electricity, and work that can be done round the clock, it makes sense that some of us are early birds, and some are nocturnal creatures.

Here are some thoughts and suggestions for changing your morning moods:

➤ If you have kids who have trouble getting up in the morning, can you change your schedules? Sounds radical, but why not? Some of us are locked into commutes and early morning school starts—others have more flexibility, and should think about taking advantage of it. When I was in high school, I had a choice of what time to begin school. Being a morning dove who wanted out early, I often took a preperiod PE class at 7. The idea of such would send shudders of horror down the spine of my slug-a-bed—oops, I mean my work-the-night-away—husband.

➤ Consider your own morning modeling. Are you a *Night of the Living Dead* zombie, arms outstretched, staggering into the kitchen moaning, "Cah-ffee, cah-ffee," or are you Hyper Harriet stressed about being late to work *again!* even though the last time you were late was five years ago? Work a little on your own morning attitude. Your child will learn that no matter how crummy you *feel*, it's important to be civil.

Tales from the Parent Zone

I know a couple who almost broke up because he bounded out of bed every day with a cheery "Good morning!" and she needed at least a half an hour—and a lot of coffee—to feel human.

➤ In Japan, where many people live crowded together in small spaces with thin walls, the tradition is to "not see" people until they're dressed, washed, and ready for the day. You might try it; it works for some families.

➤ Watch your pace. A child who feels rushed may resist by getting slower, and sl-o-w-e-r. Nagging, moaning, and screaming might get her out the door now, but tomorrow morning, it'll be the same thing. Allow more time. Get her up earlier, or set an alarm clock of her own for 10 or 20 minutes earlier. This is counter-intuitive, but sometimes works, as she can go more at *her* speed, or play a little in her room, and slowly get used to being awake.

➤ If *you're* the slug-a-bed and she's a crack-o'-dawn type of kid, let her get up—and be your alarm clock at an established time. Maybe she can participate by helping with family breakfasts and lunches! (More on family participation in Chapter 13.)

➤ Get it done the night before. Organize the backpacks, jackets, homework, sports supplies, and put them near the door or, better, in the car. Pack lunch, choose clothes. Some parents even let their kids sleep in their (comfortable!) clothes and roll right out of bed into the car (breakfast in a plastic bag on the way). Whatever works for you.

➤ Get into a rhythm and routine so your child (and you!) can operate on cruise control without having to *think*. (Thinking in the morning can be quite a challenge.)

➤ If your child is having a particularly difficult period in the morning, determine if life at school or in her social life is okay. If you are facing a hard day, you don't want to get up either!

➤ When feasible, set consequences. ("If you're late, you need to walk" or, perhaps more effective, "Since you're so tired in the morning, you need an earlier bedtime for now.")

➤ No matter *how* well your family has done that morning, always kiss or hug your child good-bye.

➤ Don't forget the positive reinforcement! When your kid's had a better morning, mention it! Bring it up that evening!

Beastly Bedtimes

We all want serenity at the end of the day, a slow wind-down, a gentle cuddle, and drifting off into sweet dreams.

Well, dream on. For many families, bedtime is the major battle. Since bedtime comes in the evening when everybody is exhausted, tempers fray easily. As the parent, you may be *so* tired and wanting to spend a quiet half hour with your partner that your tolerance is out the window. At the same time, your kids begin their wildness. The more fatigued they get, the more resistant to bedtime—and you.

When Bedtime Is Agony

If your child has a hard-to-impossible time going to sleep, consider that he might be a night owl, and when the sun goes down, he's just kicking it into high gear. There may be other reasons for his resistance:

➤ Did he get enough exercise? Kids need to *move* and the child who's been in school all day (at a desk), comes home to homework (at a desk), sits down to dinner (at a table), and now is asked to lie down (on a bed) may need to physically move his body in order to release. I know a woman with sons who takes them to a park every evening. "I'm taking the boys out for a run," she jokes. They sleep better when she's "run" them.

➤ On the other hand, he may need some time just to *be* at his own pace. Life is conducted at a rush rush pace, without a lot of time to just be a kid anymore. He rushed out of the house, concentrated at school, did his chores, ate dinner, did his homework. Now he wants to be a *kid* for a while.

➤ Sometimes kids want their limits stretched, and resist bedtime because they feel they should be allowed to stay up later.

➤ Some kids, especially little ones, need a physical release, such as provided by laughing hysterically or crying before their bodies are relaxed enough to sleep. They won't know this, of course. They are acting on a purely instinctual basis when they rile you up until you yell. Then they cry, and then they drop off to sleep like babies.

It's a Good Idea!

A responsible 10-year-old can self-organize his bedtime and all that entails: finishing homework, washing up, brushing hair, getting into pj's, whatever you do in *your* household before bed. Tell him he's got an hour left, and it's up to him to get ready. The increased responsibility may lessen his resistance.

Some Enchanted Evening Suggestions

Here are some suggestions for smoothing and soothing your evenings:

➤ Rely on ritual to carry you through. The more you can make bedtimes routine, the smoother *most of them* will go. Help your child with her bedtime rituals or give gentle reminders.

➤ Establish limits. Once you set a limit, avoid nagging. Remind her of the consequence, "If you want me to sing to you, you have to leave enough time. That means getting into bed by 8:15."

It's a Good Idea!

The more reliable your daily rhythms and rituals, the more secure, and calmer, your child will be. Rituals and rhythms are the foundations of life (as spring follows winter, day follows night, and night, day).

➤ When the going gets rough, point out (once!) that the natural consequence of not going to bed is that she'll be tired in the morning. Not that this will sink in *now*.

➤ Involve yourself in bedtime. It's hard, especially when you're tired, but it's best if you can plan to focus *more* attention than usual. (I know, it's hard when you're tired.) Bedtimes can be a very special time. Your kids may feel starved for you, and reluctant to let you go. Sometimes a little added special time or attention will get them drifting off to slumberland.

Getting-There Hassles

Day-by-day hassles often involve going places, and many of the "going places" hassles involve people's varying attitudes about time. I've found that people tend to fall into one of three categories: "We're early!" "We'll just make it!" and "Relax, the world's not going anywhere without us." I call these categories *time temperaments*.

Assess your family's time temperament. Are you all "we'll just make it" types, who squeak into every event one minute before (or after) it starts? Perhaps your family has never made it to a movie preview in your life, and your pals all tell you an event starts an hour before it truly does. Or are you eager beavers, who get stressed if you're not the first ones in line? If you're all pretty much in agreement, your family will have an easier time than the family whose time temperaments clash.

Families with clashing time temperaments need to work toward meeting in the middle. Those who are chronically late need to be made sensitive to those whose blood pressure soars for every second they're not out the door. Those who are hyper about being early need to allow a little more slack, and resist the urge to nag, nag, nag as the clock tick, tick, ticks.

Words to Parent By

Time temperament refers to the way a person feels about, and handles, schedules and deadlines. Some people are chronically late, others always early, and still others exactly on time. Some are relaxed about time, "Drop in whenever," they say, and they mean it. Others need schedules.

Mealtime Struggles

For many families, the seat of the family battles is the kitchen table, and there are few areas as problematic as eating. Eating and food tends to be emotionally "loaded" in this society anyway, between the quest for thinness, the concern about nutrition, the lack of family dinner time, the increase in eating disorders, and the emphasis on fast food. Few people manage to enjoy eating together. Instead, food is a battle. It's a shame, because food is one of life's joys, and eating together can, and should be, the heart of the family experience.

Tales from the Parent Zone

Ellyn Satter, author of *How to Get Your Kid to Eat . . . But Not Too Much,* writes, "Parents are responsible for what is presented to eat and the manner in which it is presented. Children are responsible for how much and whether they eat."

Here are a few ideas for increasing your family food pleasures, and decreasing the power struggles:

➤ Let your child regulate her own intake. Don't pressure your child to eat, or to stop eating. Don't even mention it! Remember that the more fuss you make about eating, about your own weight, or your child's weight, the more it will become an issue for your child, and for your family. I know, this is truly a challenge.

➤ Present healthful food in ample quantities.

➤ Model healthful eating.

➤ Eat together. It *can* be done. I have friends who eat breakfast together every day because Francesco is a chef who works during the dinner hour. This family values eating together enough to get up 45 minutes early every morning. Some families make eating dinner together a family rule: "This family eats dinner together on Tuesday, Thursday, and Sunday nights."

➤ Engage your child's imagination for food. Food is an adventure—try new things together. Enjoy your food, and your child will enjoy hers.

➤ Involve other families and other kids into your dining. It doesn't have to be formal—a potluck once a month with a neighboring family, or encouraging your kids to have friends over for dinner (after asking!) can do a lot to build community and make eating a pleasurable, social function.

➤ Everything in moderation, including moderation, is what I always say. (In other words, healthful food in small portions is a good thing to model, and so is an occasional blow-out gorge on fabulous, rich, unhealthful food.)

Behave Yourself!

If you think your child has an eating disorder, get help! You cannot deal with it alone, as a matter of fact, parental involvement often makes it worse! See Appendix C for information on where to turn for help.

The Dirty Child

Some kids are naturally spotless or wear the average layer of childhood grime that is easily rinsed off with a daily shower or biweekly bath. Other kids are dirt magnets. They wallow in it. They walk three steps out of the house and are instantly grubby. They *hate* washing, and they'll lie to avoid soap and water ("Yes, I washed my face") even when the lies are blatant and pathetic. Much of this is developmental—kids between 8 and 10 are notoriously grimy.

What do you do? Here are some suggestions:

➤ Remember that kids don't feel that they have a lot of power in their lives, and cleanliness is an area where they can assert some control.

➤ Choose your battles, and set limits for areas you feel strongly about ("Yes, you do need to wash your hair before the first day of school!").

➤ Looks are one thing, smells are another. You have a right to breathe clean air.

Tales from the Parent Zone

I know of a small subsection of late adolescents who *never* wash their hair, bodies, or clothes, who rat their hair, and who call themselves "Crusties." They're protesting the superhygenic, uptight attitudes of the middle class, they say. *I* say, "Yuck!", look at my daughter, and cross my fingers that when she's a teenager she doesn't choose this particular form of rebellion.

➤ Problem-solve around issues you're willing to compromise on. Perhaps every other week is okay for clean hair as long as the blackened bottoms of his feet are scrubbed before bed (or vice versa).

➤ Get creative! If it's summer, turn on the sprinkler and "let" everybody run through until soaked. Then bring out the bubbles (it's soap!).

➤ Invest in a few rubber ducks, a bottle of bubble bath, or some aromatherapy. Rubber duckies can be mighty seductive, no matter *what* his age!

Food, Shelter, and CLOTHING!

What kids wear, and how they wear it, becomes an issue for many families. I imagine that cave kids battled with their parents about skins ("Grog, leopard skin skirt too short!"). Hair styles, too, have always been a bone of contention ("Get gazelle thigh out of hair, Ug. You want neighbors think you too primitive to build fire?"). Look, anything can become a battleground. Clothing and hairstyles are one way kids can assert their personal tastes, independence, and choice-making abilities. It's important to support as many of your child's choices as possible.

Getting Dressed, Getting Undressed

With kids under seven, it's not uncommon for families to wage pitched battles over getting dressed and undressed. Even little kids who are perfectly capable of dressing themselves often refuse, point blank ("No!") when you ask them to please get out of their pajamas and into daytime clothes, or out of play clothes and into their nighties.

➤ Do they need help? Little heads get stuck in turtlenecks, and small feet don't always slide easily into stiff shoes. Ask if he needs help before leaping to the rescue, and choose showing him how over doing it for him, whenever possible.

➤ Can you make a game out of it? Suggest a race between the two of you to see who can get dressed first (and make sure you lose). Or tell him to "surprise" you or your partner, leave the clothes, and leave the room.

➤ Allow more time. Little ones often feel rushed into submission.

➤ If the battle is too big, give up, get him into the car, and let him go to school in his pj's. Once or twice and that will be it. (And you won't be the first parent to try this, believe me!)

➤ Or get him in the car in his nightclothes, bring his clothes, and have him change once you get there. Change the place, change the space!

➤ Get him dressed yourself, and realize that this may be an expression of his need for emotional nurturing right then.

Don't Be Revilin' Her Stylin'

Okay, I confess, I went to high school in the '70s, and in the '80s I was an art student with magenta and purple streaks in my hair. Since I've spent so much of my life looking awful for fashion, I'm pretty tolerant about clothing and hair fads in kids. Basically, kids want to be different from their parents, and they try to attain this difference using personal appearance.

Your child may spend a good deal of her life looking utterly absurd to you. You looked absurd to your parents, didn't you? Try not to get too alarmed. Your child will customize her appearance to match her friends'. Remember that hair grows, makeup washes off, and styles in clothing come and go. Try not to make it a battleground.

Keep in mind:

➤ Kids are insecure, and they need to know that they look good. Compliment her even when you don't like her style.

➤ Clothes are expensive. Most families have to put the brakes on spending. Help your child learn about budgets by giving her one. Clothing allowances with spending guidelines can start as young as ten.

➤ Set limits. Be reasonable, but when it comes down to it, you do have a say over how high those skirts go, how low those jeans sag, and whether pierces are allowed (though your adolescent may defy you). Talk about the limits and the reasons for them.

➤ If shopping or choosing clothes to wear is a problem, provide limited choices ("You may choose one of these pairs of athletic shoes. Great. Now choose some pants. Want the gray or the black?").

➤ If your child is shocking you with her styles, assess the rest of her life. If she is dressing like her friends, doing well in school, and volunteering at the old folks home on weekends, who cares if her lipstick is black and her hair an ugly shade of green?

➤ Teach her where certain clothes are and aren't appropriate. Your daughter's pierced navel might be sexy and cute, but flaunting it is inappropriate at Great Aunt Suzie's funeral.

➤ Draw the line at tattoos. Even pierces heal. Tattoos are forever (and don't start telling me about laser surgery!).

Behave Yourself!

No, you aren't out of line when you restrict the amount of money your child spends on clothes and shoes. You can assert the value of budgeting and restraint here. Your kid will not suffer irrevocable damage if she doesn't have *this* skirt or *that* pair of shoes.

Play Dates and PlayMates

Used to be, if a child wanted to play, he stepped outside, ran down the block to Cindy's house and knocked on the door. The two of them disappeared into the woods and, some time around dinner, two grimy children wandered back with frogs and sticks in their pockets. Today, for better or worse, that scenario rarely happens. Instead, we have a new institution: the play date. Appointments are made. Kids are picked up or kids are dropped off. Then, generally two by two, kids play. There's a bit of etiquette involved. Here are some suggestions for helping play dates go smoothly for your kids (and in your relationship with the other parents):

➤ For kids under six, plan for the parent to stay for all, or part of, the first play date. Feed the parent tea and cookies in the kitchen, and listen intently to the squeals. Are those giggles or sobs?

➤ Watch the dosage. Each child has a different "play date" tolerance. Some are fine for four hours or more, some turn to soggy Rice Krispies after an hour and a half.

➤ What's your child's low-energy point of the day? Avoid those times, if possible.

➤ Don't ever chasten another person's child. If there is conflict, you can help them resolve it. If the kids aren't getting along, try a snack, separation, and/or strong supervision.

➤ Reciprocate. If a friend's family takes your child to the zoo, take their child along next time you have a picnic.

➤ Generally, the host family pays for all expenses. This is another reason for reciprocation.

➤ Any and all issues of money and timing should be worked out in advance, between parents.

Lessons and Other Activities

Our kids are busy, some say overscheduled. If your child is constantly on the go to classes, consider *why* your child has to study soccer, music, dance, French, gymnastics, *and* life drawing. If the idea is to introduce him to the joys of sports and creativity, you may be overdoing it. If it's so he can excel in life, remember that kids only learn when learning is fun, and that kids *need* down time—a chance to piddle around the house, stare into space, read a book, play.

That said, a moderate number of activities can enhance a child's life, and have positive ramifications into adulthood. Here are some suggestions for handling the issues that arise:

➤ Figure a day or so of "sick time" for every six-week session of lessons or activities. I *know* you paid for it, but activities are supposed to be fun. A tired, cranky child does nobody any good if he goes to swim class and is so wasted that he acts out, loses focus, and has a miserable time.

➤ If your child refuses to participate, don't force it. You'll turn him off to the activity.

➤ Keep music practicing to the minimum, and, if your child is having trouble focusing, sit with him during the practice period. A child (unless extremely well motivated) will have trouble sitting alone in a room and practicing scales. As he gets better at his instrument, he will learn to *enjoy* the process of practicing. He'll get into the *discipline* of it.

Behave Yourself!

Your child learns as much from playing in the backyard with friends as she does in her extracurricular activities. Granted, this learning is social, but social learning is essential to happiness and school success. Lessons are great, in moderation. Don't schedule every moment of your child's life. Let her be free!

The Least You Need to Know

➤ The more you understand your child's rhythms, the more you can avoid trouble.

➤ Daily rituals are the foundations of life.

➤ The more fuss you make about eating or weight, the more it becomes an issue for your child and family.

➤ Kids don't have much power in their lives, and clothes and cleanliness are areas where they can assert themselves.

➤ Figure in a day or so of "sick time" for every six-week session of lessons or activities.

Chapter 12

Behaviors and Relationships

In This Chapter

➤ Teaching your child manners

➤ Whining and sass and how to survive them

➤ What to do when your baby's a bully

➤ Parenting the child who lies, cheats, or steals

➤ Physical-fighting solutions

How your child relates to the world matters. In this chapter, we'll look at human relationships and the kinds of misbehaviors—like swearing, bullying, lying, stealing, and more—that interfere with your child's relationship with you and his smooth integration into society. How do we treat others? How do we want others to treat us? Children learn about behaving in relationships from watching others, and by trying things out. Much of the misbehavior kids express in relationships is experimental. It's when it becomes a pattern that it becomes a real problem.

In this chapter we'll look at these misbehaviors, both occasional and chronic, and consider how they affect your child's growing sense of ethics. But mostly we'll look at what you can do about it.

Verbal Misbehavior

"I don't like that tone of voice, young man!" "We don't use that kind of language in our house!" "Talk to me with respect, please!" Any of those phrases sound familiar? Between whining, swearing, tattling, and sass, many parents have their hands full.

Whine, Whine, Whine

There's little as annoying as a whining child. Your tolerance for whining may vary. Some parents don't mind a bit of whining, some declare a No-Whining Zone that encompasses the entire house. That's your choice. Here are a few things to keep in mind about whining:

➤ Whining is different from complaining about something that is legitimately wrong. Make sure you're hearing the message, not just reacting to that horribly irritating voice.

➤ Probably 99.9% of all kids whine, at least a little.

➤ Remember that kids whine because it gets results. Keeping your limits consistent, and only saying no when you mean it will help reduce the whining.

➤ Respond to the feelings behind the whine, rather than just trying to stop the whining. Whining is a request for attention. Often, if you stop and focus on the child, the whining goes away.

➤ If you want to establish a no-tolerance-for-whining policy, here are your scripts: "I can't hear you when you talk to me in that tone of voice," and "If you whine about it, you don't get to do it, and that's that." (If you decide to enforce this, be prepared for immediate conflict and resistance. Hang firm, one slip and your word is mud. The whining will *increase*.)

It's a Good Idea!

Remember to look for the positive intent! Your child is not evil, and all his misbehavior has a reason behind it. Look for the cause, don't just treat the symptoms.

Foul, Filthy Language

For a few months my eleventh year, I went through a cursing phase, where every other word out of my mouth had four letters. I wasn't alone, my friends were doing it, too. A few years later, so was my younger sister.

Almost all kids go through stages where profanity is intriguing and desirable. Even though some experts consider it almost a developmental norm, it can still be quite distressing and embarrassing to parents (and other adults). Kids swear to be cool, impress their friends, and shock adults. What can you do about your little foul-mouthed Felicity?

➤ Many kids experiment with foul language. Figure out where your personal indignity level is—the level of swearing, or the particular words, that you consider simply unacceptable. Establish for yourself the difference between certain words and ways of talking that you don't like and don't approve of but will let slide, and ones that are simply not okay under any circumstance.

➤ Watch what you're modeling. How's *your* language?

➤ Try "ignoring" the swearing. Your child may be doing it to see what kind of reaction it gets from you. If you downplay it as an issue, your child will probably move on, very quickly, to irritating you in some other way. There's more on ignoring in Chapters 4 and 10.

➤ Draw the line at certain terms and phrases. Racist, sexist, or derogatory language is not okay, nor is swearing *at* somebody. There's a very big difference between salty language and name-calling.

Battling Tattling

Tattling happens most frequently between siblings, though it happens between playmates as well. Here's the issue—nobody likes a "rat," but kids often get points for disclosing information. We'll talk more about tattling between siblings in Chapter 19, but here are a couple of things to keep in mind:

➤ Never reward a tattler by punishing a child whose behavior you haven't seen.

➤ Encourage kids to "tell" only if there are safety or moral issues involved. Stress that letting an adult know if something is truly wrong is not tattling.

Oh, That Sass!

"Sass" is also known as "talking back" or "spunk," and it's a quality in children that tends to elicit mixed responses from adults. The child who questions and defies is infuriating at times, and often knows just how to rile up anger. On the other hand, a child showing sassy behavior has a strong self-image, can stand up for herself, and is showing qualities that are worthy of respect in adults.

Consider why your child's sass is so upsetting to you. Is this an issue of hierarchy? Are you upset at her "sass" because you are an adult, she is a kid, and kids need to talk with respect to adults? Keep in mind that:

➤ Standing up for yourself is different from being disrespectful. True sass is great (though infuriating).

➤ The "sassy" child takes to heart the old bumper stickers "Question Authority" and "Question Assumptions." She's probably a good thinker, intelligent, and possibly underchallenged. Give this kid more responsibilities!

➤ Consider whether the child is "talking back" just to get a reaction from you.

➤ This is the child who will be fighting for your rights when you're old, gray, and decrepit. Foster the positive impulse here. How about enrolling her in debate club?

➤ Increased incidents of "talking back" might indicate something going on. Is your child very angry about something? How is she handling stress? Is something unusually stressful going on in life?

➤ All kids are impudent at times.

➤ It's great, and appropriate, for a child to express her feelings and opinions. She can do it with vehemence, she can do it in a sassy fashion, but she can *not* do it in an abusive manner.

Tales from the Parent Zone

I have a six-year-old daughter who questions everything—authority, assumptions, you name it. The other day I was telling her "Goldilocks and the Three Bears" for the umpteenth time, and she interrupted me. "Is Goldilocks the same size as Baby Bear?" "I guess so," I said, adding, "That's why his chair is 'just right' for her." "Good," she said, and paused, "but if they're the same size, why does Goldilocks break the chair when she sits in it?" Geez. Mind like a steel trap. The Grimm Brothers didn't write the answer to *this* one.

Aggressive and Nasty Behavior

Up to 30% of kids occasionally or regularly engage in aggressive behavior. Fewer do it on a regular basis. Is your baby a bully? According to Dan Olweus, a Swedish psychologist and an expert on bullying, bullying involves repeated, aggressive behavior with a negative intent from one child to another, where there is a power difference.

Hara Estroff Marano, in *"Why Doesn't Anybody Like Me?"* noted, "Children who are rejected because of aggressive tendencies are not 'bad.' They are unable to decode or 'read' emotion effectively, so they misperceive and misinterpret social signals in others."

When Your Baby's a Bully

A child who is chronically aggressive feels out of control, and tries to get what he wants and needs by taking it from others or otherwise asserting his power over them. While bullies are usually strong and social, the bully doesn't have many friends. Kids, ultimately, reject a bully.

Here's a bit more information about chronic aggression and what you can do if your child is engaging in bullying behavior:

➤ The child who is bullying others wants social success, but doesn't know how to attain it. He's grabbing for it, instead of being kind, interested in others, and empathetic.

➤ Your child doesn't need your rejection or anger, he's getting more than enough of that at school. He needs your support, and your skills.

➤ Kids who bully are hypersensitive, and often feel a bit paranoid, as though people are out to "get" them. They aren't skilled at reading social situations, and they often register unintentional slights or accidents as direct attacks.

➤ Kids tend to initially like a child who bullies; they try to please him, follow his lead, and want to be his friend. This doesn't last—as kids become more frightened of him, he loses clout.

➤ Your child may need help understanding social structure. He doesn't know how to contribute to others, or to share.

➤ "Boys will be boys" is not a valid excuse for bullying behavior.

➤ The kid who is bullying others often gets into trouble, but always has a scapegoat.

➤ Don't label or let others label him a bully. People *can* change, and aggressive tendencies can be channeled.

➤ Consider that chronic aggression may be a sign of a learning disability or other problems.

➤ Don't pity your child, but take action to improve his communication skills. Let him know why is having trouble making friends, "Joe, kids aren't friends with people who hit them and are angry all the time."

➤ Engage your child in a problem-solving session (Chapter 19), or brainstorm ways for your child to get his friends back or make new ones (guidelines in Appendix E). Make sure the ideas come from your child, or, at least, are adopted by him.

➤ Bullying an aggressive child will not teach him anything.

➤ Be specific, consistent, provide a *lot* of positive reinforcement, and set very clear limits. Show *no* tolerance for aggressive behavior. The only way to truly stop bullying is to create a climate where aggressive behavior is consistently not tolerated.

Cruella de Kid

Classic bullying is more common among boys, while girls tend to manifest their aggressive behavior in other ways, namely cruelty, or psychological warfare.

Kids who are more subtly aggressive try to control the social dynamics by excluding other kids, talking behind others' backs, saying mean things, and withholding friendship ("I won't invite you to my party unless you..."). Kids are often cruel because they fear being excluded themselves.

➤ Victims of even one seemingly small instance of cruelty often hurt for a long time, and sometimes they never forget it. Cruelty damages.

➤ Children often exclude others because they've been excluded themselves.

➤ If you see your child being cruel to another, show her your disapproval, and talk with her about appropriate ways to talk with and play with people.

➤ Support your child's efforts to reach out to friends. Encourage her to invite friends for dinner, for overnights, to special events.

➤ It's easier to avoid cruel behavior in a one-on-one play date, rather than during group social time.

When Your Child Has Been Excluded

All kids feel unpopular or excluded at times. Alas, sometimes they really are. Group dynamics are always changing. Cliques, especially among girls, are part of the developmental process of discovering what it means to be a member of a group. When your child feels excluded, be a big ear and listen well. Calm her by listening (advice doesn't usually help) and help her by involving her with other groups and activities as well.

When Your Child Is Chronically Victimized

If your child has become victimized in more than one social setting, then something else is going on, and she needs some help to become more adept socially. Don't let victimization slide. Work with her to develop more assertive behavior, to deflect teasing, and to show her strength. Victims often remain victims because they reward their tormentors by crying or cringing. A child who can stand up to a bully (and this doesn't mean beating the crap out of him, it's more a psychological thing) often stop being targeted.

Lying, Cheating, and Stealing

Many kids lie, cheat, and steal. It's not cute behavior—and if it continues into adolescence, it can have serious consequences. We'll look at "serious" episodes of misbehavior in Chapter 22. Here, we'll concentrate on the kind of common, low-level, amateur lying, cheating, and stealing behaviors many kids participate in.

Lying Larry

We all expect honesty from our kids. Most adults understand that all kids occasionally lie, yet, when the day comes that your own sweet little boy or girl stares you straight in the face and tells you something you *know* isn't true, understanding that it's "normal" doesn't make a bit of difference. It just doesn't wash, it's not okay. You may feel shocked, betrayed, angry, and that you've failed to instill good values in your child. Where are his ethics?

Ethics and Lies

Before you turn in your parenting badge for lack of raising a good, ethical kid, consider that building ethics takes time. Use your child's lying as a teaching opportunity, and model honest behavior. Ethics cannot be forced, they have to seep in. Ethics, especially in kids, are not absolutes, either. Try not to worry too much about lying, and try not to focus too much on the behavior. Even a mostly ethical kid will occasionally lie. Her ethics, her personal sense of right and wrong, are still being developed.

It's a Good Idea!

Lying is related to cognitive development. A small child doesn't—can't—"lie" with the same intent as a teenager. Keep in mind your child's development as you look for her intent.

Why Do Children Lie?

Lies come out of children's mouths for a variety of reasons:

➤ Fear. When kids are scared of the consequences of their actions, they often lie to cover up. (Are the rules too strict? Are the limits too tight? Does your child feel free to talk with you?)

➤ To protect somebody else (tattlers aren't admired, see earlier in this chapter, and Chapter 19).

➤ Because she is imaginative and the truth is boring.

➤ To avoid an unpleasant task. ("Did you brush your teeth?" "Yes, Dad!")

➤ By mistake. Sometimes lies seem almost involuntary, and a lie just slips out, especially if your child gets caught in a misdeed. ("Who broke the antique chair? "I didn't!") Then, soon enough, it's Sir Walter Scott: "Oh, what a tangled web we weave, When first we practice to deceive!"

➤ For love, for approval, and because kids like to impress people quickly and effectively.

Behave Yourself!

Stretching the truth? Lying? White lies? Fibs? Lying by omission? If you think about it, lying isn't black and white in our culture. Lying exists in many shades of gray. Be honest with yourself—what kinds of prevarication do *you* accept? Be clear with yourself, and be clear with your child.

Lie Prevention Techniques (And That's the Truth!)

No, you can't keep your children from lying, but you can make lying a less rewarding activity. Many lies come from self-protection, and you can help by not creating a situation where your kid feels pressured to lie or suffer the consequences.

➤ Keep the conversation focused on what happened or what the problem is, rather than casting blame.

➤ Don't cross-examine ("After you left school, which route did you take home? And this was at precisely 3:10 P.M.?"), forget the fierce white lights and the sleep deprivation techniques. Remember that the object of talking with your child is to communicate. Grilling will make him close down, not open up, to you.

➤ Looking for the positive intent? Lies are a misguided survival technique.

➤ Lies are easy to slip into, and even easier to compound themselves, lie upon lie. Many kids slip into lying as painlessly as sliding into warm, tropical ocean water. It's more painful getting out (shiver, shiver).

➤ When your kid has misbehaved, don't trap him into a lie, or set him up in a no-win situation. Confronting him with leading questions is more likely to elicit a lie than talking calmly with him about what happened. If Tony comes home with a black eye and you scream at him, "I swear I will *kill* you if you got into a fight! Did you fight today?" you are putting Tony into a situation where he's either got to lie ("Oh no, I walked into a wall." "Oh honey, get an ice pack for that") or face your wrath. A better approach would be, "Oh my! What happened? Let's sit down."

➤ The truth is hard to tell. It's risky to confess (and risk is always hard). If your child confesses a misdeed to you, you need to 1) thank him for the truth, and give him positive reinforcement for his bravery and his sense of ethics, and then 2) deal with the misdeed by applying appropriate consequences. Doing step 2 but not step 1 is as bad a mistake as doing step 1 without step 2. He needs to have positive feedback for telling the truth *and* he needs consistent consequences. The positive feedback will make the consequence easier to take, and help build his ethical sense.

➤ Don't reprimand your child for telling the truth.

➤ Before you talk with your kid about a lie he's told, make sure that he did lie. A false accusation, or not believing a child when he is telling the truth, can devastate.

Behave Yourself!

Grilling is for barbecues, not children.

Seven Quick Steps to Dealing with a Lie

Discovering your child has lied can be quite distressing. Lies are often an additional layer of misbehavior (the child misbehaves, and then lies about it) and it's this layer that often makes parents go ballistic. ("I'm furious that you stole my silver coin collection and bought candy with it, but the fact that you *lied* to me about it, too, well, I *can't stand it!*") If you've discovered a lie ("layered" or simple), try this:

1. Focus on the misbehavior, not the lie your child used to cover it up.

2. Breathe, run around the block, take 10, calm down. Take as long as you need to take in order to deal with the situation, not the lie, or the fact that your child wasn't honest with you.

3. Talk with your child. Let her know that you aware of the truth. (Be as calm and level-voiced as possible.)

4. Talk about values, and let her know that you don't value lying.

5. Give her the benefit of the doubt (she may be caught in a compound lie).

6. Once the situation she lied about is resolved, talk with her about the problems lying can cause. Knowledge (and your obvious disapproval) will help her avoid lying in the future.

7. If you don't want a child who lies, don't label her a liar. Kids tend to internalize the labels we give them.

It's a Good Idea!

Consistent, compulsive lying is rarely an isolated problem; it's usually a symptom of something else wrong in your child's life. Look at what else is happening. Is she trying to escape an ugly reality? Are you expecting too much from her in terms of behavior limits? Is she getting a lot of attention for her lying?

Cheating Child. Charming? Not!

If your child is caught cheating on a test in school or during a competitive activity, your first reaction is likely to be rage, the second, betrayal and shame, and the long term, suspicion. Even though cheating is legion in our society, nobody wants a "cheat" for a child.

Here's the deal: Cheating is *very* common (whoa, hold on, I'm not asserting that it is okay). Lawrence Kutner, author of *Your School-Age Child,* cites surveys showing that up to 70% of all students admit to having cheated at least once in high school. That's a lot of cheating. Why?

Competition is fierce in this world, and kids understand very early in life that they are expected to achieve. Since they are still developing their sense of ethics, most kids see nothing wrong with the fastest path between two points, even if that path uses cheating.

This culture gives people a silent message that cheating, as long as you are smart enough not to get caught, is perfectly all right. Going against cultural messages is hard, and the parent who tries to do so risks being labeled old-fashioned.

If your child is caught cheating:

➤ Try to understand the *why* of the cheating. Cheating is a symptom of other problems, and the best way to get your child to stop cheating is to treat the underlying problem.

➤ Check the competition level in your child's life. Cheating is often a sign of too much stress being placed on grades or winning. Try switching to noncompetitive sports for awhile to take the stress off.

➤ Don't expect too much from your child. Cheating is often a sign of a child having trouble with parental expectations. What is your message about grades and achievement? Is your child feeling too pressured? Would a tutor or coach help? Stress the *process* of good study habits and time organization, not just the grades that result.

➤ Give your child the message that cheating is not acceptable. To do this effectively, you'll need to examine your own behavior. The parent who cheats on taxes and keeps the extra change is teaching his child that those behaviors are acceptable.

➤ Don't label him a cheater. Kids tend to adopt their labels—they believe them, and they become them.

➤ Show your child that you understand, and sympathize with, the stress he's under.

➤ Talk with him about the cheating incident, but watch that you don't corner him into lying about it.

Stealing Sid

Point 1: Kids steal. Little kids steal a lot—from poor impulse control. It's a developmental stage; they want it, they take it. Older kids often steal, too. Your child is probably not evil or destined for life in prison.

Point 2: Of *course* it's not acceptable. It's embarrassing, shocking, and angering.

In this section, we'll talk about petty, occasional small-scale stealing. For big crimes, turn to Chapter 22.

Kids steal for any number of reasons:

➤ Poor impulse control, as I mentioned above.

➤ To be cool and impress her friends.

➤ When somebody else has a one-of-a-kind something she wants or needs.

➤ To get back at somebody (stealing a bully's lunch money).

➤ When she wants or needs something, she doesn't have enough money, and you can't afford it either.

➤ When she's afraid to ask you for the money for this particular object (condoms, a bra), or feels too embarrassed to purchase it.

➤ When she may not be able to legally purchase something (beer, cigarettes).

➤ Because it's fun; kids enjoy taking risks, and in a society that is careful to protect kids as much as possible, stealing provides a risky, thrill-provoking activity.

➤ During times of stress. What else is going on in your child's life?

Here's what you can do if your child is caught stealing (or if you catch her yourself):

1. Use disapproval. Immediately make it clear that you don't tolerate this behavior. No, it's *not* okay.

2. Talk with your child. Try to determine why she's stealing, what the motivation is, if this is a regular thing, if she's done it before. Don't grill her (you might want to review the suggestions for proactive listening in Chapter 8. Don't berate, embarrass, scare, or ridicule your child, unless you want to end the conversation and gain no information at all.

3. Talk about values and ethics. Keep this part short, not a lecture, just a reminder.

4. Have the child make restitution, helping her if you need to. This means she needs to return the merchandise, or pay off damages.

5. Tell your child that you are watching her behavior, that she has lost some trust, and that she needs to re-earn it.

6. Assess the situation. Be honest with yourself. Is there a pattern here? If your kid is stealing frequently, or the stealing is combined with other misbehaviors, seek professional help.

It's a Good Idea!

When your child is caught stealing, try to emotionally separate yourself from the action. The fact that your kid is stealing is *not* a reflection on your parenting skills. Take comfort in the fact that most kids who steal do it only occasionally, as a crime of opportunity. And most do it poorly (which *is* why they get caught).

It's a Good Idea!

If your child needs to pay off damages and she doesn't have any money, you can pay the damages and have her work off her debt. Be fair now! Consider keeping the consequence more in line with the misbehavior than the actual monetary amount of damages. The *main* idea is to teach her to never do it again. You might take some of it as a financial loss, with an eye for the future.

Tales from the Parent Zone

Tony's mom Roxanne discovered that Tony had stolen collectable comic books from a local store with the reputation for having a "no-tolerance" policy for theft, that is, they reported all shoplifters to the police. As Tony's parent and ally, her job was both to discipline (teach) Tony not to do it again, *and* to protect him. Before he walked in to return the books, she called the store to find out its policy about returning stolen goods. As a parent, she had to decide if an arrest, trial, and possible record was the best thing for Tony (in some cases, though not usually, it may be). Roxanne talked with the store manager and "made a deal" for Tony to make restitution that taught him the desired lesson but didn't have lifelong consequences.

Little Kids and Stealing

Five-year-old Hannah came into the house, a pack of gum in one hand, an eyeglass repair kit in the other, and a hangdog expression on her face. Her crimes had just been discovered by her dad as he got her out of the car. It was late—there was no time to go back to the store that night to return the booty, so her parents let her know that stealing was unacceptable, illegal, and wrong, and removed the stolen goods.

"People who steal things can go to jail," her mother told her. "Not if they're little kids, and not usually for small things, but you *could* be arrested."

Hannah's eyes grew wide and scared. The next day, her mother took her back to the grocery store. On the way, they planned their approach.

"Will you say it, Mommy?" Hannah asked.

"Yes, but you'll hand back the stuff you stole," her mother said. At the cash register, Hannah listened as her mother said, "Hannah took this yesterday without paying for it. She is sorry and won't do it again."

Unfortunately, the clerk didn't understand the lesson. "That's okay, honey," she said to Hannah, "We didn't even notice they were missing."

"It's not okay," her mother corrected, firmly. "It's illegal and it's wrong."

Then the clerk understood. "Thanks for returning these things," she said to Hannah. "Don't do it again."

Despite the clerk's slow response, Hannah was deeply affected by the experience. Hannah had tried a behavioral experiment and the results had alarmed her. Because the feedback wasn't enjoyable, Hannah hasn't stolen anything in the three months since the incident.

Fighting Physical Fighting

Whether or not your child will be involved in physical fights is strongly influenced by your own attitudes, and the attitude of the subculture around you, about fighting. For some people, fights are a part of childhood, and kids are encouraged to be tough. Other people (and their subculture) are horrified by any kind of physical violence. Certainly, if your child sees you fighting, or hears, "Don't let him push you around, hit him back, harder!" (or a similar message) coming from you, he's likely to fight. There are more details about fighting in Chapter 19, but before you get there, here are a few things to keep in mind:

➤ Physical violence in the family tends to influence kids toward solving their problems through physical violence.

➤ Hitting and fighting do *not* have to be a standard part of childhood.

➤ In classrooms where classroom meetings have been held as part of an attempt at teaching kids nonviolent resolution, the number of incidents of fighting has dived.

➤ A physical fight rarely resolves issues. Nonviolent conflict-resolution approaches, such as talking and doing problem-solving exercises, are far more effective.

The Least You Need to Know

➤ Breathe, cope, and don't flip out—much of the misbehavior kids express in relationships is experimental.

➤ Kids whine because it gets results.

➤ Most kids go through a "profanity" stage.

➤ An aggressive child wants social success, doesn't know how to attain it, and needs your help.

➤ Don't label kids who lie, cheat, and steal as liars, cheats, and thieves.

➤ Look at what else is going on with your child.

➤ Most kids occasionally engage in lying, cheating, and stealing. It needs to be dealt with, but doesn't doom them to a life of crime and prison walls.

➤ Teach kids who are fighting physically other conflict-resolution skills.

Chapter 13

Teaching Responsibility

In This Chapter

➤ Taking family responsibilities seriously

➤ Chores and children? Yes, they *can* mix!

➤ Hassle–less homework how-to's

➤ All about allowance

When it comes to running your household, how's the balancing act going? Is your child considered a guest, slave-in-training, or participatory member? Does your kid live like a pasha with you in attendance? (Perhaps you've got your kids trained to give *you* the royal treatment!) Here's the dream situation: a child who is a full, participatory member of your household with age-appropriate responsibilities. Is it only a dream? Could it possibly be a reality?

Most parents instinctually agree that kids should take some responsibility within the household, and their instincts are correct. Kids who are trusted, who contribute to the family, and who feel their contributions are valued, feel great about themselves. These great-feeling kids are less likely to engage in "problem" behavior, and are on their way to becoming wonderful, responsible members of their communities.

How much responsibility parents give their children (and what they expect from them) varies widely from family to family. In this chapter we'll look at family participation and individual responsibilities such as chores and homework. We'll also look at allowance, how it should be used, and the role it plays in teaching children responsibility.

What's *YOUR* Job?

Here's the reality, and American society's dirty little secret—many kids don't learn how to wash their clothes, cook a meal, mow a lawn, make a bed, or even effectively wash a dish until they've moved out of the house. (In other words, you're not the *only* one with a demanding slug for a child!) Yet, most people agree that kids do benefit from having a role in the daily operations of the family.

Figuring out the right amount of responsibility is a balancing act. Kids work very hard. Between schoolwork, learning to deal with social situations, and, for many kids, their many extracurricular involvements, kids have very little "down" time. They need a chance to play, relax, daydream, nap. At the same time, teaching children life skills (and I'm talking kids of both sexes here, by the way) has a number of benefits:

➤ A person who enters college, or an independent living situation, with life skills will have a far easier time living with roommates.

➤ Family responsibilities teach basic discipline.

➤ The skills learned from having family responsibilities include time management, prioritizing tasks, and general organizational abilities.

➤ With family participation, the parents don't have to slave their life away serving the royal offspring.

➤ Most importantly, the child understands that he is part of a community (your family) and that as a member of the community, he needs to share responsibilities to keep the community going.

It's a Good Idea!

Think about the benefits of family responsibilities as more than just learning survival skills. It's the participation that matters. Participating in family responsibilities helps a child develop essential social skills.

Chores as Teaching and Consequences

Chores teach kids responsibility, and the skills to start, work at, and complete a job. Most parents believe that kids should help out around the house, even if it's just taking responsibility for straightening their own rooms. Some families assign specific jobs, and some ask their kids to help as the need arises.

Other parents don't expect their kids to do any household work at all, feeling it's not worth the agony of trying to get their kids to do it, and then having to do them over themselves because they were done so poorly. This is a valid point of view, but these parents should figure out alternative ways to have their kids learn responsibility.

Chores are used by some parents as consequences for misbehavior. Remember that consequences need to fit the three R's; they need to be related to the misbehavior, respectful to the child, and reasonable in their scope and duration. (There's more on this in Chapter 9.) As long as a chore fits within these parameters, chore away! For example, if a school-aged child scribbles on the walls, an appropriate consequence would be to clean the wall and, perhaps an adjoining stain or two as well. It would, however, be *unreasonable* to have her clean the whole house. It would be *disrespectful* to have her do it in front of all her friends. And it would be *unrelated* to have her mow the lawn.

Chores as Earning Power

Some parents pay their kids for all the "work" they do. More often, parents pay their kids only for special, optional jobs. Paying your child for average, maintenance types of tasks strikes me as putting your entire family into an economic model. I don't like it. Your child will be participating in family life because he's being paid for it, not because he's a member of your family community. Of course, if you have an extra job, and your child is interested in making some money, why not hire him?

If you're going to hire your child, make sure that you:

➤ Establish your job expectations ahead of time, both in terms of what your child will do, how well he needs to do it, and how much he'll be paid.

➤ Treat him like a professional on the job, as much as possible.

➤ Pay promptly and fairly.

Tasks for Kids

When you're assigning tasks, you might choose to simply rotate responsibilities, you might decide to give each child (and adult, too) an area of responsibility, or you might do both. There are advantages to each approach (but I suggest you try number 3!):

1. **Chore rotation** works well when there's a similarity in skill and independence level among the kids in the household, and there's a variety of household tasks to be done (some more unpleasant than others). Rotating chores means that sometimes you get off easy with folding laundry, and sometimes you're mucking around in toilets, but everybody has an equal chance for easy and hard jobs. The advantage is that, because you're changing jobs all the time, nobody gets bored, and nobody gets stuck forever with the "yucky" stuff.

2. **Chore ownership** is a system where each person has responsibility for a certain chore, or chores. "Danny cleans the birdcages and Cindy wipes down the counters before bed." The advantages to chore ownership are that, should there be a breakdown and something doesn't get done, you don't have to go searching for a schedule, kids can gain a sense of pride in "their" jobs, and that pride will reflect in the quality of their work. Also, lots of experience in one area leads to increased skill. Downside? A bathroom that doesn't ever *quite* get clean (see "But I Tried" later in this chapter) and boredom. If you decide to assign permanent or

semipermanent tasks, make sure you're being equitable (even if it isn't equal) and involve the kids in the decision about who does what jobs. They'll have preferences, try to accommodate them.

3. **The big combo factor.** I believe the secret to making chores work for your family can be found in one word: options. If you assign certain chores (such as cleaning bedrooms and, say, taking out the trash) as "owned" chores, and rotate others (say, the bathroom and mopping floors, 'cause nobody loves doing it all the time), then your child will feel better about the chore system. Use family meetings as times to set up rotating chore charts, and allow your kids to choose from a variety of options.

You can also provide "trade-in" chores. Say Paula is scheduled to clean out the refrigerator, but she just can't stand the idea. She can trade in her refrigerator chore for the chore of washing the car, or cleaning the attic. (See the sample chore chart, below.) Kids also sometimes like to trade chores. Develop a policy that trading chores should happen at family meetings, or with the agreement of a parent, to ensure that the trading is fair, and nobody gets the shaft.

It's a Good Idea!

Most household chores (unless they involve toxins or sharp edges) can be done by a small child with adult support. As time goes by, the child can "grow into" them.

Which Chores for Whom?

What types of participation should your child be asked for? It's really a matter of "know your child." A lot of books list tasks for kids and the ages the jobs become appropriate. I don't like to do that because kids vary so widely, in their development, skills, and interests.

This list of household tasks is here to get you thinking. Choose tasks that you (and your child) think are appropriate, both in terms of development and temperament. Remember, this is only a starting place:

Emptying wastepaper baskets

Washing and folding laundry

Setting the table

Clearing the table

Doing the dishes

Loading and unloading the dishwasher or drain

Straightening family areas

Dusting family areas

Vacuuming family areas

Organizing the bookshelves

Organizing the videos and CDs

Cleaning the attic

Cleaning the garage or storage shed

Clipping coupons

Polishing doorknobs, railings, or silver

Mopping floors

Cleaning toilets or sinks or showers

Caring for the pets (walking, grooming, feeding, cleaning cages)

Exterior of house (windows, mowing, raking, gardening)

Washing the car

Organizing the recycling

Taking out garbage

Making a shopping list

Shopping

Washing dishes

Cooking meals

Charting the Chores

Parents rely on a variety of motivators and reminders to get their kids to do their chores. Some schedule the responsibilities on chore charts. Some paste gold stars on the calendar every time the child completes them. Some use a chip system—add a coin (or chip) to a jar every time a chore is done. When the jar is full, the child can trade the chips in for special treats. Use whatever works in your family.

No matter what method you choose, one thing is clear: Organization is key, and the bigger the family, the better the organization needs to be. If you are trying to set up a chore chart, you can use the example here as a model (notice that *all* the kids, even the little ones, are included):

Rotating Chore Chart

For the week of _____

Who?	What?	By When?
Maria	Take out all trash	Tuesday evening before bed
Maria	Set the table	5:25 P.M. every night
Maria	Empty dishwasher	Tuesday and Thursday after school
Tony	Clean parakeet cage	Tuesday evening before bed
Tony	Clear table and load dishwasher	After dinner every night
Tony	Empty dishwasher	Monday and Wednesday after school
Little Liz	Help Mommy with the grocery shopping	Wednesday afternoon
Little Liz	Hold the parking lot ticket	Every morning

Trade-Ins:

You can trade in one of your jobs this week in exchange for:

1. Ironing the pile of clean shirts in the laundry room, or

2. Spot cleaning the carpet (ask Dad for the spot remover), or

3. Cooking Sunday brunch *and* cleaning up! (Reminder: Grandma and the cousins are coming. This is a big job. Dad will be your assistant.)

Getting Chores Done

Once you decide to implement chores, the battles begin. No self-respecting child is going to want to *work!* Here are some tips for making it go smoothly.

➤ Be clear that this is a positive step in raising a responsible, resourceful, well-behaved child. Your confidence will be catching (and remember that kids *love* limits, even if they'll never, ever admit it!).

➤ Chores can be boring. What about scheduling one of the weekend mornings as family clean-up day, and doing it all together?

➤ Keep your chore expectations in line with your child's age and development.

➤ If your child is highly resistant to chores, consider that she may be maxed out on activities. Between school, other activities, and scheduled play dates, she may have too much on her plate to handle work, too. Consider eliminating some of her outside commitments. Family time and family commitments are very important. (While you're at it, leave her time to just hang out and play. Your child needs some "down time." Something has to give. You don't want that "something" to be your child.)

➤ Teach your child *how* to clean. Sweeping is a skill, it requires practice. Knowing how do the laundry, or to clean a bedroom (see Chapter 6), requires practice, too. Be patient, don't redo her work, and give her positive reinforcement for her efforts.

➤ Stop listening to the other parents when they brag about how responsible their kids are. They may be exaggerating. Most kids don't do chores until college (and many don't do them even then!).

Behave Yourself!

Don't be so judgmental about your child's attitude about chores. It's the rare kid who loves doing household chores. Toss the shoulds ("He should start doing his own laundry, he's old enough") and take a walk down memory lane. Then, when Junior starts reacting, rebelling, and refusing to even hit the hamper with his gym shorts, you'll have some empathy. And that's a good place to start.

Need More Responsibility?

Some kids can't wait to grow up. You know 'em, from the time they're a toddler, the very idea of being a child rankles. It's particularly hard on these kinds of kids if they have to deal, not only with being a *child,* but with the added indignity of being a younger sibling. The cure for a child like this? More responsibility. Put her to work. Make her feel important.

In general, kids don't always know when they want or need more responsibilities. Often they'll ask for them in reverse, by being less responsible than usual. Sound bizarre? Hey, lots about kids is bizarre, but this really isn't. It's an issue of ownership (remember chore ownership, above?). If your child feels useless, and that everything will always be done for her, why should she try to be responsible?

Take the story of Jeannie, who had very few responsibilities other than occasionally straightening her room. She began pushing her limits, never bringing the trash out of her room, leaving her clothes in great, wrinkled piles, and, most of all, arriving late to meals, complaining about the food, and never helping to even clear the table. Finally her parents put her in charge of cleaning the entire kitchen. "The kitchen is your domain, Jeannie," they said, and sat back to wait. Jeannie whined, moaned, and (after a few unpleasant logical consequences such as having to stay home to complete her chores), got organized. Soon she was complaining when people left dirty dishes in the sink. And, amazingly, soon her room was even less of a mess (at least there were no dirty dishes moldering in corners!). Jeannie had claimed ownership of the kitchen, and her pride in her work began to "leak" into other parts of her life.

Putting a child in charge (you can be the "helper," available when needed) will give her a sense of responsibility. Put your son in charge of doing laundry and imagine this scenario: Little Doug arriving at your bedroom door saying, "Dad, please strip your sheets before this afternoon so I can wash them." Like the idea? I do.

It's a Good Idea!

Responsibility breeds responsibility.

"In a Minute, Mom": Dealing with Procrastination

Chores are harder for some kids than they are for others, and temperament plays a big role in why.

Here's a true story: Robbie was 10, Matty was 9, and they both had Saturday responsibilities—straightening their rooms, picking up their toys from the rest of the house, and helping to clean the kitchen. The deal was that they needed to finish their responsibilities before they could go out to play. Matty, even though he was younger than Robbie, was very businesslike. Saturday mornings, he leapt right in, did his jobs, and was finished in 45 minutes. Robbie, on the other hand, tended to daydream, procrastinate, cry and whine about it, get distracted by toys, play, get reminded and yelled at, procrastinate again. It often took him most of the day to get his chores done.

If you have a child, like Robbie, who procrastinates, it's important not to feel sorry for him (all that sighing and moping). Once you take over and "rescue" him, he'll get the message that his responsibilities are optional. His modus operandi will become to stall until you take pity on him. He'll think, "If I wait long enough, Mom will get impatient enough to do it for me."

Kids procrastinate for many reasons. If your child is having trouble with procrastination, consider why:

➤ Is he a perfectionist, afraid to start or finish for fear the work might not be good enough? (See Chapter 5 for more on perfectionism.)

➤ Does he know *how* to do the job at hand?

➤ Is the task too much, too long, or too hard?

➤ Is he getting enough positive reinforcement when he finishes the job?

➤ Is it the solitude of working alone that is bothering him? (Can you make his work time more social, encourage him to break it up with "people breaks," or work together as a team?)

"But I Tried"

So, Eliza finishes scrubbing the bathtub, and the ring is still there. Pop quiz! Do you:

A. Yell, "Eliza, this is terrible! Do it again!"

B. Say, "Nice try, Honey, I'll get this looking better in a jiffy," as you roll up your sleeves and improve her work.

C. Say, "Wow, you sure have been working hard. Tell me what kind of cleaning stuff you were using. Just a wet towel? That's a good idea. Next time, you might try adding a little of this bleach, you may hate the smell, but it will save you a lot of elbow grease."

Answer: C. When it comes to chores, look at the effort, not the results. If you need to give feedback for improvement, keep it positive, and *never* take over or redo your child's job. Keep in mind that you have two objects: getting the work done and teaching your child about responsibility, work ethic, and family participation. So the bathtub has a ring this week. Will the sky crash down? Eliza's ego certainly won't! Eliza tried, and effort counts. Criticizing the quality of her work would be counterproductive. She has years to learn how to clean a tub, but she'll only learn if she's motivated.

Homework Hassles

Not every educator agrees with the principle behind assigning homework. The arguments against homework include the following:

➤ If a child understands the concept, why have her repeat it over and over again at home?

➤ If a child does *not* understand the concept, she won't get it by sitting alone in a room.

➤ Kids are "overworked" as it is, and can use some down time when they are not in school.

➤ Rather than continuing to do schoolwork, shouldn't the child be learning how to participate in family life, communicate, and share times with her parents and siblings?

The arguments *for* homework include the following:

➤ Homework during childhood allows students to practice what they've learned in school.

➤ Homework develops self-discipline, personal study habits, and time management.

➤ Homework helps kids learn to persevere.

No matter where you stand (or fall) on the great homework question, the reality is that most schools do assign homework. Another reality is that homework is a miserable experience for many families—kids procrastinating and groaning, parents yelling or correcting, kids resenting and pulling away.

Whose Homework Is It, Anyway?

Homework may be hard to handle for kids, and it certainly is for grownups. We all want our kids to do well, and it's often hard to take the long view, let the child figure it out, and avoid rescuing her. In other words, parents tend to help (or even do) their children's homework in a misguided effort to help them succeed in school. In their book, *7 Strategies for Developing Capable* Students: *Responsible, Respectful, and Resourceful*, H. Stephen Glenn and Michael L. Brock write, "Homework is the child's, not the parents' responsibility. By enforcing that early—with encouragement, empathy, and support—we lay the foundation for our children developing as capable young people who understand the meaning of personal responsibility." Kids need to learn their own work processes, they need to take responsibility for how they do in school, and sometimes it takes them awhile to figure it out. As a parent, you have a couple of difficult questions to consider:

1. Can you let your kid fail in the short term to succeed in the long term?

2. What is your reaction when homework is being done, but not as you would have done it, or would like to see it done?

Here are some thoughts, ideas, and suggestions for reducing your child's stress about homework (and also lessening your own):

➤ Stay aware of your child's progress in school. That means visiting the school, asking for periodic conferences with the teacher (even when things seem right), and generally being involved with your child's education. Did you know that a parent's attendance at open house night is the number-one signifier of

It's a Good Idea!

When, *where*, and *how* your child does his homework is negotiable. *Whether* he does it is not.

whether or not a child will succeed at school? The more involved you are with your child's schooling, the more clearly you'll know if he is having trouble with "homework: the concept" or "homework: this particular assignment."

➤ Stop taking responsibility for your child's homework. If you complete it, correct it, or take over, *you* may be learning, he will not be.

➤ Participate if he asks questions or asks for your suggestions. Gently guide him on the path to the answer (but do not provide it).

➤ Express your empathy and confidence in your child. ("Yep, this looks pretty challenging. I know you can figure it out, though.")

➤ Take a child's time temperament into consideration when you schedule time for homework. If your bright-eyed and bushy-tailed morning dove prefers to get up at dawn to complete his assignments, why not? He'll probably work better than in his brain-dead presleep period in the evening.

➤ For very active kids, it's torture to do homework after sitting in school all day. Plan an exercise break.

➤ Talk with your child about where to do homework. Some kids love to work in solitude, some prefer the hustle bustle of the kitchen table.

➤ Some kids actually work best with music blaring or in front of the TV. (This was true of my stepdaughter Rachel, who is now working toward her Ph.D. in chemistry!) Allow your child to try it, and monitor the results. Get him earphones so you won't have to try it, too.

➤ If your child is homework resistant, persevere. You can say, "When you're done, I'm looking forward to a board game with you" (or any other special time activity), so he knows you are interested in spending time with him—but that doing homework is nonnegotiable.

➤ A child should never be rewarded for good grades. Instead, encourage him to feel good about the process of learning. Celebrate the process and its completion, rather than the grade earned.

➤ Be open to the possibility that your child might need tutoring. You can talk with the school about what is appropriate, and where to find it.

➤ Don't try to be your child's teacher.

➤ Be available to offer guidance when he gets stuck. Share your approach, any tricks, resources you might know about.

➤ Don't reward procrastination.

Tales from the Parent Zone

Then there's the story about the frustrated teacher who barked at the student, "How could one person make so many mistakes on a homework assignment?" "Well," replied the student, "It wasn't just one person. My dad helped a lot."

Should Reading Ever Be a Consequence?

Should reading *ever* be a disciplinary consequence? In a word, *no*. Reading should only be associated with pleasure, because the people who enjoy reading are the people who become good readers. Keep books and discipline completely separated.

Kids and Money

For many families, talking about money is taboo. The adults make it, the kids ask for it, end of story. Yet financial experts agree that understanding cash, credit, and consumerism is possible, and important, for building a sense of financial responsibility in children. How can you teach your kids about money? What kind of message should you teach them? Let's talk about money.

The ABCs of Do-Re-Me

Kids need to know how the economy works. No, not stocks, interest rates, and world markets! I mean the basic ins and outs of a family economy. You can start when your kids are very young by helping them understand the difference between needs and wants, that money comes from working, what money looks like, and that everybody has a job (a kid's job is to learn things, to play, and to participate in the family). As they get older (once they know that a nickel is worth less than a dime, even though it's larger), you can talk with them about credit cards, bank interest, and so on. Kids can learn about budgeting from the time they are about seven. Remember that a solid money education is one of the best tools you can give your kids—it will aid them the rest of their lives.

It's a Good Idea!

Ask your child about what a credit card is and how it works. Tell her it's a way to borrow money, and teach her that, unless you pay it back every month, everything you buy with a credit card is far more expensive than it would be if you paid cash. Model a cash economy yourself. Teach her the discipline of credit cards and you'll be doing her a very big financial favor.

Ethics Through Sharing

Part of a solid money education includes teaching your kids that, as a member of a community, as a responsible person, and as a world citizen, they have a responsibility to other people outside themselves and their family. That means sharing. We all live on a small planet together, and we are all linked. Teaching your kids a sense of social ethics includes a sense of charity or giving.

You can help your child develop a sense of social responsibility by:

➤ Setting an example, modeling charity. Some families tithe to a church or temple, others put aside a certain amount of money every year to give to charity or service organization.

It's a Good Idea!

Steve Otfinoski's book *The Kid's Guide to Money: Earning It, Saving It, Spending It, Growing It, Sharing It* is unusual for a book on finances for kids in that it stresses the importance of both financial *and* social responsibility (that's the "sharing it" part of the subtitle). Most similar books have nothing about giving. A loss, if you ask me!

➤ Sharing your work specialty with others who can't afford it is another option for people who are knowledge or service "rich" but cash "poor." Donate your services to a worthy cause of your choice, and bring your kids along with you. They'll learn a valuable lesson as you participate in improving the world.

➤ Volunteer work. People participate in giving programs during the holidays, but don't forget the rest of the year. The nursing homes are filled with amateur entertainers in December, and empty from January through November.

➤ Individual participation. Stress to your child that it's not enough that the family give, that every individual needs to participate, too.

➤ Giving. It's not how much you give. Every little bit helps.

➤ Donating. Kids can donate old clothes, toys, time, or a percentage of their allowance.

Allowance

Parents use allowance in several ways: to teach their kids about handling money, to provide them with a share of the family's money as discretionary funds, and, in some families, in exchange for successfully completing chores or jobs. How and why you give your kids allowance is up to each family to determine, but here's my approach:

➤ Allowance should be a small amount of money given every week to a child, just because she exists.

➤ Allowance can be spent, saved, lost, or given away. It's the child's choice. Allowance is your child's opportunity to try out her money management skills, make mistakes, errors in judgment, and learn from them.

➤ Allowance should not be tied to chores. Every child should have responsibilities as part of her participation in family life, and those responsibilities have nothing to do with money.

➤ Paying your child for additional jobs shouldn't affect her allowance in any way.

➤ Allowance should not be tied to behavior. I don't believe in withholding allowance from a child for misbehavior (unless it's a very, very rare occasion where the misbehavior is directly related to the allowance).

➤ Don't mistake allowance with, say, a "clothes allowance" or a "lunch money" allowance, which is really a budget for your child's needs. Allowance is not about needs, it's about wants.

How much allowance your child should get depends on how old he is, where you live, how much money your family has, and what other kids his age receive. Obviously, it shouldn't be too much, and it shouldn't be too little. You can pay allowance weekly or monthly. A good guideline for a 10-year-old would be a weekly allowance of enough to go to a matinee movie (and you can kick in for the popcorn). For a little kid (four to nine), a monthly allowance of $1 for each year of life sounds about right. Many families divide this sum into weekly increments.

Behave Yourself!

Money and schoolwork have absolutely nothing to do with each other. Don't try to tie them together!

The Least You Need to Know

➤ Family responsibilities increase a child's self-esteem and reduce behavior problems.

➤ Your child is a member of your family community and should participate in keeping your community going.

➤ Reward the effort, not the results.

➤ Let your child be in charge of her homework. Don't butt in!

➤ Allowance should never be tied to behavior, chores, or homework.

Chapter 14

Discipline at School, at the Neighbor's, on the Road

In This Chapter

➤ Your child, an utterly different being (away from you)

➤ The child in school, and in the principal's office

➤ When other parents discipline your child

➤ Manners of a princess or manners of a pig?

➤ The pros, cons, and survival techniques of taking a vacation

You *know* your child. You know pretty much how she is going to act and react, what she likes, and what she despises. Yet, since you also know a little bit about human nature (being a grown-up, and all), you have a sneaking suspicion that you don't always know the whole story. Let me confirm your suspicions: Your child is *different* away from the house, and she's different when she's away from *you*.

This chapter focuses on your child's behavior with or without you when she's away from home—at school, at friends' houses, at public events, and on vacation. It focuses on ways to prevent problems and keep your child well behaved out of the house. You'll also find suggestions for dealing with trouble, trouble, trouble.

Behavior and Misbehavior Away from Home

All kids go through phases when their parents find them almost unbearable. Yet, at the same time as you're feeling the most terrible about your child and your own parenting abilities, you may start hearing wonderful things about your child through the grapevine. "He's such a little angel," you get told by another parent or a teacher.

Behave Yourself!

The grass is always greener on the other side of the fence, and that goes for children, too. Before you start thinking about what a great kid that Jones boy is and how you wish your little Johnny would behave like him, consider what kind of grief Jonesy might be giving his parents at home.

It's a Good Idea!

The rule of the public child: Kids are different in public than they are at home, and usually for the better.

"That's absurd," you might think. But before you start rolling your eyes and watching that parent or teacher for foaming at the mouth or other signs of rabies, consider that the misbehavior you're seeing at home may be a release after your child's good behavior during the day. Your child might be working really hard at school, playing by the rules, and turning into a demon at night. You are the parent, so you have the honor of seeing the worst side of your child, the nasty, rude, cranky, over-wild, beastly side. (Well, I guess it has to come out somewhere!)

Kids are mostly well behaved away from their parents (or at least better than you expect), but what if your child *doesn't* behave beautifully when she's at school or at a friend's house? Let's look at school first.

School Discipline

The days are gone when kids were sent to the principal's office to be spanked with the Ping-Pong paddle he kept hanging on the wall, or when frustrated teachers slapped students on open palms with rulers. Corporal punishment is banished from many schools, and good riddance. Kids still get sent to the principal's office, but usually for a good talking to, detention, a note to the parent, a call home, a parent conference or, if the crime is really rough, suspension.

What should your response be when you get a call from the school, telling you that your child is in trouble?

➤ If it sounds reasonable, you can choose to let the school handle it completely. However, schools are *not* always reasonable, and it's a good idea to get as much information about the incident and the consequences as you can.

➤ If you can, march on down there and find out what is going on. If you can't, try for a telephone conference with the teacher and/or principal. Don't be afraid to butt in. This is your child, and this is the schooling you paid for (through tuition or taxes) and you have a right to know the facts.

➤ Don't immediately side with the school. Remember that you are your child's ally, and you need to stick up for your child's rights. Schools, teachers, and principals are not always right.

➤ Neither are schools, teachers, and principals always wrong. Listen closely to what they say, they may have new information about your child.

➤ Don't "double-dip" consequences. If the school has disciplined your child, it's not fair *or* useful to punish him again for getting into trouble. You can and should talk about it, but keep as a framework the feelings, "How did you feel in the principal's office?" "No, Mr. Ng probably shouldn't have thrown the erasers."

Socializing Struggles and Success

You send your child out into the world (scrubbed, neat, and shining like the sun, though that's never certain), and from the time she's very little, she's got a life of her own. Friendships, rivalries, heartbreak, love—it all happens and happens again and again, beginning early in childhood. You can support your child's struggles, but you have little control over what happens in her life.

Not all is muddy and unclear. You may get a glimmer of what is going on from your child (depending upon the strength of your communication relationship, her temperament, your temperament, and her age). You may get a sense from watching her with her friends and peers. You may also occasionally hear something from another parent. Often it will be good, occasionally it won't be.

Problems at a Friend's House

It's not a good feeling when your child's friend's parent approaches you with, "Sarah had a little problem today," or, "I need to talk with you about Todd's behavior this afternoon." You need to determine:

➤ What happened. This entails hearing the story from a couple of sides, including your child's, and keeping your cool.

➤ How the other parent handled it. Did the other family "discipline" her, and do you approve of their approach? Did they have your permission? (There's more about disciplining with a partner in Chapter 18, and in this case, the other parent is your partner.)

➤ Whether or not you'll live through the embarrassment of having your kid behave so badly. You will.

Other Parents and Discipline

For small matters—the kids are squabbling over a toy and the friend's parent removes it, your kid hits the other and the parent reprimands him, or the kids make a mess and they are required to clean it up—there's no question that the parent in charge should handle the problem. By agreeing that the other parent is caring for your child, you've put that parent in a position of authority, and the parent should be able to assert that authority without it being judged by you.

For serious concerns, the other parent should let *you* handle your own child's discipline. If there is a serious problem, it's up to the other parent to contact you, *not* deal with it alone. And *nobody* should ever hit, verbally abuse, or severely punish your child.

If your child has gotten "into trouble" at a friend's house, you'll need to talk with him about it, and possibly impose consequences (once you've gotten home). But don't apply consequences for the crime of having gotten into trouble, too—that's double-dipping.

Events, Shows, Parties

What about your child's behavior when he's out with you in public? Some parents feel very comfortable taking their kids to the opera, a trade show, or a cocktail party. If you start young, and make the family rules very clear and nonnegotiable in terms of rudeness and noise-making in public, you'll end up with a child comfortable in almost any setting.

➤ Keep your expectations clear. If your child is acting up and disturbing others, take him out. Immediately.

➤ Modeling counts here, big time. Train your child by example as well as by experience.

➤ Be a hands-on parent and don't relinquish responsibility for your child just because there are other adults there engaging him.

Behave Yourself!

Want your child to feel relaxed and self-confident? Expect the best at home! Manners take practice, and unless a child practices at home, he'll have a hard time holding his fork correctly, for example, when he's out. And, unless manners are second-nature for a child, he'll feel self-conscious and uncomfortable trying to use them in public.

Restaurant Rowdiness

What a combo—a hungry child trapped in a small space, waiting for food, forced to be quiet. Some kids are fine in restaurants, even the most solemn and ornate ones. For other kids (the high-energy ones), you might as well chain them to the wall, it's *that* uncomfortable. At their worst, kids in restaurants can become the *opposite* of well behaved. You, the parent, can have the *opposite* of a relaxed, calm dinner. The chances for humiliation are endless.

Luckily, while restaurant nightmares happen, they happen less frequently than you might think, and there are many ways to avoid unhappiness and disaster. The rule of the public child comes into play here. Here are some restaurant survival tips:

➤ Almost any restaurant is fine to take your child to. Don't feel restricted to just fast-food joints, coffee shops, or pizza parlors. If your child is not very restaurant experienced, hold off on the fancy, romantic, candle-lit ones until she's learned the restaurant ropes.

➤ Don't take your child to a restaurant when she's hungry. This is totally counter-intuitive, I know; after all, you go to a restaurant to get fed, but a hungry kid is rarely as well behaved as you like. The solution? Snacks in the car, just enough to take the edge off. There's often bread at the table, too.

➤ Bring toys, books, and coloring books for the long wait until food arrives.

➤ Let your child eat what she wants to eat (within reason, of course).

➤ Order some "safe" things (well, there's always the bread), but encourage your child to taste at least one new thing.

➤ Encourage, encourage, encourage.

➤ At the least sign of trouble, out you go for a walk until the food arrives. This is mostly true with babies and toddlers, but there are eight-year-olds who lose it and need a break.

On Vacation or On the Road

Your child is different out of the house and away from you. Your child will also be a different beast than usual when you are there but the environment is different, for instance, during vacations and other trips.

Vacations and travels as a family (or as a parent/child combination) are often an odd blend of great and horrible, relaxing and stressful, and easier and harder than life at home.

On the one hand: Spending so much time together without breaks can really *bond* you.

On the other hand: All those niggling little irritants that usually don't bug you as much (because your child is at school and you are at work all day and you have limited time together) come out of the woodwork. By day four, you fear you'll go insane if you hear Jerry click his teeth one more time, or have to listen to Sarah chanting the "driving-down-the-highway fart song" yet again.

On the one hand: The weather is great! And isn't it terrific having the only decisions of the day be, "Shall we go to the beach or the pool now, or shall we eat first?"

On the other hand: Getting there can be truly challenging. Planes, boats, trains, busses, cars—all have their stressful elements, especially when you're traveling *en famille*.

On the one hand: You wish you could be this stress-free all the time (yawn, stretch, nap).

On the other hand: You are never, ever, ever going on a trip again with these ungrateful kids, at least not until next year.

It's a Good Idea!

If you're planning to travel—down the block or around the globe—with babies or kids under five, check out my book *Baby Maneuvers: For Parents On-the-Go, Anywhere and Everywhere with Babies and Tots.*

When the Going Gets Tough, the Tough Get Cranky

Much of the processes of assuring that your child will be well behaved out of the house is planning, taking precautions, and thinking ahead. A "trip" can be as short and as local as a restaurant or the zoo, and as grand as a year around the world, including Samoa, Bangladesh, and summer in Rome.

Making your trip a success is largely a matter of relaxing certain standards (such as food restrictions and bedtimes), tightening others (anything to do with safety) and plan, plan, planning. Here are three brief sections on the elements of traveling that worry most families: car travel, airplane travel, and staying in hotels and motels.

Tales from the Parent Zone

Good morning! All over the country, parents are gulping coffee and steeling themselves for the task of chauffering children to and from school, to soccer practice, to gymnastics, to swim practice. Since driving a carload of screaming kids is enough to drive the coolest Zen master bonkers, it's a testimonial to parents' strength that the mental institutions aren't filled with car pool drivers who've cracked under the pressure.

Car Craziness

From the day you bring your baby home from the hospital, strapped carefully into his new infant car seat, little lamby blanket tucked gently around him, cars have been part of his existence. Some kids love car rides, some don't. When you're tearing your hair out about car rides, remember that:

➤ Kids need to move their bodies; it's not optional, it's a biological need. Between car seats for little ones and seat belts for bigger ones, car trips can be a challenge.

➤ Car rides can be boring. Making it worse is the fact that many kids, maybe most, can't read or focus on something small like a drawing without getting carsick. That leaves talking, word games, singing, and socking your sister. (You can see how this would be a problem.)

190

➤ For brothers and sisters with tensions between them (and that's kind of a redundant statement, isn't it?), sitting right next to each other, confined, can feel almost unbearable. That's why car fights between screaming, pinching siblings are so common.

Tales from the Parent Zone

Cartoonist Lynn Johnston's son was a very active child. When he was little, Lynn wrapped his toys in lots and lots of paper and tape, and handed them back to him, one at a time. He'd be entertained for long periods of time by unwrapping and discovering his favorites.

So, are there solutions to these problems? No solutions per se, but there are ways to reduce car troubles.

➤ If you're on an extended car trip (more than a couple of hours), stop frequently. Plan breaks ahead of time by marking them on the map, about 45 minutes apart, and stopping, even if for five minutes, for a stretch break.

➤ Separate siblings with pillow barriers.

➤ Entertain kids with car tapes. Music is wonderful for changing the mood when the mood needs changing.

➤ Try word games. Find an object out the window beginning with each letter of the alphabet. Try a round of 20 questions. Even little ones can play "I Spy."

➤ For older kids, try books on tape, available at your local video store or from the library. The whole family can enjoy the classics.

➤ Goody bags of toys, surprises, and game suggestions are helpful. Allow them a new treat once an hour, or, when desperate, once every half hour.

➤ Avoid sugary snacks, sodas, juice, and candy as much as possible. Why hype the kid up any more than he already is?

➤ Rely heavily on food. I don't mean meals (you'll need mealtime as a chance to stretch the body), but healthful snacks. Bottles of water are a must, as well.

➤ Travel at night and let the kids doze.

Behave Yourself!

Beware of driver's fatigue! Most fatal accidents happen in the wee hours of the morning because drivers fall asleep at the wheel. Don't push it!

Airplane Agony

Fear of flying? Many parents rapidly develop this syndrome when they consider the challenges of flying with their kids. In reality, flying with kids is easier than driving with them (and driving is something you do every day). As with any other form of travel, the secret is preparation. As you begin your preparation, here are a few special tips for keeping your children well behaved high in the sky:

➤ Examine your own expectations—you don't have (and won't ever have) storybook children who are polite, neat, and never speak until spoken to.

➤ Schedule your flight times to coincide with your child's normal sleeping schedule (in other words, the red-eye).

➤ Contrary to popular belief, nonstop is *not* always best. An hour or so break in an airport in the middle of a long journey can actually be a good idea.

➤ Airplanes get you from point A to point B quickly. If you think of them as giant cattle cars in the sky (with you as a family of cows, unrespected and uncared for as individuals), you'll prepare enough entertainment and supplies. Pack coloring books and pens, books to read and to be read to, cards, dolls, stickers, toys, and stuffed animals. Segregate them into sealable plastic bags and only allow one activity at a time per child. Keeping things around your seats fairly organized will save you from a five-minute panic period as you try to stuff everything away as the plane descends or the plane enters a pocket of turbulence ("Look Ma, our stuff is flying! Cool!").

➤ Consider a small tape or CD player with earphones that fit your child. Then you don't have to pony up four bucks for a headset that doesn't fit to listen to music that nobody likes.

➤ Some airlines still provide in-flight complimentary activity packets. Don't count on it, and consider it a nice bonus if it does happen. Ask the flight attendant (if possible, out of earshot of the kids).

➤ Keep your kids well fed so they don't get cranky. Bring your own supplies of sandwiches, fruit, and snacks in sealable plastic bags. Airline food is as bad as, well, airline food.

➤ A pillow or small quilt from home is a good idea (as long as you aren't traveling too light). Airplanes are cold, and your child won't be able to truly get comfortable under one of those thin sheets that pass for airline blankets.

Behave Yourself!

Toys to avoid on airplanes: anything that makes noise, Play-doh or anything sticky, balls and other round objects, Legos and other toys made up of little bitty objects, Frisbees, board games (they have too many small pieces and take up too much room).

➤ Let your kids wander as much as allowed, and let the flight attendants be your guide as to what is allowed, not the uptight businessman in row 12D.

➤ Try and keep yourself from saying "shhh" every two minutes. Measure your kid's behavior against that of the other passengers, not against your idea of the perfect, silent child. As long as he is relatively quiet and isn't bonking other passengers on the head or harassing the flight attendants, your child is far less obnoxious than the loud couple of sports fans chugging beer and tying up the bathrooms for hours.

➤ Hope, hope, hope for other kids on the flight. (And hope that their behavior is impossible and unacceptable so that your kid looks like a little dreamboat in comparison.)

➤ Remember that some people don't like children, no matter how well behaved. Unfortunate, but true. Look at the joy they're missing!

➤ Stay active. Certain types of behavior are simply unacceptable, up in the air or down. You may need to haul your child to the bathroom for a talk.

➤ If your child's reputation is irrevocably sullied, that doesn't mean yours has to be. If other passengers see that you are dealing with the behavior, they will cut the whole family some slack.

Hotel Horrors and Motel Misery?

Traveling with kids means sleeping away from home. Many meltdowns, episodes of misbehavior, and parental losses of temper happen at night, at the end of the day when everybody is tired and for some parents, the idea of hotels and motels with children is grim. Questions arise: How will I get my child to sleep? How will we handle a screaming meltdown when the walls are thin, and the situation elegant?

Here are a few suggestions. Once again, they stress prevention as a tactic.

➤ When making sleeping reservations, consider your family's needs. How many rooms? If you need more than one, try to find an establishment that has adjoining rooms. That way you can "build" a suite. Also, many hotels have junior suites. Not as fancy as the "senior" models but with enough room for a small-to-midsized family.

➤ Discuss the hotel's or motel's attitude about children with the establishment before you

Behave Yourself!

Hey, take a break! Just because you're on vacation together doesn't mean you have to spend every second together! Maybe your partner can take the kids to the playground while you work on your tan. Then you take them swimming while she shmoozes with the museum docents. Meet over dinner and dessert to share your adventures.

make the reservation. Listen carefully to the response. They often aren't allowed to *say* they don't like kids, so you'll have to pick up the icy chill in the voice, or the gushing warmth. Go for the gushing warmth.

➤ Ask about kid-friendly amenities like Magic Fingers vibrating beds, swimming pools, and ice machines.

➤ Avoid the quaint and quiet. Go for the larger, and noisier. Your family will blend right in.

Pride and Joy at the Well-Behaved Child

You see your child primarily at home or, at least, in her normal circle of activities (soccer and dance class, hanging out with her cousins). You see her in her "private" mode, where she can really let down her hair, and let loose with all her problems and tensions. As a result, you see her not only at her most relaxed, but also at her worst.

It's also hard to judge how well your teachings are sinking in. No self-respecting child will fully let you know how effective you're being as a reasonable parent.

Seeing your child in public and hearing the public response to your child—her intelligence, sensibility, manners, attitude, charm—is one of the places where the gratifying part of parenting comes in. No, your child is *not* rude, sloppy, and spacey. A sense of pride washes over you. A sense of relief, too—this child will make her way in the world. Yes! Here's proof at last that your modeling and teaching is paying off.

It's a Good Idea!

Did I say reserve? By all means, reserve when possible. You can always cancel, but since you're traveling as a family, you have needs, and the hotel or motel needs to know in advance. (Plus you may save yourself hours of wandering from hotel to hotel in the middle of the night.)

The Least You Need to Know

➤ Your child is different away from the house, and when she's away from you.

➤ Children often "save" their misbehavior for their parents.

➤ If your child gets into trouble at school, get involved and be a peer, but don't "double-dip" consequences.

➤ The parents of your child's friends are in charge of dealing with misbehavior when she's with them unless the misbehavior is serious.

➤ Nobody should *ever* hit or humiliate your child.

➤ Traveling with children can be easy and joyous, when you've planned ahead.

Part 5
Positive Discipline for Complex Families

General principles and suggestions aside, what about your *situation? You've got a toddler? Part 5 is for you, Baby. You had a toddler once, a long time ago and now it seems like you've got a toddler again? Yes, I've got a whole chapter on "the tall toddlers," otherwise known as adolescents.*

Perhaps your family doesn't look like a Norman Rockwell picture. Never fear, if you're one of almost half of all families in the United States living "in step," you have a whole chapter of your own here.

And for everybody working with a parenting partner—and that includes just about everybody reading this book—once you include your child's baby-sitters, teachers, coaches, and family members—come on in.

Yes, life is complex. But wouldn't it be boring if it weren't?

Little Kids

It's kind of a cliché to say that discipline is taught from day one, but it's a cliché for a reason: It happens to be true. Okay, so it's day one. Your baby is born, she's little, she's squalling, she sees everything as a black-and-white blur, and she's totally into her bodily functions. Teach her to behave? Are you crazy? Nope. From day one you are teaching, through modeling, the most important aspects of being a well-behaved child. You are giving her unconditional love, showing her patience, using her positive reinforcement, and being attentive to her needs.

Flash forward a couple of years. She understands simple consequences (if I cry, Mama will come) and she even understands limits ("All gone!"). She's got it down, and it's smooth sailing from here on. All you need to do is be reasonable to your child, and the little tike will learn to be reasonable herself.

Wait! Of course it's not so easy. The first five years of life can be *quite* the challenge. Little kids are lousy to their parents. They kick, bite, scream "No!", use profanity around the grandparents, wear diapers on their heads, gleefully smear food into the carpet, run into traffic, and never fall asleep when you want them to. It's a good thing they're so cute and loving.

In this chapter, we'll concentrate on the toddler set. Let's look at why little ones misbehave, learn how to set limits, explore ways to deal with misbehavior, and develop positive discipline techniques that work with toddlers and preschoolers.

No Such Thing as a Bad Baby

Let's get one thing clear, little kids are not devious. When little kids misbehave, it's not planned, it's not deliberate, and they aren't doing it to hurt anybody. It's more like a science experiment. ("What happens if I poke Mommy with a pin? Will she pop?")

If you assume positive intent and seek to understand *why* your child is acting or reacting the way she is, you'll be able to figure out the best approach to correcting the misbehavior.

Limits: You Set 'Em, They Test 'Em

The world is one big chemistry kit and your little one is a mad scientist. Little children understand very little about the world. Everything is new, everything is to be discovered, and it's your job to set the parameters of the experiment, and let your child play within them.

Setting limits for little kids is like setting limits for any age child (see Chapter 7). They should be effective, reasonable, and well communicated, and take your child's temperament into consideration. "Lilly may have *one* cookie, and only after dinner."

Why Little Ones Misbehave

In Chapter 8, we looked at Rudolph Dreikurs's *Four Mistaken Goals of Misbehavior* to try to understand why kids misbehave. Child developmental theorist James Hymes, author of *The Child Under Six,* takes a slightly different approach to understanding what's going on with your little one. (Neither approach is better or worse, they are just different tools to help you learn more about your child.)

It's a Good Idea!

Hymes's theories are described in detail in the terrific book *Becoming the Parent You Want to Be* by Laura Davis and Janis Keyser, a "must" for the bookshelf of every parent of a kid under five.

Hymes says there are four sources of difficult behavior:

1. *Developmental.* This is behavior that can be explained by the different stages we all go through (remember hearing your parents say, "it's just a phase"? Maybe it was!). You have a couple of choices for dealing with developmental misbehavior: redirection, or waiting it out. We'll look more at those options later.

2. *Unmet emotional needs.* This is behavior that is essentially a "cry for help" based on emotional needs that aren't met. A change in the family (increased parental stress, a new sibling) or

ongoing abuse can lead to difficult behavior. A child with unmet emotional needs will benefit from more attention, special time, and being truly heard.

3. *Lousy local conditions.* A quiet restaurant, a confining car seat, a rainy day and a busy parent, all may be lousy local conditions for your little one that are adding to his difficult behavior. Sometimes the best solution is to remove the child. Sometimes you can change the conditions so they are less challenging (putting fragile objects at a friend's house out of temptation's way, for instance). Sometimes you have to tough it out. Understanding why your child has turned into a beast will help you be patient with him as you hold his flailing, screaming body.

4. *When a child hasn't been taught yet.* This should be looked to as an explanation after the other three possible sources have been explored. Limits, explanations, appropriate directions, encouragement, and patience should be used. If the child isn't catching on, though, look back to one of the other explanations.

It's not always easy to figure out which of the four sources your child's misbehavior is coming from. Like all other approaches, Hymes merely provides another way "in" to the mystery.

Tales from the Parent Zone

Three-year-old Paula and her family are moving, and Paula is flipped out. She won't stay in her own bed, and she's hitting her little sister. Her parents understand that Paula's upset about the turmoil, but nothing they do seems to help. Laura Davis and Janis Keyser, in *Becoming the Parent You Want to Be*, remind parents that just because you figure out *why* your little one is misbehaving, and just because you say and do all the right things, your child may not stop the misbehavior. At least not right away. And just because you understand *why* doesn't mean you won't still feel angry or inadequate. "Even though our buttons get pushed and we get frustrated sometimes, children still benefit from our thoughtfulness about their behavior," Davis and Keyser write.

Value the Struggle

It can be endlessly frustrating dealing with toddler behavior. It's also endlessly fascinating, watching your little one develop willpower, independence of thought, and autonomy. Try to keep it in perspective.

The Power of the "No"

Saying the word *no* is a necessary part of being a toddler. Kids this age are driven by the need to make their own decisions, to be autonomous, and to control their world, and the way they express these needs is through the word *no*. If you're the parent of a toddler, you'll hear it morning, noon, and night.

Don't try to talk your little one out of it, and don't forbid it. "No" is not optional. Kids this age *can* be worked with, however. If you encourage their feelings of autonomy and power, you'll lessen the number of "no's" in your family. Here are a few suggestions:

It's a Good Idea!

Think about how hard it would be to live in a house set up for giants—chairs, tables, and sinks too tall, drawers too heavy, stairs too steep. Making your house more child-friendly will enable your little one to become more independent, more resourceful, and less frustrated.

➤ Give your child choices so she feels a sense of control over her world. "Apple juice or carrot juice?" "Would you like me to help you into your stroller, or do you want to do it yourself?"

➤ Encourage independence by letting them do things for themselves, and setting up their environment so they *can*. This may mean putting toys in bins, keeping cups for water on low shelves, putting stools near sinks, and generally making your home more child-friendly. It's hard for little kids to be as powerless as they are—let them experiment. (Let them experiment, but don't relinquish your supervision. Be sure that their experimentation happens within a safe setting.)

Tales from the Parent Zone

Pammy was helping her mother bake Halloween cupcakes. Pammy's mom noticed that Pammy had taken a finished cupcake and was lifting it toward her mouth. "Pammy! Don't eat that!" she said, alarmed and annoyed. Pammy stopped. "Don't worry Mommy, I'm not eating it, that would be stealing. I'm just licking off the frosting."

➤ Enroll your child as your assistant. Let your child be a participant in family work (this was discussed in Chapter 13) and she'll feel needed and powerful in her ability to help.

➤ Don't expect your child to always be nice, and don't take her "no" personally. Your child is not defiant, angry, or negative—she's a toddler saying "no."

Positive Reframing

Chapter 5 discussed how your expectations of your child depend on whether you are an Eeyore, with a generally pessimistic approach, or a Pollyanna, with a generally optimistic approach. Just as your expectations can be adjusted, so can your general attitude toward your child's traits. Every potentially negative personality trait can be "reframed" in a positive way. Since toddlers can be such a challenge, it helps to actively reframe their traits in order to help you take the long view. That screaming, defiant child pounding her head on the floor, for instance, isn't stubborn and bullheaded—she's asserting her strong will, and isn't it a great thing that she has such a strong sense of self? (It really is!)

Positive reframing is essential, not only for your own survival, but for your child's self-esteem. Your child knows what you think of her, and she will internalize it, and take it on as part of her own self-image.

Mary Sheedy Kurcinka, author of *Raising Your Spirited Child,* uses a positive reframing exercise that I've adapted here. It can be very useful to try, and to keep in mind when your little one is pushing every button you have.

Words to Parent By

Positive reframing means to recast a potentially negative situation or personality trait in a more positive light.

The Positive Reframing Exercise

In this exercise, think for a minute about each trait in the left-hand column, then frame it in a more positive light in the right-hand column. I've done the top few for you. There is no "right" choice.

When you're done with the ones I've started, add some of your own child's "negative" traits in the left column, and do a positive reframing in the right.

Here are some positive reframing choices to choose from (or create your own): imaginative, verbal, assertive, cautious, reserved, soft-spoken, energetic, thoughtful, deliberate, flexible, leaderlike.

Negative Trait	Positive Reframing
In the terrible twos	In the terrific twos
Stubborn and bullheaded	Persistent
Impulsive	Spontaneous
Spaced out	

continues

continued

Negative Trait	Positive Reframing
Noisy and a chatterbox	
Anxious	
Shy	
Wild	
Slow	
A troublemaker	

Disciplinary Techniques That Work with Little Children

Part of a child's development involves learning social rules. It's your job as a parent to teach your little child how to be well behaved.

Many of the problem-prevention techniques and disciplinary consequences designed to help you raise a well-behaved child, and described earlier in this book, are also effective with little kids, with a few adjustments for their age group. I'll describe nine techniques that work especially well for toddlers and preschoolers. Some of these you've seen earlier (geared for older kids), and some are here for the first time:

➤ Stop the action

➤ Look for the positive intent

➤ Educate

➤ Set clear verbal limits

➤ Set physical limits

➤ Provide choices

➤ Natural consequences

➤ Use active listening and the "sportscasting" technique

➤ Time-out techniques

➤ Redirecting the action

Stop the Action and Look for the Positive Intent

Say Helen shoves Mira off the swing. First you stop the action. "Helen, stop pushing. What's going on?"

Once you have the children's attention (and this may mean providing a physical limit, too; see below), you can look for the positive intent (more on this in Chapter 8). No matter how terribly your toddler or preschooler expresses her feelings (whether curiosity, anger, or whatever), it's important to honor the positive intent and impulse behind the behavior as a part of how you respond to her. That does *not* mean *only* acknowledging that it's there. The misbehavior is not okay, and you need to deal with it, but until you let the child know that you understand *why* the misbehavior happened, any consequences will not be fully effective.

What's Helen's positive intent? Helen may be feeling angry at Mira and unclear how to best express it, she may be trying an experiment to see what happens to Mira when she falls, or she may simply want the swing.

"Helen, it seems as though you want Mira off the swing," you might say. You don't know exactly why she's pushed Mira, but you're honoring the fact that Helen has a reason, or an emotion, behind her behavior. When you look for the positive intent, you're trying to find an impulse or a need in your child that you can support, so that your correction comes from a place of empathy.

Educate

Your little one also needs to know the impact of her actions. "Helen, when you push Mira off the swing, it hurts her." Helen may simply be unaware of how strong she is, too. Giving her information about the consequences of her actions is part of teaching her to make decisions on her own.

Set Clear Verbal Limits

Obviously, it's not okay for Helen to push Mira off the swing. You set limits with your voice, "Helen, you may not push Mira. We are gentle with our friends. I'd like you to come down now." Even when kids are very verbal and understand what you are saying (and why), they may not have self-control, and they may *not* be capable of stopping themselves or obeying your requests. It's important to set the limits verbally, even when your child is too young to fully understand you. You're teaching your child that your family uses words to settle problems.

Set Physical Limits

Because it is rare with little kids that words are enough, follow up verbal limits with physical limits (and do it before you get angry, so there's no punitive quality to it). A physical limit is imposed when you stop a child from drawing on the wall with both your words—"No Padma, we don't draw on walls. I'm going to take you into the bathroom, now, and then we'll both clean it up"—and your actions.

Hitting them, beating them, and chaining them to the wall—we've already established that these are *not* options with your kids. (Actually, I shouldn't joke about this. For some people, it's not so self-evident.) Kids don't always listen, and their bodies sometimes need help stopping dangerous activity. If your two-year-old is running into traffic, saying, "Pookie, that's not such a great idea," is not such a great idea. *Pick up your child!*

Physical limits—like removing the pen from Padma's hand—are different from physical disciplinary techniques (like slapping the pen from her hand). Physical disciplinary techniques are *not* okay with one exception: Sometimes little kids need to be physically restrained. Physical restraint is like a very strong hug, and, without hurting a child, simply restrains her until she can calm down.

Provide Choices

Choices are a part of daily life with toddlers ("Do you want to wear the red sweater or the blue one?") and they are an essential part of teaching them discipline. Giving a kid choices ("Will you stop throwing sand or should I help you stop?") teaches her that she's entitled to opinions, and that she has some say in her own life. It shows her respect, and it demonstrates your trust. Remember that kids may not always be able to choose from the choices you've given them. Here's the thing: No matter whether or not they can, you need to give them options. The more experience they have with making choices at a young age (especially when under stress), the better they'll do when they're teenagers faced with larger, more life-threatening choices (like, "He's really cute, and so are his friends. If I have a few drinks with him, he's really gonna like me even more.").

Behave Yourself!

Allowing natural consequences to teach your child is only appropriate when it is safe, and the consequences aren't too severe or long lasting. Letting kids walk on cliffs to learn what happens when they fall (yes, it's a natural consequence) is absurd. But so is letting a two-year-old play with a champagne glass. Yes, she'll learn that glass breaks, but oh, the possible ramifications.

Natural Consequences

Little kids are rarely logical enough to understand logical consequences, so the *best* approach is to allow, and point out, natural consequences. (You can review consequences, both natural and logical, in Chapter 9.) "You hit Davey, now Davey is sad and crying, and he doesn't want to play with you anymore today." "You threw your cereal on the floor, now it is all gone."

Use Active Listening and the "Sportscasting" Technique

Active listening (as explained in Chapter 3) mirrors back to the speaker what she's said. Since little kids are not very verbally skilled, using active listening with little kids relies more on "hearing" what they are saying through their actions, than does on listening to their words. It's a way of letting them know what you understand about their feelings, *and* it's a way of helping them clarify how they feel.

"Sportscasting" is related to our old friend, active listening, though it concentrates more on the events, rather than on the feelings involved. In sportscasting, you observe and describe what is going on. "Judy, I see you are dumping sand out of the sandbox and throwing your trucks. I saw that Henri laughed at you." As a result, your child is able to figure out why she's feeling bad about the event. Like active listening, sportscasting can be used to help resolve conflicts. You're merely the announcer, describing events and letting each child see that he's been seen, and that there is somebody else, too, who has a point of view on the subject. That's a step toward kids' resolving their own problems (there's more on this in Chapter 19).

Time-Out Techniques

There are details about time-outs for older kids in Chapter 10, but here's the discussion geared for the younger set:

➤ A time-out is a way of separating your child from the moment, person, or object that is causing the trouble. It's a way of saying, "C'mon, Dude, take a rest from it."

➤ It's not a "punishment" and it shouldn't be threatened. ("Jerry, stop biting or I'll put you in a time-out!") A time-out should simply be imposed, immediately, when appropriate.

➤ Keep it very brief. The idea is to break the action and mood (not the child!) and allow a little cooldown. For little ones, keep a time-out to one minute per age.

➤ You can put a child in a time-out in a separate room (more on this in the "Behave Yourself!" sidebar) but a better idea is to keep the child near you, perhaps in a special chair.

Behave Yourself!

Like all discipline, time-outs are a teaching tool. If you just slam a kid in a room and say, "Think about it," he'll learn that when he's frustrated, angry, or too much trouble, people don't want to be around him. Many of us only learn to deal with anger and frustration when alone, rather than in a supported situation. Is this healthy?

Tales from the Parent Zone

Remember how Dennis the Menace's mother used to make him sit in a rocking chair in a corner when he was naughty? I guess that was an archaic form of a time-out!

➤ When a child returns from a time-out, *don't* put him back into the environment (or activity) that was part of the problem. Start him on a new activity (redirection—see below) and immediately find something positive to reinforce. For example, say Lance is throwing food and Vikas and Katie are laughing hysterically. Lance won't stop, so you separate him from the action for three minutes in another room. When you bring him back, don't put him back at the table with Vikas and Katie. Give him painting materials and positive feedback ("What great colors!").

Redirecting the Action

Most disciplinary techniques for toddlers and preschoolers involve redirection. It may be the most basic disciplinary technique of all. If you don't like a baby grabbing at your hair, you give him a rattle to hold. As kids get a little bigger, redirection becomes *part* of almost every disciplinary action, whether active listening or sportscasting, imposing verbal or physical limits, or using natural consequences, time-outs, and so on. Redirection is a way to move through the misbehavior and onward to something else, and keeps the discipline from becoming punitive.

Working with Trouble

Perhaps the biggest trouble that little ones cause their parents is when they throw temper tantrums, and engage in hitting, biting, hair pulling, and other violent acts.

It's a Good Idea!

Kids are basically reasonable, and once you understand them, you can usually reason with them.

It's a Good Idea!

Sometimes you have to operate on "toddler time." If you slow your pace, your child will become more serene.

Temper Tantrums

Toddlers throw themselves on the floor, flail around, bang their heads, scream. How do you deal with it?

➤ A temper tantrum is a loss of control. Do not treat it as a disciplinary situation (in other words, don't ever impose disciplinary consequences on a child for having a tantrum).

➤ Say your child is having a temper tantrum. Get on the floor with him, and make sure there's nothing sharp around. Sometimes holding a child while he screams and cries is the best option.

➤ Tantrums often happen when kids feel pushed. Are you rushing from one errand to another? Slow down, and let your little one help determine the pace.

➤ Tantrums show trust. If your child didn't feel utterly comfortable with you, he wouldn't let fly.

➤ Little kids have their own agenda. If Brad is busy making mud pies, and then he plans to feed them to the dragon, he may lose it when forced to "Come inside, *now!*" Honoring his experience and giving choices will make Brad feel *seen* and sometimes avoid a *scene.* "Brad, the pies are going to bake until tomorrow. Turn on the oven and tie up the dragon. You can choose to come inside now, or I can help you come in."

➤ Little kids *hate* to be misunderstood. Frustration levels run very high, especially when children's internal development is greater than their ability to verbalize. They *know* what they want to communicate, they just can't manage to do it. Knowing that this is happening (and spending the time to try and understand his communication) can help avoid many stormy moments.

➤ Tantrums have a purpose. Sometimes a child is so tense and upset that he needs to cry hysterically and blow off some steam. Be there, let it blow, and experience the wonderful aftermath as the weepy, exhausted, red-faced little tyke drops off for a long, delightful slumber.

Biting, Hitting, Hair Pulling, and Other Violent Acts

Biting, hitting, hair-pulling, and other violent acts are caused by a variety of reasons, everything from curiosity to anger to fear to frustration to, you name it. Violent behavior is *not* okay, and you do need to address it directly.

➤ Honor the emotion, look for the positive intent, and respond to her impulse. ("I see you are angry at Sophie.")

➤ Educate and provide a verbal limit. Keep it brief and simple. ("We do not bite people. It hurts. We touch gently.")

➤ Provide a physical limit and physical education. ("I will not let you bite her again. This is how to touch gently.") Take her hand and make her hand stroke your hair.

➤ Provide an alternative. "If you are angry, you may stomp your feet and say, 'Mommy, I'm mad.' Let's see you try it."

➤ If necessary, separate her from the environment.

➤ Do *not* bite her or hit her back. It's cruel, and she'll learn that violence *is* acceptable.

Behave Yourself!

Don't label your child a "biter." It will only lead to more of the behavior.

The Least You Need to Know

➤ Discipline *is* taught from day one; it's the approach to parenting you take with your child.

➤ Little ones misbehave for developmental, emotional, environmental, or educational reasons.

➤ Hearing the word *no* is a necessary part of being a toddler.

➤ Every one of your child's potentially negative personality traits can be "reframed" in a positive way.

➤ Many problem-prevention and disciplinary techniques can also be used for little ones, if adjusted for age and development.

➤ Little kids *hate* to be misunderstood, and understanding is a big step toward having a well-behaved child.

Chapter 16

Discipline and Your Adolescent

In This Chapter

➤ Interspecies relationships—you and your teen

➤ Keeping your cool in the face of raging hormones

➤ Adolescent life and work

➤ Positive things you can do to help your adolescent cope

➤ Preparing for bye-bye

Oh my. The hormones are flying at *your* house. Welcome to the world of adolescence! If you're like many parents, these are years you've dreaded since your little one was little. Adolescence is about topsy-turvy children stretching into odd shapes, with odd emotions to match, and styles and tastes that change daily. And, for many adolescents, rebellion causes more breakouts than a hormone/stress cocktail. Make a limit, they break a limit. Quite a challenge for parents, huh? You bet.

At the same time, living with an adolescent is thrilling and always interesting, a fun-house carnival ride. And it's fulfilling, too, watching them develop into young adults—thoughtful, kind, reasonable, and (sometimes even) well-behaved.

You've spent a lot of time teaching your child to be well behaved, and part of being an effective teacher is letting your student go out into the world with his knowledge. It may sound contradictory, but your adolescent, even in the throes of rebellion, is hearing the faint strains of the disciplinary graduation march, for these are the years when discipline and values are internalized, and ethics are solidified. Your role as a parent changes too, from teacher to advisor, and you need new tactics so you both make it through.

This chapter concentrates on discipline for the adolescent, that delicate mix of "not-too-little" and "not-too-much."

Teens, a Different Species

You've dreaded the moment for years, still you're surprised by it the day it happens. You look over at your child, and you need to look *up* to see if his face is dirty. It is, so you wipe the dirt with your hand, and you realize it's not dirt, it's hair. Boo-Boo has a beard. Or, out of the corner of your eye, you catch a glimpse of a hot chick walking down the street and as you turn to stare you realize with horror that it's your 13-year-old daughter, and "My, what *is* she wearing!" Your 11-year-old isn't rolling in dirt anymore, she's spending hours in the shower. Your 12-year-old no longer likes your jokes. Adolescence has struck.

It's a Good Idea!

Discipline is like housework: It's never done. We work on it all our lives.

It's a Good Idea!

Many parents dread adolescence, and it does have its challenges, but it's a *good* time, too! Your baby is really coming into her own now. What an adventure!

Behave Yourself!

Adolescence is scary for adults, and many parents express their fears for their child by becoming more protective, more restrictive. You'll have an easier time if you loosen, instead of tighten up. Demonstrate your trust.

New Tactics Needed

He may be taller than you, he may drive and pack his own lunches. He's still a child, still *your* child, and he still needs guidance, just not in the same way. Here are some things to keep in mind about the strange creature that has taken over your child's body and is living in your house:

➤ Contrary to popular belief, your adolescent *doesn't* want a fight any more than you do. Look for the positive intent!

➤ Many communication problems happen because parents and adolescent children have different world views and interpret events in very different ways."

➤ His "world view" is influenced by the natural hormones surging through his body. Between two people coming from such different perspectives, communication becomes even more important.

➤ Your cover has been blown. Your adolescent is painfully aware that you are only human, and he may feel betrayed.

➤ Your adolescent child is fragile and new, but he doesn't need to be protected against the world completely. Actually, he needs his limits reset wider.

Expectations, Again

Adolescence begins for different children at different times, and at different ages—social *and* physical. Often development is uneven (think of the husky, unshaven boy running around with toy cars "vroooooom vroooom!" and the skinny, undeveloped girl dolled up in sexy clothes).

The way you react to when and how your child's adolescence begins will largely be a function of your own adolescent experience. Parents whose middle name was "Trouble" will tend to feel distrustful of what their child is up to (more on this in Chapter 21 when we talk about sex and drugs). Parents who had a great time in middle and high school (and who maybe are on the committee to organize the school re-unions) tend to look forward to their kids' adolescence. Parents whose teen years were riddled with angst and social mockery will dread their child's own experience, and either threaten to place the child in deep freeze at 11 and remove her at 19, or buy that sailboat and take the family on a six-year round-the-world adventure.

Remember that you cannot predict what kind of adolescence your child will have, and you cannot predict how events in your child's life will play themselves out. Watch closely with interest.

Tales from the Parent Zone

Tania was a stormy child from day one; it's no wonder her adolescence has brought trouble and high drama. Tobias, on the other hand, was sunny and serene as a two-year-old, and calm and humorous as a teen. While it's true you cannot predict your child's experience in adolescence, you *can* sometimes get a clue as to what kind of adolescent your child will be by looking at her toddlerhood. Temperament is built-in, and the very challenging toddler may well be a challenging adolescent. (It's not foolproof—maybe she "got it all out of her" when she was two. Or, maybe she's grown into rebellion.)

Keeping Rebellion in Perspective

Rebellion and pushing against limits are part of being an adolescent, and part of establishing autonomy away from you. There may be some years where your child does everything she shouldn't, just to prove to herself that she can make her own decisions, and that she isn't *you*. If it's her job to separate, your job becomes the very tough one of staying sane. She needs something to push *against* after all.

Behave Yourself!

From the time of toddlerhood, you've been your child's trampoline, something for him to propel himself from, something safe and bouncy to land on. When your adolescent leaps and pushes off from you, he's not deliberately hurting your feelings. He's pushing toward his adulthood, leaping toward that sky.

It's a Good Idea!

For some people, it helps to keep their own adolescence in mind. Did you really do those awful things? Did you really survive? (Most of us do. Our heads battered and bloodied, but unbowed.)

Given a rebellious, hormonal child, how do you stay strong and reasonable? That's often a function of being able to keep some perspective on what's up with your child. The best way to gain perspective? Education. What's "normal" rebellion? What are all the other kids doing? (and just how miserable are *their* parents?). Knowing what to expect helps. Having a strong perspective will help you prevent, or deal with, the more destructive (and self-destructive) forms of adolescent rebellion.

Educating Yourself About Adolescence

So how do you find out what's normal? Well:

➤ Read the rest of this chapter, for a start. Then read Chapter 21, all about sex and drugs, and Chapter 22, which has details about teenage misery.

➤ Then read some more. There are a number of books listed in Appendix B that may help.

➤ Talk with other parents.

➤ Get involved with your child's school, and observe the other kids.

Life as an Adolescent

What is your child going through? You may *think* you remember adolescence, but keep in mind that your memories are colored by your hormones, and that every person's experience is his own.

Who Am I Today?

Your adolescent is in flux. She may try on identities like hats: punk, slacker, social activist, financier. Changing "costumes" (including hair styles and world views) is an important part of your child's self-discovery. Stay back and watch her explore. Making an issue out of hair color or skirt length is often not worth it. You risk alienating your teenager. Remember, choose your battles.

Young adolescents often go through a year or more where they and their friends seem to meld, and become one, giant, hormonal mass of jumbo adolescent. They dress the same, talk the same, tend to wander the world in packs, and also tend to do stupid, risky things to *prove* how grown-up they are (thereby proving they are not). Whether or not the behavior is stupid, the need to conform is not. It's a developmental stage, and the kid who is pushed to be nonconformist will suffer. In a couple of years, don't worry, most kids both calm down (in terms of risks) and start looking like an individual again. As much as you can, keep them safe, but let them look like (and run with) the pack.

➤ If your child is looking totally cloned, don't make an issue about it. (It's just hair, clothes, and attitudes.)

➤ No matter what's up with the identity, stress to your child that the family values statement and family rules still hold, at least in *your* household.

➤ Shifting identities is healthy, but watch your child for major shifts in behavior. Adolescents are at high risk for depression, drug abuse, and eating disorders.

Piercings, tattoos, brandings, and other scarifications are a more serious issue because they are irreversible (or only reversible after a tremendous amount of effort and money). Many tattoo and piercing parlors now require parental permission before they will work on minors, but there are always ways around that. Ugly ways. (At least at a tattoo parlor, the work is done by an artist or trained professional who follows health and safety precautions.)

Sometimes kids test their parents by threatening to get tattoos or body pierces. If your kid really wants a tattoo or pierce (and is deigning to talk with you about it), try not to overreact ("You *what!*"), and treat it as a topic for discussion. Discuss the pros and cons (and your own personal opinions) in as level-headed a manner as you can, and let *her* make the decision. Remember that 1) adolescents don't really understand the concept of "irrevocable," 2) talking about it might be an attempt to get some support for a "no" decision, and 3) no matter what you say or think, she *will* make the decision for herself. Don't alienate her, and you *may* get some input.

Tattooing is a centuries-old art form (not one that everybody supports, but an art form nonetheless). Piercing and branding are also done for style reasons by many, many people. They can also be a signal that your child is depressed or having difficulty coping emotionally. If your child comes home "altered," try to determine if it is for style reasons, or for other, less happy purposes.

It's a Good Idea!

If he's insistent on permanent body decorations, you can help practice "creative damage minimization" by supporting a few extra ear pierces, or a small tattoo on his shoulder rather than the six eyebrow pierces or the full-body dragon he's hankering for. Take him to a reputable body shop where you know they change the needles (dirty needles can spread hepatitis, AIDS, and other nefarious diseases).

Body Image Problems: What Do I Really Look Like?

It's not just kids with eating disorders (Chapter 22) who have warped or negative body images and who suffer from lowered self-esteem because of it. We all suffer from the image promoted by the media of what the perfect body looks like (and it's hard even for adults to shake the impression that life would be better if we only had thinner thighs, bigger breasts, a more manly chest, or another two inches of height).

Behave Yourself!

Never criticize your child's looks or weight, even when the criticism is couched in suggestions ("Martina, what about that new exercise program Nadia is doing? It's really firmed *her* up!"). She knows (far more than you do) where her "failings" are. Even constructive criticism usually isn't.

Your adolescent, already hyperself-conscious, may be terribly affected by these messages, so insidious that they seem to float through the air and water into her head (even if you only allow her to watch public television). The girl who believes that she's somehow lacking because she isn't skinny like Kate Moss or busty like Pamela Anderson, the boy who measures his chest development and looks against Brad Pitt's, suffer a distorted self-image and a lowered self-esteem.

While you cannot avoid these media messages, you *can* help your child build a strong self-image through encouragement, trust, love, limits and consequences. Model good self-imaging. Stop comparing your *own* thighs to those of Kate Moss (does she even *have* any?). By concentrating on strength and ability (sports, dance, or other activities that make her feel good about her abilities), you can help transcend (or at least lessen) society's stress on appearances.

It's the Pals That Matter

What do you remember most about junior high and high school? Besides that evil, ruler-wielding Miss Slicker who taught German, and cranky, slobbery Mr. Glubb, the bane of the math department, it's your friends, right?

Tales from the Parent Zone

Then there's the time when Katherine, age 16, was shopping for a prom dress. She found the perfect one. "I'll take it!" she told the saleswoman. "Wait. Just in case my mom likes it, is it returnable?" Teenagers struggle hard to find their independence. Asserting her own taste (and denying her mother's) was, for Katherine, an essential part of this process.

During adolescence, social relationships are at least as important as family, sometimes more so. As your child goes through the soul-searching journey of who she is and how she's going to spend her life, it's her friends who are her companions. You, her parent, take a lesser role.

Demoted!

It would be great if adolescents were content to simply shift their loyalties to their friends, while still giving you some respect. No dice. Sometimes it seems as though they're on a mission to burn every bridge, to humiliate you into submission. Did you know just *how* square, boring, dorky, and embarrassing you were? (If you have an adolescent, you do now!)

Being treated like this can be very disconcerting, to say the least (especially if you had *any* pretenses that you were at all cool, or at least interesting). While you may understand intellectually that this kind of treatment is merely part of your adolescent's job, to separate from you, it still can be very painful and hard to handle.

There are a couple of things you can do:

➤ Work on gaining some psychological distance from your child. Just as it's her job to separate from you, so, too, you must learn to get along without her (at least for a number of years).

➤ Take care of yourself through self-nurturing activities (more on this in Chapter 23). If your adolescent is like most, you can use some support. If your kid is miserable, you are apt to feel miserable yourself.

It's a Good Idea!

In Biology 101, we learned that there is no growth without stress, and that goes for adolescence, too.

The Work of the Adolescent

Your adolescent actually has five tasks, writes Ava L. Siegler, author of *The Essential Guide to the New Adolescence*. According to Siegler, the tasks are to separate from his family, to create new bonds (with friends, and other adults), to establish a mature sexual identity, to formulate new ideas and ideals, and to consolidate his character, that is, to unify the parts of his character he has been building since he was a small child.

Not only does he have to do these tasks, but he has to do them in a climate that presents a lot of challenges. The adolescent is becoming an adult in a world that presents him with ethical problems, financial worries (either his own or others'), environmental concerns, and racial issues. How much your child "takes on" is a function of how much he is exposed to, and what his temperament is. And all this on top of school, family, and social pressures (plus a whole new body to get used to). It's hard to be an adolescent.

Whether your child is a worrier or easygoing by temperament, the daily stress of adolescent life can really wear away at confidence. Almost all adolescents feel, at least part of the time, that they are alone. Watch for self-destructive patterns (more on eating disorders, risky behavior, and self-abuse in Chapter 22).

It's a Good Idea!

Teens get a bad rap. Yes, they can be terrible to their parents. They can also be sweet, thoughtful, supportive, and a true joy. You get the good with the bad, the bitter with the sweet. It's worth it!

The Struggle Between Dependence and Independence

Remember when your adolescent was a toddler, and remember your struggles over food ("Just one more bite, Pookie"), cleanliness ("I didn't *hear* the water running, Sallie"), and coming in from playing ("Come in *now*. I said 'five minutes' at least 10 minutes ago!")?

The struggles are the same, just a little bigger and more serious now (bingeing or refusing to eat, getting him to wash his filthy hair, and curfew battles). Both toddlers and adolescents are playing out the same issues with these struggles, trying to answer the question: "Who am I and what is my place in this world?" Your adolescent is ambivalent about your input. He still wants and needs it, but damned if he's going to show *you* that!

What You Can Do

There's a lot you can't do as the parent of an adolescent. You can't *force* her to be well behaved or make good choices. A lot of parenting an adolescent involves a kind of Zen practice—breathe deeply, trust that you've taught her well, and practice letting go.

Lateral Job Shift!

I told you back in Chapter 1 that you have influence but no control. It's even more true for adolescents. Michael Riera, author of *Uncommon Sense for Parents with Teenagers*, says that during your child's early life, you are the manager. As the parent of an adolescent, it's time to shift your role, from manager to consultant. As a consultant, your job is a lot more hands off. Back off on the "shoulds" and the "shouldn'ts" (before you step over a cliff).

If you try to "manage" your adolescent, she'll go out of her way to defy you in order to make her *own* decisions. If you say, "Tonia is too wild, you shouldn't hang out with her," you'll be lucky if you ever see your child alone again. If you say, "I saw you smoking and I'm very upset, you should quit," be prepared to find cigarette butts from now until a very long "then" from now. As a consultant (rather than a manager), your job involves more trust and "back up" and less direct decision-making. Here are a few tips for "hiring on" as parental consultant:

➤ As a consultant, you are still deeply involved, though your job is more passive. Make yourself available, continue special time and other family involvement, and let your child come to you.

➤ Be a sideline cheerleader and ally. "Go team, go!"

➤ Remember to continue to provide the love, limits, structure, consequences, and all that other good positive parenting "stuff."

➤ Don't feel abandoned by your adolescents. You may not know they are listening, but they are.

It's a Good Idea!

Got a message with a moral to transmit? Do it indirectly. Tell a story about somebody you both know, or use a media example. Keeping it one step slightly removed will make it easier for your child to hear the message.

Conversation Counts

The sullen adolescent is a common beast. So is the busy one, out the door at dawn, back to fall into bed late at night. The time of just hanging out as a family and letting conversations develop naturally are gone. At the same time, communication is more important than ever. Here are a few ideas for maintaining (or gaining) communication flow:

➤ Listen, and know that you don't and won't have the answers to some of the things that are bugging your adolescent. This is a time of formulating new ideas and ideals, and your child may be paying more attention to the world than he ever has. Nobody has all the answers to the world's ills and injustices, but it's important to think about them, and to help your child develop critical thinking skills by talking and expressing opinions and feelings.

➤ Your moody, moody adolescent is "processing." Stand back! Don't pry! Don't assume that, just because the timing is good for you, it's good for her. If you want to talk (or have her talk), make an appointment.

➤ Focus on treating your child with compassion, trying to understand the situation, and allowing (and encouraging) your child to use her resourcefulness to deal with difficult situations. Just yelling or condemning her behavior will just cut you off from her.

It's a Good Idea!

Adolescence is a time when kids develop their own sense of morals and ethics. For some, this is a time of intense political or religious activity. And woe to the hypocrite! Adolescents have little to no tolerance for hypocritical behavior, especially parents.

➤ Talking about sex, drugs, and other "touchy" issues is really hard. There's more on this in Chapter 21.

➤ Expect a certain level of lying, even if it's just lies by omission. Your child is building her private world, and protecting her friends. A lot of lying, or elaborate lies, signify either a relationship where your child doesn't feel safe in telling the truth, or a very high level of insecurity. Look at your expectations—are you expecting too much? Are your limits too tight? What are you modeling?

Tales from the Parent Zone

It's worthwhile to spend time listening to your child, even when you disagree (or, worse yet agree but want to move on to another topic). When my stepson was a teenager, he often wanted a forum for his burgeoning political and social ideas. Some of his thoughts weren't yet well developed, but it was important that he be heard, and that he knew that his thoughts and thought process were respected by us. The older he got, the better his argumentation, and the deeper his perceptions.

Relaxation!

Stress, stress, stress. Yet what do far too many adolescents do? Stress their bodies even more through eating poorly, not sleeping well, playing too many computer games, drinking, and smoking (see Chapter 22). You can help by teaching him coping strategies. Enroll him in a yoga class, spring for a massage, get him involved in a volunteer effort. By diversifying your teen's activities, you may find at least one area in a teen's life that is stress free. Kids (and adults) can also learn to rely on self-relaxation techniques (more on this in Chapter 24).

Gaining Distance

You'll be happiest and probably most effective as a parent of an adolescent if you can remove yourself psychologically (even just a bit) from your child's plight. It's *his* angst! (If you are getting gray hairs over your child's adolescent agonies, you're probably not doing this.) You'll also do better if you can distance yourself just enough that you're not as invested in how well behaved or successful your child is. Is this possible? Probably not completely, but it's something to strive for.

Look to Your Child

So much of what we do for our kids in general is in response to our own needs and experiences. If you wanted to be doctor but were foiled in your interests, you might push med school. Don't give him what *you* needed, give him what *he* needs.

Positive Reframing

Adolescents can be as infuriating as little kids, and it's helpful for both of you to stay as positive as you can. If you find yourself judging your teen ("That lazy slob!" "That obstinate kid!"), I suggest you review the positive reframing exercise in Chapter 15. It applies for big kids as well.

It's a Good Idea!

Enlist yourself as your adolescent's ally. Let her know that you know life is difficult, and that you are available to help her figure it out. (You're *not* in charge of figuring it out!)

When Life Gets Hard

How a kid handles her stress and her developmental tasks depends on the child. Ava L. Siegler writes that kids have five basic responses to the stresses and fears of adolescence: anxiety, rebellion, depression, withdrawal, or overattachment. All kids will experience some or all of these responses, and the only time to really worry is if your child gets "stuck" in one of them. If your child doesn't seem to be moving through to a resolution, it's time to get some outside help. Chapter 24 has information about the role of therapy and support groups, and suggestions for finding help.

Tales from the Parent Zone

Regression! Fifteen-year-old Amy had just broken up with her boyfriend and her parents found her in bed, snuggled up with her old baby quilt, begging for warm milk and a story. Sometimes it's the flu that lays them flat, sometimes just the stress of daily life, but one day you'll find a very large three-year-old staring you in the face, overwhelmed by choices, and needing a little babying. Take pity. Put her to bed, give her hot chocolate, and read her her favorite children's book. Give her a limited choice of stories: "*Babar* or *Madeleine*?"

Finding Adult Allies for Your Teen

Sometimes things are simply too tense between you and your child, and it's time to take drastic measures—sic him on somebody else! The extreme version of this is to have your child live with another family for a few months (or you can trade kids—see Chapter 19). Less extreme is encouraging a friendship with a concerned adult.

Many people fondly remember an influential adult from their teen years—*not* a parent—who was concerned and involved. Friendships between adolescents and adults can be highly valuable to both, as they each gain new perspectives.

It's a Good Idea!

The parent who wants a child to be a disciplinary "success" should do everything possible to set her up for that success, and then stand back.

Behave Yourself!

Want your child to hang out *all the time* with that "bad element"? Just express disapproval. Want your child to hang out with the right crowd? All you can do *is* stress your values, listen and talk with your child, and trust that the good, the true, and the beautiful will win out over the forces of evil!

Adolescents are ripe for adult input (and I'm not talking about the stuff that comes from *you*). Developmentally, they seek role models to show them how to "be" in the world. (They're also prone to hero worship, which can make them quite vulnerable to betrayal.) If your child has a special adult friend:

➤ It's wonderful for your child to have somebody else to hash things out with. Remember that confidence in friendship is sacred. Respect your child's privacy, don't pry, and don't feel bad if she has secrets. Know that by asking your child to divulge confidences, you are essentially forcing your child to lie.

➤ In a similar vein, don't ask the adult friend to betray your child's trust, even if you are worried about your child. Get your information elsewhere—the friendship's sanctity should not be broken.

➤ The vast majority of people are reliable, trustworthy, and will not harm your child. If you don't like your adolescent's adult friend, don't say a word about it unless you fear for your child's safety or you sense something sexual is going on. This is your child's friendship, not yours.

➤ If you sense something illegal, immoral, or sexual happening, deal with it by talking with your child. Present yourself as an ally. If your child has gotten in over his head in a hard situation, be there to run interference.

Letting the Little Bird Fly

I'm sure momma birds feel a bittersweet pang as they shove the little ones from the nest and watch them fall, flutter, falter, and finally fly. You will too. Watching your child open up, develop and march out into the world is a truly amazing transition (though not as dramatic or definite as that of the bird kingdom). You are metaphorically stepping away from the edge of the nest every time you let him make his own choices about when to go to bed or what to cook for dinner on his cooking night. Adolescence is a process, and you're spending these years finishing the process you began the first time you left him at day care, or kissed him good-bye on the doorstep of the classroom.

Adolescence is a stage of life, and most kids make it through reasonably intact. They make it through as thinking, feeling people. Because of the emotional storms and experiences of adolescence, they'll come through the other side veterans of love, loss, wonder, joy, and beauty.

The Least You Need to Know

➤ For parents, living with an adolescent brings agony, but it also brings joy.

➤ Adolescents still need unconditional love, support, limits, and consequences.

➤ You cannot predict how your child's adolescence will play itself out; or predict what image your child will project tomorrow.

➤ Rebellion and pushing against limits are important parts of being an adolescent.

➤ Wanna have a conversation with an adolescent? Make an appointment!

➤ Shift your role from manager to consultant.

➤ Look to other adults as allies for your teenager, too.

Chapter 17

The Well-Behaved Stepfamily

In This Chapter

➤ The step-something

➤ The disciplinary evolution of a stepparent

➤ Getting through and beyond disciplinary issues

➤ Disciplinary tips for the stepdad and stepmom

➤ When your kids have a stepparent

If you're like almost half of the population, you've got a step-something in your life. (By the year 2010, 50% of all families will be stepfamilies.) Since the strategies for raising a well-behaved child differ when everybody isn't biologically or legally related, it's vital that we devote a chapter to the stepfamily. We'll look at the well-behaved child during and following divorce, how to deal with disciplinary issues as a stepparent, what to do when the rules are different in your child's "other" household, and other common issues faced by people living "in step."

Step Lingo for Step-Somethings

The stepparent literature is chock-full of terminology all its own. It can be confusing, so here's a brief glossary:

Stepfamily: A family where there are members who are not biologically or legally related to each other.

Stepparent (stepfather, stepmother): The relationship between the adult partner of a parent and that parent's children. There's no biological or legal relationship between a stepparent and a stepchild.

It's a Good Idea!

Many people refer to stepfamilies with two sets of kids (one from each partner) as "blended" families. I use the term *combined*. When families join together, the goal shouldn't be to blend into one bland mess. Instead, they are combining, while maintaining their individual characteristics. Much more interesting, much healthier.

Behave Yourself!

Divorce is an injury to everybody in the family, and every family member will heal his wounds differently, and on his own timeline.

Behave Yourself!

Be careful! In a household where the foundations are already shaky, disciplinary issues can be fatal, collapsing the house of cards into rubble. An extreme difference in disciplinary approaches and values reflects other differences in approaches and values, and is sometimes enough to split a family apart.

Step-siblings: Kids in a stepfamily who are related to each other only because of their parents' commitment to each other. When parents of unrelated children marry or "get together," the children become step-siblings. (Each parent becomes a stepparent to the other parent's kids.) There's no biological or legal relationship between step-siblings.

Half-siblings: Kids who share either a biological (or legal) mother or biological (or legal) father, but not both.

Biochild: The biological (or legal) child of a parent.

Bioparent: The biological (or legal) parent of a child.

Blended family: see *combined family*.

Combined family: A stepfamily with two sets of kids— one set provided by each adult partner.

Semi-blended family: see *Semi-combined family*.

Semi-combined family: A combined stepfamily where at least one set of kids lives in the household only part of the time.

Discipline During Divorce

Before there are stepfamilies, there are families of divorce. In general, parents often have differences of opinion about how to handle discipline. During divorce (when nobody is getting along), those small differences may be magnified. Parents may pit each other against the kids, disagree for the point of disagreeing, or simply be so upset that they can't think clearly enough to remain strong and reasonable.

Divorce also generates misbehavior. Kids are terribly upset when their parents split up, and may show it by acting out in a variety of ways. As a parent going through a divorce, you have a few difficult tasks:

➤ Take care of yourself so that your children don't have to take care of you.

➤ Let the rest of your child's support system (his teachers, adult friends, coaches) know about the divorce so they can help him through, and also let you know if they see any behavioral shifts you should be aware of.

➤ Do your best to set aside differences with your ex, and look to the best interests of the kids. (I know, this is far easier said than done.)

Discipline as a Stepparent

Once you become a stepparent, or invite a new person into your life to stepparent your child, you'll be faced with the issue of discipline, the scariest, most confusing, and biggest challenge of stepparenting. It's vitally important that you talk with your partner about parenting approaches, and disciplinary do's and don'ts. Unprepared, the stepparent may face enough resistance or resentment from the kids to make him run screaming, struggle with feeling "evil," walk on eggs to keep from crossing into inappropriate discipline, and feel undervalued.

Talk about it. You and your partner (whether you are the stepparent, your partner is, or you both are) have some decisions to make and some questions to answer. How do you discipline a stepchild? Should you discipline a stepchild? What parts are done by the stepparent, and what parts by the bioparent? Relax, don't flee yet. I have suggestions and ideas for you.

The Disciplinary Evolution of a Stepparent

Jamie K. Keshet, author of *Love and Power in the Stepfamily,* suggests a five-stage approach she calls the Stages to Stepparent Authority. How long your stepfamily has existed will affect what step in this approach you are in now. A new stepparent should be at stage 1, a Back Room Consultant, and spend her time whispering her thoughts to her partner in the bedroom. One who has been an established member of the family for several years may have completed all five stages. Each family should take its own time to develop through these five stages. You may do it quickly, or it may take years.

I've adopted (and adapted) Keshet's stages, which follow:

1. Serving as back room consultant
2. Standing up for your own needs
3. Operating as designated enforcer (when the bioparent isn't around)
4. Collaborating with your partner
5. Performing spontaneous disciplinary decision-making. (No, this is not like spontaneous combustion!)

Serving as Back Room Consultant

This is where you start. As a stepparent, your role is to observe, advise silently, and avoid taking a direct role. That means that establishing limits and enforcing consequences is not up to you. Defer to the bioparents (yes, both of them!) for the decisions and the implementation.

Does this mean withdrawing and saying "Whatever" with a shrug? Absolutely not. You are a concerned party, and you have a great deal of influence. Just keep your suggestions between you and your partner for a while. If you're feeling powerless, remember that you do have a strong, active role to play: modeling behavior, respecting your stepkids and your partner, practicing positive reinforcement techniques. Patience. Your stepchild is a small wild animal in the woods. You need to tame her and convince her you won't bite. Then and only then she'll listen to you.

Tales from the Parent Zone

Whether at the park, during a rocky bedtime, or when she was eating too much Halloween candy, it took a couple of years for my little friend Stephanie to listen—at all—when her stepfather corrected her behavior. Experts say that it takes about two years of stepfamily life for kids to accept discipline from a stepparent. Experts also say it takes about two years for strong, trusting relationships between stepparents and stepchildren to form. Coincidence? I don't think so.

Standing Up for Your Own Needs

At the same time that you are leaving disciplinary matters to your partner the bioparent, you need to stand up for your own rights and needs as a member of the household. You have the right to consideration and privacy. You have the right to being considered a full member of the household, and a partner to the children's bioparent. If you're feeling squashed or quashed, you can and should assert your rights. This may lead to conflict, so enlist the support of your partner before you begin. (Standing up for your rights is part of modeling proper behavior, and also part of feeling good about yourself and your situation.)

Behave Yourself!

Save the whips, chains, and punishment until you've built up a reserve of respect and affection with your stepkids. And then take those whips, chains, and punishment and throw them in the trash can where they belong!

Operating as Designated Enforcer

As time goes on, your stepchildren should begin to understand that you and their bioparent are a disciplinary unit (check out the concept of the "Unified Front" in Chapter 18). As time goes on, they will begin to see you as more of an authority figure. Now you can begin being a designated enforcer of already established rules and limits. Step lightly! Your role is an enforcer, and your line, if questioned, is: "Hey Buddy, I'm just an officer doin' my job!" (or something along those lines). Try citing the authorities: "Your dad wants you to hang your clothes in the closet, Suzanne," and, "The family rule says, "No eating between dinner and bedtime."

Even though you are now an enforcer, you should not be the only enforcer. The bioparent still takes the primary role (and in most combined families, it will stay this way).

Collaborating with Your Partner

Of course, you've been doing some collaboration all along, even though much of it has been behind closed doors. Now it's time to start actively participating in family meetings (Chapter 6) and family decisions, and lending your opinion and feelings about family values and rules. You'll help divvy up responsibilities (and possibly hand out allowance), and help decide on limits, expected behavior, and consequences. In short, you are now one of the authorities in the household. And as an adult, you do have more decision-making power than the kids.

Keep in mind that this is still wholly collaborative, and you are helping, not making the decisions on your own. You will always be a collaborative member of the partnership (as is your partner, the bioparent). The fifth and final step (below) doesn't wipe out the collaborative aspects of all discipline in a stepfamily.

Performing Spontaneous Disciplinary Decision-Making

Sometimes a spontaneous, instantaneous decision is called for, and you're the only one there. This step, performing spontaneous disciplinary decision-making, should only be done by you if you've lived together as a family for a while, and everybody is comfortable with your role. Save your solo decisions for times when your partner is not available for you to confer with and there are no established consequences for this particular misbehavior that you can fall back on.

Behave Yourself!

In all families, and especially in stepfamilies where people don't have a lot of experience living together, kids need to understand the expectations, the rules, and the limits.

It's a Good Idea!

It's not just the kids who will feel uncomfortable if you start imposing discipline too soon. Your partner may be uncomfortable, too. You may have some intimacy and relationship issues to work on before the bioparent is ready to let you make disciplinary choices.

Whatever You Decide: Respect the Established Family Values

Don't march in with your own ideas, values, limits, rules, and consequences and override the structures and beliefs already in place. Any decisions you make should be based on family values, rules, and limits. You need to know what these are, and you shouldn't have to guess. Have them defined for you (this will help everybody get his expectations in order).

What if you don't agree or approve? Of course, things can change. But take any change very slowly, or you'll come smack up against a giant wall of stepchild resistance.

It's a Good Idea!

It's not just discipline that's complicated when you're living in step! For information on everything from dating a parent to dealing with the ex to stepparent adoption to the complicated legal aspects of writing permission slips for stepkids, every stepparent or potential stepparent needs *The Complete Idiot's Guide to Stepparenting* by Ericka Lutz (yup, that's me!).

Stepfamily Discipline Issues

All families have issues. Stepfamilies, however, while sharing the average issues with fully biological families, have a set of issues particular to their circumstances and configuration. Here are a few of the major, common issues stepparents face, and some suggestions for getting through them. You'll see that there are special sections for stepfathers and stepmothers, too; that's because, while most of the issues are the same, there are some issues particular to stepparents of each gender.

Who Are You, Anyway, Bub?

You live with this child, share her life, and suddenly, "You're not my parent, you can't tell me anything!" Ouch. That hurts (and believe me, your stepchild knows it). What can you do? Presuming you haven't moved through Jamie K. Keshet's stages too fast (see above), you can try the following approach. It will soon defuse the situation:

1. Remain utterly calm, and look as detached as you can possibly be.

2. Acknowledge the truth by saying, "You're right, I'm not your parent."

3. Follow it up with, "But I am an adult living in this house, and I'm in charge. These are the rules." Or, "I live here, and this is my house, so yes, I do have some input." You can even assert, "I'm your stepparent, and you're wrong, you do need to listen to me."

The secret here is the calm manner. Dig down deep, and get serene.

When Two Sets of Family Rules Collide

Different households have different approaches to life. When there's more than one family involved in a child's upbringing, life can get very complicated. Shared custody or frequent visitation are usual in most divorces, so, as a stepparent, you'll likely deal with the issue of different disciplinary approaches in each household. Here are some things to keep in mind:

➤ Kids are smart. They can handle different sets of rules and limits, provided those rules and limits are explicit.

➤ You and your partner have little control over the rules and customs at the ex's house. All you can do is stress your own values, and trust that your behavior modeling will rub off on your stepchild.

➤ When it comes to your partner's ex, don't butt in. Their relationship (including their own possibly unhealthy dynamic) is none of your business!

➤ The only time you and your partner should interfere with life at the ex's house is if you suspect or know that there is abuse—mental, emotional, sexual, or physical—going on. As your stepchild's ally, you do have a responsibility to do something. See Chapter 24 for suggestions.

Behave Yourself!

When your stepchild pits you against his bioparent—"But at my dad's house we"—you might want to reply sarcastically, "Do I look like your dad?" Refrain. Sarcasm might feel good to you at the time, but kids don't understand this kind of humor, and it only confuses or hurts them. Carefully explain (again!) that different households have different ways of doing things.

Discipline as a Stepdad

Stepdads have their own set of issues, and though many areas of stepparenting are easier for stepfathers than stepmothers, discipline is an area of particular concern. Discipline is a no-win situation for many stepdads. As a stepdad, here are some things to keep in mind before your start taking a disciplinary role with your stepchild:

➤ Many stepfathers jeopardize their relationship with their stepchild by stepping in as a disciplinarian. Laying down the law, being harsh, raising your voice, demanding action, or applying punishment will get you nowhere.

➤ You're not the child's dad, and the more you try to be, the less you'll be accepted. Before you can effectively teach a child discipline, you have to gain her trust and respect.

➤ It's often made worse because many biomothers expect their new partner to take on this job. (Other moms may resent your taking over their parenting roles.)

➤ Little kids are pretty easy to stepfather. They're very likely to accept all aspects of your parenting, even discipline. It's the preteens and teenagers who are more problematic—they'll be very resistant to your authority. Review the parenting style continuum in Chapter 2, and focus on being reasonable, gentle, and strong.

➤ Move slowly into your role as an authority. You have time. Start as a buddy, a mentor, an uncle, or a confidant. Rely on your partner for the authority aspects for quite a while.

Tales from the Parent Zone

Thom, like many stepfathers, is having a hard time because he's been cast as the "heavy" in the family (both he and his new wife Mona are responsible for this). He's trying to impress Mona with his control of the situation, and at the same time, he's struggling to get comfortable with another man's children. Thom's situation is not uncommon. Sometimes a leap into discipline by a stepfather comes from not understanding any other way to deal with a lack of respect. Or sometimes it's in a misguided attempt to "straighten up" a child who is in real disciplinary trouble.

Laying off the authority can be very difficult, especially if your stepkids are out of control, treating you or their mother terribly (or ignoring you completely). First, understand that it's not necessarily personal. Many kids newly "in step" have been used to a lot of independence during and after their mother's divorce. Then, rely on your partner to take control. She is the mother, after all, with all the love, history, and biological ties to give her authority. Communicate with her about what you both want and need from the situation. (Communication is essential for shared parenting; see Chapter 18.) She may need some help with behind-the-scenes support. Do it, and resist the urge to step in and start (metaphorically) swinging.

Here's the rule: The rougher things get, the more gentle you get. Stay involved and concerned, stay positive; provide verbal encouragement and other positive reinforcement. Show respect for your stepkids. Work on liking them (it's not a requirement). Positive prevention truly works.

Discipline as a Stepmom

The word *stepmother* unfortunately conjures up images of Cinderella's and Snow White's evil stepmoms. Stepmothering is a tough job, and according to most experts, it's the most difficult role in the stepfamily. (At the very least, it's the most demanding.) As stepmother, the rest of the family looks to you to be all things to all people, and there's very little thanks involved. Stepmothers often end up feeling overworked and unappreciated (and, alas, sometimes even evil!).

Tales from the Parent Zone

Two years into a stepfamily, and everybody feels fairly comfortable. Discipline by the stepparent is accepted, and trusting relationships have been established. But experts say it takes about seven years to *completely* combine a family. As a longtime stepmother myself, I can tell you that in our case, the experts were right. About seven years into our stepfamily adventure, we all finally felt like a "real" family.

Perhaps the most difficult of all stepmothering tasks is discipline. How do you work through the difficulties and gain satisfaction? Believe me, it's possible; it just takes time, patience, and planning. Here are some suggestions for handling disciplinary issues and thriving as a nonwicked stepmother:

➤ It's not your job. Don't let your partner dump the discipline on you! Work as a partnership, following the progression of the "The Disciplinary Evolution of a Stepparent."

➤ Never, ever, ever badmouth the biomother. I don't care how horrible, crazy, and demanding she may be. It will lose you the trust of your stepkids; it will begin a war with the stepmom; it's bad news. Confide in a friend, vent (privately) with your partner, but never let your stepkids hear a peep out of you.

➤ Part of modeling good behavior is letting your stepkids, particularly your stepdaughters, see you as a strong woman. Don't put up with being a pushover, don't let yourself be taken advantage of, and stand up for your own rights. You're doing your kids a favor to model a strong, reasonable person.

It's a Good Idea!

If all the parents (both biological and step) get along (or at least appear to), a tremendous weight is lifted from the kids. Try as hard as you can. Bite your tongue. Be noble. Pinch yourself. Do whatever it takes to maintain civility in front of the kids.

➤ At least for a while, think about presenting yourself in an alternative role to "mother," especially if the kids' mother is still living. How about taking the model of an aunt, a big sister, a wise older friend of the family? This role is less threatening than marching in and trying to "mother" the kids.

Combined Stepfamily Issues

You've got a family, your partner has a family, and when the two combine, you may face a collision of parenting approaches, family values, limits, and consequences. (Your kids might have some conflicts, too, and there's more on this in Chapter 19.) The preliminary work here happens between you and your partner, as you talk about what is important to both of you, and how you are going to teach those values.

➤ Where there have been different approaches to discipline, try and incorporate some of each approach as you move toward a middle way of doing things. Suddenly switching to one family's customs would be a disaster in the making.

➤ You're altering patterns (and kids hate this), so go slowly. You'll need to hash out a new family values statement, and create new family rules that everybody can live with. Start doing this in family meetings.

➤ As you move toward a more cohesive parenting partnership, each of you should follow "The Disciplinary Evolution of a Stepparent" approach with your stepkids, while remaining the primary parent for your own kids.

➤ Remember that limits are particular for individuals (no matter whose biological child he is, his limits should be appropriate for him, and his development).

➤ Be explicit with your partner about who can enforce what rules with whom. This will help you avoid fighting about or feeling defensive over how your partner is treating your child (and vice versa).

Who Lives Where, and with Whom?

Stepfamily life can get complicated. Maybe the kids of one partner live with you, and the kids of the other do not, and only visit occasionally. Maybe you and your partner have full custody of her two stepkids. Maybe there's only one child (yours), and you have him all summer every summer, and not in between. Or perhaps there's a bunch of kids from each of you—and they sometimes live with you, sometimes don't. There's no one configuration of stepfamilies, so it's hard to make generalizations about disciplinary issues (hey, it's hard to make generalizations about anything!).

When You're a Custodial Stepparent

When you are the stepparent of a child who lives with you (at least part of the time), you have some real authority. It's your home. Yes, of course you make decisions. Actually, the dangers arrive when you are too assertive about the rules. At least at first.

➤ Your stepchild will feel best about the family rules when she has at least a minimal say in them. That's what family meetings are for!

➤ You can speed the acceptance process (you of her, she of you) by spending special time and time as a family together on a regular basis (more on these in Chapter 5). The better you know her, the better you can assure that both of you are having your needs met. Spending special time with a kid who doesn't much want you in her life can be very unpleasant. If it's not working (or if she refuses to go out with you), start small. Watch her favorite TV show with her. Bring her hot cocoa when she's studying for a test. Keep inviting her out. And when she does agree, keep it short (an hour trip to the beach or the mall). Keep the conversation light—this isn't the time for a heavy encounter session.

➤ A stepchild who has moved into your house, or joined you and your partner in moving to a new place, will feel rootless, especially if her parents have only recently split up. Give her some responsibility for making family choices such as how the living room is going to be laid out (that means relinquishing your tight grasp on how the living room looks!). It's better that your stepchild feels comfortable, and that her opinions and tastes are welcomed, than it is that your living room is laid out perfectly.

➤ Make sure your stepchild's privacy is respected, and make sure she has a place (maybe even just a shelf or a cubby) where nobody meddles. Then don't meddle! Respect is a big part of teaching discipline.

The Half-and-Half Custodial Step

More and more divorced families share child custody. Sometimes the child moves back and forth from one bioparent to another once a week, more often it's every few days. It's a complicated arrangement (and complication is always a challenge!). The toughest period will always be around transitions, the comings and the goings. Transitions are where you'll see the most misbehavior, and the most distress. Give your stepchild time to adjust. Be compassionate—and back off! Some families develop rituals to aid the child. (For instance, Dad picks him up at the bus stop Friday night and they immediately go to the video store to rent a movie for the weekend, they come home, read a book together, and then join Stepmom for dinner.)

Remember that the child is under a lot of stress every time he changes houses: He's reminded that his parents are no longer together (and even if this is a good thing, it still hurts) and he has to remember two ways of doing everything.

Visitation Discipline

At least, if your stepchild lives with you full- or part-time, you have some say over her behavior. If you don't, your partner does. If you don't have custody over your stepchild, you probably will have to deal with "The Visit." Perhaps "The Visit" happens regularly (in which case you all have a chance to get to know each other). But what if your stepchild only visits once in a long while?

The child who doesn't live with you is getting virtually all of her disciplinary teachings from somebody else. Sometimes you won't agree with the way she's being raised. Unfortunately, in terms of issues like manners and speech patterns, you can't do much but model the behavior you would like to see. Try to be lenient. Utterly gross behavior is always unacceptable, but it will cause tensions and resentment if you try to give her a crash course in manners. (It also won't "stick" if she's going back to the same environment after a short visit with you.)

For other behavior and misbehavior, the family rules still apply, of course, and it's up to your partner to use education and reminders to make sure that they are held to ("In this house, we use words to solve our problems, Joannie, and we don't hit.").

When Your Kids Have a Stepparent

If there's a stepparent in the house (and it's not you), your challenge is to let them develop their own relationship while continuing to be the primary parent.

If it's your ex who has a new partner, things can be rougher. Perhaps you'll get lucky and like your ex's new partner. People aren't always that lucky. If you don't like your ex's new love, it can be very upsetting when you think about your kids spending time in that household. Your children's stepparent can feel very intrusive (particularly since she does have some influence on your kids). Here's where you need to breathe deeply, and trust that your own influence is vital to your children.

It's a Good Idea!

It's hard to fathom, but your child's stepparent (your ex's new love) may even have some good things to teach him. The world is a big place, and there's room for many influences in your child's life, both good and bad. You're raising a resourceful child who can make positive choices. Trust him, and trust your teaching.

➤ Your ex's new partner may actually become an ally, at least where your child is concerned.

➤ You are allowed to hate your ex's new partner, but don't badmouth! (It's your ex who has to spend time with that horrible person. Isn't there some satisfaction in that?)

➤ You may not get an accurate picture of the disciplinary details at your ex's house. Kids often leave essential details out of their stories.

➤ If you have disciplinary differences with the way they do things in that other household, deal with your ex, rather than with your ex's new partner. But remember, unless there are real abuses going on, you really have no right to make an issue of it.

➤ Don't try to undo or remedy your ex's disciplinary mistakes. Support your child, and concentrate on doing what you can at your house.

➤ If you have complaints with your ex, try to deal with them away from your child. Don't put him in the middle! Don't force him to choose sides! (Everybody loses in that scenario.)

The Least You Need to Know

➤ Almost half of the population is in a stepfamily.

➤ Divorce generates misbehavior. Expect behavior shifts and problems to be magnified.

➤ Discipline is the biggest challenge to the stepparent.

➤ Go slow! Taking too active a disciplinary role too soon is a stepparenting disaster.

➤ The better all the parents get along, the smoother stepfamily life.

➤ Don't ever badmouth a child's parent or stepparent (no matter how despicable they may be).

➤ It takes time to combine a family. You'll get there!

Chapter 18

Double Discipline: The Tag-Team

> **In This Chapter**
>
> ➤ Introducing your parenting partner!
>
> ➤ Deciding on discipline and presenting a unified front
>
> ➤ Tips for when your partner's away
>
> ➤ Working with friends, neighbors, and the extended family
>
> ➤ Holding firm to your disciplinary values

In this great adventure of child rearing, you are not alone! A child is raised by his parents, his extended family, and his personal network of teachers, adult friends, baby-sitters, mentors, coaches, and other community members. That means that no matter how your particular family is configured, you, the parent, have at least one other parenting partner. Most parents have a number of other adults around who are involved, and influential, in their child's upbringing.

This chapter is devoted to your relationship to the other adults in your child's life including the primary one—your child's other parent—and the extended family, the baby-sitter, and the village meddler.

Parents, Team Players, and the Unified Front

No two parents take exactly the same approach to running a household, hanging with the kids, resolving conflict, or granting privileges. That's okay. Kids easily accommodate to the differences in parenting styles and activities.

Kids do, however, need to know what is expected of them. When your primary parenting partner is your child's other parent, the most important disciplinary issue is consistency. (Let's assume the two of you live together. I discuss the issues of single

Words to Parent By

A *parenting partner* is any adult who shares parenting or child care responsibilities with you. It includes any adults who have direct involvement with, or influence on, your child's life.

Words to Parent By

A *unified front* is an agreed-upon approach to an issue. In disciplinary matters, it's best to at least have the appearance of total agreement. For instance, say you think dessert is to be eaten only after dinner, and your partner feels that anytime is the right time for chocolate. You might give in, for the sake of the unified front, but continue to negotiate privately.

parents with their ex and the challenges of stepparenting in Chapter 17.) Consistency doesn't mean "sameness." It's fine to apply values and beliefs differently, as long as there's a basic family understanding of what is important. Kids need clear, consistent guidelines, and they need a basic family commonality of valuesand beliefs (there's your family value statement in Chapter 6).

Just on a purely pragmatic level, you and your partner need to establish some disciplinary guidelines: rules, limits, and consequences. Unless you're joined at the hips (I mean permanently!), you're not going to be able to check with each other about every little thing.

You and your partner are not Tweedledum and Tweedledee—you are separate individuals and, though you may share some values and ideas, there is likely much you don't agree about. This carries over to discipline. There will be times when the two of you just don't agree about an approach, a limit, a consequence, a response. How then, can you be consistent with your child about discipline?

Consistency can be planned for! Parenting and value differences are for you and your parenting partner to work out, privately. In "public," in front of your kids, consistency is vital. If you're not consistent, your kids are going to play you off, one parent against another. You need to develop a unified front, that is, an agreed approach to the issues.

How do you develop a unified front? And how do you do it when you have different values or different approaches to parenting?

Developing a Unified Front

Working out your unified front may not require a "big" discussion, though it probably will be an ongoing process. If you've developed a family value statement and worked out family rules (Chapter 6), then you're well on your way. Here are a few essentials about the unified front:

➤ If you have a question about family policy, discuss it with your partner.

➤ If your partner makes a snap decision, you need to support it. If you make a snap decision, your partner should support it. You can (and should) discuss your responses, beliefs, feelings, and suggestions for the future. But do it later, when the two of you are alone.

➤ As much as possible, avoid having one person make unilateral decisions (especially if you tend to disagree).

When You Need to Talk About It

Every partnership will have differences of opinion on how to handle certain disciplinary issues. Undiscussed, these differences will fester. It's important to clearly establish where there is a difference in disciplinary approach, and where there is a difference in the underlying values. Ideally, your partner shares your values about the importance of taking a positive, rather than a punitive, parenting approach. (Say, maybe your partner needs to read this book!)

What if you love your partner, shiver under his touch, adore the French toast he makes you every morning, but, alas, differ with him on certain parenting values, including disciplinary approach? It can be a scary thing to contemplate discussing something as volatile as discipline (since it cuts right to the heart of parenting philosophy), but it's crucial, for the sake of all of you.

As you meet to "hash out" your feelings, keep an open mind. Plan ahead and make it pleasant—take an evening drive and park near a view, have a wine and cheese date. Make the grandparents take the kids out for the evening. When you're relaxed, loving each other, and in a good mood—now's the time to discuss discipline.

➤ Bring up disciplinary values issues privately. This isn't a conversation for the kids! Make sure the atmosphere is safe for raising disagreement—try active listening, and try for an open mind as you listen.

➤ Each of you might consider spending a little time defining your basic disciplinary philosophy (you may think you know how you and your partner feel and believe, but give it a try anyway. There is something very defining, powerful, and often surprising about putting your philosophy and feelings into words.

It's a Good Idea!

At times, you and your partner will disagree about an issue, yet one of you will feel more strongly than the other. She: "I cannot allow the kids to talk about bodily functions at the table!" He: "Well, I don't love it, but I feel issues need to be addressed when they come up. But, I see it really matters more to you than to me, so let's go with your feelings."

Behave Yourself!

Discussions about discipline should, ideally, be planned. Why ruin a good (and rare) date? Picture this: You're dressed to the nines, your sweetie looks terrific, and you gaze at each other across the table through a haze of delicious food, wine, and raging pheromones. A leg brushes yours under the table. Your eyes lock, and your darling whispers, "If Mary socks Marty one more time, I'm going to ground her for a year!"

➤ Your partner may be taking a different path to achieve the same goals, of respecting your children, honoring their autonomy, and nurturing their needs. Look for the positive intent!

➤ Clarify the problem. Is this really about differing values? Or do you have the same value, but a different approach?

It's a Good Idea!

If things get too "hot" when you're talking about discipline with your partner, take a break, focus on transforming the "heat" into passion, and leave the discipline for another day.

➤ If you are meeting about a specific incident, try to separate out the incident from old hurts and disappointments.

➤ Discipline is about learning—in order to be a "well-behaved" parenting duo, you two may need to do a little problem-solving (see instructions for the problem-solving process in Chapter 19).

Discipline is a tough area for all parents. It touches deep nerves—our values, our histories, our sore spots. We all get passionate about these issues. Watch that, in your passion, you aren't burning each other.

Manipulation: It's Not Just for Politicians Anymore!

Hoorah! You've created your unified front! You and your partner are consistent and supportive of each other's decisions (at least in public).

Uh-oh. Problems. Darling Darla likes warm milk before bed. You've been concerned about her teeth, and last night you laid down the law, "No. Darla, if you want warm milk, you have to tell me early enough so that you have time to drink it before you wash up, because if you don't, the milk will cause cavities during the night." Darla complains and whines and cries, and whine and cries and begs, and finally goes to sleep. The next night, it's your partner's turn to get Darla to bed. Alas, you've forgotten to tell her about your conversation with Darla. "May I have some warm milk?" she asks. "Well," your partner answers, and, not knowing the history of this issue, agrees. Ooh, manipulative Darla! How could you have raised such a devious little skunk!

Look, Darla is a kid, and that means she doesn't really have much power over much of her life. Manipulation is a common way for kids to gain control over their lives, and a certain amount of it is normal and healthy. On the other hand, you won't have to fall into your child's little trap quite so often if you and your partner train yourselves to check with each other as often as possible—even in as benign a situation as this.

When You Don't Agree

Say you've hashed it out, and you just don't agree. Is that it? The end of the relationship? Or does one of you need to give in now, just lay down like a carpet to get walked on? Of course not. Discipline is a process. There are areas where you will agree, and use those as a foundation to build from. Try problem-solving your way to a unified front (there's tools for that in Chapter 19). Remember that you may disagree, but you need to respect each other's opinions.

Discipline is hard—it may be the hardest part of parenting (well, those early years of sleep deprivation are right up there). Commit yourself to working out your differences, and realize it may take some time. Differences in opinion are a common cause of break-ups, though, so it's really worth it to spend the time. You may even need to spend money (therapy isn't cheap)—but it's worth it to clarify and enhance your relationship.

But What If? The Unanticipated Situation

Back in Chapters 7 and 9, I discussed setting limits and consequences ahead of time. Of course, you can't anticipate everything. Parenting is a think-on-your-feet activity. What do you do when Georgianne suddenly and surprisingly is discovered painting the cat, or Paul is busted for roller-blading through the halls at school? I highly doubt you and your partner have prepared for those exigencies!

That's Between You, Me, and the Kids?

The time has come for a little discussion to figure out what to do next. So, will this discussion be conducted as a private chat between the two of you from which you'll return as a unified front? Or, will Georgianne or Paul be invited? Should you, perhaps, mark it down as an agenda item for the next family meeting? Where and how will you and your parenting partner figure out the correct course of action? You have a few approaches possible to you:

The Very Private Partners—These are the parents who discuss and decide everything in private before coming back out of the bedroom. "We'll see," "Let me talk with your mother," and "We'll discuss it," are the three most common statements in the household. In this kind of family, the child goes to the parents, presents her "case" and then waits for the judges to return from chambers to announce her decision. These parents have the concept of "unified front" down. The advantage? She can't turn one parent against the other, because she doesn't know either parent's perspective or know if there are any conflicts between them. The problem? Little Juniorette never sees a decision in progress. She doesn't understand how to resolve conflict, because she's never seen fair fighting or conflict-resolution in action.

The Everybody's-Got-a-Vote Family—This family spends so much time airing their dirty laundry that the kids have forgotten what it looks like clean. All members of the family are equal, and if Mom and Dad disagree about a disciplinary issue, they all work it out together—often after a loud, loud argument. When things are resolved, everybody knows how the decision was reached. The kids have grown into young conflict resolution experts who know firsthand that people who love each other can scream, disagree, and then problem-solve their way to serenity. Alas, poor Junior and Juniorette never have any privacy and, because they know exactly where each of their parents stands on an issue, there's lots of side-taking and power-mongering as part of daily life.

The Perfect People—This family doesn't exist (let's get that straight right now), but if they did, they'd act like this: Mom and Dad have a deep intuitive understanding about when to discuss it in the bedroom, when to discuss it alone with their child, and when to raise it as an issue in a family meeting.

Good Cop, Bad Cop

Don't gang up on the poor kid! Just because you're working closely with your parenting partner doesn't mean you both have to be involved with every conversation, every active and proactive listening session, or every problem-solving process. At times, two parents is overkill. Take turns with the discipline (I don't mean a scheduled rotation, just an informal sharing). It can help to have only one parent play the "heavy." Just make sure that it's not a permanent role. Worried about it? If you've effectively established your unified front, your kids will understand that discipline comes from the both of you, no matter which of you is laying down the law.

When the Partner's Away

Your parenting partner isn't always around to consult with, and neither are you. How do you maintain the unified front if there's only you? When should you make speedy decisions, and when should you wait until you can talk with your partner?

Wait a Moment

Okay. Your partner is away for a few hours or a few days and something big comes up, something you've never talked about, something bizarre. Allen wants to pierce his tongue. Or Suzanne has pierced her tongue. Roberta is caught stealing kids' lunch money at school. Lance belts the teacher, Louise sasses the preacher. You're the only parent around, so you have to decide what to do. Wait a moment. Do you?

Here's a revolutionary thought—why can't you wait? Come on. You've been talking about the need to slow down in your life (I've heard you!). So take five—minutes, hours, days—and wait to make a decision until you can consult with your partner. Tell your child that you need to talk with his other parent, and that your response will happen—after a little while. Most of the time, important things can wait.

"And I Mean Now!"

Then again, time and tide wait for no parent, and it may be up to you to make a quick, reasonable, unilateral judgment call. Aha! You and your partner may not have discussed this particular emergency, but all those discussions and negotiations laid the groundwork for the decision you're about to make. You can make an educated guess about what your partner will think.

Partners Need Trust

Step back and trust your partner to parent your child. It's sometimes hard to believe that your parenting partner knows as much as you do, cares as much as you do, and makes the right decisions as often as you do. When your partner makes a judgment call, support it, even as you know that you would have approached the issue differently.

Parenting together means trusting that your partner's intentions are good. People have different ways of doing things, even within a family. You might allow your child to eat candy before dinner—as long as she eats dinner, while your partner may insist that dinner happens first. It doesn't matter, as my old pal Peggy used to say, "There's more than one way to skin a cat," and either approach gets dinner eaten. Appreciate the ways your partner enhances your child's life. There's room for more than one approach. Kids easily learn to tolerate differences.

"Wait Until Your Father Gets Home!"

Way back in the olden days (oh, 30 years ago or so), almost everybody divvied up the responsibilities by gender and the statement, "You just wait until your father gets home, young lady" echoed throughout the land. Hoorah! We're not so limited now! Don't push disciplinary responsibilities, decisions, and actions onto your partner, and don't let them be lumped onto you. Keep both parents empowered. While you might want to wait until you see your partner to make any big decisions, it's cruel and ineffective to leave your child completely hanging. At least have a talk about it!

Tales from the Parent Zone

Life sure is better for women since the Women's Movement began, but the break-neck pace of Millennium living has stresses of its own and sometimes, Mama, I'm just so tired. As the old jingle goes, these days, women are expected to: "Bring home the bacon. Fry it up in the pan. Never, never let you forget you're a man." Alas, we're also expected to: Raise the pig for the bacon. Slaughter it. Cure it. Slice it. Remodel the kitchen and add a fan over the stove. Forge the steel for the pan. Light the pilot for the stove. Fix the stove if it breaks, and so on.

Discipline and Other Adults

Along with your child's other parent, your primary parenting partner, you have a number of secondary parenting partners. This section is about your relationship with them.

First, Flexibility

I once heard a story about Charles Berlitz, the guy who invented the Berlitz language courses. He grew up in a family where his mother, father, and live-in grandmother each spoke a different language to him. Instead of being chronically confused, little Charles thrived. Not only did he understand and speak all the languages, he knew with whom to use which language, and when very young, he began inventing his own language, because he thought that's what humans did.

Behave Yourself!

I said "flexible," not "floppy!" Flexibility is vital, but kids need to know what *is* expected of them. The basic message about values, rules, limits, and consequences within the family must be consistent!

Just as kids who are raised in families where every adult speaks a different language thrive and become multilingual, so exposing your children to a variety of disciplinary styles fosters flexibility. Flexibility is key to mental health.

Your child will experience other parenting and disciplinary styles from relatives, friends' parents, teachers, coaches, and members of the community. As your child expands her horizons, keep checking in with her. Keep communicating—you want your child to come to you if she has an uncomfortable experience with another adult.

Tales from the Parent Zone

Few families currently resemble the classic 1950s description of the perfect nuclear family—mom, dad, two kids, dog, white picket fence. I know a lot of people, but none of them match that old Norman Rockwellesque "norm." Hey, what's with that fence, anyway? Symbolically, it shuts out the rest of the world. Unfortunately, it also fences the little family in.

Good Behavior and the Extended Family

The shape and configuration of family structures has changed radically, and many families miss the intense involvement of other relatives in child rearing. They get by without the cousins to baby-sit and Grandpa to teach little Lulu to drive. It's too bad—actively involving other family members in your child's life is good for everybody concerned. You get a break, your child has a wider circle of people to love and learn from, and Grandma, Gramps, and the aunts and uncles get to share the love and involvement, too.

Hey, of course it's not always a walk in the woods! Relationships are hard! The more parenting partners you have the more complex the situation. What should your response be when Aunt Prunella and Junior lie to you about sharing a beer, or Grandpa keeps threatening to "whup his little heinie if he can't use his dang fork." Here are a few suggestions:

➤ It's easy to get overwhelmed by family members or in-laws. This is your child, and you and your partner make the rules and limits, especially about moral and safety issues. Assert yourself ("Susan is too young to drink and that is that!"), don't listen to mocking ("Aw, loosen up, you were drinking beer at 11!"), and let your primary parenting partner know that you expect back-up. If your partner confronts the relative, be an active, supportive ally.

➤ Let the relatives know your position on spanking and other corporal punishment. Everybody has a bottom line. ("Nobody hits my child.")

➤ You are your child's ally too, and, now matter how uncomfortable it makes you feel, it's your responsibility to stand up for him ("Aunt Lucy, don't ever call Jimmy 'stupid.'").

➤ Be flexible, yourself. Different people have different approaches to child-rearing, and the trade off for the gift of having extended family in your child's life is a loss of control. Things won't always get done your way.

➤ Ideas have changed about child rearing, and different generations understand children and discipline differently. If your parents or in-laws are part of the fabric of your child's life, you may experience some conflict. Some you can explain to your child as a difference in age or style: "In Grandma's day, children were to be seen and not heard. We know you have a lot to say, and that you have a right to say it. Tell you what, at her house, let's all respect her beliefs as much as we can by trying not to interrupt."

Grown Friends: Indulgence and Love

My daughter Annie is a fortunate child; like a small but powerful spider, she's woven a sticky web around her, and caught a large number of adults. Friends of mine, friends of my husband's, members of our community—all are deeply "stuck" on Annie, and all have, over the course of time, developed individual relationships with her. For the most part, these relationships with her adult friends have little to do with "discipline." Annie is possibly at her best behaved when she is with her adult friends (why not? She's showered with love and attention!). On the other hand, they have everything to do with discipline! She's learning how to behave in the world both through noticing how other adults do it, and by experiencing the positive feedback she gets when she is considerate, thoughtful, charming, and intelligent.

Baby-Sitters

Baby-sitters, like substitute teachers, "don't get no respect." The most well-behaved child—say, the child who doesn't have bedtime issues—will often turn into a demon-possessed little terror. You can't expect baby-sitters to enforce family rules (you just aren't paying them enough) but you can expect them to respect your family's values. Establish the guidelines with your child and let him know that you expect him to adhere to them. "Bedtime is eight o'clock. When Sherri tells you to wash up and go to bed, I expect you to march." If there is a history of trouble, advise him of the consequences. "If I hear that you were rude to Sherri by refusing to go to sleep, you will spend tomorrow evening writing her a note of apology instead of carving your Halloween pumpkin." Note that, in this example, the emphasis of the consequence is on the rude behavior, not going to bed late. The baby-sitter deserves to be treated respectfully.

On the other hand, it's important to listen to your child's experience with the baby-sitter. If your child has a lot of trouble with her, or is seriously unhappy, you should consider getting another sitter.

Often baby-sitters bring their own beliefs and disciplinary values into your household. A short-term baby-sitter should not be actively teaching your kids discipline. Instead, she should rely on modeling and respecting the family values. A longer-term baby-sitter should enforce family rules, but be careful about asserting her own.

When I was a child, my mom went away for a two-week trip, and my parents hired a woman to take care of my sister and me during the afternoons until my dad came home from work. This woman was convinced that my sister, Jessica, and I were lacking in discipline, that is, we couldn't resist temptation. One day, she placed a plate of nonpareil chocolate candies in front of us on the table, and told us we weren't allowed to eat any in order for us to learn self-control. Then she left the room, leaving us

It's a Good Idea!

The disciplinary relationship between kids and baby-sitters is well explored and documented in the comics. Remember "Calvin and Hobbes"? Remember "Dennis the Menace"?

It's a Good Idea!

Child-care workers and baby-sitters are undervalued in this society. As parents, it's important that you like and respect your baby-sitter, and that you demonstrate your respect, and the value you place on her role in your family, by paying her a fair wage.

alone for a good 20 minutes. I don't remember if we did or didn't resist—I do remember that my dad fired her the next day after we came to him crying. She had overstepped her bounds—it was not her responsibility or her right to give us behavior tests. (She was also going about teaching us discipline in the wrong way by testing our self-control before she'd taught it. The message she sent to Jessica and me was that we were weak, undisciplined children, and that self-control is misery.)

A regular or long-term baby-sitter will be teaching your children discipline. It's important that he understand your values and family rules, and it's important that you ask him, in the initial interview, how he teaches discipline, and how he handles conflict. If you cannot come to an agreement, he's probably not the sitter for you.

Other Kids' Parents

It's instructive for your child to learn how other parents parent. As your child begins to spend more time socially in other families, you may hear your child whine a little ("Laura's mom lets us eat cake as a snack! How come we can't?"). On the flip side, your child will learn just what a lucky child she is to be parented by you!

There's more about other parents parenting your child in Chapter 14, "Socializing Struggles and Success," and Chapter 19, "Wanna Trade?".

Tales from the Parent Zone

While, alas, it's not against the law for some other kid's parent to berate your child, hitting your child isn't allowed. This issue should rarely (if ever) come up. Even parents who might use corporal punishment on their own kids would probably never use it on yours. Spencer's best friend Taylor's parents regularly spanked Taylor, but never (luckily!) touched Spencer. I think they believed, on some level, that Taylor was their "property" and that Spencer (who was not their child) was the property of his own parents. They respected Spencer's parent's "property," and left "it" up to them.

The Influence of Teachers and Coaches

When it comes to teaching your child discipline, the "other" adults in your child's life (his teachers, his coaches) can be just the ticket. Your child won't always listen to you—shocking, but true! Fourteen-year-old Anthony desperately wanted a motorcycle. His parents, dead set against it, refused to even consider it. They talked with him. They showed him pictures of motorcycle accident victims. They pleaded. They cried. Anthony began saving his allowance, working odd jobs, and papering his room with motorcycle posters. His parents, in despair, called in his soccer coach to help.

Coach took Anthony out one day in the afternoon to get some ice cream. They were a long time coming home, and when Anthony returned, he went immediately to his room and turned the music on, loudly. Anthony's parents asked Coach what they'd done. "We stopped off to see my brother," Coach said. "He showed Anthony his ankle-to-hip scar from his accident. Of course it took him a while to explain, it's kind of hard to understand him since he got knocked so hard in the head. At least he was wearing a helmet."

Anthony didn't suddenly change, rip down the motorcycle pictures and join the Glee Club at school (those kinds of epiphanic moments happen mostly in the movies). Over time, however, his parents noticed he was talking less obsessively about bikes, and putting more time into his schoolwork and less into his odd jobs. Anthony had heard his coach, even though his parents had told him the same thing. Sometimes kids find it easier to listen to anybody and his third cousin on his mother's side rather than their parents.

It's a Good Idea!

Want perspective? Step back! At times, people who are concerned and involved in your child's life but who are slightly removed from the situation have a better view of your child's reality.

Ex-Partners and "Other" Parents

If you or your partner shares kids with an "ex," you have a whole other kettle of fish to fry. Check out Chapter 17.

Nosy Neighbors

Everybody has an opinion, especially about raising children, and especially about how you are raising yours! We cannot raise our kids in a vacuum, nor do we want to. And, while it's true that "it takes a village to raise a child," not every single bozo in the village should have equal input. Some people—the cruel and bigoted commissioner, the town creep, and the nosy neighbor—should have little influence at all. Yes, they're part of your child's "village" too, but it's their job to provide examples for your child of how *not* to behave! Not everybody should have a say in your child's upbringing. Especially in the area of discipline.

In some ways, dealing with the "nosy neighbor" is most challenging for parents. This is any person (and it could be a family member) who can't keep silent about your parenting techniques. "I'd never let my son get away with wearing those pants, they're sliding off his rear!" the lady at the post office says. Or it's the man in the supermarket who, mistaking my tiny six-year-old daughter for a much younger child, grabbed the gum from her hand and announced loudly, "Children can choke on gum! You're a terrible mother!" Or, it's the woman who walks by as your eight-year-old is screaming and yelling at you in public (something you're not happy about, either) and says, "Take a belt to that boy. You're letting him get away with murder. He's gonna be out shooting up schoolyards if you don't get him under control."

It seems easy to dismiss criticism like this from people who obviously don't know you, your child, or the situation. You're the parent, you know what's going on, they don't, and why should you care what they think? Yet you do. Parenting is far from a science, and none of us are positive what works on every occasion. Parenting matters to you, you would like approval for your parenting, and hearing criticism—even when it is from clueless strangers—can hurt, and even make you question your approach ("Gee, maybe I should forbid those baggy pants."). While self-questioning is often positive and necessary, too much can be counterproductive. Make your decisions and hold firm—you're doing it for your kids.

The Least You Need to Know

➤ A parenting partner is any adult who shares parenting or child care responsibilities with you. You probably have a number of parenting partners.

➤ Kids can handle flexibility in disciplinary styles, but within the household, they need consistency of values, rules, limits, and consequences.

➤ Hash out your disciplinary value differences privately. This conversation isn't for the kids.

➤ Family members may have different approaches to discipline. As the parent, you determine the bottom line.

➤ At times, other adults can get a "message" through where a parent cannot.

➤ When it comes to parenting decisions, think it through, make a decision, and then hold firm in the face of criticism.

Part 6
The Hardest Parts

Arghhhh!! Those kids! Sometimes life as a parent just feels so hard that you wonder if you'll make it through the next five minutes, let alone the rest of your life.

Nobody ever said it was going to be easy. It can be easier.

Part 6 focuses on the yucky stuff, family fighting, sex (scary!) and drugs (scarier!), challenging children, depression and abuse, and real trouble—the kind where the police officer arrives at your door.

Inside these chapters is a lot of information and support, plus specific tools for handling crises. You'll find conflict resolution exercises and a step-by-step approach about what to do if your child is ever arrested. Read it, take a deep breath, and hang in there.

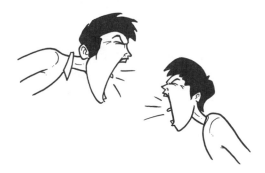

Chapter 19

The Fighting Family

In This Chapter

➤ Hot and cold running anger

➤ Conflict-resolution and fair-fighting techniques

➤ Disengaging from sibling squabbles and tattling

➤ When step-siblings are "involved"

➤ Trading kids? Why not?

As a parent, few things are scarier than the hot, raging, out-of-control feeling that comes when you're truly angry with your child. Few things are worse than the brittle tension in a household where people aren't speaking to each other. And few things are more unpleasant than family fights—between you and the kids, and between siblings. Certainly, conflict and anger are a normal part of life in a family but the destructive energy of both repressed tension and firestorms—yours and your children's—can damage the quality of family life. In this chapter we'll look at rage, anger, and icy withdrawal. We'll look at conflict-resolution skills, and ways to make family fights fair and less destructive. There's lots here on siblings, too.

The Hot Winds of Rage

Rage is a hidden issue in parenting, and a parent with a temper is also often a parent who carries a sense of shame. The vast, vast majority of parents lose their temper, at least occasionally (and the ones who don't, well, we just won't talk to them!). It's not so bad—anger is a valid emotion. People have tempers, and it's good for children to see that:

➤ There are safe ways to express, and then deal with, anger.

➤ Feeling angry will not destroy you.

➤ Parents are human!

Your rage can also be a highly destructive force in your family. As a wanna-be reasonable parent, what happens when you "lose it"? Perhaps you scream, perhaps you spank (even when you don't want to). You may not want to have your children frightened of you, but a parent with an unpredictable or short temper is intimidating. And it feels terrible to lose control like that.

You can begin to control your rage by making a conscious decision to let things fly by, taking yourself out of the situation (a parent time-out!), or, if you feel really out of control, getting some professional counseling to help you decelerate, rather than accelerate, when you get angry. It helps to track your anger, to figure out what makes you angry, and when. (There's more on anger tracking in a moment.)

Tales from the Parent Zone

Robert gets mad and it infuriates his father, who has to fight his instinct to strike back (both physically and verbally). How do *you* handle your child's rage? The challenge comes in resisting this urge, acknowledging the validity of the rage, and getting or keeping the entire situation under control.

Respond, Don't React

Way back in Chapter 8, I gave you a process to go through before responding to something your child has done. Here it is again (annotated for our little anger discussion):

1. React. (Here's where rage tries to take over.)

2. Cool down and gain a little distance. (That's the parent's time-out part; or you can close your eyes and count to 458.)

3. Separate the deed from the doer. ("It's not *you* I hate, it's what you are doing!")

4. Listen to your child, look for the message behind the action, determine the child's needs, figure out how to "honor the impulse," determine your own needs.

5. Then (and only then), respond.

Track Your Anger

If you are having continuing difficulties with rage control, try tracking your anger. Get out your little teeny notebook (the one you got for the exercises in Chapters 4 and 5). Now, simply write down the times you get angry, what you are angry about, and what you do when you are angry. When you begin to understand the causes of your raging as well as methods of anger control and avoidance, you'll be better able to enjoy your child and your life as a parent. Here's a sample "anger tracker" form:

When (date and time)

What made me angry

What was my response?

Wednesday, 7 A.M.

Marjorie absolutely refused to get dressed. Tony chimed in yelling, and we were eight minutes late getting out of the house.

I screamed, and forced Marjorie's shoes on. I totally lost it with Tony, and grabbed his arm, not *very* hard, but a little harshly. I sulked as I drove them to school.

Thursday, 3:47 P.M.

Marjorie and Tony were squabbling about the TV, and kept coming to me to whine about it while I was paying the bills.

I took away TV privileges for the night.

It's a Good Idea!

Is your child suddenly unbearable and losing control? Are you? When was the last time you ate? Scientists have been unsuccessful in proving that blood sugar levels are related to activity and mood, but ask any parent. We know. Got a cranky kid? Feeling rather testy? Did you miss a meal? Food is magic.

Impatience! Tsk, Tsk

Rage and anger are often triggered by impatience. Kids are designed to irritate, it seems, to know and push every button you have. It's normal to sometimes feel irritated and impatient with your children ("Suzanne, stop acting like such a child!" "But I *am* a child, Daddy!"). Yes, you'll be challenged by the task I set before you, but it's an important one: Kids need their parents to be patient with them. Here are some patience tips:

➤ Take a deep breath, let your shoulders relax, and pretend you are a Buddhist monk meditating in a high mountain kingdom, with the world at your feet and all eternity stretching before you. You have time. (Say it often enough, and you might even believe it!)

➤ Empathize with your child. She's on another timeline, she's got her own agenda, and she's got little hands and feet (at least compared to your big dogs!). Remember what it was like to be a kid, with everything moving faster than you?

➤ Understand your child. Seeing her realistically, knowing her strengths and limitations, will help give you patience.

➤ For parents of teens: Keep in mind that your child is on serious, mind-altering "drugs" (otherwise known as raging hormones).

The Icy Chill of Withdrawal

Some people turn their rage inward, withdraw, and simply don't say a word. And the pressure builds. And the pressure builds some more. And though the angry, withdrawn person looks like icy tundra, inside he's like a seething volcano, holding molten lava deep in his core. Perhaps he'll blow, perhaps not. If he blows, it all spews out—old ashes of memory, molten rocks of resentment, lava flows of fury. If he holds it in forever, the internal organs start to go from the pressure of holding in all that rage. Watch out—will it be a heart attack, migraine headaches, or a stroke?

I'm merely suggesting that holding anger in is not a good solution. You may think that nobody will notice, but nobody can avoid noticing that icy glare, or the way you leave the room when the person you are angry with walks in.

How to Use, Not Abuse, Your Anger

Anger is a strong emotion, closely related to passion, and it can be a productive emotion. When you're furious, and you express your anger cleanly and fairly, you teach your child that angry feelings can be expressed in a way that doesn't harm anybody.

How, then, can you manage your anger in a positive way? How can you redirect it? How can you problem-solve your way out of conflict? Here are few suggestions for dealing with anger, frustration, and so on:

➤ Make sure to take enough space so that you can see clearly, without the blood pounding through your eyes and creating a fine, red, veil of rage. Go pound a pillow, cry, tear old newspapers into tiny shreds, or meditate and relax. How about pounding the pillow and crying, then relaxing?

➤ Watch that you're not responding to the lowly straw that broke the camel's back as though the straw is the only reason the back is broken. In other words, if you've had a rough day—you dumped a pot of tea over your lap in the morning, you forgot your report at home before a major client meeting and had to go back for it, and you spilled shoe dye all over your pants, shirt, floor, and wall when it "exploded" as you were trying to open it—don't lose it and belt your kid when he calls you a "dork."

➤ If the world is a grim, hard place today, warn your family that they're in the presence of an ogre. This doesn't give you free rein to act like an ogre. Or, let them know that you're like an airplane out of control. Putting out warning lights on the runway as you attempt an emergency landing might keep others from being crushed as you crash.

➤ Even if your reaction is to utterly blow it, try to pull it together to respond effectively.

➤ Work as hard as you can to express your anger clearly. Use language that demonstrates your emotions, needs, and values. Using "I" statements to state what you are angry about, and what you would like changed, shows your child how strongly you feel about her, and her behavior. (I show you how to build "I" statements in Chapter 3.)

➤ Once a conflict has been resolved, check in with yourself to see how you really feel. Is the anger still there? Find a friend or shrink to vent on, or jot it down in a journal. Don't bottle it up (see "The Icy Chill of With-drawal," above).

It's a Good Idea!

The trick is to use your anger to effectively teach your child discipline while improving your relationship with your child. How? By being clear, direct, and genuine.

Resolving It Right!

There are always conflicts, and that's a good thing! When effectively resolved, conflicts between people can lead to improved understanding and increased closeness. Here are some general tips for resolving conflict (and we'll get into specifics in a moment):

➤ Listen, listen, listen.

➤ Use "I" statements to express your feelings and perspectives.

➤ Don't interrupt.

➤ You can ask questions to clarify, but stay away from "why." ("How" is a better choice.)

➤ Keep your arguments in the present, and stay specific.

➤ Don't dig up old dirt from the past.

➤ Avoid "globalizing" the argument (by using words such as *always, never,* or *should*).

➤ Taboo subjects are taboo—there are certain nasty comments that are off-limits in all relationships.

➤ Keep your requests for behavior changes very specific. Don't ask for a personality transplant.

The Four Ways of Resolving Conflict

When you and your child are having a conflict, there are four basic ways the conflict can be resolved:

1. You can decide how to resolve the conflict. This is the "because I say so," unilateral approach to conflict resolution. It may work, but Junior isn't going to feel any kind of satisfaction.

2. Junior can be the winner of the big decision-making contest. It's he who decides the outcome of the conflict. Feel good? I doubt it.

3. You have the option of resolving the conflict through compromise. If you compromise, you give a little, Junior gives a little, and you come to an agreement. Neither of you necessarily feels great about it, though.

4. Ah, problem-solving! You and Junior can collaborate for a "win-win" (as they say in business school). Yup, it sometimes takes some time to get here, but doesn't it feel good? You bet!

Here It Comes! It's the Problem-Solving Process!

The six-step problem-solving process I'm about to describe applies the talking and listening techniques we've looked at all throughout this book. This process can be done one-on-one with your child, or in a group—for instance, at a family meeting. The problem-solving process's main purpose is to resolve problems and conflicts, but it's more than that—it's a disciplinary technique in that it teaches respect, empathy, logic, and empowers a child by using him as a collaborator on his own problems. Once your child has been through a problem-solving process a couple of times, he'll have had experience in thinking seriously about a problem, applying logic and creativity, arriving at solutions, and acting respectfully and responsibly throughout the process.

Step 1. Understand the child's perspective. It's time to define the problem as your child sees it. Use active listening (introduced in Chapter 3). As you paraphrase what your child has said, make sure to include his feelings as well as his words. Allow him to clarify and correct you. "Jerome, you're upset and angry because Dad and I don't want you to wear your fatigues to school. You say that fatigues are comfortable, that all the other kids wear them, and that we're interfering in your individuality. You also think we are hypocrites, because we've always said we don't believe in school uniforms and dress codes. Now you feel let down and betrayed." Don't jump in with your own opinions, judgments, advice, criticisms, or analysis. You'll have an opportunity to put in your own two cents later.

Step 2. Empathize. Let Jerome know that you understand the problem. "My mother let me wear anything I wanted to school. That is, until I bought a skirt I loved, but that she thought was way too short. Bam, she was back to being the boss! I was furious." Don't go on and on, here. This isn't about you and the miniskirt, this is about Jerome and the fatigues. Step two is simply so Jerome knows you understand his feelings and his point of view.

It's a Good Idea!

As a parent, one of your primary roles in the problem-solving process is as an active listener. Your child probably has more answers to his problems than he knows. Kids are smart. If you listen hard enough, they may just give you the answers you, and they, need.

Step 3. Express your own feelings and opinions. Here it comes—it's your turn now! As you express your feelings and opinions, follow the general tips for resolving conflict, above, including using "I" statements. Keep blame far, far away. "Jerome, I'm concerned about you wearing fatigues to school for a few reasons. One, I know a lot of the third and fourth graders are wearing fatigues and playing war games—throwing fake grenades, forming commando units, shooting, and I don't support that. The teachers held a meeting with the principal to express their concerns that the fatigues are helping create an environment that celebrates war, and I agree. As you know, we've never allowed pretend shooting or toy guns in this house. Also, I understand there have been some problems with kids getting upset because they don't have fatigues. I'm not interested in squashing your creativity or individuality, but I am feeling very concerned and distressed."

Step 4. Hold a brainstorming session to find potential solutions. (Check out Appendix E to find out how.) As you brainstorm ideas, let the ideas flow free but avoid the phrases "You should," "I would," "I think," and "If you ask my advice." (Nobody is asking you your advice.) You and Jerome might come up with (in our example): "Jerome gets to wear a fatigue top or bottom, but not both," "Jerome can wear his fatigues once a week," "Jerome burns his fatigues and starts wearing only tie-dye," and "Jerome drops out of school and joins the army!" Remember that no idea should be evaluated, judged as silly, or squelched as they are coming out.

Step 5. Evaluate the ideas and decide on a trial solution. "Jerome will wear his fatigues once a week, as long as he isn't participating in war games." After you evaluate the brainstorming ideas, agree on a trial solution, think about the four ways of resolving conflict, and try not to compromise, give in, or win. Most problems do have a solution—and your creative brainstorming session may well provide a surprising, and wonderful, answer.

Step 6. Follow up. Put the idea to work, and see how it goes. Then follow up! Check back in with your kid after a couple of days or a week to see how the idea is working out. Is it working? Is it too early to tell? Or is it back to the drawing board?

It's a Fair Fight

What if it's not a problem to resolve—what if it's a fight? What if you really have a bone to pick? Fighting's not always negative. A good, fair fight can clear the air and resolve family problems. Here's a fighting technique that works well with older kids who can understand and want to apply the rules. It's particularly useful when you find your family's fights tend to meander off into old hurts and happenings. In this technique, first the event or situation that provoked the fight is resolved, then any residual feelings about the fight are resolved.

Schedule the fair fight. "Hey Bub, I've got a bone to pick with you about the continuing mess in the bathroom. Let's have one of those fair fights tonight. How's 8, in my bedroom, while the rest of the family is watching that video Dad brought home?"

Find privacy, and a long, appropriate time slot. Allow enough time to really do your fight justice. (You can't do it in 20 minutes—schedule an hour, and if you're done early, make popcorn and celebrate!) Don't plan your fair fight the night before a final, a major swim meet, or the day a major report is due. Plan it to occur in a place where you won't be bothered or distracted.

Ready to go? Either one may begin. The first person describes the events or problems from her point of view. The second person practices active listening, knowing that she will get her chance in just a moment. After she has paraphrased the first person's thoughts and feelings to her satisfaction, it's the second person's turn to state her version of the situation, while the first person listens actively. Her version may be similar, or it might differ tremendously from the first person's point of view. Now the first person paraphrases the second person's feelings and opinions (to the second person's satisfaction, of course).

Don't stop! Just discussing the issue and events is not enough, even if you've cleared up misunderstandings, and gained empathy for each other's position. Part of fair fighting includes resolving feelings about the situation. I call this the "metafight," the fight about the fight.

Begin the metafight! The first person describes her emotional reactions to the whole situation—what she feels like now, what she felt like then, and how she feels about the fight. The second person listens actively, and then paraphrases what the first person has said she feels. Then it's the second person's turn.

Words to Parent By

A *metafight* is a fight about having a fight. In the fair fighting technique, after the situation that prompted the fight is resolved, the participants resolve their feelings about fighting with each other.

Reach a resolution. Each person (taking turns, of course) states her hopes for the future. If one person has wronged or harmed the other, the injurer should provide amends or restitution. If both people are equally at fault, both people can use the opportunity to reaffirm their commitment to having a good relationship, and celebrate the end of the tensions.

Seal it with a kiss. Or a hug or a handshake—some sort of nonverbal acknowledgment of the resolution.

Sibling Struggles

Where are most tensions in the household? Between siblings, of course! Brothers and sisters share parents, family, love, jealousy, resentment, admiration, and, a lot of times, a bedroom. You can help keep tensions to a minimum.

➤ Keep your kids safe from each other, and teach them how and where to put their angry feelings. ("Use your words, not your fists!")

➤ Acknowledge their difficult and ambivalent feelings about each other.

➤ Treat your children equitably (remember that *equitable* and *equal* are not the same). Refrain from comparing them. Focus on giving each what he needs.

➤ Don't let anybody label any of your children.

➤ Try not to make one sibling responsible for the other.

➤ Allow them to solve their own disagreements and battles.

➤ Focus on each child's abilities, not failings or disabilities.

➤ Make siblings share family time activities, and one-on-one time. They need shared experiences to build their relationship, and to have a testing ground to learn conflict resolution. Maybe a special class together? Yes, they'll act resistant, but try anyhow.

Behave Yourself!

Worried about rivalry? Don't make it worse! Your attitudes are catching—your children internalize what you think of them. Don't make value statements about your kids. ("Jane's the smart one, but Amanda is going to be a little heartbreaker!")

Fighting

Let the kids resolve it on their own. Of course, at times, you may need to facilitate. Here are the guidelines for when to step in, and, if you do step in, what to do. They're based on ideas from *Siblings Without Rivalry,* a helpful guide by Adele Faber and Elaine Mazlish.

Condition Green—Your kids are bickering, squabbling, mildly arguing, and bugging each other. So what else is new? They need to learn how to live with each other (and others) and how to resolve conflicts. If you interfere with bickering, you exacerbate it, you encourage it, and you probably raise your own blood pressure as well. Hum a tune, go for a walk, think of it as low-level background music. You are not involved.

Condition Yellow—It's not a bicker, it's a real argument. Time to wake up and smell the coffee.

➤ "Boy, you guys are pretty pissed at each other, huh?" Saying this acknowledges their emotions.

➤ Translate. (This is a version of sportscasting, which you'll find described in Chapter 15.) "Paulette, you are angry because you were in the chair first and when you came back from the bathroom, Brian was there. Brian, you are angry at Paulette because she always 'calls' the chair, and, you feel that if she got out of it to go to the bathroom, it was empty and therefore up for grabs."

➤ Don't denigrate the problems or the emotions. "It can be really hard when two people want the same thing."

➤ "I know you'll come up with a good solution," you say, showing your confidence in their ability to solve the problem.

➤ Then leave.

Condition Red—They are really going at it. You need to determine if they are play-fighting by mutual consent. You may have family rules about use of language, use of physical force, or use of violent play (like guns)—if so, remind the kids of the rules, and go away.

Condition Blue—Okay, they are really fighting now!

➤ Stop the fight. Keep in mind your ultimate goal, to teach your kids to mediate their own disputes.

➤ Separate the kids, and give them a cooldown period (this may need to be enforced through time-outs). Cooling down is not a punishment, and it should be applied and enforced equally.

➤ You are not a contender, you aren't even a mediator (yet). Don't take sides. Take yourself out of the fray. You are not on either child's "side."

➤ After cooling down, bring them together and encourage them to resolve the issue themselves.

➤ If they are unsuccessful, you or your partner should step in as mediator, and help them with the problem-solving process or the fair fight technique (both above).

Tales of Tattling

Tattling between siblings is very common as a way for kids to gain attention and parental favor, to get revenge, as a form of manipulation, or as a power play. Tattling is a form of aggression, and it should be stopped.

➤ Let each child know that you expect her to be responsible only for her own behavior, and that you won't listen to tales about siblings.

➤ If your child tattles, label the behavior as tattling, and let her know you don't approve.

➤ Ignore it. Don't reward the aggressor by responding coolly, "We don't tattle in this family. Work it out."

➤ Never scold a child whose behavior you haven't witnessed.

➤ A child who tattles frequently may need some help with interpersonal skills.

Speaking up about danger or speaking out against true injustice is not tattling. It is always okay to let you know if somebody is in danger of being hurt, or if somebody is being unsafe. Reassure your child that you are always available to help, and that she can always come to you if she's frightened.

Behave Yourself!

No parent wants a tattletale child. Think back to your youth (those many eons ago)—remember the tattler in the group? In general, kids who tattle tend to be unpopular (it's a nasty pattern for a child to get into).

Help Rebalance the Power!

Power plays between siblings can be intense! You can help balance the power by giving attention to the kid who's been injured instead of the aggressor. If Linda is picking on Lucy, talk to Lucy. "Linda was pinching you, wasn't she? I bet you feel hurt by this."

Step-Sibling Squabbling

Sibling squabbles are normal and average. Step-sibling squabbles are too, but since the entire stepfamily relationship can be loaded with issues, there's often an added dimension of worry when step-siblings go at it with each other. As with other sibling conflicts, your primary job is to teach them how to resolve their problems themselves.

It's a Good Idea!

Here's an idea to help solve step-sibling rivalry and enhance together-ness at the same time: When there is a conflict or problem, have all the kids take responsibility for it. If they are annoyed enough at you, they'll ally themselves together. This will help build a sense of sibling-hood.

When Squabbling Covers Up Step-Sibling Sexual Interest

Step-siblings are not related to each other and, since they often haven't been raised together, the natural taboos against family members having sex with each other don't always kick in. You may think there's no chance of it happening in your house (and I don't want to make you paranoid), but preteen and teenage hormones are strong stuff.

It's normal for step-relations to feel sexual attraction (it's not okay for them to act on it). Here are a few precautions and suggestions:

➤ Little kids are far more likely to follow the normal sibling taboos. There's something about diaper changes and years of stomach flu and "cooties" that decimates romantic ideals.

➤ Watch for intense feelings between step-siblings, even if the feelings manifest themselves as extreme disgust or dislike. "You are disgusting!" may cover up intense attraction.

➤ Discuss this issue with the kids, even if there are no overt signs of attraction between them. Reassure them that the feelings are normal (though acting on them would not be all right).

➤ If there is a sexual charge, discuss it. Ignoring it won't make it go away, while discussing it will probably help diffuse the issue.

➤ Stress the risks of step-incest: family breakup, emotional breakdown, plus the usual risk of pregnancy and (possibly) disease.

➤ Here's the rule: If it happens under your roof, you have a say. It's not just their business. Adolescent, sexually involved step-siblings (who are unwilling to stop being involved) may need to be separated. Or both may need to move out. It's for the health of the entire family.

➤ You do not have any control over involved adult step-siblings who do not live with you, but you should express your feelings and opinions.

➤ A therapist may be able to help.

Wanna Trade?

Family fighting getting you truly down? Just not getting along with one of your kids? Besides counseling (covered in Chapter 24), I've got an idea for you. It doesn't work for everybody, and it probably is only appropriate for adolescents.

We all have a light side and a dark side, a Dr. Jekyll and a Mr. Hyde. If all you're seeing these days is your child's Hyde, and that's all she sees of you, when the dynamics truly stink, if things are very, very tense in your household, then try this on for size: Exchange her for another model. Consider doing a short-term swap with another parent for awhile. Oh, it's only temporary!

Try it for a week or two. You'll get a bit of a break (though you'll still be caring for a child), your child will get a bit of a break, and you'll both have a chance to cool down. Your child will learn the flexibility of accommodating to another household, and, because the tensions won't be there, will probably have a great time. Taking care of another person's child will make you appreciate (and miss) your own, and you'll likely be delighted to see each other.

➤ Trading kids only works if everybody is into it. You don't want your child to ever feel or think that you don't want him anymore. Propose it as an experiment, and talk a lot about how it's going to be before it happens.

➤ Spend time with your child, even if he's sleeping in somebody else's house. Make a special date, go out to lunch, and then drop him off at "home."

➤ No nagging, third-degreeing, or reminding him how to act. Let the other family handle it their way. You concentrate on your borrowed child for a while.

➤ The "borrowed" child is a member of the family, not a guest, and he should be subject to the same expectations and family rules. Make sure he's briefed on what they are, and provide a lot of positive reinforcement. It's a challenge for him (as it is for your own child at the borrowed child's house).

➤ Before the experiment, meet and talk with the other parents about discipline, expectations, and your own family rules. Make sure everybody is clear about these things in advance.

The Least You Need to Know

➤ Rage is a hidden issue in parenting, and in families.

➤ Expressing clear, direct, genuine anger to your child teaches her that angry feelings can be expressed in a way that doesn't harm.

➤ Don't compromise; work toward win–win solutions.

➤ Give siblings the support to solve their own disagreements and battles.

➤ Don't reward a tattler by listening to her tales.

➤ Active dislike of a step-sibling might signify sexual interest.

➤ Trading kids allows you and your child a break, and lets you see each other in a new light.

Chapter 20

The Well-Behaved Challenging Child

In This Chapter

➤ When your child is simply more

➤ The dreamer, the dynamo, the discoverer—the Edison trait

➤ About attention deficit disorder—diagnosis, therapy, and what you can do

➤ Tips for successful events and activities

You've tried it all—you've been loving, affectionate, and attentive. You've provided consistency, limits, and consequences backed up by lots of talking, listening, and positive reinforcement. You're a good parent, yet your kid is high-spirited or volatile, not doing well in school, disruptive or daydreamy, unhappy, highly energized, easily distracted or too highly focused, or obsessed by a hobby.

Is it temperamental? Or could it be biological? Is your child highly energetic, creative, and bright with a twist—acting a little different or learning a little differently from the norm? Does he have what author Lucy Jo Palladino calls "the Edison trait"? Or does he indeed have a neurobiological difference, warranting the diagnosis Attention Deficit Disorder (ADD)?

Whole books are written about "challenging" children. In these short pages, I can only begin to give you an introduction to the subject. Since this book is about how to raise a well-behaved child, we'll focus on specific strategies for improving your child's behavior. As you probably figured out, this chapter is for the parent of the child with a difference.

The Child with a Difference

Who is the child with a difference? In the descriptions below, you'll notice that Attention Deficit Disorder (ADD) and Attention Deficit Hyperactivity Disorder (ADHD) are medical diagnoses, and being "spirited" and having the Edison trait are not. What do they all have in common? Why am I lumping them together?

Behave Yourself!

Don't "type" your child! Descriptions such as "spirited," "Edison trait," and "ADD" are only useful as tools to help your very individual child get along better in the world. They are hurtful when they are used to define who your child is, or when they limit what he can do.

➤ Children who are spirited, kids whose thinking is divergent rather than convergent, and kids with ADD and ADHD all need special attention to maximize and focus their distinct qualities and assets to become happy, productive people.

➤ Even though the descriptions and "symptoms" for these challenges vary, there are enough commonalities and overlaps that many of the suggestions I provide should help you work to improve the behavior of your child.

The Spirited Child

Spirited children are, as author Mary Sheedy Kurcinka writes in her book *Raising Your Spirited Child*, more. "They are normal children who are more intense, persistent, sensitive, perceptive, and uncomfortable with change than other children." A spirited child does not have ADD or ADHD, although there are some characteristics that may overlap, as you will see below. The spirited child's challenges come in the area of temperament traits. (There's an introduction to temperament in Chapter 5.) Understanding your child's temperament, your own temperament, and how they mesh and clash will help you work with your child, not at cross-purposes. Not all spirited kids will exhibit the same temperament characteristics, but each will possess enough of them to make them, as Kurcinka says, "stand out in a crowd." It can be quite a challenge to teach your spirited child to be well-behaved.

Spirited Kids Are More Intense

The spirited child may be loud and noisy or quietly focused inside, but her reactions to life and emotions are always powerful. There's nothing blasé about these kids. Too often, spirited kids get the message that their intensity is a negative force. On the contrary, when understood and managed, intensity makes kids enthusiastic, passionate, and ambitious. Spirited kids need to learn to notice when their intensity is about to overwhelm them. As a parent, you can provide soothing activities and use humor and time-outs as ways to help your child learn to calm herself.

Spirited Kids Are More Persistent

Some spirited kids "lock in" to an activity, and can concentrate on it for hours (many ADD kids also have this ability). On the plus side, people with this focus, commitment, and determination make the world work, and persistent kids need to know that you admire and value their ability to hyperfocus. It's hard to parent a very persistent child, though. Power struggles abound, and getting persistent kids to change their minds (even their activity!) can be like moving mountains—slow and arduous. Increased communication skills—like the problem-solving process in Chapter 19—can help. Make sure your family rules are explicit, too.

Spirited Kids Are More Sensitive

Spirited children are usually deeply aware of their environment—the sounds, smells, lights, textures of the room, the tension in the air between you and the cute bank teller. A sensitive spirited child knows when you are angry, even when you are hiding it from yourself. She can't stand tags on clothes or belts that touch her belly button, and she may burst into tears in a crowd.

Sensitive spirited kids are the "feelers" of the world—their friendships are deep and lasting, they fight for justice, they're often gifted in the artistic fields. They need to know their gifts are appreciated. You can help your sensitive spirited child get along in the world by reducing environmental stimulation, teaching her the words to describe the sensations and emotions she is feeling, and teaching her to recognize (and pull away) when she's getting overstimulated.

Spirited Kids Are More Perceptive

Spirited kids are often so perceptive to everything going on in the environment (people, conversations, animals, colors) that they become distracted. It's this trait of noticing everything that sometimes gets confused with distractibility, a trait of Attention Deficit Hyperactivity Disorder. A perceptive spirited child is not suffering from an attention deficit; she can focus on the task at hand when interested. A child with ADHD isn't able to, even if she wants to.

Perceptive spirited children have keen senses, "eagle eyes," the ability to observe things others do not. They are often wise beyond their years. Until your child learns how to sort out the important information from the dross, he'll become unfocused and unable to concentrate. You can help your perceptive child by reinforcing the importance of his creativity and keen awareness of the world. You can help him pay attention and learn by using multimedia (touch, talking, writing). Keep your messages simple, and limit the number of instructions you give. The suggestions in the "Planning for Success" section below will be particularly helpful.

Spirited Kids Are More Uncomfortable with Change

Spirited kids tend to have a hard time adapting to new situations. They often hate surprises, and they hate transitions (a special concern for kids with two households— see Chapter 17). You can help your child by planning ahead, alerting your child about what's coming up, and allowing more time between activities. You can also help your child by learning to appreciate the importance of planned transitions.

Spirited Kids Are More Energetic

Some, though not all, spirited children are more energetic—moving from morning to night, discovering, exploring, skipping, and existing in a blur of activity. Spirited kids who are more energetic need to move their bodies. High energy may be confused with the energy typical of a child with ADHD. The difference is this—the ADHD child cannot stop moving and focus on a task, while the energetic spirited child may bounce in and out of her seat, but will be able to focus enough to finish her work. You can help your energetic spirited child by planning for movement and high energy (a long car ride without hourly breaks is sheer physical torture, for instance). Your child needs to hear that you appreciate and value her energy. (It's not a lie—you probably do appreciate it. When you're sitting on the couch at 8 P.M. clock-watching and waiting until you can get the kids to bed and yourself to blissful sleep, wouldn't you like some of your child's zoom?)

It's a Good Idea!

Mary Sheedy's groundbreaking book, *Raising Your Spirited Child: A Guide for Parents Whose Child is More Intense, Sensitive, Perceptive, Persistent, Energetic,* is a must-read reference, and the source of much of this information.

The Edison Trait

In *The Edison Trait: Saving the Spirit of Your Nonconforming Child,* author and clinical psychologist Lucy Jo Palladino describes and discusses the qualities of the Edison trait.

If spirited kids are characterized by being "more," Edison-trait kids are recognizable by being "divergent" rather than "convergent" thinkers, demonstrating thinking patterns that characterize many high-achieving artists, inventors, and business people. The Edison trait is named for Thomas Edison, inventor extraordinaire who, though brilliant, was thrown out of school because he wasn't functioning in the environment. When misunderstood, the Edison trait may cause social and learning problems. Edison-trait people include Maya Angelou and Bill Gates. Edison-trait kids may (or may not) have personality traits of spirited kids, and they may (or may not) have ADD qualities. They are not ADD kids. They are, like the spirited child, normal, nondysfunctional kids who may provide a challenge to parents and schools. (Not because of any failing in the child, but because of a limit in the range of expectations of what is acceptable.)

Convergent Versus Divergent Thinking

Edison-trait kids (and this includes 20% of all children) don't conform easily. They show brilliance, active imaginations, strong opinions, and a wild, courageous sense of adventure. They don't think in a convergent manner, where many thoughts all reduce to a single thought. Instead, they are divergent thinkers—one thought stimulates many others. Edison-trait kids excel in coming up with their own ideas, getting deeply involved in those ideas, starting projects, and imagining new worlds and possibilities. They have difficulty focusing on other people's ideas, letting go of their own ideas, remembering tasks, following through on thoughts, and finishing projects. You'll find a lot of Edison-trait people on Wall Street and as emergency room techs, where their risk-taking traits are an asset. Many artists and probably most poets are Edison-trait people. And so are many entrepreneurs. Life with an Edison trait child can be quite a challenge, as well as a joy!

Our schools, and our ideas of "right" thinking and "wrong" thinking, all say that convergent thinking is correct, and that there is something wrong with the divergent thinker. Divergent thinkers generally fare better once they get out of school and into the real world, where their abilities lead them, in strong numbers, into the arts and adventures. Kids with the Edison trait need their special talents nurtured so that they feel successful. Only then can they learn how to accommodate in a convergency-based world.

Edison-trait children often, but certainly not always, qualify for an ADD diagnosis. Almost all kids who have ADD also have the Edison trait but, in addition to this trait, they also have serious impairment and dysfunction (and we'll discuss that later in the chapter).

According to Palladino, Edison-trait kids fall into three temperament categories:

➤ The dreamer

➤ The discoverer

➤ The dynamo

The Dreamer

The dreamer lives in a world of the imagination, a world of "possibility," far away from clocks and schedules. Her mind wanders, inventing intricate universes, yet she under-achieves at school because she forgets to bring her homework home, or she forgets to do it, or the beauty of an oil slick in a puddle makes her late for class. Give her a problem to solve, and she'll look at it from an entirely different angle than the teacher intended. Push her to finish her work on time, and the dreamer may burst into tears. Edison-trait dreamers are usually highly intense, perceptive, and sensitive (see the descriptions above under "The Spirited Child").

The Discoverer

The explorer, the limit-tester, the little four-year-old scientist who pours all the condiments onto the table and stirs them with the contents of the sugar bowl to make a "periment"—these are the discoverers. Discoverers need surprise, change, and excitement. A discoverer will have trouble completing a sheet of math problems because he's easily bored. He's highly spontaneous, yet persistent when he wants to be. An Edison-trait discoverer is intense, persistent, and energetic (see the descriptions above under "The Spirited Child").

It's a Good Idea!

In all these descriptions of temperament traits and thinking patterns, you'll see a lot of overlap. Kids are not like bugs, they cannot be easily classified. These descriptions are merely tools to help you understand your child.

Words to Parent By

Attention Deficit Disorder (ADD) is a cluster of traits that reflect a child's inborn neurologically based temperament. ADD traits include spontaneity, creativity, and the ability to hyperfocus on tasks. It also often causes inattention, impulsiveness, distractibility, and hyperactivity (ADHD). Kids with ADD/ADHD are at high risk for developing learning disorders and behavioral difficulties.

The Dynamo

Does your child go from morning to night? Does he overexcite, rile up, and blow? He might be a dynamo. Many top athletes are. The child who has broken six bones by the time he is eight, who can seduce and delight with his enthusiasm and brilliance, who has the determination of a champion, is a dynamo. An Edison-trait dynamo is intense, persistent, and energetic. (See the descriptions above under "The Spirited Child.") In a way, he's a discoverer, too, though his discoveries tend to be more grounded in his body.

ADD and ADHD

Attention Deficit Disorder (ADD) and Attention Deficit Hyperactive Disorder (ADHD) are the most commonly diagnosed psychiatric illnesses among children, though to call them "illnesses" doesn't do them justice. About 7 to 10% of all school-age children (mostly boys) are currently on medication for these disorders.

ADD and ADHD are biological disorders. They are inborn neurological traits, and nothing a parent does can prevent them from occurring. You can minimize the impact of the disorder, much as you can work with spirited or Edison-trait kids.

ADD is characterized by selective attention, impulsivity, difficulty with prioritizing, a tendency to get lost in fantasy, and distractibility. For an ADHD diagnosis, hyperactivity must be present, as well. All people show these traits from time to time—the difference is that children with ADD/ADHD show them frequently, and for greater duration. Sound like a spirited child or a child with the Edison trait? Yes, the traits are the same (that's why I combined them in this chapter!). The difference is that in the ADD/ADHD child, these traits are extreme enough to cause significant impairment. In order to qualify for an ADD/ADHD diagnosis, your child's behaviors must be out of line with the behaviors of other kids of the same age, and be causing his functioning at home and at school to be significantly impaired.

Don't Leap to ADD!

ADD/ADHD is a psychological and biological diagnosis, and it's not easy (you can't do it yourself, and neither can your child's teacher). There is no physical test to detect it. Most ADD/ADHD diagnoses occur when the child is fairly young, when a parent, teacher, or both requests a workup based on the child's difficulty at home or at school. As a parent, look for problems with distractibility, selective attention, impulsivity, and hyperactivity. Remember that it's ADD only when your child's functioning is significantly impaired.

William Sears and Lynda Thompson, authors of *The A.D.D. Book: New Understandings, New Approaches to Parenting Your Child,* suggest six steps to help you clearly identify your child's challenges:

1. **Complete an ADD checklist.** Specialists have developed a variety of checklists enabling parents to pinpoint where their child has difficulty with attention span, spontaneity, activity levels, and emotion. They are too long to reprint here, but they are usually available from your child's school.

2. **Assess the severity of the problem.** All kids show the ADD traits from time to time. It's important to notice not only which behaviors and traits your child demonstrates, but how often, how severe, and how much impact.

3. **Gather information from others.** Ask your child's teachers, baby sitters, and extended family members to give you feedback on your child's behavior. Perhaps your child does fine at home but loses it at school. Perhaps the problem is only with one particular baby sitter (in which case it's not ADD, and it's time to change sitters). ADD kids generally have problems in many areas.

4. **Focus on your child's positive attributes.** Time to do some positive reframing (focused on in Chapters 15 and 16).

It's a Good Idea!

Unfortunately, an ADD diagnosis focuses on terminology such as *deficit, disorder, impairment,* and *disability* instead of *solutions, creativity, original thought,* and *spontaneity.*

It's a Good Idea!

When it comes to medical and psychological practitioners of any kind, get references, and don't disregard your gut instincts! Only you know who is right for your child and your family. (And listen to your child's feelings, too! He needs to feel comfortable with his care.)

5. **Keep track of the problem.** How is it progressing? Children develop at different rates, and a behavior or learning problem that improves over time doesn't cause the same concern as development that stalls out.

6. **Find the right professional help.** Several kinds of professionals focus on ADD/ADHD: psychologists, neurologists, pediatricians, speech pathologists, audiologists, and occupational or physical therapists. Your child will probably need to be seen and diagnosed by a number of these professionals. A visit to your child's pediatrician should be your first stop, to rule out other disorders (hearing problems, allergies, neurological impairment), and to get references for other professionals.

A professional assessment will probably include some or all of the following: medical and psychological history; psychological and academic tests; parent and teacher questionnaires; and tests for learning disabilities.

If Your Child Is Diagnosed with ADD or ADHD

If your child is diagnosed with ADD or ADHD, you will need all the support and information you can get. There are many books available about ADD—I've got some recommendations in Appendix B. You can also contact CHADD (Children and Adults with Attention Deficit Disorder), a nonprofit organization with 650 local branches all over the world. Most of the CHADD staff either have or are parents of kids with ADD (so they'll know what's going on with you). CHADD publishes *Attention!*, a magazine designed for parents of children with ADD or ADHD. Their address is in Appendix C.

Remember that your child is not her diagnosis, and that much of her eventual success will depend on how her ADD or ADHD is handled. ADD/ADHD can lead to learning challenges and lowered self-respect, yet many, many productive and brilliant citizens, as well as a tremendous number of artists and highly creative people, have ADD/ADHD. Most ADD/ADHD kids have average or above average intelligence.

Your ADD/ADHD child needs a strong, reasonable parent who keeps the lines of communication open, structures the child's life, and provides positive reinforcement, as well as serves as an ally and liaison to the outside world.

It's a Good Idea!

ADD/ADHD kids are easily over-stimulated. They intend to finish what they begin, but they are so easily distracted that they cannot complete their tasks. Careful direction, reduced environmental stimulation, and strong limits can help immensely.

What About Drugs?

Many kids are treated for their ADD/ADHD with drug therapy, which is effective in about 65% of kids who are medicated. I believe that while there are many instances where drug treatment can help, it's not always successful, it should always be part of a larger treatment program, and it's wise to try other alternatives as well, including neurofeedback (described below). No matter what you believe about the ethics or success of treating ADD/ADHD with drugs, it's important not to leap into it. Get a second opinion, talk to other ADD/ADHD parents, and educate yourself.

If your child is given drug therapy:

➤ He will most likely be given Ritalin. Other drugs are Dexadrine, Adderoll, and Cylert. These are all amphetamines, types of "speed" that work in the child as you might not expect—instead of making your child more hyper, they help organize the brain so that he can focus and pay attention more easily.

➤ Drug therapy should never be done without accompanying individual and family therapy. ADD may be your child's condition, but it is the whole family's challenge.

Neurofeedback Training

Neurofeedback training (a type of biofeedback) is an "alternative" therapy for ADD that helps the child retrain her brain waves so she can improve her mental flexibility and learn to better concentrate. In neurofeedback, a child sits in front of a brain wave readout, similar to an electroencephalogram (EEG) machine. Tiny electrodes measure the brain's neural output. They don't put anything into the brain, and they can't read the child's mind, they simply read the brain waves (the electrical patterns produced by neurons). The pattern of the brain waves shows whether the child is sitting still and concentrating.

On an EEG, brain wave readouts look like wavy lines. In neurofeedback training, the brain waves are computer-translated into graphic "games." As the child watches the screen and concentrates, a fish moves through the ocean, for example, or colorful graphics display. The child can win prizes or points for focusing on the game. When her mind wanders, the graphics stop, the colors fade.

Behave Yourself!

Ritalin and other drugs do not cure ADD/ADHD! They relieve some symptoms. They are effective only when taken regularly and when the doses are adjusted as the child ages. They must be taken long term—in some cases, indefinitely. A child never grows out of ADD/ADHD, he just develops successful coping strategies.

Words to Parent By

Neurofeedback training is an alternative therapy to drugs for ADD. Using real-time computer readouts of a child's brain waves in the form of graphics or games, it teaches the child to alter her neural output by concentrating. Neurofeedback training gives the child direct practice in and positive feedback for paying attention, and in the process, retrains her brain so that she is better able to focus in daily life.

It's a Good Idea!

Neurofeedback training is designed to be fun and successful for kids at all levels. Even the kid whose ability to pay attention is limited will feel successful at the same time as she is producing positive changes in her daily attention pattern.

It's a Good Idea!

Focus on making life simpler for your child. As the world becomes less challenging, so will she.

The better the child concentrates, the faster the graphics move. Exercising her neural pathways like this actually changes her brain physiology, and enables her to learn more effectively.

Planning for Success

The challenging child who has ADD, is spirited, or has the Edison trait needs structure and parental support. What can you do? Everything you've learned in this book applies here. The approach to improving a "challenging" child's behavior is the same as for any child—the difference is that your challenging child needs more: more understanding, more structure, more communication, more limits.

Whether your child has ADD, is spirited, or has the Edison trait of divergent thinking, he may benefit from the following approaches.

Identify Your Child's Challenges

This may mean looking at his temperament, analyzing his thinking (convergent/divergent), or doing a full ADD/ADHD assessment. It also means acknowledging to yourself in what ways your child is challenging for you. Identifying the challenges doesn't mean labeling—labeling your child restricts her ideas (and your ideas) of who she can be. But properly identifying what is going on is essential to helping her achieve her potential.

Identify Your Child's Strengths and Gifts

Your child is more than the sum of her symptoms—she has strengths and gifts that are the building blocks of success. If you are having difficulty seeing your child's assets, try "reframing" her personality characteristics in a positive way.

Identify Your Child's Behavior Problems

You're trying to improve certain aspects of your child's behavior so he can get along better in the world. You aren't turning him in for a new model! Identify which behaviors interfere with his functioning at home and at school, and focus on those. Pay attention to sleep patterns and food intake, too. Progress, not perfection, is the goal. This chart below can help clarify which behaviors are the biggest problem for your child:

What is the problem?

When does it happen?

Why?

What Is the Problem?	When Does It Happen?	Why?

Structure, Structure, Structure

Challenging kids need structure and limits in their lives. Here's how you can help:

➤ Provide step-by-step lists for tasks. Challenging children do best when the expectations are very clear and precise.

➤ Keep to regular routines and schedules so your persistent child (whether spirited, Edison-trait, or ADD) knows when the changes in activities will be, and what they will be. Understanding the routine will help him shift activities with less distress.

➤ Post the family rules (Chapter 6) in a central place to help remind your child of his limits. Charts can help your child focus on his progress. Kids with ADD often enjoy complicated tracking systems that provide rewards at the end for good behavior. I've included a sample in Appendix E.

It's a Good Idea!

Kids with ADD often think visually. If you can illustrate your instructions, they often "get them" better.

Provide Physical Outlets

Understand that spirited kids, dynamos, and kids with ADHD need to move their bodies. Plan time for exercise. Take your kid out for a run before bedtime, and encourage organized athletic activities (competitive or noncompetitive).

Minimize Distractions

Focus on creating a gentle, simpler lifestyle with fewer environmental distractions and less stimulation. Does this mean moving out to the woods and living "off the grid" without electricity and running water? Let's not go to extremes! It's true, however, that a regular dose of nature will help calm and focus. (And that goes for all of us!)

Simplify Instructions

Challenging kids sometimes have difficulty remembering elaborate sequences. Keep your instructions short and simple. This may take practice, but in time, you'll see a difference in frustration levels—yours and your child's.

Consistency, Consistency, Consistency

In your schedules, in your limits, in your consequences, in your responses, in your undying and unconditional love and affection. Keep in mind that some temperaments have an easier time being consistent (and that definitely goes for me!). It may be a struggle for you, too. Keep struggling—it's important.

Create Successful Events and Activities

Planning and thinking ahead can make a tremendous difference in how well your child behaves at events and during activities. Before you throw your child in the car and dash off to that party (ah, remember the good old days?):

➤ Try to predict how your child will react to the environment. Consider the setting, the number of people, the climate, the energy level.

➤ At times when you have control over the setting, plan activities to occur in a place where your child will do well—perhaps a park, rather than a restaurant; maybe a friend's house, rather than at an amusement park.

➤ Keep the activities appropriate. A very active child may not be ready to sit through an evening at the symphony. A very sensitive child may have a disastrous time at a street fair.

➤ Work with your child to establish signals ("When you scratch your nose, I'll know that you're getting anxious") or eliminate problems ("Let's sit near the door. That way, if you get too antsy, we can split.").

➤ Build in breaks.

➤ Focus on success. Don't overanticipate problems, and focus on what is going well rather than what isn't.

Relax Yourself

Parenting a challenging child is, by its very nature, a challenge. You can help your child's behavior improve by being calm and collected yourself, and feeling positive about your parenting. Read Chapters 23 and 24 for self-nurturing and relaxation suggestions. Encourage self-nurturing and relaxation in your child, too.

Outside Assistance

Don't tough it out alone. There are support groups and classes for spirited kids and kids with ADD/ADHD (you'll find some places to begin in Appendix C). Raising a challenging child can be extremely stressful for a family.

Listen to Your Child

When you carefully listen to your child, you will discover all you need to know about how to raise her. Don't compare your child with others—look at who she is and respond to her needs. We are all individuals, we all develop at different rates, and we all have challenges and provide challenges. Respond to those, and the rest will take care of itself.

The Least You Need to Know

➤ Challenging children need special attention to maximize and focus their distinct qualities and assets toward becoming happy, productive people.

➤ Most challenging children are highly intelligent.

➤ Spirited children are normal kids with more extreme temperamental traits than other children.

➤ Edison-trait kids think divergently, rather than convergently. Some, but not all, have ADD.

➤ ADD/ADHD is diagnosed when a child shows selective attention, impulsivity, difficulty with prioritizing, a tendency to get lost in fantasy, distractibility, and sometimes, hyperactivity to the extent that functioning is significantly impaired.

➤ You can help by understanding the problems and providing an environment and activities where your challenging child can thrive.

Chapter 21

Sex and Drugs and the Well-Behaved Child

In This Chapter

➤ Drugs, alcohol, what to say, what to do!

➤ When *is* it using, and when *is* it abusing?

➤ Puberty and the prepared parent

➤ Aids, pregnancy, and other risks

➤ Talking about your own sordid past

In any discussion about raising a well-behaved child, the time comes when you have to talk about drugs and sex. Okay, now's the time! Sex is wonderful; it is powerful, important, life enhancing and life creating, and one of the joys of being alive. Drugs (legal or illegal) have been used by every single world culture to alter the mind, mood, and body. But, what about for your kid?

The urge to experiment with sex and drugs is an older version of the same urge your toddler showed when he played with water toys in the bathtub and squirted the cat to see what would happen. Yes, the "toys" are scarier and more destructive, but the desire to experiment is healthy, age appropriate, and necessary for healthy social and emotional development. Most kids will want to experiment with drugs, alcohol, and sex at some point, and it's your responsibility to educate them as well as you can about the truth of what awaits them.

Let's look at the situation realistically. Drugs are available to kids who live in cities, towns, and rural areas in their high schools and middle schools (sometimes even in grammar school), and for many teenagers, sex isn't a matter of whether, it's a matter of when and with whom. The grand problem with combining drugs and kids and/or sex

Words to Parent By

A *drug* is any pain-relieving or perception- or mood-altering substance that is ingested into the body. Drugs include alcohol, nicotine, and caffeine, inhalants, and over-the-counter medications as well as illegal pain-relieving or perception- or mood-altering substances.

and kids is that the dangers are huge, and the amount of guidance in this society is small. Your child is called upon at a relatively young age to make major choices about drugs and sex, choices that can alter his life forever.

How will you prepare your child to face these challenges and make the decisions that are right and healthy for him? He needs to be educated about drugs and sex, and he needs to have the inner boundaries to know when to say no when he's not ready for sex, or doesn't want to use alcohol or drugs. How does he get these inner boundaries?

The entire point of positive discipline is to raise a reasonable, resourceful child who can make smart decisions. This chapter discusses drugs and sex and kids, provides education about the dilemmas facing kids today, and offers suggestions about what you, as parents, can do to help your child through the challenges.

Drugs, Alcohol, and Your *Baby!*

It doesn't matter where you live—high on a mountain, deep in a valley, or in the toughest inner city, where there are people, there are drugs, and your kids will be exposed to them at an early age. Cigarette smoking is on the rise, especially among young people. Alcohol abuse is everywhere. Drugs are not going to go away, and every child has to establish his own relationship (or nonrelationship) with mind-altering chemicals. You have influence, but no control.

Yes, of course you are concerned. You should be! What can you do about it?

➤ Educate yourself

➤ Educate your child

It's never too early or too late to start talking about drugs. And it's never too early or too late to begin modeling a positive relationship to them yourself.

Talking with your kids about drugs is scary for many parents. But with drugs (and I'm including cigarettes and alcohol) as an established fact of modern life, it's part of your job as a reasonable, positive parent to be as honest and up-front as you can be without getting all hot and bothered and sliding into lecture mode.

The Frightening Facts

Kids use drugs. Alcohol is the most widely used and abused drug. In the past month, about a quarter of this country's eighth graders have used alcohol (and a good number of them have been drunk). Between eighth and tenth grade, those numbers go up.

Almost five million teenagers have a drinking problem. In general, alcohol abuse is the fourth largest health problem in the country. Many alcoholics start young. Smokers start young, too. Most kids try cigarettes before eighth grade. Smoking is a leading cause of death in America, a country in which three million teenagers smoke.

Tales from the Parent Zone

Robin crashed the family car into a tree after a couple of beers. Nadia and her friends did tequila shooters and then went hiking on the sea cliffs at night. She slipped and fell to her death. Benny drank a bottle of vodka before accidentally drowning in the lake. What's one of the leading causes of death for teenagers? Alcohol-related accidents.

And kids don't just rely on the standard choices of alcohol and nicotine. What about marijuana, "huffing" (that is, sniffing household chemicals), ecstasy (or "E"), heroin, crack, the list goes on and on.

And it doesn't work to instruct your kids to "just say no." The "War on Drugs" is a total failure, and parents need to rely on education and their children's fortitude and ability to make choices.

Tales from the Parent Zone

Hide the air freshener, the barbecue lighter fluid, and the marking pens! In the Anderson family, the giggles coming from the shed weren't as harmless as they appeared—thirteen-year-old Suzanne and her friends were risking life and limb by sniffing cleaning substances to get high. Health journalist Robert Davis writes in an article in *USA Today* that about one in five eighth-graders have "huffed" household chemicals (slightly fewer than the number who have smoked marijuana). Hundreds of people die every year from household chemical abuse, and kids may not understand the risk of inhalants.

Choices, Choices

This is where all that choice-making practice pays off. Even kids younger than 13 often have important decisions to make about drug use. Whether your child becomes harmfully involved with chemical substances will depend to a great extent on his own personal development. While you cannot make his choices for him, you can help him learn to make strong choices. A child who knows his own strengths and weaknesses is less likely to have problems, and that includes drug problems. By using positive reinforcement, encouragement, and limits, your child will learn to respect his body and his mind. Perhaps he'll feel strong enough to resist the pressures around him.

The Joy of Drugs

People use drugs because they make them feel good. Sounds pretty radical, but it's true. (That's one difference between drugs and medicine, and it's one of the reasons why there's great societal resistance to using marijuana and heroin for medical purposes—because, along with their medically therapeutic purposes, they are also pleasurable.)

Before you start condemning your child for even considering trying drugs, think about your own drug use and the behavior patterns you are modeling. What drugs do you do? Caffeine, aspirin, Prozac, beer, nicotine, cognac, chocolate? (Hey, I'm "on" caffeine right now!) How do you talk with your child about your use of drugs—legal, prescription, and (perhaps) illegal?

Of course there's a difference between moderate, controlled adult use of mind- or body-altering substances, and a child's usage (though your adolescent may not see the difference). I'm not a proponent of drug use, I'm just pointing out reality as your adolescent may see it.

What if you weren't exactly the vision of clean living when you were a kid? Your child seems so young to you. She is young. How old were you when you started having coffee for breakfast or chocolate for dinner? Or, sneaking sips of your parent's booze, smoking bong loads behind the bungalows at school, or going to kegger parties? Ouch. While you probably would flip if you knew your child was doing what you used to do, what can you do about it? How much control did your parents have over you? What are you going to do?

Behave Yourself!

If your child is told "just say no" too many times, he's likely to rebel, and just say "yes."

First, all parents need to realize why their children are at risk for experimenting with drugs. Kids use drugs and alcohol for many of the reasons adults do:

➤ To try something new.

➤ Because drugs make them feel good.

➤ Because drugs provide a built-in social scene.

➤ Because drugs help some kids feel less self-conscious.

➤ To relieve the stress of school, relationships, family pressures, concerns about the future

➤ To relieve boredom.

No, No, I Didn't Say It Was Okay!

Most drugs are dangerous and stupid, you'll get no argument from me! And it's a far, far different thing for a few adults to have a couple of glasses of wine together over dinner (or even a nostalgic toke before a Rolling Stones' concert) than it is for a group of preteens to huff lighter fluid in the garage, smoke forbidden cigarettes, or score hash and crack in the school bathroom.

What's Wrong with Using Drugs?

It may seem self-evident, but it's always good to review these things:

➤ Drugs affect concentration, mood, and the thinking functions.

➤ Drug use can disrupt the learning process and the process of social development.

➤ They make it hard to set personal boundaries and limits, especially around sex (combine drugs and freshly minted hormones, and watch out!).

➤ A number of drugs are addictive, and many that are not physically addicting can become emotional crutches.

➤ Many drugs have long-term health ramifications.

➤ Use of drugs that distort reality can be confusing for adolescents, who are working on defining their own identity.

➤ Just as adults can use drugs experimentally or socially without moving along the continuum to habitual use, abuse, or addiction (see the Drug Use, Misuse, Abuse Continuum, below) and others cannot, the same is true of kids.

➤ For at least many drugs, it's against the law! (Remember though, that your child is receiving a mixed message from society about drugs.)

It's a Good Idea!

Don't like "Just say no"? Try "Just say know." That's the slogan of Nancy Rubin, author of *Ask Me If I Care: Voices from an American High School.*

How Are You Gonna Cope?

The mere idea that your child may be experimenting with drugs (or worse, using them on a more regular basis) makes most parents feel stressed to the limit and crazy. Here are some ideas for coping with reality. (None of these ideas include avoiding reality through drugs, yourself!):

➤ Learn about them. Drugs are different from each other in terms of danger, how they're taken, effects, and addiction rates. If you start lumping together marijuana and speed, cigarettes and melatonin, or LSD and crack, you're gonna be in trouble. Your child won't listen to you, and you may be setting yourself up for a lot of sleepless nights. Most schools have drug education programs. Join your child. Or visit the public library. Or surf the Internet. There's a lot of great sources of information out there.

➤ Understand that there is a difference between drug use and drug abuse, and just because your child has experimented with drugs (or even uses them on a social basis) does not necessarily imply that he is a drug addict who will never achieve anything in life. Yes, the dangers are real and significant, but hysteria doesn't help.

➤ Let your child know what you expect from him. He may not always hold to your clear expectations, limits, and consequences, but it's important for him that you state them. If he's feeling social pressures and wants to back out, he'll have your limits to fall back on, strong and reliable.

➤ Model a good, moderate relationship with alcohol or drugs. Chapter 22 has more information about drug abuse and addiction, and the relationship between a parent's and a child's uses and abuses.

➤ Keep your child's health and safety as your first priority. Express to your child that you don't want him to do drugs, yet acknowledge that you know he might experiment. Let him know you are available, and will not condemn him if he calls for a ride home because either he or his ride have been drinking or using drugs.

➤ Keep talking. Keep your conversations noncondemnatory. Be the big ear, and listen, listen, listen. The briefer the advice, the more powerful.

Tales from the Parent Zone

Barney is the parent of a twelve-year-old girl. Barney drinks wine. When his daughter asked, "Why can't I?" Barney told her, "I am an adult, and the risks I take are as an adult who is responsible for myself in all sorts of ways. You are my child and I have a responsibility to take care of you physically, emotionally, and legally, as well as financially. When you are an adult in all these ways, then I will be more comfortable with you making your own choices around drugs."

It's Legal. So What?

What about legal drugs? Parents tend to minimize the risk of drugs they are familiar with, and for many parents, that means alcohol and tobacco. But in terms of health, some legal drugs are more damaging than illegal drugs. Here's an interesting statistic: Over 500,000 deaths every year are directly attributed to alcohol and tobacco, and zero are directly attributed to marijuana use. (That doesn't mean that smoking marijuana is good for you. Marijuana affects short-term memory, it leads to lethargy, it can impair judgment and coordination, and it's never healthy ingesting smoke into your lungs.)

Using, Misusing, Abusing

Not all drug use is the same. Drug use, misuse, and abuse happen along a continuum:

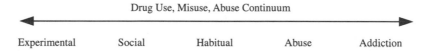

Drug Use, Misuse, Abuse Continuum

Experimental	Social	Habitual	Abuse	Addiction

Just as many adults never get past the first two stages, the same is true for kids. How soon a child begins drug experimentation is largely based on exposure (and we've already established that most kids are exposed very early). How fast (or whether) any one person moves along the continuum is largely based on biological predisposition, though peer and parental environment is influential as well. Kids with alcoholism or drug abuse in the family tend to move from the experimental stage to addiction very rapidly, while kids without a history of family abuse will tend to experiment a few times and stop, or spend years of casually and socially using drugs before (perhaps) moving to habitual use, or abuse, or addiction.

Tales from the Parent Zone

Between 5,000 and 6,000 deaths every year are attributed to cocaine, crack, and heroin use in the United States. Remember Len Bias, that famous basketball player who OD'd while celebrating being picked by the NBA?

Pressure!

Alcohol and drug use is very often a social thing, at least for kids in the first two stages of the Drug Use, Misuse, Abuse Continuum. Friendships are built on shared experience (and in this case, getting loaded together is how your child is bonding with her friends).

It's not going to work to tell your child to just say no, not without a lot of support. If drugs or alcohol are an important part of her social scene, she's risking losing friendships, not because she'll be perceived as "chicken" or "uncool," but simply because she won't be sharing the same experiences her friends are. And these friends may even respect the decisions she's made! Peer pressure doesn't usually take the form of ridicule. It's a more subtle pressure. For adolescents and preadolescents who desperately want to be accepted and welcomed by their peer group, the decision to do drugs may come despite knowing the risks.

A child who decides not to indulge in drugs or alcohol can use some peer support for the decision, and understanding from you of what she has given up socially.

It's a Good Idea!

Who spends time with your child everyday? Her teachers, of course. Check things out with her teachers. You don't need to ask about drugs—have a few teacher conferences just to find out how your child is doing. If her teachers have noticed anything troubling, this is an opportunity for them to let you know.

It's a Good Idea!

Stuck? The Planned Parenthood Federation of America can help you with resources for talking to your child about sexuality and birth control. It's in your local phone book, or you can call 800/230-7526; the Web site is www.plannedparenthood.org.

"Yeah, Mama, I'm Smokin'!"

What's the real gateway drug, that is, the drug most likely to lead to experimentation with other drugs? (Nope, it's not marijuana.) It's nicotine, the most addictive drug of all. Ready for the scary facts? According to the American Cancer Society, 40% of all grade school children experiment with cigarettes, and more than one million teenagers in the United States annually become smokers. Watch what you model. It's a fact that the younger a child starts smoking, the harder it is to quit later in life.

When Your Child Is Abusing

For many kids, use can far too easily become abuse. Alas, you, the parent, are often the last to know about it. So then, how can you know? Chapter 22 has more details about what to look for, and what to do when your child is in trouble.

Sexuality and Your Child

Drugs are one thing—not every child is interested, not every child indulges. But puberty and sexual awareness comes to all, relentless in its transformation, and when it hits, *wow!*

Puberty Marches In

Whether it happens at 9 or 16, puberty changes everything. More kids are reaching puberty at a younger age (most girls now get their period before they turn 13), and the age kids start having intercourse is also lower—one-fourth of girls and one-third of boys have had intercourse by the age of 15, and half of all teenage girls have had sex by the age of 18. That means there's a lot of nooky happening among the teenage set. It also means that (if you haven't already begun) it's time to start talking with your child about sex.

Talk? About sex? Absolutely. Kids need their sexuality supported. (If you don't support it, it's not going away, it will only cause trouble.) And it's clear that sex education works. Teenage pregnancy rates are finally going down, due to the success of sex education programs (and the availability of birth control). The World Health Organization draws a link between sex education and the age at which kids start sexual activity, and they state that sex education leads to an increase in safer sex practices, and a decrease in overall sexual activity.

Words to Parent By

While sexual intercourse may never be totally free from the risk of transmitting sexually transmitted diseases (STD), the risks can be reduced. *Safer sex* refers to sexual activity with reduced risks—using condoms, dams, and sexual activities that don't share bodily fluids.

Sex Ed: It's Not Just a School Thing

Many schools offer a sex education class or two, but it's a cop-out to think that you're off the hook here. Many school districts provide inadequate programs, plus, no matter how wonderful the program is, it can't substitute for your own ideas, wisdom, values, and understanding. You may feel squeamish about talking graphically with your child. Do your best. Read together, draw anatomically correct pictures, take a deep breath, and talk!

Tales from the Parent Zone

"No, Mom, Sabrina is *not* physically precocious," Alana explained. Grandma Rose began menstruating at 17—it's no wonder she was surprised when Sabrina started her period at 12. The average age that a girl reaches puberty has plunged in the last 100 years, from 16 to less than 13 years.

When Should You Start Sex Education?

As soon as kids start asking questions about sex and bodies, parents should start answering them—truthfully and casually. Little ones should get as many details as they can comprehend. Listen closely to their questions and answer what is being asked, being careful not to overwhelm them. Older kids should get the gory details. What, you say your child and you already talk about sex? Are you sure? In *Venus in Blue Jeans*, a fascinating book that portrays 15 teenage girls and their mothers, and describes how they talk with each other about sex, author Natalie Bartle describes how each of the mothers believes that she and her daughter communicate openly about sex, while the daughters believe they never talk. Same conversations, different conclusions.

What Should You Say?

Kids need to know how their bodies work, and they need to know how to prevent pregnancy and disease transmission. Say whatever comes into your head to start, as long as it's true. Sex education is a process, and it's far more than one brief, uncomfortable conversation. It's a process of building trust with your child. Use your listening techniques (Chapters 3 and 8). Never penalize your child for telling the truth about sex (or drugs, or anything else, either). Let him talk, confide, and trust. Stay cool. You have "later" (in private) to react. Your child needs you to be an ally.

The risks for your sexually active child—pregnancy (I said the rates are going down, not that it doesn't happen), disease, and emotional damage—are great. Your child needs to know the plain facts, but that's not enough. And it's not enough to stress an abstinence-only education (it won't work, anyway). Try for abstinence-based education. That will leave room for conversation.

Your child also needs to know that:

➤ Desire is one of the joys and wonders of being human, but it takes a long time to know how to handle it (and many people never learn!).

➤ Sexuality is a natural part of adolescence, though it doesn't necessarily mean beginning sexual activity.

➤ Any sexual involvement should be by mutual consent.

Tales from the Parent Zone

Jason was observed blinking frequently, staring obsessively at his hands, popping breath mints, and applying zit medication every few hours. Finally he confessed to his parents. He had been doing "it" and he'd heard through the grapevine that "it" would give you hairy palms, make you go blind, cause bad breath, weaken the blood, and cause pimples. His parents hastened to reassure him that masturbation is a normal part of sexuality, and just about everybody "does it."

When talking about sex:

➤ Follow your child's lead. If the conversation is going in a direction you didn't expect, take a deep breath and go there, too.

➤ Express your values (and these might be anything from "if it feels good, do it" to "after the gown, the rice, the best man's toast, and the champagne, and not until then!") but don't lecture. Just the facts, puh-*leeze*.

➤ Kids need to know about birth control, how it is used, and where they can go to get it. Your child may also need direct support in the form of birth control and information and supplies to practice safer sex. When done in a caring manner, and when it's provided as prevention rather than encouragement, this knowledge and equipment won't cause your child to have sex. Just 'cause they have access to birth control does not mean they'll be out catting around tomorrow night. Your child knows where the kitchen fire extinguisher is too, right? Is he going around lighting fires?

➤ Every 11-year-old child should certainly understand the male and female reproductive systems—and know how to prevent pregnancy.

➤ Stay calm. Don't overromanticize sex ("Like the smell of blooming roses, like fireworks, transcendent, spiritual") or scare your kid ("The first time you'll bleed, it hurts, you'll feel terrible").

➤ Stress that no matter what happens, you are there for your child.

Ideally, you want your child to be able to make smart choices, freely and without pressure. Discuss the following warning signs (these should make little blinking lights go off in your child's head):

➤ When they aren't practicing safer sex to prevent STDs, and using birth control to prevent pregnancy.

➤ When they're responding to peer pressure to be sexually active.

➤ If one partner is pressuring the other.

➤ When the partners aren't peers, when they aren't roughly the same age.

It's a Good Idea!

When is sex "sex?" Is it flirting, kissing, intercourse, or an "Arkansas howdy?" More legalistic minds than mine have tormented the country over this one. While every kid has to decide what level of sexual involvement she feels comfortable with for herself, they are strongly influenced by where you stand (even if where you stand is "I think you need to figure it out for yourself, Honey.").

Behave Yourself!

Most pregnant teens have been impregnated by older boys or men.

AIDS and Other Sexually Transmitted Diseases

Safer sex is vital when you consider the risks of STDs (sexually transmitted diseases). Some of these include herpes, syphilis, gonorrhea, chlamydia, genital warts, pelvic inflammatory disorder, and, of course, HIV/AIDS. Here's the thing: Despite warnings and extensive sex education, 75% of all teenage pregnancies occur as the result of using no form of birth control. The message about safer sex and birth control is not always getting across, or the importance of sex and love (even risky sex) overweighs concerns. We need to redouble our efforts to let kids know specifically what they can do to make sex safer, how to take responsibility for their own sexual lives, and where they can go for help.

Pregnancy: It Still Happens

In the terror of AIDS and other STDs, and the encouraging statistics about teen pregnancy, it's hard to remember that teens still get pregnant every day. Fifty percent of premarital teen pregnancies occur within six months of first intercourse, and one in five teenage women who are sexually active become pregnant. Open your mouth, and talk about birth control.

When Your Kid Is Sexually Active

You've talked, you've listened, and somewhere in that process of communication you've discovered that your child is "doing it." Or if not exactly doing "it," doing something sexual. The reality is that there's not much you can do. You can forbid it. Do you think that's going to work? People who want to have sex will find places and times to do it.

A better approach is to treat your child's decision to be sexually active as you treat all her important decisions: with discussions of your own feelings, suggestions for other options, support for the positive intent (the desire to be held? the need for acceptance?), and unconditional love.

Any kind of romantic involvement comes with the risk of heartbreak, but there are other emotional risks to teen sex as well. Is your child trading sex for love, self-esteem, or social standing?

While you have no control over the emotional risks involved in your child's romantic life (though you may well suffer along), you do have influence over the physical risks (especially for young kids). If it's a daughter, talk, talk, talk with her, get her birth control, or verify that she is using it. If it's a son, talk, talk, talk, and provide condoms. Sex can be dangerous, and this is not the time to be squeamish or puritanical.

Behave Yourself!

Do curfews keep kids from sexual activity? No way! Most kids get into "trouble" in broad daylight, after school and before dinnertime. Nobody said sex only happens after dark.

Talking About Homosexuality

Almost 10% of the population is gay, lesbian, or bisexual, so whether or not you suspect or know your child is gay, it's vital to talk with him about homosexuality as a part of his sexual education. Remember, if he's not gay, a number of the people he knows are gay, and there is still tremendous homophobia and violence against homosexuals in our society. If he is gay (or suspects he might be), he'll need all the support you can give him to accept himself, and make his way in a nonaccepting world.

Homosexuality appears randomly through the population. It is not "caused" by anything you or your partner did. It can't be prevented or cured. Let your child know that homosexuality is just another form of diversity. Gays, lesbians, and bisexuals only want the same acceptance and caring everybody else wants. As a respectful person, your child should accept this difference as she would accept any other.

If your child suspects or knows she might be gay or bisexual (and many kids know this about themselves at a very early age), she may feel extremely troubled about it. Because of society's lack of acceptance, gay and lesbian youth are at a high risk for depression and risky behaviors, and are far more likely to try to commit suicide (the Center for Population Options says gay and bisexual youths comprise 30% of all annual youth suicides). There's information on resources for your gay or bisexual child in Appendix C.

It's a Good Idea!

Sex play is normal among kids under ten. It's not unusual, and it's not necessarily a sign of sexual orientation, for play and experimentation to take place between members of the same, as well as the opposite, sex. At around age ten, this play may change to exploration and experimentation (and doesn't mean a commitment to a particular sexual orientation, either).

What About Your Own Misguided Youth?

Okay, you were no saint yourself. With all this open and honest conversation about sex and drugs going on, many parents have concerns about what to tell their kids about their own, somewhat sordid past. Here are some questions to consider when you think about whether or not you should "reveal all."

➤ Will you set a bad example?

➤ What about behavior modeling?

➤ Will your kids think you're a hypocrite for saying, "Do as I say, not as I did?"

Some parents decide to go the "no-disclosure" route. Of course, they risk being discovered. Discovery will make it harder for your children to trust you again, and that is why I believe in honesty (though not confession). Let your children know what you tried, and when, and what your experience was, both the good and the bad. That doesn't mean digging out the old lava lamp and bong to reminisce about getting stoned and listening to the Stones, or describing the feel of Jimmie Johnson's soft hands going up your shirt the first time you went to second base. Keep your dignity, and your stories. But answer honestly when asked. When you talk about your own past, and the issues of sex and drugs:

➤ Show that you take the issues (and your child's question) seriously. Don't ignore them or brush them off.

➤ Express your opinions and your values, and use your own experiences as examples of how you learned what you know.

➤ This is not a time for yelling. (Is any time?) Take it easy, take it slow. No lectures, please!

➤ Never use the "Don't do what I did" or the "Drugs are different—stronger—these days and the social scene has changed" rap. Whether or not it's true, it won't go over well, it will probably piss your kid off, and it won't work. Be honest, express your feelings, and make sure your child knows the facts.

The Least You Need to Know

➤ Kids are exposed to drugs, and they're wired for reproduction.

➤ Experimentation with sex and drugs is developmentally normal (and that has nothing to do with the risks).

➤ Three words you need to know: education, education, education.

➤ Your child needs to know your values and expectations.

➤ Your child also needs to have your trust.

➤ Supplying your child with birth control and safer sex supplies doesn't mean you've given her carte blanche, it just means you're protecting her health.

➤ When it comes to your past, tell all, but subtly. No, we don't want details!

Chapter 22

Trouble on the Home Front

In This Chapter

➤ Knowing when your kid is in trouble

➤ About self-abuse, eating disorders, depression, and abusive relationships

➤ Nine actions to take when your child is arrested

➤ Reducing violence in your child's environment and in your child

---

Brutal violence, suicide, murder—it's always horrifying when it happens, but it's somehow more shocking when the perpetrator is a minor. The vast majority of kids will (thankfully!) never make headlines in this horrific manner. But what about the heartbreaking "little cousins" of these breaking news stories? Depression, self-abuse, addiction, school troubles, eating disorders, running away, vandalism, arrest—these are the unpleasant but necessary subjects of this chapter.

This book focuses on problem prevention techniques, but sometimes, no matter what you do, your child continues (or begins) behavior that is just not acceptable, at home or out in society. When this happens, parents are filled with self-doubt and despair: "Am I a terrible parent? Is my child corrupted forever? Is there anything I can do?" Kids do get into big trouble sometimes. It's important to both understand what to look for when kids are having trouble and what to do when things go wrong.

How Do You Know If Your Child Is in Trouble?

Sometimes trouble is obvious. Your child's life is a disaster, and so is your household. Tension, fighting, lies and deceptions, messes—both physical and metaphorical. Your child is incorrigible, depressed or manic, starving herself or carving herself with ugly black tattoos. Or she's come home with a black eye, and you find home pregnancy test wands in the bathroom wastebasket. Perhaps it's just her grades—plunging from B's to D's in one semester. Or you dread the phone ringing, fearing it's the cops—vandalism, again. You fear for her, you blame yourself (and a part of you hates her for bringing this all on you). As for you, you've barely slept in weeks.

Okay, get a grip, your child is in trouble. While there may not be any quick solutions, there are approaches. And of course the first approach is to realize that there is a problem, and that you are in over your head.

When the Skies Are Cloudy

Sometimes it's not quite so obvious that your child is having problems. "The clues were there, if only I'd looked!" cries the mother of the juvenile delinquent. It's not always true that you can tell in advance when a child is getting into big trouble (and it's unfair to beat yourself up after the fact—see Chapter 23). But there are often clues that not all is well. Clue number one: Look for changes in behavior. The older your child gets, the closer you should watch for signs of serious trouble, depression, or self-abusive behavior (especially in the teen years).

Changes at School

Most kids find a groove at school and slide along it; doing extremely well, getting along fine, or just getting by. A change in your child's pattern warrants a "What's up?" Is he suddenly missing a lot of school? Is he staying home, or is he cutting? What about his grades? Have they dropped? It may be that there's something terrible going on at school itself (which means a trip or a phone call) or it might be a response to other things going on in his life. Either way, you should investigate.

Changes in Friends

Hangin' with a different crowd? Or maybe she's gone from hanging with a crowd to having only one friend, a new boyfriend she seems too close to, or no friends at all. Don't jump to conclusions. Adolescence does odd things to kids. Almost all kids play with identity and peer groups (see Chapter 16) and if the rest of her life seems fine—she's still in the Drama Club and getting good grades—there's probably little to worry about. If

Behave Yourself!

It's been said that the hardest part of making change is realizing the need for it.

It's a Good Idea!

School involvement is an excellent way to keep an eye on your child's well-being. Teachers respond to kids whose parents are involved. If teachers know you are a concerned parent, they'll be more attentive to your child, and will be able to tell you if anything is amiss. Don't rely on those overworked teachers to call you. You call them!

It's a Good Idea!

A sudden raise in grades warrants a "What's up?" too—though it usually doesn't mean trouble.

her old friends don't want her around, her behavior is "off," and school isn't working out, check it out. There may be trouble brewing.

Changes in Behavior at Home

You know your child, and, if you stop to really look at him, you'll probably get a sense that something is not right. You may not know what is bugging him—that's a whole different subject. How is he treating you? (If he's an adolescent, he may be treating you terribly; that's often par for the course.) If his weight, appetite, or personal hygiene has altered drastically, if he's exercising frantically or spending all his time listening to death rock and painting the walls of his room black, if the tensions between you are unbearably strained, there may be some problems here, and your family may need some additional help.

What You Can Do and What You Cannot Do

Positive parenting means persisting in showing your care, concern, and positive reinforcement, even when your child is treating you terribly. Often a child (even an older child) perceives his parents as an outside extension of himself. The worse he feels about himself (and the more trouble he is in), the worse he'll treat you. Yes, you do deserve to be treated with care, respect, and concern. Even as you protest the way he's talking to you, persist in treating your child as you would like to be treated. Believe me, he will hear the care in your voice, and it matters. Giving a child a sense of his own strengths will help him learn to respect his body, respect and care for himself, plus feel confident enough to resist peer pressures.

Many problems that kids have can be solved within the family, or by enlisting the aid of teachers, coaches, and other important adults in your child's life. Sometimes problems are larger than that. When do you go for outside help? The general rule is that you need help when the health or safety (of anybody) is threatened, and you are powerless to do anything about it. The hardest part is assessing the situation to figure out if you are powerless. Once you do decide to get help with your child's situation, you'll find that there are many resources available. We'll devote all of Chapter 24 to getting assistance.

It's a Good Idea!

You need outside help with your parenting when the health or safety of anybody in the family is threatened, and you are powerless to do anything about it.

It's a Good Idea!

The anger, angst, and despair of teenagers—and the behavior they express in their pain—is the darkest part of adolescence for parents, too. We want our kids happy and healthy, and it is extremely distressing when they are not. If life is very hard for your child right now, you need and deserve some support, too.

Self-Abuse, Eating Disorders, and Addiction

Many kids turn their misbehavior inward, toward themselves. This is part of adolescence's dark side for many kids—depression and self-destructive behavior such as eating disorders, sexual misconduct, and drug abuse abound. Here's a brief discussion of some of these misbehaviors, and the danger signals you should look for in your child.

Self-Abuse

Life for older children is increasingly stressful. When stress and depression turn inward, many kids turn against their own bodies. While eating disorders and substance abuse and addiction are all forms of self injury, many distressed teens perform self-destructive behaviors that include cutting themselves, burning themselves, and extreme risk-taking.

Behave Yourself!

Piercings, tattoos, and branding may be the style, but there's a difference between minor risk-taking and keeping up with the crowd, and major self-damage caused by depression. Just how extreme are those piercings, anyway?

Self-abuse may be hidden behavior (sliced arms under long sleeves, cigarette burns on the torso) or may be clearly visible—if you are looking for it. And some of it is a matter of a judgment call. Is that lower lip pierce a statement celebrating pain? Self-abuse has recently become so rampant among American teenagers, mostly female, that it's been dubbed "the anorexia of the '90s." Self injurers cut or hurt themselves to relieve extreme anxiety. If your child is injuring herself, she needs help. Check out the resources in Appendix B.

Tales from the Parent Zone

In high school, I knew a boy who burnt his arms with cigarettes when he was upset. A dear friend's mother pokes compulsively at the pores in her face until she bleeds. These people are not rare. Currently, it's estimated that around two million people in America self-abuse.

Eating Disorders

Eating disorders plague numerous bright, motivated girls. Many parents have some knowledge about the two most common eating disorders, anorexia (self-starvation) and bulimia (bingeing and purging). Though these eating disorders are extremely common among teenage girls and younger children (primarily girls), many are shocked when they discover that their daughter is suffering from an eating disorder. That's true for several reasons:

➤ Parents see their child every day and her loss of weight may be so gradual that they don't realize she's becoming anorexic.

➤ Many bulimics are of normal weight.

➤ Parents have natural defenses against accepting very painful realities.

Eating disorders are related to poor body image (see Chapter 16) and stress. They are sometimes triggered by the loss of control children feel when their bodies start to show signs of development. Eating disorders are serious problems that, in the last number of years, have been recognized and heavily researched (even as the number of girls suffering from them has grown). There are many resources available for parents who think, suspect, or dread that their daughter has an eating disorder:

➤ Your daughter's school might have an educational program about eating disorders (many do) and probably has school staff or counselors with resources or information.

➤ Read. You'll feel less panicked the more informed you become. There are many books on the subject available in the public library, and many articles on the Internet.

➤ The American Anorexia/Bulimia Association offers support, literature, and information about anorexia, bulimia, and other eating disorders. See Appendix B for contact information.

If you think your child is suffering from an eating disorder, don't ignore it, it probably won't just go away. Get help. You can't do this one alone. Start with your child's school and doctor's offices—they very often have on-site resources or recommendations.

It's important to understand that you cannot regulate your child's eating. Control and independence are two of the important reasons behind your child's eating disorder (the positive intent of it), which means that parental involvement will probably make it worse. (And worse often means hospitalization and permanent damage to her body—yes, this is serious stuff!) Back off, baby, and get her some professional help. With professional help, you may be able to help your child set her own goals and limits. Take care of yourself, too. Consider individual or family counseling. Being the parent of a child with an eating disorder can be very stressful.

Words to Parent By

Anorexia is an eating disorder characterized by self-starvation because of a distortion of body image. *Bulimia* is an eating disorder characterized by cycles of bingeing (overeating) and self-induced purging (vomiting or overuse of laxatives).

Tales from the Parent Zone

She walks through my neighborhood every day, a woman I knew as a teenager. Back then, she was just very thin. Now, after years of anorexia, she's a walking skeleton, her hair fine, her skin leathery from years of abuse and starvation. I have trouble understanding how she can still be alive. According to the American Anorexia/Bulimia Association, 90% of all teenagers with eating disorders are female. One percent of teenage girls in the United States suffer from anorexia, and up to 10% of those who suffer from it may die from it.

Depression

Childhood is a time of fun, adventure, and joy, free from the cares of the adult world, a kind of paradise on earth: *garbage!* Contrary to this idealized view of childhood, the facts are that 10–35% of boys and 15–45% of girls suffer from depression.

Society has a hard time realizing that kids get depressed, and childhood and teen depression is sometimes difficult to diagnose. As a result, only about one-third of all depressed kids get treatment. Here are a few facts and suggestions for parents whose child might be depressed:

➤ Kids can't always express their feelings. Your child may not have the skills to let you know that she is depressed. Instead, you'll see it reflected in her behavior.

➤ Depression in kids is often confused with attention deficit disorder (see Chapter 20).

➤ Other symptoms of depression may include irritability, rage, and moodiness, sleeping problems, a change in interests (or loss of interests), disruptive behavior, unexplained fears, or a preoccupation with death.

➤ Depressed kids often complain of stomachaches, tiredness, and headaches.

➤ If depression is untreated, the depressed child is at high risk for drug and alcohol abuse.

➤ Depression in kids and teens is often successfully treated with psychotherapy (and in many cases, with drug therapy as well).

➤ Bring your child in for a check-up, express your concerns to the doctor, and make sure the doctor rules out physical causes.

Substance Abuse and Addiction

In Chapter 21, you learned that drug and alcohol use is different from drug and alcohol abuse, and that many, many kids experiment with mind-, mood-, or body-altering substances in their teen years. It's one thing to tolerate normal exploration, it's another to ignore a serious problem your child is having.

Drug abuse and addiction is serious and scary, and devastates lives—the life of the abuser, and everybody close to him. Many substance abusers begin their abuse very young, and there is an enormous increase of abuse in teenagers who have parents who are alcoholics or addicts.

If you compare a child whose parents don't abuse alcohol and drugs with a child whose parents (or parent) do, the numbers are shocking. According to Darryl S. Inaba and William E. Cohen (*Uppers, Downers, and All Arounders: Physical and Mental Effects of Psychoactive Drugs*), a child with one parent who is an alcoholic or an addict is 34% more likely to become an alcoholic or suffer from a drug addiction than a child who doesn't have an alcoholic or addicted parent. If both parents suffer, a child is 400% more likely to have addiction problems. And if the child is male with both an alcoholic or drug addicted father and grandfather, a child is 900% more likely to abuse alcohol or drugs than the male child whose father and grandfather do not abuse alcohol or drugs. Is this nature or nurture? Probably a little bit of both.

This means that if you have substance abuse problems and you don't want your child to follow in your footsteps, you need to take action. (There are suggestions for help in Chapter 24 and in Appendix C.)

Tales from the Parent Zone

"What do we live in, a country of drunks and druggies?" my friend Paloma asks. "Sometimes it seems like everybody I know is the adult child of an alcoholic, or a drug abuser." Paloma's exaggerating, but she's not so far off. Twenty-eight million Americans have at least one alcoholic or drug-addicted parent.

It's not just kids of substance abusers who abuse substances, though. When a child or teen is stressed out, use can easily turn into abuse. How can you know when your child is in trouble with drugs or alcohol?

➤ It's not always as obvious as your child roaring home stinking of booze, slurring words, and crashing into walls. Those are pretty good signs, though.

➤ If your attitude is that "Kids will be kids," you should still consider that perhaps your kid is being a "kid" a bit too often for her health.

➤ Garbage cans full of gin bottles, scary people calling all hours of the day and night, track marks—these are all obvious signs. But most young substance abusers are more devious (or not so far gone) and hide their activities. Look for more subtle clues (like the ones detailed above in "How Do You Know If Your Child Is in Trouble?" above). Troubles can't be compartmentalized (though when we're having them, we often delude ourselves that we can). If your child is abusing or addicted, there are probably other clues.

Relationship Abuses

Teenage girls are particularly vulnerable to relationship abuse, especially if their partners are older boys or men. Watch for changes in your daughter's social life. How does her boyfriend treat her? Has she lost touch with her friends because she's spending all her time with him? Does she truly seem happy? She may just be in love. Then again, she may be involved with a boy/man who is overly possessive.

When Your Child Runs Away

If life gets tense enough, your child may run away from home. Running away is often portrayed in books and movies as a grand adventure, an opportunity for a young person to find himself and come of age away from his staid, grumpy old parents. In reality, running away is very dangerous, and very scary (often for the kid, too!).

Kids run away when there is big trouble in their lives. A pregnancy, a failed class, a friend's suicide, threatened violence, a drug dealer seeking owed money, unbearable tension with you, or sexual or physical abuse are some of the reasons a child may choose to leave home. For some kids, running away seems the only way out of a bad situation. The vast majority of the time, they are wrong.

The world is not a benign place, especially for kids who've led a sheltered life and who aren't street smart. (These are often the kids seeking the glorious adventures promised in books and movies.) Young boys and young girls often end up abused and on the street, sometimes prostituting themselves for money.

If your child threatens to run away, take it seriously. You diminish her issues when you sarcastically pack her bag and put it by the door. If she does leave, look for her immediately. Contact her friends (though expect them to lie for her). If you have any reason to believe she has gone further than her best friend's attic (where she might be, taking a break from the world), contact the police. If she calls, swallow your anger and let her talk.

Once she returns (or is found), realize that this is a crisis, and a big call for changes and for help. Professional intervention will help all of you. Running away is a drastic step. What is too painful in your child's life? What is she avoiding?

When You Discover Misbehavior

If you discover your child in the middle of serious illegal misbehavior, you must stop it, and then you must decide how to deal with it. Do you turn in your own child? Do you apply consequences yourself?

➤ Stop your child, and if you cannot stop him, let him know that you will call in authorities. Let your child know clearly that you cannot condone or ignore the misbehavior. Express your dismay, horror, shock, and disapproval. Keep it calm— don't rant and rave (the calmer you are, the clearer and more effective your message will be).

➤ Acknowledge to yourself that your child has put you in an impossible situation.

➤ Get the child to a neutral place. Before anybody does anything else, allow some time to cool down.

➤ Your child should make restitution to anybody who has been injured by the misbehavior. How that should happen depends upon what's been done to the person's property or person.

➤ In some cases, restitution may be the only necessary consequence. In other cases, you may consider taking legal action, and calling in the police. Before you do this, think it through. This may have serious, long-term ramifications for your child, and for your relationship. Your relationship may never recover, as your child will likely perceive your act as breaking the trust between you, no matter how positive your intent. There's a big debate about the significance and effectiveness of "scaring a kid straight" by letting him have a taste of the justice system. Think long and hard before taking this step.

➤ If you decide not to have your child arrested, let him know there is a no-tolerance policy in effect, and any single breech of it will mean legal action will be taken.

➤ And yes, you need to find professional help for your child. Immediately.

Outside Misbehavior: Legal Misbehavior and Crimes

It's miserable enough to have a miserable child who is hurting himself or others with his behavior. It's even more miserable to have that child busted for that behavior, or in trouble for hurting other people or their property.

When You Get That Call

The phone rings, it's your child using his "one call" from jail to let you know he's been busted. Or the doorbell rings, it's a police officer, telling you your sweet baby is locked up in juvenile hall. However it happens, it's every parent's nightmare. How will you respond to this tragedy? Should you ever find yourself in this horrible position (and I sincerely hope you do not), here are a few suggestions:

1. The minute you get the word, your first response will be to take action, any action, whether it's screaming, throwing up, fainting, running to the car, calling the bail bondsman, socking the informing officer, or killing yourself. This is normal. You're in terrible shock, and the human response to terrible shock is "fight or flight," and sometimes both. Please try not to react too fast; you'll only make things worse. Gather your strength and, for a moment or two, try to concentrate on your breathing (don't hyperventilate!).

2. You need the facts. You need to know what has happened, when, why, as much as you possibly can know. You have a lot to process, and you need to have as many facts as possible at your disposal. Ask questions. If you can find a pen and a piece of paper, write down as much information as you can. Wait, did you find out where they are keeping your child? Is there a phone number? Will you be allowed to see him? You need details. Don't talk, ask. The one thing to stress, if you are talking to your child, is that he shouldn't say anything until you get him a lawyer.

3. Get off the phone, say good-bye to the cop, dismiss the other people who are there, or excuse yourself to the bathroom. If you can, set the kitchen timer for 15 minutes. I know it sounds extreme, in the middle of such a crisis, but you need the time to calm down and figure out your approach. Do you meditate? If you do, try to. If not, sit quietly with your eyes closed, breathing deeply to calm your beating heart and slow your hot anger. There are two things that you need to remind yourself. First, you are your child's ally. That means you are on his side, no matter what has happened. That doesn't mean that he is right, or that you will make excuses for him. It just means that, as his parent and ally, you will work to get him out of trouble, not fight to keep him in it. Second, there's always his side of the story, and he is innocent until proven guilty.

4. As you ponder what your course of action should be, think about what your child needs to have happen in this situation. His needs might be very different from his wants. (He wants for it never to have happened, and he wants to go home and forget about it.) Does he need to experience the full natural consequences of his actions? Does he need to be shown how strong of an ally you are? It's easy to say in advance how you would feel if your child were arrested; people usually fall in one of two camps—"Let my baby go!" or "Let her rot!" Reality is always different from fantasy. How do you feel now?

5. Consider what options for action you have here, based on the limited information you have. Much of this will depend on what your child has been arrested for. Is this a victimless crime like prostitution, a violent crime like assault, or something in between? Can you provide bail, talk the arresting officers out of pressing charges, hire a good lawyer, or merely attend the trial?

6. What would happen if you didn't do anything? (Hey, you have to consider all actions, here!) If your child has been busted for possession and you don't post bail, she'll stay in jail. Juvenile hall can be a devastating experience. Will she learn a positive lesson about the dangers of breaking the law, or will she be more injured than helped?

7. What do you need to have happen? This is number 7 on the list because it is of lesser concern, in this crisis, than what your child needs. Don't skip this step though. Staying in touch with your own reactions and needs will keep you focused now, and, later when you are dealing with the fallout from this incident, it will give you information to help you process it.

8. As you start deciding just what approach and action you will take, try to separate your fury at your kid from your decision. Yes, you're angry! You should be! But you need to do the right thing, no matter how much you want to kill your child (remember that two wrongs make a very long prison sentence).

9. Make your decision, gather your fortitude, breathe deeply, and perform calmly.

Facing Your Child

So then there she is, your child the criminal, and you're facing her for the first time. She's going to feel mixed about seeing you—almost as mixed as you feel about seeing her. Remember, as the two of you work through your shock and shame, that she's still your child, the same person who you held, rocked, potty trained, and taught to make latkes or to change a flat tire. You'll get through this.

Your first task? To listen, listen, actively listen. You need all the empathy you can get (and active and proactive listening build empathy). You also need information about what happened, and those listening techniques will bring that to you. If your child doesn't want to talk about it, be patient. Stay open, receptive, and loving. Yes, you can and should express your anger and moral outrage, but try not to stay in it.

Your child is ashamed of herself. Try to resist the urge to punish her, get tough with her, or to rub it in. Try to bring a positive influence into her life—a walk in the snow, an art project, a run on the beach. She needs to heal, and the only way she'll learn from this incident is if she is given room to heal. It's time, too, to look for a good therapist. Don't treat this as a phase. Something is definitely out of hand.

Getting Help

Therapy is now a nonnegotiable issue. Your child may have veto power over who he sees (therapy is a personal relationship, and people don't always "click"), but not over the fact that he must go to his sessions. There are suggestions for choosing a therapist in Chapter 24.

It's a Good Idea!

If your child has had a criminal incident, show love, compassion, empathy, and zero tolerance.

How Bad Is Bad?

Once your child has been bailed out or released, once you've dealt with the immediate crisis and had your initial confrontation with him, you'll need to assess the long-term damage. Here are some questions that might help you get a sense of how bad things really are:

1. How old is he? (The younger a child begins criminal behavior and patterns, the more serious it is, and the harder the patterns are to break.)

2. How serious was the crime? Was it "victimless" or "violent"? Did it involve drugs? Was it gang related? The "worse" the crime, the bigger the need for immediate help.

3. Is this the first time the child has been in trouble? Even one time is terribly concerning, but a one-time crime can be a mistake, while "big trouble" incidents more than a couple of times signify a child who is seriously disturbed.

4. How is your child doing, generally? Was this his idea, was he influenced?

5. What caused the crime? Try to find a "positive intent" to respond to (even as you condemn the actions, and press your child to make restitution).

The Private Face, the Public Face

When your child is in big trouble, you're likely to feel furious and betrayed. When somebody is destroying his life (and, it often feels like, your life, too), anger is an appropriate emotion. You're also probably going to feel very worried, perhaps even hopeless. Parents of kids in trouble also talk about wanting to put emotional distance between themselves and the troubled child—"He's your son, you deal with him!"

How you deal with the situation in public (attending the trial, defending your child to strangers, pleading with the judge) may be very different from your private reaction. In public, you have to be heroic. You are your child's ally. (Yes, you can be furious for being called upon to be heroic.)

The Violent Child, Our Violent Society

There's no simple way to reduce violent impulses in your child. Kids who are violent may have attention deficit disorder or impulse control problems, or they may have simply picked up violence as a way to handle conflict from the society at large.

No wonder. Human beings are violent (no other animal species has organized wars), plus, we are a culture that celebrates violence. Our heroes are boxers, action fighters, soldiers, and police with drawn guns. Playground politics often promote the toughest kid to the ruler of the roost.

Whether or not your child has had a "violent episode," even if the level of day-to-day violence in your household is only physical fighting ("Ben and Jerry! *Stop punching!*"), if you are trying to raise reasonable, well-behaved kids, you should reduce the violent influences in your child's life. Stress other ways to resolve conflict. Just because human beings struggle against violent tendencies doesn't mean violence is acceptable in your child or in your household.

Reducing a child's violent tendencies is difficult, but one direct and effective thing you can do is to reduce her exposure to violence. (This is tough and it requires strong personal commitment. Raising gentle human beings is tough.) Here are two suggestions:

➤ Model nonviolent behavior. This is one area where behavior modeling is highly effective, as shown in many studies. Discipline your child without resorting to corporal punishment. Violence of any kind escalates and tends to create more violence. A child who is hit may well take out her frustration on another child. A person who is exposed or subjected to domestic violence as a child very often becomes an abuser as an adult. If you or anybody in your household is having trouble with rage control, or there is any physical abuse going on, you need support to change the situation. It's not just for your sake, it's for the future of your child. Call the National Domestic Violence Hotline at 800/799-7233. *Now!*

➤ Between Saturday morning cartoons, video games, and violent movies, your child is exposed to visual violence far more than is healthy. Experts estimate that by the time an American child is 14, she'll have seen 11,000 murders (and that's just on TV!). The more violence a child sees, the more desensitized she is to it. And the more likely she is to turn to violence as a solution to her own problems. Am I saying "turn it off"? Only kinda. TV is such an established part of American life that most people aren't ready to take this step. I am saying, "Screen what your child sees, and reduce her television watching time." Bonus: Less TV means more exercise, more quality family time, a less passive child, and a more creative one.

Behave Yourself!

Violence escalates, and only creates more violence.

Behave Yourself!

You can think what you like (and sometimes thinking "I'll hit you so hard you'll sail all the way to China" might even make you feel better), but never threaten violence out loud. It can feel extremely threatening to a child, and damage the trust and respect between you.

The Demonized Teenager

Headline news stories about kids with guns shooting up school yards have fed into the societal myth of the "superpredator," a new, evil breed of kids without education and conscience. People are terrified of older kids and teenagers. It's true that crime rates among teens are too high and teens have far too much access to firearms—one recent study by the U.S. Justice Department's National Institute of Justice showed that, of 734 high school males surveyed, nearly one-third had at least one firearm. Teens, however, are not as menacing as we are led to believe by the media.

Last Resorts

What can you do when your child is in deep trouble—internal or external, and nothing has worked? You've gone the therapy route, you've learned far more about the court system than you ever wanted to learn. If your child is at risk of injuring himself or somebody else, you may need to take it a step further.

Here are three last resorts (and they're listed briefly because you should rarely need to get this far).

➤ *Intervention.* Intervention is a special confrontational meeting (usually held immediately after a crisis) where people who love the child and who are involved in her life confront her as a group, express their concern about her problems, and tell her the impact her problems are having on their lives. Intervention is quite extreme, and sometimes quite effective (*especially* with young people who don't always consider other people's lives).

➤ *Residential treatment.* If your child is suffering from severe behavior problems, mental illness, drug or alcohol addiction, or a severe eating disorder, you might consider a residential treatment program. The success rate for residential treatment programs is decent—though not total (and it will need to be followed up stringently with outpatient care).

➤ *Having your child declared incorrigible, or "turning her in."* These are very serious actions with possible lifelong ramifications. Ramifications may include being labeled as a trouble-maker forever, missing out on important, developmental milestones such as graduating from high school. You may also lose all parental claim to your child if she is made a ward of the court. Having your child declared incorrigible, or "turning her in" should never be done in the heat of anger, and they should never be done without long, hard consideration, and then, only after every other possible avenue is explored. You risk losing your child forever.

Rebuilding Trust, Rebuilding Confidence

A brush with trouble, a dip in disaster—these are things that can shake a parent to the core. It's hard to regain trust in your child when he's done something terribly wrong, or gotten deep into emotional disaster. It's hard to have confidence that things will change, improve, and mellow out!

Think about all the crises in your life, the changes you've been through, the mistakes you've made. All of us face trouble—some big, others small. But things fluctuate. Life is long, traumas subside, crises are resolved, things and people change. Your pain will pass. Take a walk down a quiet country road on a moonless night. Walk along a foggy beach. Hold a baby. These things will help you regain your perspective and regain your sense of hope. Onward! There are things to be done!

The Least You Need to Know

➤ Problems leak! By observing changes in your child's behavior, you may be able to tell if she's headed for trouble.

➤ Get outside help when the health or safety (of anybody) is threatened, and you are powerless to do anything about it.

➤ You cannot regulate your child's eating.

➤ Many teens suffer from depression, but the symptoms may be masked by other behavior.

➤ If you are a substance abuser, your child has a much higher chance of becoming one, too.

➤ If your child is arrested, you will probably feel furious, hurt, and betrayed.

➤ You are your child's ally, and need to work to get her out of her problems.

➤ Violence breeds violence.

➤ There is always hope.

Part 7
Finding Balance and Serenity

Raising a child (well-behaved or not) is a balancing act. If you're out of balance, the rest of your family will be, too. Part 7, the last part of the book, is all about getting to smooth. First you—we'll talk about ways to treat yourself well so you can nurture your child, and techniques for getting rid of all that random guilt that seems to be floating everywhere.

Yet sometimes you and your family just can't do it alone. It's hard to reach out for help, but here in Part 7 I'll try to make it a little easier. I'll explain when to get therapy (for your child, family, or self), how to find a therapist, and what to look for.

The well-behaved child lives in a well-balanced and well-behaved family. The last chapter of the book focuses on nurturing and building a stronger family—using family time, art, food, reverence, and community service—and looks at the family's role in the larger community, and in the world.

Chapter 23

You're Human Too, You Know

In This Chapter

➤ Looking at, and respecting, your own struggles

➤ Getting rid of parent guilt

➤ Real parents laugh

➤ Creating a self-pamper list

➤ About mistakes, failures, and changing

What won't you do to become a good parent? For most of us, parenting matters as much as anything else in life. So much is at stake. Worry about parenting decisions keeps us up nights, turns our hair gray, and makes our teeth fall out (okay, maybe I'm exaggerating about the last one). All parents want the best for their kids. We need them to turn out all right—happy, healthy, satisfied.

None of us are perfect at parenting. All of us are desperately flawed. "It's so hard, and I'm such a mess at it," I've heard parent after parent cry. Yet we continue to ask more questions, read new books, try new approaches. What does it take to persevere in the face of the facts that there are no guarantees, and that anything we do as parents is likely to be wrong? This is a chapter about imperfection—about what we expect for ourselves, the ways we fail, what we can do about it, and how we can take care of ourselves in the process. That means diffusing guilt, using laughter, and making apologies and changes.

Respecting Your Own Parenting Struggles

Boy, do we expect a lot from our kids, almost as much as we expect from ourselves. It's not enough to be a decent parent or a decent worker anymore, we have to eat right, look good, make money, and be a room parent, too. Remember the old pressure cookers? You screwed the lid down with the vegetables in it, turned on the heat, and boy, did that food cook quickly! But if the top wasn't on right, or you released it too fast—boom! Smushed vegetables all over the ceiling!

Parents and kids are under so much pressure—time pressure, work pressure, academic pressure—that it's not surprising there are so many explosions.

As parents, it's easy to feel like a failure. (It's also easy to feel as though your child is letting you down. This is something to work on!)

When the Going Gets Tough

When parenting gets rough, when your child is unhappy or behaving poorly, it is tough to maintain your own pride and self-respect in the parenting process. Yet your self-respect is essential, both for your own emotional survival, and for the sake of your child.

As a parent, I'm trying to teach my child to respect herself, to stand up for her rights and the rights of others. If I don't feel good about my parenting, she won't either. Why should she listen to me about discipline—or about anything else?

Tales from the Parent Zone

"Gah, my mother is such a *geek*," Patty says to her friend Wai-Ching, who looks at her in dismay. Wai-Ching would never talk about her mother in that way (at least not openly). Denigrating the role of parenthood is tied in with Western cultures. In many other societies, kids don't react the same way. Yeah, in other cultures, parents get some respect!

This Family Is Not Dysfunctional!

With all the current discussion of dysfunctional families in this society, parents (especially mothers) tend to get really slammed. No matter what kind of parents we are. Our reputations are mud.

When your child reaches preadolescence, she'll start being humiliated by the fact you exist—and have to drive her to school in that dorky car. Whether or not this is a normal developmental step (some experts feel it's necessary for separation), it doesn't feel very good, and it's hard to trust and respect yourself when your child, and every cultural message around, says that you're clueless and embarrassing at best, and destructive at worst. Understanding that these cultural messages exist can help you dismiss them and get on with the important business of parenting.

Tools for Improving Your Self-Respect

Teaching good discipline requires self-trust and self-respect. If you do not respect your own parenting approach (especially on the disciplinary front), nobody, including your child, is going to respect it either. How, then, do you build up your own self-respect?

It's a Good Idea!

Just because your child doesn't want you within two miles of her friends doesn't mean she doesn't need you and, underneath that sullen exterior, love you and want you around. Keep your pleasures furtive—take special time in another town (where nobody will see her) and wait until there's nobody around before you crank the David Bowie CD so the two of you can dance wildly.

Self-acceptance and self-responsibility are vital to increasing self-respect. Look at yourself for who you are. Change the circumstances that you can change. And give yourself a break. In short:

➤ Give yourself a lot of credit for caring (and reading this book counts!).

➤ Be honest about your failings.

➤ Ignore society's negative messages.

➤ Think about the kind of parent you want to be (and ignore that ugly little word *should*).

➤ Take good care of yourself.

➤ Take action to change and improve yourself, your family life, and the world.

➤ Give yourself even more credit for improving!

➤ Listen for positive feedback from the world. Since the world won't always tell you what a good job you're doing (or give you bonus points and parenting awards), you'll need to stand in for the world, and give yourself the credit you deserve.

Tales from the Parent Zone

Marie knows her kids will respond to her limits, and they do; Paul doubts his son will ever obey him, and he's got a recalcitrant child as a result. Your parenting—especially disciplinary—successes will come fast and best when you approach your tasks with the belief that you will succeed. (Here's where the Pollyannas of the world have a leg up—they have attitude down.) The Stanford Research Institute says that success is 88% attitude. Of course, success requires a lot more than attitude. But it's a good place to start.

A Strong and Reasonable Parent: A *REAL* Parent

Throughout this book, we've discussed setting appropriate expectations for your child and for your family. Here's the big question: What do you expect from yourself? The strong and reasonable parent that you're striving to be:

➤ Shows his struggles and her faults

➤ Laughs at the wrong times

➤ Makes mistakes

In short, he's very human.

Tales from the Parent Zone

Jonah was seven when he began to hear—and fret—about the Holocaust. His mother was distressed that he had found out how evil the world can be, but his dad felt it was important that Jonah be educated. What do kids need to know about war, pestilence, natural disasters, famine, genocide, murder, death, child molestation? Enough to link them with the world, but always told within the context of keeping them safe, and always taking their age and development in mind. Don't lie, but don't terrorize them either. Keep the conversation calm, reassure them, and tell them you will be there for them as much, and as long, as you can be, and that other people are watching out for them, too.

At times, parents who question their parenting ability attempt to shield the "awful" truth about who they are from their kids. Do you try this? You can't, of course. Putting a fake smile over a heart of pain or anger may fool you, but it sure won't fool your child. Kids know. Once you begin to act phony and lie and deceive your child, you lose your credibility. What and who can they trust if not you?

Does this mean blubbering all over your kids about the mess you've made of your life, and the awful, hopeless "reality" of life as we know it? No, no, no. Don't lie, and don't frighten—you can tell the truth and still transmit hope. Part of being real is modeling your own humanity. Your child needs to learn the process of messing up, reconsidering, thinking about it, changing your mind, apologizing or making amends, and improving. And that goes for how the world works, too.

Guilt: The Good and the Gross

Guilt! Guilt seems to be an intrinsic part of parenting, at least for the good parents (and that's the good news—if you feel guilty, then you may be on the right track to improvement).

We all have things we feel rightfully guilty about—things we could have done better but flaked off on, or times we blew it big-time and did something against our values or family rules. There are times we feel guilty for working too hard or too little, or for where we work. And sometimes we just feel guilty. Guilt can incapacitate, and guilt can also teach.

At its best, guilt can be like one of those obnoxious car alarms that talk to you when you get too close— "Warning! Step back!"—demanding your attention and letting you know that you do, indeed, need to step back and look at the whole picture. If you can use guilt as a way to gain and improve your perspective, than it's a good thing. Healthy guilt can lead to more self-respect.

Words to Parent By

Guilt is a form of self-blaming—"I shouldn't have done that!" Not all guilt is appropriate. Watch for guilt that keeps you in a situation rather than moves you forward.

The Millennium Lifestyle: A Cause for Guilt

We are all stretched too thin, trying to work too many hours, care for our kids' physical and emotional well-being, and still become self-actualized. The day only has 24 hours, and, as much as you might skip sleep, you still may be falling behind. On top of all this time crunching, you no doubt feel guilty that you're not able to put in more effort. You feel guilty when you're lazy, you feel guilty for relaxing, you feel guilty for not relaxing. If you're a mother, you feel guilty for staying home or working in the home or working out of the home. If you're a dad, you feel guilty for working too little or not making enough money or working too much. Is there anybody here who doesn't feel guilty?

Well, maybe you don't, but most moms and dads do. Look, a lot of this guilt is a function of the current society we live in. "Busy-ness guilt," as I call it, is useless, hurtful guilt because, though you need to find the lifestyle that will work for you and your family, there may be no easy solution to your situation. You are doing the best that you can.

When Guilt Destroys

Guilt is like ivy, once it begins climbing up a tree, its little sucker roots dig in tightly, its strands tightly cling, and it won't relinquish its hold. It's hard to let go of guilt, because guilt won't let go of you.

Some parents feel guilty over everything that goes wrong for their kids. If Tiny Teena's teeth need braces, they feel guilty that they gave her such lousy bite genes. They feel bad that they're not rich or, if they are rich, they worry that their Little Lord Fauntleroy isn't learning street smarts. No matter what the situation, they feel guilty that they aren't perfect parents.

What is a perfect parent? Who do these guilty parents want to be? Whoever it is, it's probably an unobtainable ideal. Close your eyes for a moment, and think of your image of the word *mom* or *dad* (choose the title that matches your own gender). Now, do you feel guilty that you aren't that perfect image?

Guilt, Be Gone!

Much of the guilt that parents feel can't be tied to specific actions or issues, it's just a vague sense that you're doing everything just a little bit wrong, or that you're just slightly inadequate for the tasks set before you. Free-floating guilt is a little message from the universe that it's time to take a break. Check out the self-nurturing suggestions later on in this chapter and, while you're at it, take a guilt-break.

Guilt Is Lousy Modeling

"Oh, that's okay; I'll just sit here, in the dark." Too much guilt, and you'll beat yourself so hard you'll turn into a martyr. Don't model martyring (please!). The more you martyr yourself, the less respect you'll get—from yourself, from your kids, from the world. Remember that kids learn what they experience. Do you really want your child, 60 years from now, to be telling her grandkids, "No, that's okay, walk all over me, I deserve it anyway."

Guilty of Guilt?

Feeling guilty is a habit that may take time to break. Don't feel guilty about feeling guilty. Just don't feel guilty. You can't go back. Concentrate on doing better next time.

Even Strong Parents Laugh

Sometimes the best parenting survival tool is humor. Allow humor to play a role in your parenting, and in your discipline. Say Tracy is clearing the table and drops a stack of dishes, sending broken plates and scraps of food all over the floor. You and Tracy could scream, you and Tracy could cry (and you still may), but if you take a deep breath and laugh about it first, it will give you the fortitude to deal with the situation and pick up the pieces (so to speak).

Or, say you're summoned to the back yard by blood-curdling screams and there you find best friends Gloria (six) and Marlys (five), fighting over who is bossier, standing nose-to-nose and screaming at each other at the top of their lungs. You settle the immediate crisis (separate and let them cool, bring them together to let them solve it, open the shed, and pull out the trikes to divert the energy). Then, exhausted, you go into the house, thinking of the image of those two sweet children standing toe-to-toe and screaming, and laugh. Laughing about a situation pulls you away from anger, worry, or fear and gives you a sense of perspective.

Laughter is a disciplining tool. It gives you perspective on a situation (so you can effectively respond), and it says "I love you." "I love you" is always a strong place to begin teaching discipline.

It's a Good Idea!

Laughter is physically healthy for your body. It relieves anxiety and promotes healing in times of injury or illness.

Egads, I Laughed!

Are you afraid of encouraging misbehavior by laughing at times you "shouldn't?" It happens, and it isn't the worst thing in the world. Just because you laughed doesn't mean that you can't correct. You can laugh and disapprove, or laugh and then apply consequences. Too often discipline is thought of and taught as a grim task. "Okay, enough pleasure. It's time to go discipline my child!" Stated this way, it's no wonder most parents are baffled, confused, and basically despise the idea of discipline.

It's a Good Idea!

Discipline does not have to be punishment.

When Laughter Is Inappropriate

At times, laugher is not a helpful response.

➤ If a child is feeling very vulnerable, laughter (even when you are laughing with instead of at the child) can injure. Laughter's gift is that it helps distance you from the immediate situation, and there are times when your child doesn't want you distanced. He needs you right in there, empathizing with him.

➤ Laughter should never be used as a weapon to hurt a person's feelings.

➤ Laughter is inappropriate when it's a response to actions that victimize somebody.

➤ Some people and families use humor and laughter as their primary mode of conversation, or as a means of emotional survival. Laughing should never be used instead of listening and talking; it's an adjunct to it.

Treating Yourself Reasonably Well

All this pressure, all this guilt—it sure isn't helping anybody. It's time to do something that will help the entire family. Nurture yourself! This section has a wide variety of suggestions—from the small to the big—to get you started taking care of yourself. The first task is to convince yourself that not only are you "worth it," but that your family is "worth it," too.

Replenishing your energy is not self-indulgent. Far from it. It is a necessary part of parenting. When the world is overwhelming and you're trying to do 12 things at exactly the same time with no breaks, it's hard to be reasonable. (You're likely to be very cranky, too.) If your child is misbehaving, you need to have distance from the situation to figure out the most effective way of dealing with it. You need to have the fortitude to go the distance—parenting is fatiguing. Hot-tempered, exhausted parents are not the best disciplinarians! To gain perspective and strength, you must separate yourself from your child and the world and replenish. All this spells out "self-care."

Give-Yourself-a-Break Suggestions

Self-care is daily, too—for the next few weeks, build in down-time, blank space, a few moments to an hour every day of time alone just for self-nurturing. Here are some suggestions to begin thinking about. The first take only a few minutes (but that doesn't mean they aren't powerful and replenishing), the later ones take longer. After you look at these suggestions, I'll give you a work sheet for you to create your own pamper list using these suggestions (if you like them) plus ones of your own:

Got 30 seconds?

➤ Take 10 long, deep breaths. In through the nose, out through the mouth, in through the nose, out through the mouth.

➤ Relax those shoulders. You are (at least in part) your body. When your body is relaxed, so are you.

Got six minutes?

➤ Turn on a CD and dance wildly for six minutes.

➤ Eat a ripe peach, slowly, alone.

➤ Eat a square of good, dark, chocolate. Okay, eat two squares!

➤ Stretch.

➤ Change your clothes into something that makes you feel really attractive.

➤ Write down three things that you did well yesterday, whether large or small. Your list might read: 1) Cleaned the birdcage. 2) Made a play date for Betty. 3) Wrote 10 pages of my book. If you do it tomorrow, it might read: 1) Washed my hair. 2) Complimented my boss. 3) Won Nobel Prize.

Got 30 minutes?

➤ Talk with a good friend on the phone.

➤ Play a card game with your partner.

➤ Take a stroll through your neighborhood.

➤ Work a little in the garden.

➤ Take a "power" nap—20 minutes of midday snuggling with the comforter and pillows. Don't worry if you don't sleep, just enjoy resting.

➤ Look up a friend or lover in the phone book (No! Not for romance!), call the person, and reminisce about the old days.

Got an hour?

➤ Treat yourself to a manicure.

➤ Put your feet up, park the kids in front of PBS (would I ever recommend commercial TV?), make yourself a pot of tea, and read a short story or a few chapters of a novel.

➤ Take a long bath with bubbles or aromatherapy oil and bath toys (borrow your kid's).

➤ Take a nature walk in the local park.

➤ Get a massage. Sometimes they'll come to your house.

➤ Have good sex (no, not with the massage therapist!).

➤ Do an art project.

➤ Set the timer and take a guilt break. For one hour, refuse to feel guilty. Stop feeling guilty about still feeling guilty, stop feeling guilty for feeling guilty about feeling guilty. If you don't feel guilty, don't feel guilty about that, either.

Got two hours?

➤ Take yourself out for sushi.

➤ Do a more elaborate art project.

➤ Try a dance class.

➤ Take a trip to the gym.

Got an evening?

➤ Hire a baby-sitter and go out to dinner with a friend you haven't seen in years. While you're at it, have some guilt-free dessert.

➤ Take the kids to a loving friend's house and go to a concert.

Create Your Own Pamper List

You spend a lot of time in your life doing the "right" thing and taking care of other people. This is a pamper list for you! When you're in the middle of a stressful period, it's often hard to remember to take care of yourself, and when you do remember, it's hard to decide what to do. Aha! You can prepare in advance! Fill out this work sheet when you are in a good mood. When big stress hits, refer to this list for ideas. You may use some of the ideas I've suggested above, though I encourage you to make up your own, too. You are the only one who knows what will replenish you.

It's a Good Idea!

Bumper sticker on my car: Serenitize your multitasking.

If I have 30 seconds, I'll:

If I have six minutes, I'll:

If I have half an hour, I'll:

If I have an hour, I'll:

If I have two hours, I'll:

If I have an evening, I'll:

I feel happier with myself when I:

It's a Good Idea!

Use your pamper list!

I feel better about my body when I:

I feel excited by life when I:

It's Unconditional *Love*, Not Unconditional *Like*

I've got a revolutionary concept for you, guaranteed to lighten your emotional load and relieve your guilt: You don't always have to like your child.

Point: It's unconditional love. Love isn't easily killed, especially when it's your child. You can love your kid to bits, be perfectly willing to throw yourself in front of a train for her, yet it might drive you crazy to be around her because of the way she's acting. No, it does not make you a bad parent. I promise there are times when she is not liking you! (Temporary dislike may even be a natural stage in development, a part of separating.)

At times, all of us are so frustrated with our kids that, while we love them to pieces, we don't particularly like or respect them. It's hard to feel that way, and it's hard to parent well in that state of mind. When you're feeling at wit's end, fill out the following asset list for your child. It can help you refocus on her wonderful qualities. Stay positive!

Behave Yourself!

Despise the deed, not the doer.

What are my child's greatest talents?

1.

2.

3.

4.

What are my child's skills?

1.

2.

3.

4.

What are my child's greatest temperamental strengths?

1.

2.

3.

4.

What do I admire most about my child?

1.

2.

3.

4.

What can I learn from my child?

1.

2.

3.

4.

Nobody's Perfect, Everybody Errs

Alas, we are all flawed. We feel guilty, we worry too much, we neglect our own well-being, we dislike our kids, and we make mistakes. Little ones and big ones. You will say and do things you regret, and you will neglect to say and do the right thing. At times you will really flame out, bite the big one, fail!

When you make a mistake, it's important to acknowledge it, apologize (if necessary), make changes (if you can), and move on.

Be gentle with yourself, a mistake is not a call to guilt or self-hatred. Try using the mistake as a learning tool (that's what mistakes and failure are for!).

The way you deal with your mistakes and failures will teach your children how to deal with their own.

Tales from the Parent Zone

A scientific study demonstrated that students whose mistakes were greeted with gentle guidance and encouragement learned material far better than students who were scolded, and that students remembered best the material they'd gotten wrong originally, and restudied!

About Failure and Trying Again

Many writers and thinkers have spoken about the importance of making mistakes. Educator John Dewey said, "Failure is instructive. The person who really thinks learns quite as much from his failures as from his successes." The key here, of course, is the "really thinks" part.

Failure and mistakes are just information, the human way of learning.

Love Is Saying You're Sorry

I've noticed that the world can easily be divvied into two types of people: those who apologize constantly, and those who rarely apologize. Which camp do you fall into?

Pay attention. When you're feeling low self-esteem, when you wonder about your parenting skills, you may be at risk of turning into a chronic apologizer, taking on everybody else's woes ("You hit me? I'm sorry!"), with "I'm Sorry" as your middle name. Too much apologizing means that your apologies won't be taken as sincere. They're also a way of giving away your personal power (and that's another subject).

While chronic apologizers may go overboard, there are certainly times for everybody when it's appropriate to apologize for your behavior. At times, an apology isn't enough, and it's important to make restitution.

It's Never Too Late for Change

Personal change requires a desire to change, and the time to change. It's also true that some things change whether or not we have the desire, or the time. Life is change, it's one of the few things we can rely on. Things will be different tomorrow, and next year. Situations, relationships, and people are constantly in flux, and none of us have full control over what happens to us—or even who we become.

When you're feeling stuck, when a situation or a behavior pattern of your own or of your child's feels overwhelming, it's hard, but vital, to remember that how things are now are not how they will remain. Some things change without your effort, and some things require your instigation, your hard work, and a leap of faith.

Change takes time. You may read this book and, filled with ideas and resolutions, leap into a completely new mode of behavior. Whoa! Slow down! A positive approach to parenting and discipline is not a conversion—take it one step at a time. Mark your progress, not in moments or incidents, but by the week or month or year.

Here are some suggestions for making changes in your parenting techniques:

➤ **Set small goals every day**. Try this: After the alarm clock rings and before you leap out of bed to attack the day, take half a minute to set yourself a couple of achievable goals. ("Today I will give Perry positive reinforcement for his struggles with math." "Today I won't scream.")

➤ **As you drop off to sleep, check with yourself (again, this shouldn't take more than a couple of minutes) to see how you did with your goals**. Didn't make them? It's not a reason for insomnia! Let it go. In the immortal words of Scarlett O'Hara, "Tomorrow is another day!"

➤ **Don't "force" the suggestions in this book**. Work within your own vocabulary and parenting style. I'm not trying to script your life. Translate the words I suggest into language that feels comfortable for you.

➤ Identify the problems you want to work on with your kids, and then take them one at a time. Here's the interesting thing: Behavior problems are often linked even when the links aren't evident. If you clear up one problem, often other problems correct themselves as well.

➤ Celebrate yourself and your family's progress. Don't put your slow progress down or denigrate your victories—no matter how small.

➤ Remember that were there were no difficulties, there would be no triumphs.

The Least You Need to Know

➤ There's a lot of pressure in society for both parents and kids to be perfect, yet the strong and reasonable parent is necessarily flawed.

➤ Teaching good discipline requires self-trust and self-respect.

➤ Guilt is largely destructive—though it can be used as a wake-up call.

➤ Laughter says "I love you"—always a strong place to begin teaching discipline.

➤ Replenishing your energy is a necessary part of parenting.

➤ You don't always have to like your child.

➤ Change takes time.

Get a Grip: Get a Helping Hand

Effective parenting is a balancing act. Most of the time, you'll manage to maintain a rhythm between the ups and downs. Sometimes, though, your family's balance will become so firmly out of whack that you'll feel like a couple of unmatched children on a seesaw—either the little kid, light, ungrounded, stranded high in the air, or the big kid, too heavy, unable to leave the ground and soar. At these times, you may not be able to rebalance yourselves. You may need assistance. This chapter discusses how and where to turn for help. It focuses mostly on traditional therapy, but we'll talk a bit about support groups and parenting classes as well.

Turning to Others for Help

Anorexia, criminal behaviors, suicide attempts, self-injury, Attention Deficit Disorder (ADD) symptoms, alcoholism—at times, it's pretty clear when the family (or one person in the family) is out of balance and in need of help. Other times, it's not so obvious. Is your family's vague misery and constant tension normal, or is it time to bring in a fresh perspective? Part of your decision to find support, therapy, or a parenting class will depend on your previous experience with outside help (if any!) and the community you live in.

It's a Good Idea!

Effective therapy is a tool for healing, learning, and self-nurturing. It isn't punishment.

At times, your own community network of friends and family can give you the support and answers you need. Other times, it's just not enough. When do you know it's time to turn to a professional or an organized support group? A good time to try looking for solutions outside your network of friends and family is when you feel stuck, when you've tried everything you can do to get yourself and your family out of the problems you're in.

Deciding that your problems are too big for at-home solutions is not easy. Yet it's sometimes the very best choice you can make for your family. Seeking therapy doesn't mean your family is a disaster, that you're a failure as a parent, that you've done something wrong (and are being punished for it), or that any of you are off your rockers, have bats in the belfry, or a screw or two loose. It's a tool, a learning experience, and a way to heal old wounds. Therapy is positive.

Tales from the Parent Zone

Mary moved to a small community from the San Francisco Bay Area (where there seem to be three mental health professionals per square inch, and everybody and her sister is on her third therapist). In the course of conversation with her new neighbor, she began a sentence with, "As my therapist said," and then realized her neighbor was looking at her in horror. In Mary's new town, getting mental or emotional therapy is considered odd, and marks you as a little nuts. Let me stress: While too much therapy itself can become an "addiction" (witness Woody Allen with a zillion years on the couch and counting), a little help at the right time is the opposite of nuts—it's utterly sane.

People are touchy about therapy. Once you've decided to get outside assistance, you may face resistance from the rest of the family. Your child may not be ready to admit she needs help, your partner may pooh-pooh therapy's effectiveness, or feel that the family's problems are private, and that it's inappropriate for you to go outside the family for help. If you're facing a lot of pressure to drop the subject:

➤ Don't give up. Many times, people are initially resistant (and frightened).

➤ Even if you believe it's your child or the entire family who should be seeing a therapist, go by yourself for the first couple of times, if necessary. When they see you're still the sweet, sane person you always were, just with some new insights and more patience, they may join you.

Who Gets the Help?

Maybe it's your child, maybe it's you, maybe it's all of you. If your child is having problems, that affects the rest of the family. The problems may even be caused by the rest of the family! If a child is in crisis, the entire family should be seen, at least for an assessment or initial support. Very often, effective therapy with troubled kids involves a parental component.

Other times, the root of the problem is based in your relationship with your partner. Maybe once you two have worked through your issues, your child won't act out so much. And if your child is going through a hard time or having problems (even if they don't really relate to you), you may still need some extra support. Perhaps it's a friend's shoulder to cry on. It may be a support group or a weekly therapy session. Take care of yourself.

Finding a Therapist

Whether you are looking for a therapist for yourself, your child, or the whole family, there are many resources available as you perform your search.

Who Will It Be Now?

You've made the big decision, "We can't handle this alone." What's the next step? There are a wide variety of types of therapies and many different types of therapists and counselors—all with different training, approaches, and styles. You'll need to think, at least briefly, about what you want in a therapist, and what form of therapy she practices. Do you want group therapy, family therapy, individual therapy?

It's a Good Idea!

Look for outside help when you are stuck, going around in circles, or caught deep in a maze with no apparent way out.

It's a Good Idea!

Depression is often frustration that has been turned inward. Take some time off!

It's a Good Idea!

Therapy doesn't give quick solutions. It's about the process of self-discovery, and it can create deep, profound changes.

These days, therapy is rarely a classical analysis (lying on the couch and relating your dreams in a stream of consciousness to a Freudian analyst). More likely, you'll be searching for and benefiting from talk therapy—sitting up, talking with the therapist to get at the root of your feelings, and gaining insight and tools for solving your own problems. As you begin the process of finding the right therapist, remain open to format suggestions. You may not know what you need.

Getting One

In many communities, therapists and other mental health professionals advertise in community papers. Getting a referral from your doctor or pediatrician is another way to begin. Here are some suggestions for places and ways to locate the perfect "shrink" for you, your child, your partnership, or your family:

➤ Personal referrals. Say you have a buddy who's been in therapy for a while. Ask him to ask his therapist for a referral. You could go to your buddy's therapist, but neither of you may want that to happen. It may feel just a tad too close.

➤ Other parents, particularly if your kids share the same problems. If your friends the Joneses send their daughter who has ADD and suffers from erratic behavior and low self-esteem to a wonderful doctor in the next town, and your son has similar issues, perhaps you can get a referral from the Joneses.

➤ Don't know the Joneses? Use the Internet, parenting e-mail lists, and the "community grapevine" to locate other families with similar problems. Local parents can also tell you who, specifically, to stay away from. Nonlocal parents can tell you what kinds of things to look for, and what kinds of things to avoid.

➤ Your child's school can be an excellent resource, especially if it is "in the loop" with what's happening with your child. It may have listings of its own. At the least, it should be able to put you in touch with social service agencies that can help you find what and who you'll need.

Tales from the Parent Zone

Sometimes it's you who needs help. When you're feeling sad or depressed, your tolerance is reduced, your empathy dries up, your patience is gone, and it's hard to be an effective parent. You may need to withdraw, to replenish yourself. On the other hand, withdrawing isn't fair to your child. Brandy faced this situation, when she found she was too upset and depressed to care about the hard time her twins were having in school. She realized she had a responsibility to take care of herself so that she could be an effective parent. (For Brandy it meant therapy. For you, this may mean a bath and a massage, or you may need a therapist, too.)

➤ Look in the "Government" section of your phone directory for "Health and Human Services" (or similar) listings. All communities should have access to a family service agency.

➤ The National Association for the Advancement of Psychoanalysis (212/741-0515) can give you referrals to psychoanalysts and psychotherapists in your area.

➤ In some parts of the country, mental health professionals advertise in local weeklies or monthlies. Call the ones that sound good, and then interview them deeply (there's more about this below).

What's with All Those Letters?

The initials after a therapist or mental health professional's name reflect the type (and amount) of training she's received, and their licensing regulations. Generally, it's more important to find a therapist that you or your child "click" with than it is to match the degree to what you think you need. It's nice to know what they mean, just the same.

An *MFCC* is a marriage, family, and child counselor. An MFCC holds a master's degree in psychology, has spent numerous hours counseling people as an intern (see below) under supervision, and takes a strenuous written and oral exam before being certified. Some MFCCs concentrate on the "marriage" aspect, some on the "family," some on the "child," and some just do individual and/or group therapy with adults. You'll have to ask.

An *LCSW* is a licensed clinical social worker. The emphasis for an LCSW is slightly different than it is for an MFCC, as her master's degree focuses on social work. She also goes through a rigorous hands-on training as an intern (numerous hours of counseling people under supervision), and takes an oral and written exam. Her interests and areas of expertise may vary, too.

An *intern* is an MFCC or LCSW candidate working through her counseling hours using the license, and under the supervision of, a certified therapist.

A *psychiatrist* is an M.D., a medical doctor, who specializes in psychological treatment. Psychiatrists have varying approaches to treatment. If you or your child are being treated by any mental health professional and medication is indicated—these would be things like antidepressants, Prozac, Zoloft, and so on—then a psychiatrist will enter the picture, too. Only a doctor can prescribe medication.

Then there's the other kind of doctor, the *Ph.D. in psychology*. (We're not talking about other Ph.D.s here—only somebody who has trained in psychology or a related field can provide psychological counseling.) Many psychologists have other clinical training or certification, too (perhaps in psychoanalysis, pediatric psychology, or another therapeutic approach).

Other mental health professionals may be available, too. Make sure that whomever you see has been well trained, and that you like him.

Getting a Good One

How will you know if a particular therapist is right for you or your child? You won't, until you talk with him, and perhaps try a session. Shop around, try a few people. After your child's first session, ask him how he feels about going back. Don't ask for *any* details about what happened during the session. What is between your child and his therapist is confidential. The feelings your child has about the therapist do not need to be.

Tales from the Parent Zone

When Dan was looking for a therapist, he found he was so choked up whenever he thought about talking with somebody that he'd hang up before leaving a message. He would stare at his list of referrals and feel utterly overwhelmed, afraid each therapist would think he was nuts if he started to cry just setting up an appointment. Alas, looking for a therapist is often like looking for a roofer in a rainstorm—it's a crisis, so you need somebody now and it's hard to be choosy about whom you pick. Forget the panic for a moment and make the call. Allow yourself to get as emotional as you need to, and see how the therapist responds. Does this feel like somebody you can trust?

Paying for It

If you have medical insurance, it may cover mental health care, usually for short-term therapies only. One problem with having your insurance or HMO pay for your therapy is that you may need to be diagnosed as having a psychological problem. Being "diagnosed" sounds uncomfortable and limiting, but it's not always an evil thing, and your insurance company may consider it necessary. It's worth finding out about. Are your records going to be sealed? How many sessions will they pay for in a year?

Individual therapy not covered by insurance is expensive. On the other hand, it may be the best money you've ever spent. It may save your life, your child's life, and your family's happiness. All are worth it.

Many therapists operate on a sliding scale, so if you are a student or lower income, you may still be able to afford it. It's worth asking about. If you have no money and no insurance, your county social service department may have programs that can help you. Your city may also have free or low-cost clinics. And, for very short-term emergencies, there are a number of hot lines you can call for free crisis advice. Check out the listings in Appendix C.

The Interview and Initial Session

As you look for your therapist, you'll need to ask her a number of questions about her areas of expertise, her training, and her overall approach. Here's how it's going to go:

After you leave a message on the therapist's voice mail (I think there's a law against therapists answering their phones), she'll call you back and you'll have an exploratory phone conversation. You'll probably feel nervous. This is normal, though if you think about it, it's odd, she's the one who's having the job interview!

This conversation has at least two components. You'll talk about you or your child, she'll tell you about herself and how she works. You'll get personal, she won't. Welcome to the world of therapy. This is usually the only time you'll be able to get a sense of your therapist's history, experience, training, and approach, so it's worthwhile to really grill her (I'll give you some sample questions in a second). Don't be shy—if you hire her, from here on out, she'll ask the questions, and you'll answer. Don't forget to jot down a few notes as you go. Finding a therapist is stressful, and you may not fully get everything she's said unless you write it down.

As the conversation progresses, listen to how the therapist answers the questions as well as what she answers. Does she act like it's strange that you're asking questions? (If so, find another therapist.) When you talk about your family or your child, does she listen empathetically, wisely? Or does she jump to conclusions? Listen for reasonable, respectful, and related responses. You may need to talk to several therapists. Just having the right degree and licensing doesn't guarantee empathy, wisdom, and insight.

Here are a few questions to start with:

➤ Ask her about her training and degrees. "What is your training?" "Where did you do your course work, and how long have you been in the field?"

➤ Some therapists specialize in certain problems—eating disorders, fathering and intimacy issues, children of alcoholics, people who drown their problems in food, stepfamily dynamics, young women with self-esteem issues, sex addicts, marital counseling, autistic children, inner-child issues, you name it. If you are struggling with a particular issue, it's worthwhile to find out how much experience the therapist has had working with people with similar problems. "How do you generally approach _____ (the problem you're seeking help for)?" "How much experience do you have working with _____?" "Are you affiliated with any associations, organizations, or support systems that specialize in _____?" "Have you done any additional training or certification in _____?" (The answer doesn't have to be "yes," but it certainly is a bonus!)

➤ Ask about the therapist's style of working. "Will the entire family be involved? Just my child? All of us? Will you meet with us individually, or as a group?"

➤ Some therapists do assessment tests, many just talk with you. "How do you evaluate problems? Will you be doing any testing, or just talking with my child (me, my family)?"

➤ Now the big question. "What do you charge, and do you have a sliding scale?"

➤ You also need to know how often you'll meet. Much of this can't be determined until the therapist meets with you (and/or your child). You can get an idea of this therapist's trend, though. "How often do you generally meet with your clients?"

➤ And, if you're feeling pretty good about the conversation, "When can you meet with me (us, my child), and can I call you back to confirm?" Like buying a new car, it's best to sleep on the decision.

Behave Yourself!

If your child needs therapy, you and your partner may need to put your feet down and insist that he attend. You do the initial phone screening and set the appointment. He does get to nix who you send him to see (after a session or five), but he doesn't get to nix that he has to go.

After the phone conversation, check in with yourself a couple of hours later. Did you like her? Did you feel as though she's somebody you'll be able to trust? Do you think your child will respond to her? If there's any nagging, niggling feeling that there's something not quite right, listen to it. There are other therapists out there, somebody just right for you and for your family.

When it's time for the initial session (that is, if you get that far with a therapist), keep an open mind. Here's the thing: Unless the therapy is just for you, it's not just up to you. Each family member in therapy has to approve of the therapist. Therapy builds a very tight relationship between client and therapist, and if the two people don't click, no good work will be done.

Support Groups

Going to a professional therapist or psychiatrist is not your only choice for getting help with your problems. You may find help from your peers, groups of people who are going through similar problems, or who have similar situations. Members will provide support (often outside of group meetings) and provide a pool of common experience and information. Sometimes these groups have a leader, sometimes meetings are facilitated in turn by group members. Depending upon where you live, you may be able to find support groups for a myriad of problems.

Here's a sampling of support groups I found advertising in my community's local weekly paper: Stepparenting Support, Adult Children of Alcoholics, Foster Parents Support, Incest Survivors, Parents of Kids with Eating Disorders, and so on. Then there are the 12-step-program groups: Alcoholics Anonymous, Alanon, Alateen, Marijuana Anonymous, Narcotics Anonymous, Sex-Addicts Anonymous, Nicotine Anonymous, Overeaters Anonymous.

Support groups have saved many a parent from going out of her skull. They usually are free or very inexpensive (what a nice change from therapy!). You might consider a support group as a great backup to therapy (if your child is being treated by a therapist, think about a support group for yourself). Some support groups are guided by a particular philosophy (such as the 12-step programs) and some are more free-flowing. Check your local newspaper or phonebook for listings, and give it a try.

Parenting Classes

Sometimes it's not therapy or "support" you need, but a specific set of parenting skills. We all have room for improvement in our parenting. Nobody is born knowing how to parent, yet it's one of the few areas in life (I guess sex is another) where we assume that we should know what to do, and how to do it most effectively. But why not take a class? You're reading an advice book, right? A class can give you even more information, tailored specifically to your needs.

Parenting classes can help parents deal with guilt and shame for mistakes they may have made. Parenting classes provide proof that you are not alone in blowing it or having a troubled child, and combine that knowledge with a set of new skills.

People also seek parenting education when they're faced with an unexpected situation. How do you parent a spirited or ADD child? What can you do to make your divorce as smooth as possible for your child? How can you discipline through gentle, positive parenting, when your upbringing was the opposite? Short-term parenting classes and workshops are offered through community colleges, churches and temples, and hospitals. Often, parenting classes spin off into support groups so that parents have resources to check in with, as they put their new skills into play.

Alternative Stress-Reducing Therapies

Just "talking about it" may not be enough. If your child is unhappy, stressed, perhaps feeling guilty and suffering from low self-esteem for causing all these problems (yes, even if it isn't her fault), then more than her mind needs nurturing. The best healing comes holistically. Try combining a few elements. Focus on proper nutrition, a more nurturing environment, perhaps exercise, some acupressure, or a weekly massage.

That goes for you, too. (Remember the self-nurture list in Chapter 23?) You're no good to anybody else if you're no good to yourself. Your own outlook affects your family almost as much as it affects you.

It's a Good Idea!

The massage is the message!

Force Yourself to Relax!

While you're looking for help outside the family, don't forget to do what you can inside the family. Therapy, at least at first, is very intense, and very exhausting. You or your child may feel terrific after a session. On the other hand, sometimes you or your child will come home more tense and upset than before. It's all part of the process, but it can be hard on the body—all that tension makes muscles ache.

If your child is in therapy, he needs love, support, and help relaxing. So does your partner. So, for that matter, do you.

You can use this guided relaxation exercise in a variety of ways:

➤ Help your child or partner (or both!) relax by reading it slowly as he lies on his back on a warm floor.

➤ Have your partner read it to you—and let you gain the benefit!

➤ Tape record your voice reading it out loud. When you get really tense, take a psychic break, excuse yourself for 15 minutes (make sure some other grown-up is on call for the kids), lie on a warm, carpeted floor in a room by yourself. (No, forget the pillow, this isn't a nap, you're trying to get your back to relax flat.) Now you can play your tape—ignore what your voice sounds like—and use this opportunity to just release the tension.

The Progressive Relaxation Exercise

Begin reading here:

"Lie on your back with your legs folded comfortably into an upside-down V, the soles of your feet on the floor, and your arms by your sides, palms up.

"I'll be leading you through a progressive relaxation session. Just follow the sound of my voice.

"As we go, you'll be letting go of some of your tension. As the tension disappears, be aware that you may feel a variety of emotions percolating up like bubbles through you. It's fine—that's just the tension you're holding letting go. Don't bottle up the bubbles, just let them bubble up, and then let each bubble pop. If you need to cry, let the tears flow.

"Close your eyes lightly and sigh deeply. Breathe deeply and slowly, in through your nose and out through your mouth. As you breathe each breath, count to four."

(Pause in the reading here for a while.)

"When you've completed 10 breaths, continue breathing. You're doing well."

(Pause in the reading here for a while.)

"Rock your head from side to side, and gently let it rest in the middle."

(Pause in the reading here for a while.)

"Feel your jaw drop and relax. Were you clenching your teeth? Feel the lovely relief as you let it go.

"Relax your forehead. Let the tension slide off the top and back and disappear. Feel the skin on the top of your head rest gently against your scalp. Feel your eyes sinking softly and resting in their sockets. Don't hold them, just let them rest."

(Pause in the reading here for a while.)

"Feel how heavy your shoulders are on the floor. If you feel any pain or discomfort, notice where it is. Let it go. Release it, and let it bubble up. As you release your shoulders, feel the front of your chest float open, and your shoulder blades flatten and widen. Don't force it. Let it go."

(Pause in the reading here for a while.)

"Now your midback settles and releases against the floor. Breathe.

"Your lower back settles and releases. Breathe. Let your breath carry the tensions out of your body and release it into the air.

"Let your buttocks become heavy and flat. Continue to breathe.

"Feel the soles of your feet rest against the floor. Breathe in. Breathe out. Continue to let your whole body melt, like a puddle."

(Pause in the reading here for a while.)

"Now, go through your body again, checking for areas of remaining tension. When you find them, concentrate on inhaling your breath into them, breathing, and letting the tension float away with your breath."

(Pause in the reading. The person you are reading to may drift off to sleep here, or just be very relaxed. You may not be able to easily tell. You can bring her back slowly, or stop here, and let her relax or sleep. If you decide to "bring her back":)

"Slowly, without moving, open your eyes. Your body is relaxed. When you decide to get up, move slowly, rolling first onto your side. You are refreshed, revitalized, and ready to gently approach the rest of the day."

The Least You Need to Know

➤ It's hard to ask for help when there's little community or family support for therapy.

➤ Interview any potential therapist on the phone before being treated, and consider the first session exploratory.

➤ There are a wide variety of types of therapists, but the main qualification is that the therapist works well with your family.

➤ Your child needs therapy; he can choose which therapist he sees, but not that he should be seen.

➤ Consider a support group or a parenting class in addition to therapy.

➤ Reducing tension will aid your family's healing and health.

Building Family Togetherness

Strive to build a strong, reasonable, and respectful family, and you'll achieve building a strong, reasonable, and respectful child. This is the truth as I know it—a child exists within a family, and a family exists within its community and world. No discussion of raising well-behaved kids can be complete without looking at ways to build family strength and community ties through rituals, shared time, spiritual exploration, creative activities, community commitment, and celebrations of the human spirit. In this chapter we'll do just that!

Building a Strong Family Identity

Your family's identity provides a foundation for your child to stand on. Numbers and configurations don't matter. It makes no difference whether your family consists of you and your child alone, or you parent within a multigenerational brood of kids, aunts, uncles, grandparents, step-relations, close friends, and cousins.

A strong sense of family provides your child with a set of allies and a sense of belonging. Model the value of family, and prove yourself an ally to other members of the family. Reach out for the big things—attend graduations, weddings, and funerals.

Reach out for the small things—celebrate your niece's first lost tooth, and put up your third cousin twice removed when she passes through town.

Family Time

In Chapter 5, you learned about the importance of special time—one-on-one sessions with each of your kids. It's also vital to spend time together as an entire family to cement your family identity.

Shared experiences build connections. Discipline is best taught by a parent who truly knows her child's interests and reactions. This knowledge is based on shared experience. I know a family where the parents were so afraid that their kids would compete with each other that the kids were never allowed to do anything together. The family rarely spent time together—they were little more than a bunch of people who shared a house. I don't know about you, but I had more than my share of roommates in my 20s. I certainly don't want that level of unconcerned detachment from my family.

Share time together as a family. Family time—as well as family meetings (Chapter 6) and special time (Chapter 5)—prevents problems as well as solves them.

It's a Good Idea!

When it comes to family strength, "Since you can't beat 'em, join 'em."

It's a Good Idea!

Get your priorities in order! It's far more important to carve out that extra hour from your busy life to read to your kids or go out for ice cream than it is to get the old newspapers up off the floor, sweep the porch, or defrost the freezer. Life is short. Family is sweet.

Family time is an ensemble group activity—yep, you're all invited, whether it's for a game of Uno, an afternoon in the garden, or a trip to the mountains. Not only are you all invited, it's important that you all attend. Schedule it, and make it a family rule (if necessary). "We spend the last week in August at Grandma Ruthie's ranch." "We have waffles Saturday morning." "On Tuesday evenings, we walk the dog around Lake Temescal."

Family time can be fun time. Family time can also be mealtimes shared, or community service time (and we'll talk about those in a moment). The important thing is that it's time spent all together.

Family time builds family identity, and it also enhances communication. The more attention you pay to each other, the more opportunities you have to talk. Kids talk best with their parents when they're relaxed, hanging, and comfortable. You're hiking in the forest, for example, silently admiring the grandeur of the redwoods, and Junior suddenly breaks free with something that's been bothering him all week. Since (for once in your life) you're not multitasking yourself to death, you can really listen. And even if nothing significant comes up during family time, your shared experiences are the building blocks of a strong family unit.

Tales from the Parent Zone

The Pierce family members floated past each other like ships in the night, their house was like a dispatch station, with nobody staying put for more than the eight hours each day it took to sleep. Something had to change, and when they decided to focus more on family time, the Pierces were smart to take it slowly. Intimacy, when forced, can feel confining. All relationships need time to breathe. The Pierces began with weekly family time activities where they were all involved in something together, but weren't forced into only getting stimulation from each other. A coastal clean-up, a bike ride, an art class—this was the beginning of the Pierce family time tradition.

What should you do during your family time? Here are some ideas to get you started:

➤ Eat together (there's more on this, below).

➤ Participate in the community together (there's more on this, below, too!).

➤ Go to the zoo or to a natural history museum. They're fun plus they're educational—for you too!

➤ Ah, go fly a kite. Take a hike (but take the kids along).

➤ "Take me out to the ball game," and use the time between the hits, runs, errors, and screaming ("Throw the bum out!") as an opportunity to bond.

Behave Yourself!

There's no two ways about it, watching TV together does not count as family time. Turn it off, stop focusing on the screen, and look at each other!

Food for the Belly, Food for the Family

Your family identity is enhanced the more you eat meals together. Civilization was built around the dinner table. Breaking bread together, a symbolic international peace-making gesture, has more than just a political meaning, it's a vital way of touching base as a family.

Mealtimes are an important part of sharing family time together, far too often dismissed in our rush, rush, rush culture. Our family tries (and usually succeeds) in eating dinner together at least three nights a week, plus breakfasts and weekend brunches. My friend Linda and her husband, Francesco, can't manage dinners together (he works as a chef in a restaurant—he's usually busy cooking dinner for other people), so the family gets up early and all has breakfast together. I'm impressed. (It would never work for us, but it shows you a bit about the different approaches different families can take.)

Your family identity is also strengthened by the types of food you eat. Don't like your own "native" cuisine? So adopt another's. (We'll talk about celebrating your heritage, below.) Learn to cook (and cook together as part of your family time). Invite extended family, invite friends, and soon people for generations to come will be begging for the secret to your apple pie crust (lard!). Whether it's a cuisine that came with you from the "old country," or you've developed on your own, your child's taste buds and brain cells will always remember Mom's paprika chicken, Bill's chicken curry, Aunt Taki's spinach lasagna, Grandma Karla's seven-cheese brown rice casserole, and the faces and monsters Dad constructs out of pancake batter.

It's a Good Idea!

Warm soapy water feels good on tired, prearthritic hands, and the gentle white noise of running tap water soothes and relaxes. Yes, I'm talking about doing the dinner dishes!

Does this sound a little too "back-to-the-land" for your lifestyle? Are the speed dials on your phone all set to the local pizza, Japanese, and Mexican take-out and delivery spots? Perhaps you want to share dinner time, but you can't cook, you're working way too many hours, and the kids are used to catch-as-catch can. No matter where you're starting from, I've got a few suggestions for moving slowly toward a reemphasis on family mealtimes.

➤ First things first, gotta get motivated. Remember that a hot dinner cooked with love feeds more than the belly. Share the cooking tasks (you'll find no gender-related job suggestions here!) and share the cleanup, too.

➤ One meal at a time. Schedule a family dinner once a month. Once people get used to it, schedule another.

➤ If not you, who? If not now, when? Do you really want your kids to grow up without tasting Aunt Fanny's recipe for the fluffiest garlic mashed potatoes south of the cloud layer? If you have traditional family foods but your kids never have the opportunity to eat them, how will they know they're supposed to spend the rest of their life craving them?

➤ Assert yourself. Family meals are part of family time. They are mandatory. Many families choose one weekend day (often Friday, for Shabbat, or Sunday, after church) where all family members are expected to be there.

➤ When you introduce "family food," or food from your heritage, make it clear that the kids are expected to try it. Tell them, "Sharing these foods with you is very important to me. It's your choice whether or not you like it, but I do expect you try." Then, after they've had bites and the "Eeuuuus" have rung forth, let them break out a bowl of cold cereal.

➤ Invent your own food rituals and traditions. Since everybody loves "toad in the hole," explain to the kids that "toad in the hole" is now an official "family food."

➤ The television is banned from dinner time. Take those old TV trays you inherited from your parents, and turn them into junk sculpture or bury them deep in the shed until they are old enough to be considered quaint antiques.

➤ Okay, okay, even precooked food that's generated by that speed dial on your phone tastes better when it's eaten at the dinner table with everybody chatting, complaining, and socking each other in the arms.

➤ Even lousy cooks can learn to cook—get your kids a great cookbook for kids and learn together. And if little Jimmy's got the touch and you don't, that's superb, too. (Do I smell a new responsibility?)

Tales from the Parent Zone

My parents didn't do it all right (no parent does), but they did do dinner right! Growing up, my sister and I often had wistful friends join us for dinner, friends whose families ate together in front of the TV, or simply munched randomly and individually when they were hungry. Our friends loved our family's emphasis on food and togetherness and conversation. I never realized how rare our experience was—the average American family eats dinner together less than half the time. The average at-home dinner lasts only 15 to 20 minutes. So says researcher Mike Lewis, who has spent years studying the American dinner.

Family Vacations

We talked a bit about family vacations in Chapter 14. Besides the challenges and the sheer fun of adventuring, the shared experiences of family vacations are great family identity builders. This is your opportunity to present your clan out into the world.

Celebrating Your Family

There are as many ways to celebrate your family as there are families. Celebrating your family's togetherness and individual gifts is a way of asserting, "We're glad to be a family. We're glad that we love each other." You celebrate your family each time you share family time, each time you continue traditions from your heritage, tell stories about your history, and perform old and new rituals. You celebrate your family, at times, simply by standing up against depression and despair when times are hard.

Your Family Heritage and Cultural Pride

Part of what makes your family special is your cultural heritage. Where did your family come from? Whether you are immigrants or your family has been planted in the same spot for centuries, your family has a background. It matters little whether your roots are American Indian, Scottish, Jewish, Hungarian, Laotian, West African, Polynesian, Botswanan, Irish, Sri Lankan, Germanic, Japanese, or a combination of many elements of the human race. When you teach your children about their ancestors, you ground them in the flow of time, and give them a sense of history, continuity, and hope for the future.

➤ Tell your child about your culture and your culture's customs, even if you don't practice them, or have rebelled against them. They are part of her history and legacy, and she deserves to know.

➤ If your first language is different from the dominant culture's (for instance, if you are a Spanish speaker in the United States), speak to your child in your original language, too. Language is an important aspect of culture, and losing the "old" language means losing part of the old culture, too. You might not appreciate it, but your child may.

➤ It may not be you rebelling against your culture, it may be your kid. Even though she may resist your culture's garments, dances, music, and food, and find them restrictive, these things are a part of her heritage and she'll appreciate knowing about them later. No, I didn't say force, I said introduce. In small doses. As information.

Words to Parent By

Cultural pride is a sense of self-esteem and self-respect for your heritage.

It's a Good Idea!

Adoptive children often come from a dual heritage, their birth family's culture, and their adoptive family's culture. More and more, adoptions are "open" and kids know their backgrounds. Help them learn all they can—help them celebrate their unique entrance into this world, and into your family. Celebrate holidays associated with your child's cultural heritage: Cinco de Mayo, St.-Jean-Baptiste Day, Divali, Chinese New Year, and so on.

Family Stories: Real and Mythological

Celebrate your family and help build your family identity by sharing family stories. Kids love to hear about how they were born, how Grandpa Than escaped the Thai pirates on his way out of Vietnam, or how Great-Great-Uncle Jack went to jail in the 1934 General Strike.

Here are a few reasons to share personal and family stories with your kids:

➤ Stories serve more than historical purposes, they become part of the fabric of family life, even if they aren't fully true. Over time, they change, stretch, and enter the family mythology.

➤ Stories about family members tell us something about their character, or about our hopes, dreams, and beliefs in heroism and romance.

Tales from the Parent Zone

I grew up remembering the story of my parents camping in Maine when they were just young lovers. My dad, showing off his wood-chopping skills, chopped a huge gash in his leg, so my mother carried him several miles out of the forest. The true version is more mundane—no Maine, no camping, just a college man trying to impress a college woman on their wooded New York campus. Still, the story remains part of my family mythology—showing my mother strong as an ox and my otherwise fault-free father helpless before the gale winds of infatuation.

➤ Stories are a casual, nonmoralistic way to model values and consequences without making your lesson into a lecture.

➤ By telling stories about your childhood, you show your kids your humanity, your faults, your struggles on the way to adulthood. Stories build empathy, a quality your child needs on the way to ethics.

➤ Sharing your commonalities with your kids in the form of stories can help them through hard times.

➤ Historical family stories can help build a sense of place, time, and distance in your children.

➤ Stories about the extended family help with the family identity as a whole. Cousins living on different edges of the continent may meet in 15 years and find shared ground in the story of Grandpa Arthur's horse named Harry.

➤ You are only a conduit for history—your stories, cultural and personal, are a part of your children's legacy. They deserve to know both truths and mythologies.

Tales from the Parent Zone

Good stories have a life of their own. Through a fluke of fate, I was born in the same small Midwestern city where Bill, then 11 years old, was briefly living. The way the story goes, little Billy peered into a carriage one day, saw a gorgeous baby (me!), and proclaimed, "Someday that baby will be my wife!" The true story—we met for the first time in a college class in San Francisco 25 years later—doesn't have half the spice.

Building Your Own Rituals

Rituals, whether cultural or religious, are the backbone of our passage through time. They are how we mark our seasons, our weeks, and our days. Rituals are the glue we use to hold our families together, to become "intentional" families rather than haphazard groupings of people.

Family rituals range from the bedtime story-'n'-song of my childhood to the big blow-out holiday celebrations many people cherish and plan many months for. In our family, we have a brushing-the-teeth ritual (Annie's stuffed Kitty has her own toothbrush), a saying good-bye ritual ("hug, kiss, nose-cuddle, hug, take a bite of the sandwich"), a birthday morning ritual (croissants from La Farine), and countless others. We're still working out our winter holiday ritual, though we've got New Year's Eve down (complete with homemade French onion soup gratinée at the stroke of midnight).

It's a Good Idea!

The Heart of a Family: Searching America for New Traditions That Fulfill Us, by Meg Cox, has terrific information and suggestions for creating family rituals that balance, sustain, and provide joy.

In your family's search to discover rituals that are meaningful for you, you may find yourself combining rituals from your cultural and religious traditions and new rituals, ones that have meaning particularly for your family.

Rituals that are frozen in time, static, and have no meaning can be painful and may need changing. Why not create your own family rituals, incorporating the best of the old with fresh, new ideas?

Celebrating Your Children

It may not seem like so much—a "B" on a math test. For some families, it would be a disappointment. But you know your child, and it may be that for your child, a "B" on a math test represents the end of a tremendous amount of hard work. She worked hard, and got through something unpleasant for her, and that is a triumph. Then celebrate the process! Throw caution to the winds, crank up the music, and dance! Celebrate your children both for who they are, and for how proud they make you.

Family Treats in Hard Times

When times are tough, emotionally or financially, it's hard to celebrate the family. Yet this is exactly the time that you must, to clear the air, to lighten the load, to keep the family strong.

➤ You can have inexpensive or free family time just by getting out of the house and going to the park! Run with the dog, chase butterflies and come home for lemonade, or build snow creatures and come home for cocoa (depending upon the season). After a long day of job hunting or stressing over no money, take whatever food you have in the house, and go eat it outside on a blanket.

➤ Host a potluck party, and invite the extended family to bring their favorite comfort food (be prepared for a lot of soft carbohydrates). Don't forget to invite the "heart" family—dear friends who are as important to you as biological relations. Maybe the kids can create their own contributions. You supply the dishes and the dish washing.

➤ Take the family to the closest beach, lake, stream, pond, or other waterway that moves. Make paper boats with wishes for the future, and set them sailing.

➤ Write your worries on small scraps of paper, and use them to light a fire in your fireplace (if you have one). If you don't, tear each worry into as many small pieces as possible, and ceremoniously dump the shreds into the garbage can.

Spiritual Exploration

Whether it's the beauty of dust motes wandering in a shaft of morning sunlight, the god of an organized religion, or the mystery of the stars, it is the rare person who doesn't feel awe for some aspect of life. This spiritual aspect of human nature is innate in your child, too.

Most people belong to an organized religion and, whether observant or not, find a sense of community or identity within their place of worship, with other people who follow the same religion. Religious training for children is an important part of most religions. It's a way to continue the traditions, beliefs, and culture.

Other families—nonobservant believers, agnostics, or atheists—use nature as a cathedral, finding in the beauty of the outdoors a way to focus on the spiritual aspects of humanity. Gaining serenity from a waterfall, seeing God in a grain of sand, filling with awe and respect at the sight of a small sprouting seed, a grand redwood tree, or the miraculous patterns of a shifting desert.

The strongest families acknowledge spirituality (whatever the form), celebrate it, and by doing this teach their children to respect, love, and find joy in the spiritual aspects of life.

Creative Expression

Creativity—art, music, dance, writing, the performing arts—is more than just an enjoyable way to spend time. Building creativity into your family structure actually strengthens your family.

The Disciplinarian as Interdisciplinary Artist

Many parents want their kids to learn an art, though a relatively small number of people become professional artists. Becoming proficient in any of the arts requires practice—discipline. By now, you know that when I say *discipline,* I don't mean a military-style, rigid adherence to orders imposed by a big authority. I'm talking about focus, diligence, and attention.

Artistic disciplines provide paths for learning. The more creativity in your child's life, the more flexible, balanced, and attentive she'll be.

It's a Good Idea!

Artistic disciplines build internal discipline.

Taking an Artistic, Interdisciplinary Approach to Discipline

In interdisciplinary art, the artist decides on what she wants to say or explore, and then chooses the media to work with that will best help her achieve her vision. If she's working with the theme of world peace and the devastation of war, she might use old printed maps as her background, and combine painting, old films, and shrapnel in her finished piece.

Words to Parent By

Interdisciplinary art is any art form combining more than one medium. It takes an empirical approach. The artist bases her choice of media on what the artwork is attempting to say or explore.

As you work toward raising a well-behaved child (and as you work to build a strong family structure), you're approaching the task from many different angles, too, and with many different tools. Your art is the art of discipline, the art of parenting. As an artist, you use the varying media of strength and empathy, nurturing, encouragement, limits, consequences, family rules, values statements, and therapy if needed.

Creativity Supports, Nourishes, and the Child Flourishes

When things collapse, when life doesn't go well, when the bumper sticker of your internal car reads, "Life sucks and then you die," what do you have to fall back on? Hard times come for everybody, and sometimes it feels as though life is almost unbearable in its troubles. (A wise soul once said, "Life is just about as hard as it can be, and no harder.") What can you give your children, and your family, as a support system?

Making art helps. Whether it's knitting or sculpture, primal dancing or poetry, expressing trouble—having an outlet to express your troubles—can help. Art also helps in the good times. Expressing your creativity is fun and nourishing, and usually replenishes more energy than it expends. You don't have to be good at it, and you don't even have to consider yourself "creative" (most people don't). It's the action of making, doing, and dancing that can ease the soul.

Ways to Raise a Creative Child

Children are highly creative, and then, for most, their creativity is stomped out of them. You can encourage and enhance your child's creativity in a variety of ways:

➤ Model your love of playing with your child. Like to carve wood? Draw monsters? Cook? Share your experiences with your child, and let him explore as he goes. Keep your judgments to yourself, and only encourage, encourage, encourage.

➤ Encourage fantasy play and play with your child. If your child is under 10, consider a dress-up chest (yes, for boys, too). Stock it with thrift shop items like odd shirts, tacky belts, scarves galore, and hats, hats, hats.

➤ Turn off the TV!

➤ Read to your child and with your child, and have your child read to you.

➤ Stock the house with things to make things: glue, sequins, paper, pens, yarn, chocolate (for baking, not for inspiration!), clay, feathers, beads, books, and provide a place for him to explore. A back porch, a noncarpeted area of his room, a corner of the kitchen where newspaper can be laid down and messes made. (Sound like a lot of clutter? Yes! You can "bin" the materials, but remember that they are the building blocks of creativity.) (Okay, don't "bin" the chocolate.)

➤ Art should not be goal-oriented. It's the process that's fun, and if you or your kids get hung up in the results, you won't enjoy yourselves as much.

➤ Most communities have individuals who give music lessons for kids. You don't need to invest in a Stradivarius for your child who is beginning violin. A used instrument is fine—at least until your child is practicing in her spare time without being reminded, and the music teacher is brimming with pride. And then, you still don't need to get a Stradivarius.

Tales from the Parent Zone

It's hard to let go of the product, especially for kids who tend toward perfectionism. I remember the first day of my first sculpture class. We were playing with clay. As I squished and molded, I imagined myself as the next Auguste Rodin—and then I looked at my mushy mess and felt demoralized. It took a long time before I could let go and just experience the process (actually, I'm still working on it).

➤ Set aside time for practice, but don't nag your child. Lessons should be a pleasant, positive experience. For kids who can't self-motivate yet, try a teacher or class with little or no practice time.

It's a Good Idea!

If you're feeling uncreative or frustrated with your artistic process (or lack of it), check out Julia Cameron's wonderful workbook *The Artist's Way*.

➤ Look into dance, drama, photography, sculpture, and ice-skating classes. The first four used to be offered in most public schools, but rarely are today. Try community centers for inexpensive classes. It's a positive investment in your child. Skimp somewhere else.

➤ Just because you love it doesn't mean it's right for your child. Not all "art" forms are for every-body. Annie prefers cooking and dancing to drawing. Trying different art forms and classes for your child is great, even if none of them "stick." The more exposure a child has to creative work/play, the better.

Community Commitment

Where do your alliances lie? What responsibilities do you have to your community? It depends on how you define your family. What makes a family, anyway? Accidents of birth, twists of fate that throw people together—a family is built through shared experiences in the rough times as well as the smooth. Your family is your community—and it follows that your community is your family, as well.

You have a commitment to your community. Your family exists in the world, and the immediate world around you is your community. You build the strengths of your child by building the family and the community. The strengths of the community and family are reflected right back onto the child.

Community Service

Whether it's through your church or temple, through local political action, neighborhood watch, volunteer fire departments, or donating clothes, money, and time to the Red Cross in times of international disasters, your commitment to the community is important. Share it with your family. Make community involvement part of your family's life—and from it, your children will learn about the values and ethics of helping others.

➤ Some families tithe 10% of their income (and for kids, this would be their allowance) toward helping others.

➤ Try volunteer or free professional work for those who can't pay for essential services. My husband, Bill, teaches low-income, at-risk teenage foster kids reading and study skills. I host a portion of BabyZone.com, a Web site sharing and disseminating information for pregnant women and new parents, many of whom have few other sources of information. Whatever little you can do helps—and, as a bonus, teaches your kids about the value of honoring your connection to the community.

Building Your Personal and Family Support Network

Friends and neighbors matter. As you build your family from the inside, you also need to build it from the outside, and that means other people, other influences on your kids. Don't get insular, and don't neglect your friendships.

Focus on the Process

Building a strong family and raising a well-behaved child is a process. It's never done, and it's not like being in school—there's no midterm exams to tell you how you're progressing. In this way, teaching your child discipline is a process. Parenting itself is a process. Childhood is a process, too, and learning how to become well behaved is part of it.

Raising a child is a tremendous commitment of love, time, and energy. It takes a physical and emotional toll (it also gives back more than it takes). Savor the lessons you are learning and teaching. Enjoy the process.

➤ Keep your perspective. Way back when, your baby was a baby and the days stretched out wide before you all. Living in the immediacy of "baby time," it seemed impossible to imagine a time when the infant in your arms

It's a Good Idea!

Question: What do meditation, bread baking, Aikido, gardening, dance, and teaching discipline to your child have in common?

Answer: They are all disciplines where the process is as (or more) essential than the long-term results.

would be walking. Your troubles, too, seemed interminable. Would you ever sleep at night again? As your child grew, so did your perspective. Yet it's always hard to imagine the future. Things change. Hang in there. Take the long view.

➤ Undeveloped strength often appears as trouble. Your "undisciplined" child with the strong opinions and challenging temperament traits may contain the strong seeds of leadership. Focus on the strengths, incorporate them into your family stories, and celebrate the adult she will become, even as you work with her difficult behavior.

➤ Raise an adult you would like to know. Be who you would like your child to be—not in terms of career, lifestyle choice or temperament, but ethically and morally. Children learn what they live.

➤ Fill your home with affection and appreciation. Your child needs your companionship and your love. He needs to see you relaxed and loose, laughing and enjoying yourself, and him. Being reasonable and respectful doesn't mean keeping your distance from your children. Hug your kid, hold his hands, brush away stray hairs, kiss him. Play games, tell him stories, and brag about your pride in who he is—just make sure he can overhear you.

➤ Give yourself credit and celebrate your successes. Raising a strong, reasonable family with well-behaved kids is hard, important work. Pat yourself on the back!

➤ Acknowledge the wonders of now, and pay attention to the larger picture. Yes, it can be frustrating. When you're deep in the thick of family conflict, when you can't see further than your nose, take a breath, step back, and look for the joy. It's there.

Behave Yourself!

Wrestling with and tickling your kids is fine as long as they are happy, and feel their personal boundaries are respected. Watch for nonverbal signals that they're not comfortable. And, of course, "no" means "no!"

The Least You Need to Know

➤ Your family's identity provides a foundation for your child to stand on.

➤ Family time builds family identity, it also enhances communication.

➤ Family stories and mythologies are an important part of your child's identity.

➤ Fostering creativity in your children enhances their ability to nurture themselves.

➤ Model community commitment to your children.

➤ Keep it in perspective, and focus on the process.

Glossary

active listening   Trying to understand the child's thoughts and feelings by listening silently and then paraphrasing—saying back again as closely as possible without interpretation—what has been said.

ally   Somebody who is on your side, who looks out for you, and who you can trust to be there when the chips are down.

anorexia   An eating disorder characterized by self-starvation because of a distortion of body image.

Attention Deficit Disorder (ADD)   A cluster of traits that reflect a child's inborn neurologically based temperament. ADD traits include spontaneity, creativity, and the ability to hyperfocus on tasks. It also often causes inattention, impulsiveness, distractibility, and hyperactivity (ADHD). Kids with ADD/ADHD are at high-risk for developing learning disorders and behavioral difficulties.

behavior modeling   Demonstrating through your daily actions the kind of behavior you expect your children to demonstrate. (This takes a certain amount of discipline of your own.)

bulimia   An eating disorder characterized by cycles of bingeing (overeating) and self-induced purging (vomiting or overuse of laxatives).

consequences   What happens as a result of a behavior, good or bad. Consequences can be pleasant or unpleasant—they are simply the outcome of an event or a course of events.

consistency   Sameness, the same rules and consequences over time.

corporal punishment   "Punishing the body." Spanking—swatting your kid once or many times on the rear with your hand—is corporal punishment. So is hitting your child anywhere on his body, softly or hard, with your hand, belt, or any other object, one time or 10 times, frequently or once in a while.

cultural pride   A sense of self-esteem and self-respect for your heritage.

double-dip consequence   A consequence one step removed—a consequence applied because the parent is upset that a child has done something away from home that required somebody else to apply discipline. Double-dip consequences are very common, but highly inappropriate. An extreme example: A child is spanked for "earning" (and getting) a spanking from somebody else: unjust, unfair, and punitive.

drug   Any pain-relieving or perception- or mood-altering substance that is ingested into the body. Drugs include alcohol, nicotine, and caffeine, inhalants, and over-the-counter medications as well as illegal pain-relieving or perception- or mood-altering substances.

empathy   Feeling what another person feels.

family   A grouping of people—usually but not always biologically or legally related—who may live together, and who love and rely on each other.

family values statement   A general set of beliefs and behavior guidelines that apply to everybody in the family—for example, "Our family does not use violence to settle problems." It is based on your family's deep-seated beliefs.

"I" statement   A declaration of your feelings, views, needs, likes, or dislikes that begins with the word *I*. "I" statements tell the listener that you're speaking from your own point of view.

interdisciplinary art   Any art form combining more than one media. It takes an empirical approach. The artist bases her choice of media on what the art work is attempting to say, or explore.

internalizing the discipline   The process whereby a child learns how to discipline herself.

justice   A combination of integrity, virtue, and equity. Fighting for justice means fighting for righteousness.

limits   Behavior boundaries. Some are set by nature (humans can't fly, I can't keep track of my sunglasses), some by the state (you can't drive the wrong way down a one-way street), and some are set by you. It's up to you to define and make explicit each child's limits.

logical consequences   Consequences with some human intervention, and are logically related to the behavior. If Polly throws a ball in the house, it's a logical consequence for Dad to remove the ball. If Dave gets up late and misses the carpool, the logical consequence is that he walks to school. And if Anselm sneaks in an extra TV show or two after he's been warned, he loses his TV privileges for a week.

meta-fight   A fight about having a fight. In the fair fighting technique, after the situation that prompted the fight is resolved, the participants resolve their feelings about fighting with each other.

modeling   *See* **behavior modeling.**

natural consequences   The natural outcomes of behavior. The natural consequence of taking an hour-long shower is having to rinse your hair with icy cold water because you drained the water heater. A natural consequence of throwing your favorite toy against the wall is that it breaks. It's a cause and effect thing.

neurofeedback training   An alternative therapy to drugs for ADD. Using real-time computer readouts of a child's brain waves in the form of graphics or games, it teaches the child to alter her neural output by concentrating. Neurofeedback training gives the child direct practice in and positive feedback for paying attention, and, in the process, retrains her brain so that she is better able to focus in daily life.

parenting partner   Any adult who shares parenting or child care responsibilities with you. It includes any adults who have direct involvement with, or influence on, your child's life.

positive discipline   An approach to discipline that incorporates encouragement, praise, trust, and respect for children with setting firm, wise limits. It teaches them how to make their own choices, and to understand the consequences of their choices. When necessary, it provides related, respectful, reasonable, and rewarding responses to misbehavior.

positive intent   The underlying positive meaning behind any action. It's a theory (developed by Don and Jeanne Elium, authors of *Raising a Family*) that assumes that people mean well and strive for the best.

positive reframing   To recast a potentially negative situation or personality trait in a more positive light.

positive reinforcement   A parenting attitude and technique that reinforces what the child is doing right rather than concentrating on what the child is doing wrong. It increases the likelihood that the behavior will be repeated. It supports your child's positive deeds and qualities through enthusiasm, descriptive encouragement, and natural, logical rewards.

privileges   Optional responsibilities or activities allowed your child.

reasonable parent   An informed and compassionate parent who relies on reason as well as emotion to understand his developing child.

safer sex   Sexual activity with reduced risks—using condoms, dams, and sexual activities that don't share bodily fluids. While sexual intercourse may never be totally free from the risk of transmitting sexually transmitted diseases (STDs), the risks can be reduced.

self-control   The ability to deny oneself immediate pleasure for one's longer-term good or for the good of somebody or something else. Self-control becomes an issue for kids in many areas: homework (do it now or watch TV), money (spend it or save it), food (eat it all or leave room for dessert), and so on.

sympathy   Feeling for but not necessarily understanding another person.

temperament   A way of analyzing a person's adaptability and emotional style. Temperament is inborn. The 10 characteristics—adaptability, energy level, environmental sensitivity, first reaction, intensity, mood, perceptiveness, persistence, physical sensitivity and regularity—all refer to the way a person approaches the world.

time temperament   The way a person feels about, and handles, schedules and deadlines. Some people are chronically late, others always early, and still others exactly on time. Some are relaxed about time. "Drop in whenever," they say, and they mean it. Others need schedules.

unconditional love   Love that has no conditions attached to it. The person loved unconditionally doesn't have to be anybody, or prove anything, or act in any particular way to be loved, and love is neither withdrawn for "bad" behavior nor bestowed for "good" behavior.

unified front   An agreed-upon approach to an issue. In disciplinary matters, it's best to at least have the appearance of total agreement. For instance, say you think dessert is to be eaten only after dinner, and your partner feels that anytime is the right time for chocolate. You might give in, for the sake of the unified front, but continue to negotiate privately.

well-behaved child   A child who is respectful, reasonable, responsible, resourceful, loving, eager to learn, and engaged by life. It's not a child who is beaten down, cowed by you, her peers, or the "system," or who is too frightened to express her feelings and ideas.

"you" statement   A statement that begins with the word *you* and can appear to be accusatory or self-righteous.

More about family security

Books and Other Resources

General Positive Parenting Books

American Academy of Pediatrics. *Caring for Your School-Age Child: Ages 5 to 12*. New York: Bantam Books, 1995.

Cox, Meg. *The Heart of a Family*. New York: Random House, 1998.

Davis, Laura, and Janis Keyser. *Becoming the Parent You Want to Be*. New York: Broadway Books, 1997.

Dreikurs, Rudolph. *Children: The Challenge*. New York: Plume Books, 1990.

Elium, Don, and Jeanne Elium. *Raising a Son: Parents and the Making of a Healthy Man*. Berkeley: Celestial Arts, 1996.

———. *Raising a Daughter: Parents and the Awakening of a Healthy Woman*. Berkeley: Celestial Arts, 1994.

———. *Raising a Family: Living on Planet Parenthood*. Berkeley: Celestial Arts, 1997.

Faber, Adele and Elaine Mazlish. *How to Talk So Kids Will Listen & Listen So Kids Will Talk*. New York: Avon Books, 1991.

Forman, Deborah L. *Every Parent's Guide to the Law*. New York: Harcourt-Brace, 1998.

Goldstein, Robin. *Stop Treating Me Like a Kid: Everyday Parenting: The 10- to 13-Year-Old*. New York: Penguin Books, 1994.

Joslin, Karen Renshaw. *Positive Parenting From A To Z*. New York: Fawcett Columbine, 1994.

Lerman, Saf. *Parent Awareness Training: Positive Parenting for the 1980s*. New York: A and W Publishers, 1980.

Nolte, Dorothy Law. *Children Learn What they Live*. New York: Workman Publishing, 1998.

Satter, Ellyn. *How to Get Your Kid to Eat...But Not Too Much*. Palo Alto, CA: Bull Publishing, 1987.

Discipline Classics

Nelson, Jane, et al. *Positive Discipline for Parenting in Recovery*. Rocklin, CA: Prima Publishing, 1996.

———. *Positive Discipline for Preschoolers*. Rocklin, CA: Prima Publishing, 1998.

Poretta, Vicki, and Ericka Lutz. *Mom's Guide to Disciplining Your Child*. New York: Macmillan, 1997.

Windell, James. *8 Weeks to a Well-Behaved Child*. New York: Macmillan, 1994.

———. *Discipline: A Sourcebook of 50 Failsafe Techniques for Parents*. New York: Collier Books, 1991.

Special Situations

Faber, Adele, and Elaine Mazlish. *Siblings Without Rivalry*. New York: Avon, 1987.

Kurcinka, Mary Sheedy. *Raising Your Spirited Child*. New York: Harper Perennial, 1992.

Noel, Brook. *The Single Parent Resource*. Beverly Hills, CA: Champion Press, 1998.

Palladino, Lucy Jo. *The Edison Trait*. New York: Times Books, 1997.

Sears, William, and Lynda Thompson. *The A.D.D. Book*. New York: Little, Brown and Company, 1998.

For Parents of Teens

Riera, Michael. *Uncommon Sense for Parents with Teenagers*. Berkeley: Celestial Arts, 1995.

Rubin, Nancy. *Ask Me If I Care: Voices from an American High School*. Berkeley: Ten Speed Press, 1994.

Schwebel, Robert, Ph.D. *Saying No is Not Enough: Raising Children Who Make Wise Decisions About Drugs and Alcohol*. New York: Newmarket Press, 1989.

Siegler, Ava L. *The Essential Guide to the New Adolescence*. New York: Dutton, 1997.

Steinberg, Lawrence, and Ann Levine. *You and Your Adolescent*. New York: Harper-Perennial, 1997.

For Stepparents

Lutz, Ericka. *The Complete Idiot's Guide® to Stepparenting*. New York: Macmillan, 1998.

Where Can You Turn for Help?

Families in Crisis, Violence, and Abuse Issues

National Child Abuse Hotline
800/4-A-CHILD

National Youth Crisis Hotline
800/442-4676

National Domestic Violence Hotline
800/787-3224

National Council on Child Abuse and Family Violence
800/222-2000

National Organization for Victim Assistance
800/TRY-NOVA

National Clearinghouse on Child Abuse and Neglect
800/FYI-3366

National Resource Center on Child Abuse and Neglect
800/227-5242

Boys Town National Hotline
800/448-3000

Family Violence Prevention Fund
800/313-1310

Parents Anonymous, Inc.
675 West Foothills Blvd., Suite 220
Claremont, CA 91711
909/621-6184
HN3831@handsnet.org
www.parentsanonymous-natl.org

Drug and Alcohol Information and Resources

Alanon-Alateen Information Service
800/344-2666
www.al-anon.alateen.org

Alanon Family Group Headquarters
800/356-9996

Alcoholism and Drug Treatment Addiction Center
800/383-4357

Alcoholics Anonymous
www.alcoholics-anonymous.org

> *Look in your local phone book or write for referrals to local chapters:*

General Service Office
Grand Central Station
P.O. Box 459
New York, NY 10163

American Council on Alcoholism
800/527-5344

800 Cocaine
800/262-2463

Marijuana Anonymous World Service Office
800/766-6779
www.marijuana-anonymous.org

Nar-Anon Family Groups World Service Office
800/547-5800

Narcotics Anonymous World Service Office
818/780-3951
www.na.org

National Clearinghouse for Alcohol and Drug Information
800/729-6686
www.health.org/

National Drug and Alcohol Treatment Referral Hotline
800/662-HELP

Self-Injury and Eating Disorders

Secret Shame
800/DONT-CUT
www.selfinjury.com

The American Anorexia/Bulimia Association
212/891-8686
members.aol.com/amanbu/

Sexual Information and Assistance

Planned Parenthood Federation of America
www.plannedparenthood.org

Look in your phone book for a local clinic, or contact the main office:

810 Seventh Ave.
New York, NY 10019
212/541-7800.

National Resource Center on Sexual Abuse
800/543-3520

AIDS and Sexually Transmitted Diseases (STDs)

National STD Hotline
800/227-8922

Centers for Disease Control National AIDS Hotline
800/342-AIDS

San Francisco AIDS Foundation Hotline
415/FOR-AIDS

Gay and Lesbian Issues

National Center for Lesbian Rights
870 Market St., Suite 570
San Francisco, CA 94102
415/392-6257
www.nclrights.org

Parents, Families and Friends of Lesbians and Gays (PFLAG)
202/638-4200
www.pflag.org

ADD and ADHD Resources

ADDA (National Attention Deficit Disorder Association)
P.O. Box 972
Mentor, OH 44061
800/487-2282
www.add.org

CHADD (Children and Adults with Attention Deficit Disorder)
499 N.W. 70th Ave., Suite 101
Plantation, FL 33317
800/233-4050
www.chadd.org

Stepparenting Support and Information

Stepfamily Association of America
650 J. St., Suite 205
Lincoln, NE 68508
800/735-0329
402/477-7837
www.stepfam.org

Step Family Foundation, Inc.
333 West End Ave.
New York, NY 10023
212/877-3244
stepfamily@aol.com
www.stepfamily.org

Finding a Therapist

American Association of Marriage and Family Therapy
202/452-0109
www.aamft.org

National Association for the Advancement of Psychoanalysis
212/741-0515

National Mental Health Association
800/969-6642
www.nmha.org

Other Resources

Children's Rights Council (CRC)
300 I St., Suite 401
Washington, DC 20002
202/547-6227
www.vix.com/crc/

Disciplinary Examples

Here's a chart to show you some examples of use and misuse of some of the disciplinary techniques I've discussed in this book.

Misbehavior	What's the Problem, Need, or Intent?	Unrelated or Ineffective Responses	Related and Reasonable Responses
Twelve-year-old caught smoking.	Wants to fit in, look cool. Wants to assert her independence.	Grounded until end of semester. Not allowed to play with "those friends."	Education. Take her to meet somebody diagnosed with lung cancer. Sign her up for sports activity.
Ten-year-old steals, and then lies about it.	Wants adventure. Afraid to ask for desired object. Afraid of your anger.	Loss of privileges (no dessert or TV). Grounded. Spanking.	Return and restitution. Have child take back property and apologize (you escort, being ally) and have child work off damages (either work for you and you pay, or work directly). Give warning. Tell child you are "watching" him.
Eight-year-old trashes bathroom—wet towels on floor, hair in sink.	Child meant to clean up, but forgot due to time crunch—poor time management skills poor cleaning skills.	Related but not reasonable response: Child forced to clean entire house.	Related *and* reasonable response. Child cleans up bathroom. Parent shows child how to scrub toilet. They write a "work schedule" to alternate bathroom duty.

continues

continued

Misbehavior	What's the Problem, Need, or Intent?	Unrelated or Ineffective Responses	Related and Reasonable Responses
Thirteen-year-old cutting school.	School is no longer challenging—child is more interested in working on building model airplanes. Social troubles with bully.	Screams, threats, spanking, loss of privileges.	Strong supervision and paying attention to child's needs. Parent checks in with each teacher daily. If necessary, escorts and picks up child. Child allowed to work on model airplanes at night after home-work is done.
Fourteen-year-old falling behind in school. Caught falling asleep on desk many times.	Too much partying because child doesn't know how to say no. Kid afraid of math teacher. Child mocked for being dumb.	Grounded until end of semester. Given unrelated tasks (mowing lawn and cleaning entire house).	Child is grounded on weekends until work is completed. Parent demonstrates being an ally, and "takes heat" from child's peers ("Jimmy can't party tonight, because I've grounded him."). Education and help—math tutoring provided.

How to Hold a Brainstorming Session

Brainstorming is a quick and effective way to find creative solutions to problems and generate new ideas. Whether it's coming up with ideas for Grandma and Grandpa's 40th wedding anniversary or figuring out how to keep the goldfish from being overfed, brainstorming is a terrific technique to help solve problems.

Brainstorming can involve the whole family (it works really well as a family meeting agenda item), but it can also be done in pairs. Here's how it works:

First, review these rules and procedures (somebody can read these aloud). Then, go to it!

➤ Set up a chalkboard, a white board, a large pad of paper, or a blank wall that you're going to paint tomorrow.

➤ Choose a "scribe" to write down all the ideas that are generated.

➤ State the problem or situation you are brainstorming about.

➤ Now, the participants generate suggestions and ideas, as many as possible. No matter how silly, wild, and improbable they sound, write them down. Rule: Nobody is allowed to judge the suggestions and ideas. Often the most ludicrous idea inspires brilliance.

➤ If you're having trouble getting started, use turn-taking.

➤ As the ideas start to flow, you'll notice that some start "piggybacking" onto others. This is good. Get into it!

➤ Once you've run out of steam, room on the board, or time, stop. Now you can cross out the unfeasible ideas, and combine the similar ones.

➤ Look at what's left—now you have a variety of ideas to evaluate and prioritize.

➤ Once you've decided on something, write it down, and schedule a time to revisit and reevaluate later.

The Kid-Time Exercise Sheet

Just how much time do you spend alone with your child every week?

	Day and Time	Description of Kid-Times	Who else was there?	How long?	Notes
Monday					
Tuesday					
Wednesday					
Thursday					
Friday					
Saturday					
Sunday					

What's Your Priority?

Who would you like your child to be? What do you want for yourself?

As you work to define your expectations for your child, it's helpful to see where your goals for yourself overlap. In this exercise (inspired by *The Mom's Guide® to Disciplining Your Child,* by Vicki Poretta and me!), you're going to be choosing from a list of positive traits and defining which you would like your kid to have—once he's grown and gone.

It may be hard to choose—all the traits are positive. Just prioritize as best as you can.

A. Read the list below, then choose the top-10 traits you want your child to have as an adult, and jot them in the "Child's" section.

The Top-10 Traits I'd Like My Child to Have When Grown

1.
2.
3.
4.
5.
6.
7.
8.
9.
10.

B. Are you surprised by the traits you chose? Are there traits I didn't include that you would like to add? Do it.

C. Now do it again, prioritizing the top-10 traits you would like to describe you.

The Top-10 Traits I'd Like Myself to Have

1.
2.
3.
4.
5.
6.
7.
8.
9.
10.

The List of Positive Traits

Ability to form mature friendships

Ability to form mature sexual relationships

Ability to mediate and make peace

Ability to relish pleasure and celebrate life

Agent of social change

Artistic sensibility and ability

Community spirit

Complacency—sense of comfort

Ethical

Fitting in, amiable, popular

Happy

Honesty

Kindness

Independent

Independent thinker

Lasting contributor to human knowledge

Inner balance, harmony and Serenity

Loving and lovable

Loyalty—to family and friends, employer, or nation

Money brains (the ability to prosper)

Responsibility toward family

Relaxed

Respect and admiration for others

Sense of fairness and justice

Rich inner life

Strong, entrepreneurial spirit with energy and ambition

Savvy (not easy to fool)

Scholarly aptitude (good student)

Spirituality or religious spirit

Self-respect and self-esteem

Wisdom, a mature understanding of life

Food for Thought

Now that you've completed filling out the tables, here are some questions to think about:

➤ How do the two tables compare?

➤ In what ways are the traits you've chosen for yourself different from the traits you've chosen for your child?

➤ You may find that the traits you chose for your child are similar or identical to the traits you chose for yourself. Do the traits you've chosen for your child match her abilities, interests, and temperament?

➤ Was there anything about this exercise that surprised you?

➤ Look at the traits you've chosen for your child. Is your disciplinary approach likely to foster these traits? (If you've read the book carefully, I hope you can say yes!)

➤ What can you change in your parenting techniques to move your child or yourself closer to your goals?

What's Your Temperament?

In Chapter 5, we talked a lot about temperament. Sometimes parents' temperaments match their kids', and sometimes not. Either way, it's helpful (and very interesting) to see where you match up.

In the chart below, describe your child's mood, intensity, regularity, sensitivity, energy level, first reaction, adaptability, persistence, and perceptiveness. Then you'll do it for yourself.

There's no winning or losing or correct or incorrect here—but it may help you work better with your child in your mutual quest for good behavior.

Temperamental Trait	Your Child	You
Is the general mood up or down? Optimist or pessimist?		
Is the intensity high or low? How strong are emotional reactions?		
Is regularity of high or low importance? Look at sleep, eating, and bathroom patterns.		
Is physical sensitivity high or low? Consider tolerance for scratchy clothes, loud noises, fingernails on blackboards, gooey food.		
Is energy level high or low?		

continues

continued

Temperamental Trait	Your Child	You
What is the general first reaction? High risk or cautious? Do you jump right into a situation or hang back?		
Is adaptability and a change in routine easy or hard to adjust to?		
What's the persistence level? Is it high or low? Once started, is it easy to stop and move on?		
Is the environmental perceptivity level high or low? How easily distractible?		

Index